Radio and
Electronics
Engineer's
Pocket Book

Newnes
Radio and Electronics Engineer's Pocket Book

18th Edition

Keith Brindley

Heinemann Newnes

Heinemann Newnes
An imprint of Heinemann Professional Publishing Ltd
Halley Court, Jordan Hill, Oxford OX2 8EJ

OXFORD LONDON MELBOURNE AUCKLAND

First published by George Newnes Ltd 1940
Thirteenth edition 1962
Fourteenth edition 1972
Fifteenth edition 1978
Reprinted 1979, 1980, 1982 (twice, with additions), 1983
Sixteenth edition 1985
Seventeenth edition first published by Heinemann
Professional Publishing Ltd 1987
Reprinted 1988
Eighteenth edition 1989
Reprinted 1990

British Library Cataloguing in Publication Data

Newnes radio and electronics engineer's
  pocket book.—18th ed.
  1. Electronic equipment – Technical data
  I. Brindley, Keith
  621.381'0212

ISBN 0 434 90187 3

Typeset by Vision Typesetting, Manchester
Printed and bound in Great Britain by
Courier International Ltd, Tiptree, Essex

Preface

Radio and electronics reference books are, generally, quite specific in nature; often covering such narrow and detailed aspects that they are of use to only a minority. Those few books which cover more than this tend not to allow easy reference to specific details, and are expensive. My intention in revising this book was to cater for the needs of most people with interests in radio and electronics related areas, while making it easy to locate the required information – at an affordable price. I hope I have succeeded.

My main criterion in choosing what to include and what to discard has been, 'What do *I* look up?' I have tried to include, therefore, *anything* of relevance to radio and electronics referred to in literature. In this respect, a number of tables of units, conversion factors, symbols etc., are newly included. On the other hand, anything for which a calculator is better used, has been discarded.

Keith Brindley

Contents

Abbreviations and symbols

Many abbreviations are found as either capital *or* lower case
letters, depending on publishers' styles. Symbols should generally
be standard, as shown.

A	Ampere or anode
ABR	Auxiliary bass radiator
a.c.	Alternating current
A/D	Analogue to digital
ADC	Analogue to digital converter
Ae	Aerial
a.f.	Audio frequency
a.f.c.	Automatic frequency control
a.g.c.	Automatic gain control
a.m.	Amplitude modulation
ASA	Acoustical Society of America
ASCII	American Standard Code for Information Interchange
a.t.u.	Aerial tuning unit
AUX	Auxiliary
a.v.c.	Automatic volume control
b	Base of transistor
BAF	Bonded acetate fibre
B & S	Brown & Sharpe (U.S.) wire gauge
b.p.s.	Bits per second
BR	Bass reflex
BSI	British Standards Institution
C	Capacitor, cathode, centigrade, coulomb
c	Collector of transistor, speed of light
CB	Citizen's band
CCD	Charge coupled device
CCIR	International Radio Consultative Committee
CCITT	International Telegraph and Telephone Consultative Committee
CCTV	Closed circuit television
chps	Characters per second
CPU	Central processor unit
CTD	Charge transfer device
CLK	Clock signal
CrO_2	Chromium dioxide
CMOS	Complementary metal oxide semiconductor
c.w.	Continuous wave
D	Diode
d	Drain of an f.e.t.
D/A	Digital to analogue
DAC	Digital to analogue converter
dB	Decibel
d.c.	Direct current
DCC	Double cotton covered
DCE	Data circuit-terminating equipment
DF	Direction finding
DIL	Dual-in-line
DIN	German standards institute
DMA	Direct memory access
DPDT	Double pole, double throw
DPST	Double pole, single throw

DTE	Data terminal equipment
DTL	Diode-transistor logic
DTMF	Dual tone multi-frequency
DX	Long distance reception
e	Emitter of transistor
EAROM	Electrically alterable read only memory
ECL	Emitter coupled logic
e.h.t.	Extremely high tension (voltage)
e.m.f.	Electromotive force
en	Enamelled
EPROM	Erasable programmable read only memory
EQ	Equalisation
ERP	Effective radiated power
EROM	Erasable read only memory
F	Farad, fahrenheit or force
f	Frequency
Fe	Ferrous
FeCr	Ferri-chrome
f.e.t.	Field effect transistor
f.m.	Frequency modulation
f.r.	Frequency response or range
f.s.d.	Full-scale deflection
f.s.k.	Frequency shift keying
G	Giga (10^9)
g	Grid, gravitational constant
H	Henry
h.f.	High frequency
Hz	Hertz (cycles per second)
I	Current
IB	Infinite baffle
i.c.	Integrated circuit
IF	Intermediate frequency
IHF	Institute of High Fidelity (U.S.)
I^2L (IIL)	Integrated injection logic
i.m.d.	Intermodulation distortion
i/p	Input
i.p.s.	Inches per second
k	Kilo (10^3) or cathode
K	Kilo, in computing terms ($= 2^{10} = 1024$), or degrees Kelvin
L	Inductance or lumens
l.e.d.	Light emitting diode
l.f.	Low frequency
LIN	Linear
LOG	Logarithmic
LS	Loudspeaker
LSI	Large scale integration
l.w.	Long wave (approx. 1100–2000 m)
M	Mega (10^6)
m	Milli (10^{-3}) or metres
MHz	Megahertz
m.c.	Moving coil
mic	Microphone
MOS	Metal oxide semiconductor
MPU	Microprocessor unit
MPX	Multiplex
m.w.	Medium wave (approx. 185–560 m)
n	Nano (10^{-9})

NAB	National Association of Broadcasters
Ni-Cad	Nickel-cadmium
n/c	Not connected; normally closed
n/o	Normally open
NMOS	Negative channel metal oxide semiconductor
o/c	Open channel; open circuit
o/p	Output
op-amp	Operational amplifier
p	Pico (10^{-12})
PA	Public address
PABX	Private automatic branch exchange
PAL	Phase alternation, line
p.a.m.	Pulse amplitude modulation
PCB	Printed circuit board
PCM	Pulse code modulation
PLA	Programmable logic array
PLL	Phase locked loop
PMOS	Positive channel metal oxide semiconductor
P.P.M.	Peak programme meter
p.r.f.	Pulse repetition frequency
PROM	Programmable read only memory
PSS	Packet SwitchStream
PSTN	Public Switched Telephone Network
PSU	Power supply unit
PTFE	Polytetrafluoroethylene
PU	Pickup
PUJT	Programmable unijunction transistor
Q	Quality factor; efficiency of tuned circuit, charge
R	Resistance
RAM	Random access memory
RCF·	Recommended crossover frequency
RIAA	Record Industry Association of America
r.f.	Radio frequency
r.f.c.	Radio frequency choke (coil)
r.m.s.	Root mean square
ROM	Read only memory
RTL	Resistor transistor logic
R/W	Read/write
RX	Receiver
S	Siemens
s	Source of an f.e.t.
s/c	Short circuit
SCR	Silicon-controlled rectifier
s.h.f.	Super high frequency
SI	International system of units
S/N	Signal-to-noise
SPL	Sound pressure level
SPST	Single pole, single throw
SPDT	Single pole, double throw
SSI	Small scale integration
s.w.	Short wave (approx. 10–60 m)
s.w.g.	Standard wire gauge
s.w.r.	Standing wave ratio
T	Tesla
TDM	Time division multiplex
t.h.d.	Total harmonic distortion
t.i.d.	Transient intermodulation distortion
TR	Transformer

t.r.f.	Tuned radio frequency
TTL	Transistor transistor logic
TTY	Teletype unit
TVI	Television interface; television interference
TX	Transmitter
UART	Universal asynchronous receiver transmitter
u.h.f.	Ultra high frequency (approx. 470–854 MHz)
u.j.t.	Unijunction transistor
ULA	Uncommitted logic array
V	Volts
VA	Volt-amps
v.c.a.	Voltage controlled amplifier
v.c.o.	Voltage controlled oscillator
VCT	Voltage to current transactor
v.h.f.	Very high frequency (approx. 88–216 MHz)
v.l.f.	Very low frequency
VU	Volume unit
W	Watts
Wb	Weber
W/F	Wow and flutter
w.p.m.	Words per minute
X	Reactance
Xtal	Crystal
Z	Impedance
ZD	Zener diode

Letter symbols by unit name

Unit	Symbol	Notes
ampere	A	SI unit of electric current
ampere (turn)	At	SI unit of magnetomotive force
ampere-hour	Ah	
ampere per metre	Am^{-1}	SI unit of magnetic field strength
angstrom	Å	$1 Å = 10^{-10} m$
apostilb	asb	$1 asb = (1/\pi) cd\,m^{-2}$ A unit of luminance. The SI unit, candela per square metre, is preferred.
atmosphere:		
standard atmosphere	atm	$1 atm = 101\,325 N\,m^{-2}$
technical atmosphere	at	$1 at = 1 kgf\,cm^{-2}$
atomic mass unit (unified)	u	The (unified) atomic mass unit is defined as one-twelfth of the mass of an atom of the ^{12}C nuclide. Use of the old atomic mass unit (amu), defined by reference to oxygen, is deprecated.
bar	bar	$1 bar = 100\,000 N\,m^{-2}$
barn	b	$1 b = 10^{-28} m^2$

baud	Bd	Unit of signalling speed equal to one element per second.
becquerel	Bq	$1 \text{ Bq} = 1 \text{ s}^{-1}$ SI unit of radioactivity.
bel	B	
bit	b	
British thermal unit	Btu	
calorie (International Table calorie)	cal$_{IT}$	$1 \text{ cal}^{\circ}{}_{\!-} = 4 \cdot 1868 \text{ J}$ The 9th Conférence Générale des Poids et Mesures adopted the joule as the unit of heat, avoiding the use of the calorie as far as possible.
calorie (thermochemical calorie)	cal	$1 \text{ cal} = 4 \cdot 1840 \text{ J}$ (See note for International Table calorie.)
candela	cd	SI unit of luminous intensity.
candela per square inch	cd in^{-2}	Use of the SI unit, candela per square metre, is preferred.
candela per square metre	cd m^{-2}	SI unit of luminance. The name nit has been used.
candle		The unit of luminous intensity has been given the name *candela*; use of the word *candle* for this purpose is deprecated.
centimetre	cm	
circular mil	cmil	$1 \text{ cmil} = (\pi/4) \cdot 10^{-6} \text{in}^2$
coulomb	C	SI unit of electrical charge.
cubic centimetre	cm^3	
cubic foot	ft^3	
cubic foot per minute	ft^3 min^{-1}	
cubic foot per second	ft^3 s^{-1}	
cubic inch	in^3	
cubic metre	m^3	
cubic metre per second	m^3 s^{-1}	
cubic yard	yd^3	
curie	Ci	Unit of activity in the field of radiation dosimetry.
cycle	c	
cycle per second	c s^{-1}	Deprecated. Use hertz
decibel	dB	
degree (plane angle)	°	
degree (temperature):		Note that there is no space between the symbol ° and the letter. The use of the word *centigrade* for the Celsius temperature scale was abandoned by the Conférence Générale des Poids et Mesures in 1948.
degree Celsius	°C	
degree Fahrenheit	°F	
degree Kelvin		See Kelvin.
degree Rankine	°R	
dyne	dyn	
electronvolt	eV	

erg	erg	
erlang	E	Unit of telephone traffic.
farad	F	SI unit of capacitance.
foot	ft	
footcandle	fc	Use of the SI unit of illuminance, the lux (lumen per square metre), is preferred.
footlambert	fL	Use of the SI unit, the candela per square metre, is preferred.
foot per minute	ft min^{-1}	
foot per second	ft s^{-1}	
foot per second squared	ft s^{-2}	
foot pound-force	ft lb$_f$	
gal	Gal	1 Gal = 1 cm s^{-2}
gallon	gal	The gallon, quart, and pint differ in the US and the UK, and their use is deprecated.
gauss	G	The gauss is the electromagnetic CGS (Centimetre Gram Second) unit of magnetic flux density. The SI unit, tesla, is preferred.
gigaelectronvolt	GeV	
gigahertz	GHz	
gilbert	Gb	The gilbert is the electromagnetic CGS (Centimetre Gram Second) unit of magnetomotive force. Use of the SI unit, the ampere (or ampere-turn), is preferred.
grain	gr	
gram	g	
gray	Gy	1 Gy = 1 J kg^{-1} SI unit of absorbed dose.
henry	H	
hertz	Hz	SI unit of frequency.
horsepower	hp	Use of the SI unit, the watt, is preferred.
hour	h	Time may be designated as in the following example: 9^{h}46^{m}30^s.
inch	in	
inch per second	in s^{-1}	SI unit of energy.
joule	J	
joule per Kelvin	J K^{-1}	SI unit of heat capacity and entropy.
Kelvin	K	SI unit of temperature (formerly called *degree Kelvin*). The symbol K is now used without the symbol °.
kiloelectronvolt	KeV	

kilogauss	kG	
kilogram	kg	SI unit of mass.
kilogram-force	kg$_f$	In some countries the name *kilopond* (kp) has been adopted for this unit.
kilohertz	kHz	
kilojoule	kJ	
kilohm	kΩ	
kilometer	km	
kilometer per hour	kmh^{-1}	
kilopond	kp	See kilogram-force.
kilovar	kvar	
kilovolt	kV	
kilovoltampere	kVA	
kilowatt	kW	
kilowatthour	kWh	
knot	kn	$1 \text{ kn} = 1 \text{ nmih}^{-1}$
lambert	L	The lambert is the CGS (Centimetre Gram Second) unit of luminance. The SI unit, candela per square metre, is preferred.
litre	l	
litre per second	ls^{-1}	
lumen	lm	SI unit of luminous flux.
lumen per square foot	lmft^{-2}	Use of the SI unit, the lumen per square metre, is preferred.
lumen per square metre	lmm^{-2}	SI unit of luminous excitance.
lumen per watt	lmW^{-1}	SI unit of luminous efficacy.
lumen second	lms	SI unit of quantity of light.
lux	lx	$1 \text{ lx} = 1 \text{ lmm}^{-2}$ SI unit of illuminance.
maxwell	Mx	The maxwell is the electromagnetic CGS (Centimetre Gram Second) unit of magnetic flux. Use of the SI unit, the weber, is preferred.
megaelectronvolt	MeV	
megahertz	MHz	
megavolt	MV	
megawatt	MW	
megohm	MΩ	
metre	m	SI unit of length.
mho	mho	$1 \text{ mho} = 1 \, \Omega^{-1} = 1 \text{ S}$
microampere	μA	
microbar	μbar	
microfarad	μF	
microgram	μg	
microhenry	μH	
micrometre	μm	
micron		The name *micrometre* (μm) is preferred.
microsecond	μs	
microwatt	μW	
mil	mil	$1 \text{ mil} = 0.001 \text{ in.}$

mile		
nautical	nmi	
statute	mi	
mile per hour	$mi\,h^{-1}$	
milliampere	mA	
millibar	mbar	mb may be used.
milligal	mGal	
milligram	mg	
millihenry	mH	
millilitre	ml	
millimetre	mm	
conventional millimetre of mercury	mm Hg	$1\ mm\,Hg = 133{\cdot}322\ N\,m^{-2}$.
millimicron		The name *nanometre* (nm) is preferred.
millisecond	ms	
millivolt	mV	
milliwatt	mW	
minute (plane angle)	...′	
minute (time)	min	Time may be designated as in the following example: $9^h46^m30^s$.
mole	mol	SI unit of amount of substance.
nanoampere	nA	
nanofarad	nF	
nanometre	nm	
nanosecond	ns	
nanowatt	nW	
nautical mile	nmi	
neper	Np	
newton	N	SI unit of force.
newton metre	N m	
newton per square metre	$N\,m^{-2}$	See pascal.
nit	nt	$1\ nt = 1\ cd\,m^{-2}$ See candela per square metre.
oersted	Oe	The oersted is the electromagnetic CGS (Centimetre Gram Second) unit of magnetic field strength. Use of the SI unit, the ampere per metre, is preferred.
ohm	Ω	SI unit of electrical resistance.
ounce (avoirdupois)	oz	
pascal	Pa	SI unit of pressure or stress. $1\ Pa = 1\ N\,m^{-2}$
picoampere	pA	
picofarad	pF	
picosecond	ps	
picowatt	pW	
pint	pt	The gallon, quart, and pint differ in the US and the UK, and their use is deprecated.

pound	lb	
poundal	pdl	
pound-force	lb$_f$	
pound-force foot	lb$_f$ ft	
pound-force per square inch	lb$_f$ in^{-2}	
pound per square inch		Although use of the abbreviation psi is common, it is not recommended See pound-force per square inch.
quart	qt	The gallon, quart, and pint differ in the US and the UK, and their use is deprecated.
rad	rd	Unit of absorbed dose in the field of radiation dosimetry.
radian	rad	SI unit of plane angle.
rem	rem	Unit of dose equivalent in the field of radiation dosimetry.
revolution per minute	r min^{-1}	Although use of the abbreviation rpm is common, it is not recommended.
revolution per second	r s^{-1}	
roentgen	R	Unit of exposure in the field of radiation dosimetry.
second (plane angle)	..."	
second (time)	s	SI unit of time. Time may be designated as in the following example: $9^h46^m30^s$.
siemens	S	SI unit of conductance. 1 S = 1 Ω^{-1}
square foot	ft^2	
square inch	in^2	
square metre	m^2	
square yard	yd^2	
steradian	sr	SI unit of solid angle.
stilb	sb	1 sb = 1 cd cm^{-2} A CGS unit of luminance. Use of the SI unit, the candela per square metre, is preferred.
tesla	T	SI unit of magnetic flux density. 1 T = 1 Wb m^{-2}.
tonne	t	1 t = 1000 kg.
(unified) atomic mass unit	u	See atomic mass unit (unified).
var	var	Unit of reactive power.
volt	V	SI unit of electromotive force.
voltampere	VA	SI unit of apparent power.
watt	W	SI unit of power.
watthour	Wh	
watt per steradian	W sr^{-1}	SI unit of radiant intensity.
watt per steradian square metre	W (sr m^2)$^{-1}$	SI unit of radiance.
weber	Wb	SI unit of magnetic flux. 1 Wb = 1 V s.
yard	yd	

Electric quantities

Quantity	Symbol	Unit	Symbol
Admittance	Y	siemens	S
Angular frequency	ω	hertz	Hz
Apparent power	S	watt	W
Capacitance	C	farad	F
Charge	Q	coulomb	C
Charge density	ρ	coulomb per square metre	Cm^{-2}
Conductance	G	siemens	S
Conductivity	κ, γ, σ	siemens per metre	Sm^{-1}
Current	I	ampere	A
Current density	j, J	ampere per square metre	Am^{-2}
Displacement	D	coulomb per square metre	Cm^{-2}
Electromotive force	E	volt	V
Energy	E	joule	J
Faraday constant	F	coloumb per mole	$Cmol^{-1}$
Field strength	E	volt per metre	Vm^{-1}
Flux	ψ	coulomb	C
Frequency	v, f	hertz	Hz
Impedance	Z	ohm	Ω
Light, velocity of in a vacuum	c	metre per second	ms^{-1}
Period	T	second	s
Permeability	μ	henry per metre	Hm^{-1}
Permeability of space	μ_o	henry per metre	Hm^{-1}
Permeance	Λ	henry	H
Permittivity	ε	farad per metre	Fm^{-1}
Permittivity of space	ε_o	farad per metre	Fm^{-1}
Phase	ϕ	—	—
Potential	V, U	volt	V
Power	P	watt	W
Quality factor	Q	—	—
Reactance	X	ohm	Ω
Reactive power	Q	watt	W
Relative permeability	μ_r	—	—
Relative permittivity	ε_r	—	—
Relaxation time	τ	second	s
Reluctance	R	reciprocal henry	H^{-1}
Resistance	R	ohm	Ω
Resistivity	ρ	ohm metre	Ωm
Susceptance	B	siemens	S
Thermodynamic temperature	T	kelvin	K
Time constant	τ	second	s
Wavelength	λ	metre	m

Fundamental constants

Constant	Symbol	Value
Boltzmann constant	k	$1.38062 \times 10^{-23}\,JK^{-1}$
Electron charge, proton charge	e	$\pm 1.60219 \times 10^{-19}\,C$
Electron charge-to-mass ratio	e/m	$1.7588 \times 10^{11}\,Ckg^{-1}$
Electron mass	m_e	$9.10956 \times 10^{-31}\,kg$
Electron radius	r_e	$2.81794 \times 10^{-15}\,m$
Faraday constant	F	$9.64867 \times 10^{4}\,Cmol^{-1}$
Neutron mass	m_n	$1.67492 \times 10^{-27}\,kg$
Permeability of space	μ_o	$4\pi \times 10^{-7}\,Hm^{-1}$
Permittivity of space	ε_o	$8.85419 \times 10^{-12}\,Fm^{-1}$
Planck constant	h	$6.6262 \times 10^{-34}\,Js$
Proton mass	m_p	$1.67251 \times 10^{-27}\,kg$
Velocity of light	c	$2.99793 \times 10^{8}\,ms^{-1}$

Electrical relationships

Amperes × ohms = **volts**
Volts ÷ amperes = **ohms**
Volts ÷ ohms = **amperes**
Amperes × volts = **watts**
(Amperes)^2 × ohms = **watts**
(Volts)^2 ÷ ohms = **watts**
Joules per second = **watts**
Coulombs per second = **amperes**
Amperes × seconds = **coulombs**
Farads × volts = **coulombs**
Coulombs ÷ volts = **farads**
Coulombs ÷ farads = **volts**
Volts × coulombs = **joules**
Farads × (volts)^2 = **joules**

Dimensions of physical properties

Length: metre [L]. Mass: kilogram [M]. Time: second [T]. Quantity of electricity: coulomb [Q]. Area: square metre [L^2]. Volume: cubic metre [L^3].

Velocity: metre per second	$[LT^{-1}]$
Acceleration: metre per second^2	$[LT^{-2}]$
Force: newton	$[MLT^{-2}]$
Work: joule	$[ML^2T^{-2}]$
Power: watt	$[ML^2T^{-3}]$
Electric current: ampere	$[QT^{-1}]$
Voltage: volt	$[ML^2T^{-2}Q^{-1}]$
Electric resistance: ohm	$[ML^2T^{-1}Q^{-2}]$
Electric conductance: siemens	$[M^{-1}L^{-2}TQ^2]$

Inductance: henry	$[ML^2Q^{-2}]$
Capacitance: farad	$[M^{-1}L^{-2}T^2Q^2]$
Current density: ampere per metre^2	$[L^{-2}T^{-1}Q]$
Electric field strength: volt per metre	$[MLT^{-2}Q^{-1}]$
Magnetic flux: weber	$[MLT^2T^{-1}Q^{-1}]$
Magnetic flux density: tesla	$[MT^{-1}Q^{-1}]$
Energy: joule	$[ML^2T^{-2}]$
Frequency: hertz	$[T^{-1}]$
Pressure: pascal	$[ML^{-1}T^{-2}]$

Fundamental units

Quantity	Unit	Symbol
Amount of a substance	mole	mol
Charge	coulomb	C
Length	metre	m
Luminous intensity	candela	cd
Mass	kilogram	kg
Plane angle	radian	rad
Solid angle	steradian	sr
Thermodynamic temperature	kelvin	K
Time	second	s

Greek alphabet

Capital letters	Small letters	Greek name	English equivalent	Capital letters	Small letters	Greek name	English equivalent
A	α	Alpha	a	N	ν	Nu	n
B	β	Beta	b	Ξ	ξ	Xi	x
Γ	γ	Gamma	g	O	o	Omicron	ŏ
Δ	δ	Delta	d	Π	π	Pi	p
E	ε	Epsilon	e	P	ρ	Rho	r
Z	ζ	Zeta	z	Σ	ς	Sigma	s
H	η	Eta	é	T	τ	Tau	t
Θ	θ	Theta	th	Y	υ	Upsilon	u
I	ι	Iota	i	Φ	φ	Phi	ph
K	κ	Kappa	k	X	χ	Chi	ch
Λ	λ	Lambda	l	Ψ	ψ	Psi	ps
M	μ	Mu	m	Ω	ω	Omega	ö

Standard units

Ampere Unit of electric current, the constant current which, if maintained in two straight parallel conductors of infinite length of negligible circular cross-section and placed one metre apart in a vacuum, will produce between them a force equal to 2×10^{-7} newton per metre length.

Ampere-hour Unit of quantity of electricity equal to 3,600 coulombs. One unit is represented by one ampere flowing for one hour.

Candela Unit of luminous intensity. It is the luminous intensity, in the perpendicular direction, of a surface of $1/600,000 \, m^{-2}$ of a full radiator at the temperature of freezing platinum under a pressure of $101,325$ newtons m^{-2}.

Coulomb Unit of electric charge, the quantity of electricity transported in one second by one ampere.

Decibel (dB) Unit of acoustical or electrical power ratio. Although the bel is officially the unit, this is usually regarded as being too large, so the decibel is preferred. The difference between two power levels, P_1 and P_2, is given as

$$10\log_{10} \frac{P_1}{P_2} \text{ decibels}$$

Farad Unit of electric capacitance. The capacitance of a capacitor between the plates of which there appears a difference of potential of one volt when it is charged by one coulomb of electricity. Practical units are the microfarad (10^{-6} farad), the nanofarad (10^{-9}) and the picofarad (10^{-12} farad).

Henry Unit of electrical inductance. The inductance of a closed circuit in which an electromotive force of one volt is produced when the electric current in the circuit varies uniformly at the rate of one ampere per second. Practical units are the microhenry (10^{-6} henry) and the millihenry (10^{-3} henry).

Hertz Unit of frequency. The number of repetitions of a regular occurrence in one second.

Joule Unit of energy, including work and quantity of heat. The work done when the point of application of a force of one newton is displaced through a distance of one metre in the direction of the force.

Kilovolt-ampere 1,000 volt-amperes.

Kilowatt 1,000 watts.

Lumen m^{-2}, lux Unit of illuminance of a surface.

Mho Unit of conductance, see Siemens.

Newton Unit of force. That force which, applied to a mass of one kilogram, gives it an acceleration of one metre per second per second.

Ohm Unit of electric resistance. The resistance between two points of a conductor when a constant difference of potential of one volt, applied between these two points, produces in the conductor a current of one ampere.

Pascal Unit of sound pressure. Pressure is usually quoted as the root mean square pressure for a pure sinusoidal wave.

Siemens Unit of conductance, the reciprocal of the ohm. A body having a resistance of 4 ohms would have a conductance of 0·25 siemens.

Tesla Unit of magnetic flux density, equal to one weber per square metre of circuit area.

Volt Unit of electric potential. The difference of electric potential between two points of a conducting wire carrying a constant current of one ampere, when the power dissipated between these points is equal to one watt.

Volt-ampere The product of the root-mean-square volts and root-mean-square amperes.

Watt Unit of power, equal to one joule per second. Volts times amperes equals watts.

Weber Unit of magnetic flux. The magnetic flux which, linking a circuit of one turn, produces in it an electromotive force of one volt as it is reduced to zero at a uniform rate in one second.

Light, velocity of Light waves travel at 300,000 kilometres per second (approximately). Also the velocity of radio waves.

Sound, velocity of Sound waves travel at 332 metres per second in air (approximately) at sea level.

Decimal multipliers

Prefix	Symbol	Multiplier	Prefix	Symbol	Multiplier	Prefix	Symbol	Multiplier
tera	T	10^{12}	deka	da	10	nano	n	10^{-9}
giga	G	10^{9}	deci	d	10^{-1}	pico	p	10^{-12}
mega	M	10^{6}	centi	c	10^{-2}	femto	f	10^{-15}
kilo	k	10^{3}	milli	m	10^{-3}	atto	a	10^{-18}
hecto	h	10^{2}	micro	μ	10^{-6}			

Electronic multiple and sub-multiple conversion

these to → These multiply by the figures below →

these ↓

	Tera-	Giga-	Mega-	Myria-	Kilo-	Hekto-	Deka-	Units	Deci-	Centi-	Milli-	Micro-	Nano-	Pico-
Pico-	10^{-24}	10^{-21}	10^{-18}	10^{-16}	10^{-15}	10^{-14}	10^{-13}	10^{-12}	10^{-11}	10^{-10}	10^{-9}	10^{-6}	0·001	
Nano-	10^{-21}	10^{-18}	10^{-15}	10^{-13}	10^{-12}	10^{-11}	10^{-10}	10^{-9}	10^{-8}	10^{-7}	10^{-6}	0·001		1,000
Micro-	10^{-18}	10^{-15}	10^{-12}	10^{-10}	10^{-9}	10^{-8}	10^{-7}	10^{-6}	0·00001	0·0001	0·001		1,000	10^{6}
Milli-	10^{-15}	10^{-12}	10^{-9}	10^{-7}	10^{-6}	0·00001	0·0001	0·001	0·01	0·1		1,000	10^{6}	10^{9}
Centi-	10^{-14}	10^{-11}	10^{-8}	10^{-6}	0·00001	0·0001	0·001	0·01	0·1		10	10,000	10^{7}	10^{10}
Deci-	10^{-13}	10^{-10}	10^{-7}	0·00001	0·0001	0·001	0·01	0·1		10	100	100,000	10^{8}	10^{11}
Units	10^{-12}	10^{-9}	10^{-6}	0·0001	0·001	0·01	0·1		10	100	1,000	10^{6}	10^{9}	10^{12}
Deka-	10^{-11}	10^{-8}	0·00001	0·001	0·01	0·1		10	100	1,000	10,000	10^{7}	10^{10}	10^{13}
Hekto-	10^{-10}	10^{-7}	0·0001	0·01	0·1		10	100	1,000	10,000	100,000	10^{8}	10^{11}	10^{14}
Kilo-	10^{-9}	10^{-6}	0·001	0·1		10	100	1,000	10,000	100,000	10^{6}	10^{9}	10^{12}	10^{15}
Myria-	10^{-8}	0·00001	0·01		10	100	1,000	10,000	100,000	10^{6}	10^{7}	10^{10}	10^{13}	10^{16}
Mega-	10^{-6}	0·001		100	1,000	10,000	100,000	10^{6}	10^{7}	10^{8}	10^{9}	10^{12}	10^{15}	10^{18}
Giga-	0·001		1,000	100,000	10^{6}	10^{7}	10^{8}	10^{9}	10^{10}	10^{11}	10^{12}	10^{15}	10^{18}	10^{21}
Tera-		1,000	10^{6}	10^{8}	10^{9}	10^{10}	10^{11}	10^{12}	10^{13}	10^{14}	10^{15}	10^{18}	10^{21}	10^{24}

Useful formulae

Boolean Algebra (laws of)

Absorption:	$A + (A.B) = A$
	$A.(A + B) = A$
Annulment:	$A + 1 = 1$
	$A.0 = 0$
Association:	$(A + B) + C = A + (B + C)$
	$(A.B).C = A.(B.C)$
Commutation:	$A + B = B + A$
	$A.B = B.A$
Complements:	$A + \bar{A} = 1$
	$A.\bar{A} = 0$
De Morgan's:	$\overline{(A + B)} = \bar{A}.\bar{B}$
	$\overline{(A.B)} = \bar{A} + \bar{B}$
Distributive:	$A.(B + C) = (A.B) + (A.C)$
	$A + (B.C) = (A + B).(A + C)$
Double negation:	$\bar{\bar{A}} = A$
Identity:	$A + O = A$
	$A.1 = A$
Tautology:	$A.A = A$
	$A + A = A$

Capacitance

The capacitance of a parallel plate capacitor can be found from

$$C = \frac{0.885\, KA}{d}$$

C is in picofarads, K is the dielectric constant (air = 1), A is the area of the plate in square cm and d the thickness of the dielectric.

Calculation of overall capacitance with:
Parallel capacitors – $C = C_1 + C_2 + \dots$

Series capacitors – $\dfrac{1}{C} = \dfrac{1}{C_1} + \dfrac{1}{C_2} + \dots$

Characteristic impedance

$$(\text{open wire})\ Z = 276 \log \frac{2D}{d}\ \text{ohms}$$

where $\left.\begin{array}{l} D = \text{wire spacing} \\ d = \text{wire diameter} \end{array}\right\}$ in same units.

$$(\text{coaxial})\ Z = \frac{138}{\sqrt{(K)}} \log \frac{d_o}{d_i}\ \text{ohms}$$

where K = dielectric constant, d_o = outside diameter of inner conductor, d_i = inside diameter of outer conductor.

Dynamic resistance

In a parallel-tuned circuit at resonance the dynamic resistance is

$$R_d = \frac{L}{Cr} = Q\omega L = \frac{Q}{\omega C} \text{ ohms}$$

where L = inductance (henries), C = capacitance (farads), r = effective series resistance (ohms). Q = Q-value of coil, and $\omega = 2\pi \times$ frequency (hertz).

Frequency—wavelength—velocity
(See also Resonance.)
The velocity of propagation of a wave is

$$v = f\lambda \text{ metres per second}$$

where f = frequency (hertz) and λ = wavelength (metres).

For electromagnetic waves in free space the velocity of propagation v is approximately 3×10^8 m/sec, and if f is expressed in kilohertz and λ in metres

$$f = \frac{300,000}{\lambda} \text{ kilohertz} \qquad f = \frac{300}{\lambda} \text{ megahertz}$$

or

$$\lambda = \frac{300,000}{f} \text{ metres} \qquad \lambda = \frac{300}{f} \text{ metres}$$

f in kilohertz $\qquad f$ in megahertz

Horizon distance

Horizon distance can be calculated from the formula

$$S = 1.42\sqrt{H}$$

where S = distance in miles and H = height in feet above sea level.

Impedance

The impedance of a circuit comprising inductance, capacitance and resistance in series is

$$Z = \sqrt{R^2 + \left(\omega L - \frac{1}{\omega C}\right)^2}$$

where R = resistance (ohms), $\omega = 2\pi \times$ frequency (hertz), L = inductance (henries), and C = capacitance (farads).

Inductance
Single layer coils

$$L \text{ (in microhenries)} = \frac{a^2 N^2}{9a + 10l} \text{ approximately}$$

If the desired inductance is known, the number of turns required may be determined by the formula

$$N = \frac{5L}{na^2}\left[1 + \sqrt{\left(1 + \frac{0.36n^2a^3}{L}\right)}\right]$$

where N = number of turns, a = radius of coil in inches, n = number of turns per inch, L = inductance in microhenries (μH) and l = length of coil in inches.

Calculation of overall inductance with:
Series inductors − L = L$_1$ + L$_2$ + ...

Parallel inductors − $\dfrac{1}{L} = \dfrac{1}{L_1} + \dfrac{1}{L_2} + ...$

Meter conversions
Increasing range of ammeters or milliammeters
Current range of meter can be increased by connecting a shunt resistance across meter terminals. If R_m is the resistance of the meter; R_s the value of the shunt resistance and n the number of times it is wished to multiply the scale reading, then

$$R_s = \frac{R_m}{(n-1)}.$$

Increasing range of voltmeters
Voltage range of meter can be increased by connecting resistance in series with it. If this series resistance is R_s and R_m and n as before, then $R_s = R_m \times (n-1)$.

Negative feedback
Voltage feedback

$$\text{Gain with feedback} = \frac{A}{1 + Ab}$$

where A is the original gain of the amplifier section over which feedback is applied (including the output transformer if included) and b is the fraction of the output voltage fed back.

$$\text{Distortion with feedback} = \frac{d}{1 + Ab} \text{ approximately}$$

where d is the original distortion of the amplifier.

Ohm's Law

$$I = \frac{V}{R} \qquad V = IR \qquad R = \frac{V}{I}$$

where I = current (amperes), V = voltage (volts), and R = resistance (ohms).

Power
In a d.c. circuit the power developed is given by

$$W = VI = \frac{V^2}{R} = I^2R \text{ watts}$$

where V = voltage (volts), I = current (amperes), and R = resistance (ohms).

Power ratio

$$P = 10 \log \frac{P_1}{P_2}$$

where P = ratio in decibels. P_1 and P_2 are the two power levels.

Q

The Q value of an inductance is given by

$$Q = \frac{\omega L}{R}$$

Reactance

The reactance of an inductor and a capacitor respectively is given by

$$X_L = \omega L \text{ ohms} \qquad X_C = \frac{1}{\omega C} \text{ ohms}$$

where $\omega = 2\pi \times$ frequency (hertz), L = inductance (henries), and C = capacitance (farads).

The total resistance of an inductance and a capacitance in series is $X_L - X_C$.

Resistance

Calculation of overall resistance with:

Series resistors – $R = R_1 + R_2 + ...$

Parallel resistors – $\dfrac{1}{R} = \dfrac{1}{R_1} + \dfrac{1}{R_2} + ...$

Resonance

The resonant frequency of a tuned circuit is given by

$$f = \frac{1}{2\pi \sqrt{LC}} \text{hertz}$$

where L = inductance (henries), and C = capacitance (farads).

If L is in microhenries (μH) and C is in picofarads, this becomes—

$$f = \frac{10^6}{2\pi \sqrt{LC}} \text{kilohertz}$$

The basic formula can be rearranged

$$L = \frac{1}{4\pi^2 f^2 C} \text{ henries} \qquad C = \frac{1}{4\pi^2 f^2 L} \text{ farads.}$$

Since $2\pi f$ is commonly represented by ω, these expressions can be written

$$L = \frac{1}{\omega^2 C} \text{ henries} \qquad C = \frac{1}{\omega^2 L} \text{ farads.}$$

Time constant

For a combination of inductance and resistance in series the time constant (i.e. the time required for the current to reach 63% of its final value) is given by

$$\tau = \frac{L}{R} \text{ seconds}$$

where L = inductance (henries), and R = resistance (ohms).

For a combination of capacitance and resistance in series the time constant (i.e. the time required for the voltage across the capacitance to reach 63% of its final value) is given by

$$\tau = CR \text{ seconds}$$

where C = capacitance (farads), and R = resistance (ohms).

Transformer ratios
The ratio of a transformer refers to the ratio of the number of turns in one winding to the number of turns in the other winding. To avoid confusion it is always desirable to state in which sense the ratio is being expressed: e.g. the 'primary-to-secondary' ratio n_p/n_s. The turns ratio is related to the impedance ratio thus

$$\frac{n_p}{n_s} = \sqrt{\frac{Z_p}{Z_s}}$$

where n_p = number of primary turns, n_s = number of secondary turns, Z_p = impedance of primary (ohms), and Z_s = impedance of secondary (ohms).

Wattage rating
If resistance and current values are known,

$$W = I^2R \text{ when } I \text{ is in amperes}$$

or

$$W = \frac{\text{Milliamps.}^2}{1,000,000} \times R.$$

If wattage rating and value of resistance are known, the safe current for the resistor can be calculated from

$$\text{milliamperes} = 1,000 \times \sqrt{\frac{\text{Watts}}{\text{Ohms}}}$$

Wavelength of tuned circuit
Formula for the wavelength in metres of a tuned oscillatory circuit is: $1885 \sqrt{LC}$, where L = inductance in microhenries and C = capacitance in microfarads.

Resistor and capacitor colour coding

Colour	Band A	Band B	Band C (multiplier) Resistors	Band C (multiplier) Capacitors	Band D (tolerance) Resistors	Band D (tolerance) Capacitors Up to 10 pF
Black	—	0	1	1	—	2 pF
Brown	1	1	10	10	±1%	0·1 pF
Red	2	2	100	100	±2%	—
Orange	3	3	1,000	1,000	—	—
Yellow	4	4	10,000	10,000	—	—
Green	5	5	100,000	—	—	0·5 pF
Blue	6	6	1,000,000	—	—	—
Violet	7	7	10,000,000	—	—	—
Grey	8	8	10^8	0·01 μF	—	0·25 pF
White	9	9	10^9	0^1 μF	—	1 pF
Silver	—	—	0·01	—	±10%	—
Gold	—	—	0·1	—	±5%	—
Pink	—	—	—	—	—	—
None	—	—	—	—	±20%	—

Resistor and capacitor letter and digit code

(BS 1852)

Resistor values are indicated as follows:

0·47 Ω	marked	R47		100 Ω	marked	100R
1 Ω		1R0		1 kΩ		1K0
4·7 Ω		4R7		10 kΩ		10K
47 Ω		47R		10 MΩ		10M

A letter following the value shows the tolerance.
F = ±1%; G = ±2%; J = ±5%; K = ±10%; M = ±20%;
R33M = 0·33 Ω ±20%; 6K8F = 6·8 kΩ ±1%.

Capacitor values are indicated as:

0·68 pF	marked	p68		6·8 nf	marked	6n8
6·8 pf		6p8		1000 nF		1µ0
1000 pF		1n0		6·8 µF		6µ8

Tolerance is indicated by letters as for resistors. Values up to
999 pF are marked in pF, from 1000 pf to 999 000 pF (= 999 nF) as
nF (1000 pF = 1 nF) and from 1000 nF (= 1 µF) upwards as µF.

Some capacitors are marked with a code denoting the value in pF
(first two figures) followed by a multiplier as a power of ten (3 =
10^3). Letters denote tolerance as for resistors but C = ±0·25 pf.
E.g. 123 J = 12 pF × 10^3 ± 5% = 12 000 pF (or 0·12 µF).

Note that adjacent bands may be of the same colour unseparated.

Over 10 pF	Band E Resistors	Polyester capacitors
±20%	—	—
±1%	—	—
±2%	—	250 v.w.
±2·5%	—	—
—	—	—
±5%	—	—
—	—	—
—	—	—
—	—	—
±10%	—	—
—	—	—
—	—	—
—	Hi-Stab.	—
—	—	—

Preferred values

E12 Series

1·0	1·2	1·5	1·8	2·2	2·7
3·3	3·9	4·7	5·6	6·8	8·2

and their decades

E24 Series

1·0	1·1	1·2	1·3	1·5	1·6
1·8	2·0	2·2	2·4	2·7	3·0
3·3	3·6	3·9	4·3	4·7	5·1
5·6	6·2	6·8	7·5	8·2	9·1

and their decades

(continued on page 34)

RC time constants

Capacitance (microfarads)

Time (sec.)	0.1	0.2	0.3	0.4	0.5	0.6	0.7	0.8	0.9	1.0
0.1	1.0 M	500 k	333 k	250 k	200 k	166 k	143 k	125 k	111 k	100 k
0.15	1.5 M	750 k	500 k	375 k	300 k	250 k	214 k	188 k	167 k	150 k
0.2	2.0 M	1.00 M	666 k	500 k	400 k	333 k	286 k	250 k	222 k	200 k
0.25	2.5 M	1.25 M	833 k	625 k	500 k	417 k	357 k	313 k	278 k	250 k
0.3	3.0 M	1.50 M	1.00 M	750 k	600 k	500 k	429 k	375 k	333 k	300 k
0.35	3.5 M	1.75 M	1.17 M	875 k	700 k	583 k	500 k	438 k	389 k	350 k
0.4	4.0 M	2.00 M	1.33 M	1.00 M	800 k	666 k	571 k	500 k	444 k	400 k
0.45	4.5 M	2.25 M	1.50 M	1.13 M	900 k	750 k	643 k	563 k	500 k	450 k
0.5	5.0 M	2.50 M	1.67 M	1.25 M	1.0 M	833 k	714 k	625 k	555 k	500 k
0.55	5.5 M	2.75 M	1.83 M	1.38 M	1.1 M	917 k	786 k	688 k	611 k	550 k
0.6	6.0 M	3.00 M	2.00 M	1.50 M	1.2 M	1.00 M	857 k	750 k	666 k	600 k
0.65	6.5 M	3.25 M	2.17 M	1.63 M	1.3 M	1.08 M	929 k	813 k	722 k	650 k
0.7	7.0 M	3.50 M	2.33 M	1.75 M	1.4 M	1.17 M	1.00 M	875 k	778 k	700 k
0.75	7.5 M	3.75 M	2.50 M	1.88 M	1.5 M	1.25 M	1.07 M	938 k	833 k	750 k
0.8	8.0 M	4.00 M	2.67 M	2.00 M	1.6 M	1.33 M	1.14 M	1.00 M	889 k	800 k
0.85	8.5 M	4.25 M	2.83 M	2.13 M	1.7 M	1.42 M	1.21 M	1.06 M	944 k	850 k
0.9	9.0 M	4.50 M	3.00 M	2.25 M	1.8 M	1.50 M	1.29 M	1.13 M	1.00 M	900 k
0.95	9.5 M	4.75 M	3.17 M	2.38 M	1.9 M	1.58 M	1.36 M	1.19 M	1.06 M	950 k
1.0	10.0 M	5.00 M	3.33 M	2.50 M	2.0 M	1.67 M	1.43 M	1.25 M	1.11 M	1.0 M
1.5	15.0 M	7.50 M	5.00 M	3.75 M	3.0 M	2.50 M	2.14 M	1.88 M	1.67 M	1.5 M
2.0	20.0 M	10.00 M	6.66 M	5.00 M	4.0 M	3.33 M	2.86 M	2.50 M	2.22 M	2.0 M

2·5	25·0 M	12·50 M	8·33 M	6·25 M	5·0 M	4·17 M	3·57 M	3·13 M	2·78 M	2·5 M
3·0	30·0 M	15·00 M	10·00 M	7·50 M	6·0 M	5·00 M	4·29 M	3·75 M	3·33 M	3·0 M
3·5	35·0 M	17·50 M	11·66 M	8·75 M	7·0 M	5·83 M	5·00 M	4·38 M	3·89 M	3·5 M
4·0	40·0 M	20·00 M	13·33 M	10·00 M	8·0 M	6·66 M	5·71 M	5·00 M	4·44 M	4·0 M
4·5	45·0 M	22·50 M	15·00 M	11·25 M	9·0 M	7·50 M	6·43 M	5·63 M	5·00 M	4·5 M
5·0	50·0 M	25·00 M	16·67 M	12·50 M	10·0 M	8·33 M	7·14 M	6·25 M	5·55 M	5·0 M
5·5	55·0 M	27·50 M	18·33 M	13·75 M	11·0 M	9·17 M	7·86 M	6·88 M	6·11 M	5·5 M
6·0	60·0 M	30·00 M	20·00 M	15·00 M	12·0 M	10·00 M	8·57 M	7·50 M	6·66 M	6·0 M
6·5	65·0 M	32·50 M	21·67 M	16·25 M	13·0 M	10·83 M	9·29 M	8·13 M	7·22 M	6·5 M
7·0	70·0 M	35·00 M	23·33 M	17·50 M	14·0 M	11·67 M	10·00 M	8·75 M	7·78 M	7·0 M
7·5	75·0 M	37·50 M	25·00 M	18·75 M	15·0 M	12·50 M	10·71 M	9·38 M	8·33 M	7·5 M
8·0	80·0 M	40·00 M	26·67 M	20·00 M	16·0 M	13·33 M	11·43 M	10·00 M	8·89 M	8·0 M
9·0	90·0 M	45·00 M	30·00 M	22·50 M	18·0 M	15·00 M	12·86 M	11·25 M	10·00 M	9·0 M
10·0	100·0 M	50·00 M	33·33 M	25·00 M	20·0 M	16·66 M	14·28 M	12·50 M	11·11 M	10·0 M

k = kilohms   M = megohms

RL time constants

Time (sec.)	| Inductance (henrys) 10	20	30	40	50	60	70	80	90	100
0·1	100·0	200·0	300·0	400·0	500·0	600·0	700·0	800·0	900·0	1000·0
0·15	66·7	133·3	200·0	266·7	333·3	400·0	466·7	533·3	600·0	666·7
0·2	50·0	100·0	150·0	200·0	250·0	300·0	350·0	400·0	450·0	500·0
0·25	40·0	80·0	120·0	160·0	200·0	240·0	280·0	320·0	360·0	400·0
0·3	33·3	66·7	100·0	133·3	166·7	200·0	233·3	266·6	300·0	333·3
0·35	28·6	57·1	86·6	114·3	142·9	171·4	200·0	228·6	257·1	285·7
0·4	25·0	50·0	75·0	100·0	125·0	150·0	175·0	200·0	225·0	250·0
0·45	22·2	44·4	66·7	88·9	111·1	133·3	155·6	177·8	200·0	222·2
0·5	20·0	40·0	60·0	80·0	100·0	120·0	140·0	160·0	180·0	200·0
0·55	18·2	36·4	54·5	72·7	90·9	109·1	127·3	145·5	163·6	181·8
0·6	16·7	33·3	50·0	66·7	83·3	100·0	116·7	133·3	150·0	166·7
0·65	15·4	30·8	46·2	61·5	76·9	92·3	107·7	123·1	138·5	153·8
0·7	14·3	28·6	42·9	57·1	71·4	85·7	100·0	114·3	128·7	142·9
0·75	13·3	26·7	40·0	53·3	66·7	80·0	93·3	106·7	120·0	133·3
0·8	12·5	25·0	37·5	50·0	62·5	75·0	87·5	100·0	112·5	125·0
0·85	11·8	23·5	35·3	47·1	58·8	70·6	82·3	94·1	105·9	117·6
0·9	11·1	22·2	33·3	44·4	55·5	66·6	77·8	88·9	100·0	111·1
0·95	10·5	21·1	31·6	42·1	52·6	63·2	73·7	84·2	94·7	105·3
1·0	10·0	20·0	30·0	40·0	50·0	60·0	70·0	80·0	90·0	100·0
1·5	6·7	13·3	20·0	26·7	33·3	40·0	46·7	53·3	60·0	66·7

	5·0	10·0	15·0	20·0	25·0	30·0	35·0	40·0	45·0	50·0
2·0	5·0	10·0	15·0	20·0	25·0	30·0	35·0	40·0	45·0	50·0
2·5	4·0	8·0	12·0	16·0	20·0	24·0	28·0	32·0	36·0	40·0
3·0	3·3	6·7	10·0	13·3	16·7	20·0	23·3	26·7	30·0	33·3
3·5	2·9	5·7	8·7	11·4	14·3	17·1	20·0	22·9	25·7	28·6
4·0	2·5	5·0	7·5	10·0	12·5	15·0	17·5	20·0	22·5	25·0
4·5	2·2	4·4	6·7	8·9	11·1	13·3	15·6	17·8	20·0	22·2
5·0	2·0	4·0	6·0	8·0	10·0	12·0	14·0	16·0	18·0	20·0
5·5	1·8	3·6	5·5	7·3	9·1	10·9	12·7	14·6	16·4	18·2
6·0	1·7	3·3	5·0	6·7	8·3	10·0	11·7	13·3	15·0	16·7
6·5	1·5	3·1	4·6	6·2	7·7	9·2	10·8	12·3	13·9	15·4
7·0	1·4	2·9	4·3	5·7	7·1	8·6	10·0	11·4	12·9	14·3
7·5	1·3	2·7	4·0	5·3	6·7	8·0	9·3	10·7	12·0	13·3
8·0	1·2	2·5	3·8	5·0	6·3	7·5	8·8	10·0	11·3	12·5
9·0	1·1	2·2	3·3	4·4	5·5	6·7	7·8	8·9	10·0	11·1
10·0	1·0	2·0	3·0	4·0	5·0	6·0	7·0	8·0	9·0	10·0

All resistance values in ohms

Resistor and capacitor colour coding

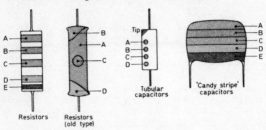

| | | Resistors | Resistors (old type) | Tubular capacitors | 'Candy stripe' capacitors |

Tubular capacitors — Tip: A, B, C, D

'Candy stripe' capacitors — A, B, C, D, E

Tantalum capacitors

	1	2	3	4
Black	—	0	× 1	10 V
Brown	1	1	× 10	
Red	2	2	× 100	
Orange	3	3	—	
Yellow	4	4	—	6·3 V
Green	5	5	—	16 V
Blue	6	6	—	20 V
Violet	7	7	—	
Grey	8	8	× 0·01	25 V
White	9	9	× 0·1	3 V
				(Pink 35 V)

Reactance of capacitors at spot frequencies

	50 Hz	100 Hz	1 kHz	10 kHz	100 kHz	1 MHz	10 MHz	100 MHz
1 pF	—	—	—	—	1·6 M	160 k	16 k	1·6 k
10 pF	—	—	—	1·6 M	160 k	16 k	1·6 k	160
50 pF	—	—	—	320 k	32 k	3·2 k	320	32
250 pF	—	6·4 M	640 k	64 k	6·4 k	640	64	6·4
1,000 pF	3·2 M	1·6 M	160 k	16 k	1·6 k	160	16	1·6
2,000 pF	1·6 M	800 k	80 k	8 k	800	80	8	0·8
0.01 µF	320 k	160 k	16 k	1·6 k	160	16	1·6	0·16
0.05 µF	64 k	32 k	3·2 k	320	32	3·2	0·32	—
0.1 µF	32 k	16 k	1·6 k	160	16	1·6	0·16	—
1 µF	3·2 k	1·6 k	160	16	1·6	0·16	—	—
2·5 µF	1·3 k	640	64	6·4	0·64	—	—	—
5 µF	640	320	32	3·2	0·32	—	—	—
10 µF	320	160	16	1·6	0·16	—	—	—
30 µF	107	53	5·3	0·53	—	—	—	—
100 µF	32	16	1·6	0·16	—	—	—	—
1,000 µF	3·2	1·6	0·16	—	—	—	—	—

Values above 10 MΩ and below 0·1 Ω not shown. Values in ohms.

Reactance of inductors at spot frequencies

	50 Hz	100 Hz	1 kHz	10 kHz	100 kHz	1 MHz	10 MHz	100 MHz
1 µH	—	—	—	—	0·63	6·3	63	630
5 µH	—	—	—	0·31	3·1	31	310	3·1 k
10 µH	—	—	—	0·63	6·3	63	630	6·3 k
50 µH	—	—	0·31	3·1	31	310	3·1 k	31 k
100 µH	—	—	0·63	6·3	63	630	6·3 k	63 k
250 µH	—	0·16	1·6	16	160	1·6 k	16 k	160 k
1 mH	0·31	0·63	6·3	63	630	6·3 k	63 k	630 k
2·5 mH	0·8	1·6	16	160	1·6 k	16 k	160 k	1·6 M
10 mH	3·1	6·3	63	630	6·3 k	63 k	630 k	6·3 M
25 mH	8	16	160	1·6 k	16 k	160 k	1·6 M	—
100 mH	31	63	630	6·3 k	63 k	630 k	6·3 M	—
1 H	310	630	6·3 k	63 k	630 k	6·3 M	—	—
5 H	1·5 k	3·1 k	31 k	310 k	3·1 M	—	—	—
10 H	3·1 k	6·3 k	63 k	630 k	6·3 M	—	—	—
100 H	31 k	63 k	630 k	6·3 M	—	—	—	—

Values above 10 MΩ and below 0·1 Ω not shown. Values in ohms.

Transistor letter symbols

Bipolar

C_{cb}, C_{ce}, C_{eb} Interterminal capacitance (collector-to-base, collector-to-emitter, emitter-to-base).

C_{ibo}, C_{ieo} Open-circuit input capacitance (common-base, common-emitter).

C_{ibs}, C_{ies} Short-circuit input capacitance (common-base, common-emitter).

C_{obo}, C_{oeo} Open-circuit output capacitance (common-base, common-emitter).

C_{obs}, C_{oes} Short-circuit output capacitance (common-base, common-emitter).

C_{rbs}, C_{res} Short-circuit reverse transfer capacitance (common-base, common-emitter).

C_{tc}, C_{te} Depletion-layer capacitance (collector, emitter).

f_{hfb}, h_{fe} Small-signal short-circuit forward current transfer ratio cutoff frequency (common-base, common-emitter).

f_{max} Maximum frequency of oscillation.

f_T Transition frequency or frequency at which small-signal forward current transfer ratio (common-emitter) extrapolates to unity.

f_1 Frequency of unity current transfer ratio.

G_{PB}, G_{PE} Large-signal insertion power gain (common-base, common-emitter).

G_{pb}, G_{pe} Small-signal insertion power gain (common-base, common-emitter).

G_{TB}, G_{TE} Large-signal transducer power gain (common-base, common-emitter)

G_{tb}, G_{te} Small-signal transducer power gain (common-base, common-emitter).

h_{FB}, h_{FE} Static forward current transfer ratio (common-base, common-emitter).

h_{fb}, h_{fe} Small-signal short-circuit forward current transfer ratio (common-base, common-emitter).

h_{ib}, h_{ie} Small-signal short-circuit input impedance (common-base, common-emitter).

$h_{ie(imag)}$ or $Im(h_{ie})$ Imaginary part of the small-signal short-circuit input impedance (common-emitter).

$h_{ie(real)}$ or $Re(h_{ie})$ Real part of the small-signal short-circuit input impedance (common-emitter).

h_{ob}, h_{oe} Small-signal open-circuit output admittance (common-base, common-emitter).

$h_{oe(imag)}$ or $Im(h_{oe})$ Imaginary part of the small-signal open-circuit output admittance (common-emitter).

$h_{oe(real)}$ or $Re(h_{oe})$ Real part of the small-signal open-circuit output admittance (common-emitter).

h_{rb}, h_{re} Small-signal open-circuit reverse voltage transfer ratio (common-base, common-emitter).

I_B, I_C, I_E Current, d.c. (base-terminal, collector-terminal, emitter-terminal).

I_b, I_c, I_e Current, r.m.s. value of alternating component (base-terminal, collector-terminal, emitter-terminal).

i_B, i_C, i_E Current, instantaneous total value (base-terminal, collector-terminal, emitter-terminal).

I_{BEV} Base cutoff current, d.c.

I_{CBO} Collector cutoff current, d.c., emitter open.

$I_{E1E2(off)}$ Emitter cutoff current.

I_{EBO} Emitter cutoff current, d.c., collector open.

$I_{Ec(ofs)}$ Emitter-collector offset current.

I_{ECS} Emitter cutoff current, d.c., base-short-circuited to collector.

P_{IB}, P_{IE} Large-signal input power (common-base, common-emitter).

P_{ib}, P_{ie} Small-signal input power (common-base, common-emitter).

P_{OB}, P_{OE} Large-signal output power (common-base, common-emitter).

P_{ob}, P_{oe} Small-signal output power (common-base, common-emitter).

P_T Total nonreactive power input to all terminals.

$r_b'C_c$ Collector-base time constant.

$r_{CE(sat)}$ Saturation resistance, collector-to-emitter.

$Re(y_{ie})$

$Re(y_{oe})$

$r_{e1e2(on)}$ Small-signal emitter-emitter on-state resistance.

R_θ Thermal resistance.

T_j Junction temperature.

t_d Delay time.

t_f Fall time.

t_{off} Turn-off time.

t_{on} Turn-on time.

t_p Pulse time.

t_r Rise time.

t_s Storage time.

t_w Pulse average time.

V_{BB}, V_{CC}, V_{EE} Supply voltage, d.c. (base, collector, emitter).

V_{BC}, V_{BE}, V_{CB}, V_{CE}, V_{EB}, V_{EC} Voltage, d.c. or average (base-to-collector, base-to-emitter, collector-to-base, collector-to-emitter, emitter-to-base, emitter-to-collector).

v_{bc}, v_{be}, v_{cb}, v_{ce}, v_{eb}, v_{ec} Voltage, instantaneous value of alternating component (base-to-collector, base-to-emitter, collector-to-base, collector-to-emitter, emitter-to-base, emitter-to-collector).

$V_{(BR)CBO}$ **(formerly BV_{CBO})** Breakdown voltage, collector-to-base, emitter open.

V_{RT} Reach-through (punch-through) voltage.

y_{fb}, y_{fe} Small-signal short-circuit forward-transfer admittance (common-base, common-emitter).

y_{ib}, y_{ie} Small-signal short-circuit input admittance (common-base, common-emitter).

$y_{ie(imag)}$ **or $Im(y_{ie})$** Imaginary part of the small-signal short-circuit input admittance (common-emitter).

$y_{ie(real)}$ **or $Re(y_{ie})$** Real part of the small-signal short-circuit input admittance (common-emitter).

y_{ob}, Y_{oe} Small-signal short-circuit output admittance (common-base, common-emitter).

$y_{oe(imag)}$ **or $Im(y_{oe})$** Imaginary part of the small-signal short-circuit output admittance (common-emitter).

$y_{oe(real)}$ **or $Re(y_{oe})$** Real part of the small-signal short-circuit output admittance (common-emitter).

y_{rb}, y_{re} Small-signal short-circuit reverse transfer admittance (common-base, common-emitter).

Unijunction
η Intrinsic standoff ratio.

$I_{B_2(mod)}$ Interbase modulated current.

I_{EB_2O} Emitter reverse current.

I_p Peak-point current.

I_v Valley-point current.

r_{BB} Interbase resistance.

T_j Junction temperature.

t_p Pulse time.

t_w Pulse average time.

$V_{B_2B_1}$ Interbase voltage.

$V_{EB_1(sat)}$ Emitter saturation voltage.

V_{OB_1} Base-1 peak voltage.

V_p Peak-point voltage.

V_v Valley-point voltage.

Field Effect

$b_{fs}, b_{is}, b_{os}, b_{rs}$ Common-source small-signal (forward transfer, input, output, reverse transfer) susceptance.

C_{ds} Drain-source capacitance.

c_{du} Drain-substrate capacitance.

C_{iss} Short-circuit input capacitance, common-source.

C_{oss} Short-circuit output capacitance, common-source.

C_{rss} Short-circuit reverse transfer capacitance, common-source.

$\bar{F}$ or F Noise figure, average or spot.

$g_{fs}, g_{is}, g_{os}, g_{rs}$ Signal (forward transfer, input, output, reverse transfer) conductance.

G_{pg}, G_{ps} Small-signal insertion power gain (common-gate, common-source).

G_{tg}, G_{ts} Small-signal transducer power gain (common-gate, common-source).

$I_{D(off)}$ Drain cutoff current.

$I_{D(on)}$ On-state drain current.

I_{DSS} Zero-gate-voltage drain current.

I_G Gate current, d.c.

I_{GF} Forward gate current.

I_{GR} Reverse gate current.

I_{GSS} Reverse gate current, drain short-circuited to source.

I_{GSSF} Forward gate current, drain short-circuited to source.

I_{GSSR} Reverse gate current, drain short-circuited to source.

I_n Noise current, equivalent input.

$Im(y_{rs})$, $Im(y_{is})$, $Im(y_{os})$, $Im(y_{rs})$.

I_s Source current, d.c.

$I_{S(off)}$ Source cutoff current.

I_{SDS} Zero-gate-voltage source current.

$r_{ds(on)}$ Small-signal drain-source on-state resistance.

$r_{DS(on)}$ Static drain-source on-state resistance.

$t_{d(on)}$ Turn-on delay time.

t_f Fall time.

t_{off} Turn-off time.

t_{on} Turn-on time.

t_p Pulse time.

t_r Rise time.

t_w Pulse average time.

$V_{(BR)GSS}$ Gate-source breakdown voltage.

$V_{(BR)GSSF}$ Forward gate-source breakdown voltage.

$V_{(BR)GSSR}$ Reverse gate-source breakdown voltage.

V_{DD}, V_{GG}, V_{SS} Supply voltage, d.c. (drain, gate, source).

V_{DG} Drain-gate voltage.

V_{DS} Drain-source voltage.

$V_{DS(on)}$ Drain-source on-state voltage.

V_{DU} Drain-substrate voltage.

V_{GS} Gate-source voltage.

V_{GSF} Forward gate-source voltage.

V_{GSR} Reverse gate-source voltage.

$V_{GS(off)}$ Gate-source cutoff voltage.

$V_{GS(th)}$ gate-source threshold voltage.

V_{GU} Gate-substrate voltage.

V_n Noise voltage equivalent input.

V_{SU} Source-substrate voltage.

y_{fs} Common-source small-signal short-circuit forward transfer admittance.

y_{is} Common-source small-signal short-circuit input admittance.

y_{os} Common-source small-signal short-circuit output admittance.

Common transistor and diode data

Bipolar transistors

Type	Case	PUL.MAT	Vce	Vcb	IC.mA	Vces	IC.mA	Hfe
AC107	GT3	NG	15	15	10			30-160
AC125	TO-1	PG	12	32	100			100
AC126	TO-1	PG	12	32	100			140
AC127	TO-1	NG	12	32	500			105
AC128	TO-1	PG	16	32	1000	·6	1A	60-175
AC132	TO-1	PG	12	32	200	·35	200	115
AC187	TO-1	NG	15	25	2000	·8	1A	100-500
AC188	TO-1	PG	15	25	2000	·6	1A	100-500
AD149	TO-3	PG	30	50	3500	·7	3A	30-100
AD161	PT1	NG	20	32	3000	·6	1A	80-320
AD162	PT1	PG	20	32	3000	·4	1A	80-320
AF114	TO-7	PG	15	32	10			150
AF115	TO-7	PG	15	32	10			150
AF116	TO-7	PG	15	32	10			150
AF117	TO-7	PG	15	32	10			150
AF118	TO-7	PG	20	70	30	5	30	35
ASZ15	TO-3	PG	60	100	10A	·4	10A	20-55
ASZ16	TO-3	PG	32	60	10A	·4	10A	45-130
ASZ17	TO-3	PG	32	60	10A	·4	10A	25-75
ASZ18	TO-3	PG	32	100	10A	·4	10A	30-110
BC107	TO-18	NS	45	50	100	·2	100	110-450
BC108	TO-18	NS	20	30	100	·2	100	110-800
BC109	TO-18	NS	20	30	100	·2	100	200-800
BC109C	TO-18	NS	20	30	100	·2	100	420-800
BC157	SOT-25	PS	45	50	100	·25	100	75-260
BC158	SOT-25	PS	25	30	100	·25	100	75-500
BC159	SOT-25	PS	20	25	100	·25	100	125-500
BC177	TO-18	PS	45	50	100	·25	100	75-260
BC178	TO-18	PS	25	30	100	·25	100	75-500
BC179	TO-18	PS	20	25	100	·25	100	125-500
BC182(L)	SOT-30 (TO-92/74)	NS	50	10	200	·25	10	100-480
BC183(L)	SOT-30 (TO-92/74)	NS	30	45	200	·25	10	100-850
BC184(L)	SOT-30 (TO-92/74)	NS	30	45	200	·25	10	250-850
BC186	TO-18	PS	25	40	200	·5	50	40-200
BC207	TO-106	NS	45	50	200	·25	10	110-220
BC208	TO-106	NS	20	25	200	·25	10	110-800
BC209	TO-106	NS	20	25	200	·25	10	200-800
BC212(L)	SOT-30 (TO-92/74)	PS	50	60	200	·25	10	60-300
BC213(L)	SOT-30 (TO-92/74)	PS	30	45	200	·25	10	80-400
BC214(L)	SOT-30 (TO-92/74)	PS	30	45	200	·25	10	80-400
BC327	TO-92	PS	45	—	1000	0·7	500	100-600

I_C mA	F_t MHz	I_C mA	P_{tot} mW	Use	Comparable types
3	2	3	80	Low noise audio	AC125–2N406
2	1·3	10	216	Audio driver	2N406
2	1·7	10	216	Audio driver	2N406
50	1·5	10	340	Audio O/P	AC187
300	1	10	260	Audio O/P	AC188
50	1·3	10	216	Audio O/P	AC188
300	1	10	800	Audio O/P	AC127
300	1	10	220	Audio O/P	AC128
1A	·3	500	32W	GP O/P	OC26,AU106
500	·02	300	4W	Audio amp.	AD165,2N1218,2N1292
500	·015	300	6W	Audio amp.	AD143,AD152,AD427
1	75	1	75	H.F. amp.	AF144,AF194,2N3127
1	75	1	75	H.F. amp.	AF146,AF185,2N2273
1	75	1	75	H.F. amp.	AF135,AF136,2N3127
1	75	1	75	H.F. amp.	AF136,AF197,2N5354
10	175	10	375	V.H.F. amp.	BFW20
1A	·2	1A	30W	H.C. sw.	OC28
1A	·25	1A	30W	H.C. sw.	OC29,AD138,AD723
1A	·22	1A	30W	H.C. sw.	OC35,AD424
1A	·22	1A	30W	H.C. sw.	OC36
2	300	10	300	S.S. amp.	BC207,BC147,BC182
2	300	10	300	S.S. amp.	BC208,BC148,BC183
2	300	10	300	Low noise s.s. amp.	BC209,BC149,BC184
2	300	10	300	Low noise high gain	BC209C,BC184C, BC149C
2	150	10	300	S.S. amp.	BC177,BC307,BC212
2	150	10	300	S.S. amp.	BC178,BC308,BC213
2	150	10	300	S.S. amp.	BC179,BC309,BC214
2	150	10	300	S.S. amp.	BC157,BC307,BC212
2	150	10	300	S.S. amp.	BC158,BC308,BC213
2	150	10	300	S.S. amp.	BC159,BC309,BC214
2	150	10	300	S.S. amp.	BC107,BC207,BC147
2	150	10	300	S.S. amp.	BC108,BC208,BC148
2	150	10	300	Low noise, high gain	BC109,BC209,BC149
2	50	50	300	G.P. amp.	BC213,BC177,BC158
2	150	10	300	S.S. amp.	BC107,BC182,BC147
2	150	10	300	S.S. amp.	BC108,BC183,BC148
2	150	10	300	Low noise, high gain	BC109,BC184,BC149
2	200	10	300	S.S. amp.	BC307,BC157,BC177
2	200	10	300	S.S. amp.	BC308,BC158,BC178
2	200	10	300	S.S. amp.	
100	100	10	800	O/P	2N3638

Type	Case	POL MAT	Vce	Vcb	IC mA	Vces	IC mA	Hfe
BC337	TO-92	NS	45	—	1000	0·7	500	100-600
BC547	SO7-30	NS	45	50	100	·6	100	110-800
BC548	SO7-30	NS	30	30	100	·6	100	110-800
BC549	SO7-30	NS	30	30	100	·6	100	200-800
BC549C	SO7-30	NS	30	30	100	·6	100	420-800
BC635	TO-92(74)	NS	45	45	1A	·5	500	40-250
BC636	TO-92(74)	PS	45	45	1A	·5	500	40-250
BC639	TO-92(74)	NS	80	100	1A	·5	500	40-160
BC640	TO-92(74)	PS	80	100	1A	·5	500	40-160
BCY70	TO-18	PS	40	50	200	·5	50	50
BCY71	TO-18	PS	45	45	200	·5	50	100-600
BCY72	TO-18	PS	25	25	200	·5	50	50
BD137	TO-12G	NS	60	60	1A	·5	500	40-160
BD138	TO-126	PS	60	60	1A	·5	500	40-160
BD139	TO-126	NS	60	100	1A	·5	500	40-160
BD140	TO-126	PS	80	100	1A	·5	500	40-160
BD262	TO-126	PS	60	60	4A	2·5	1·5A	750
BD263	TO-126	NS	60	80	4A	2·5	1·5A	750
BD266A	TO-220	PS	80	80	8A	2	3A	750
BD267A	TO-220	NS	80	100	8A	2	3A	750
BDX64A	TO-3	PS	80	80	12A	2·5	5A	1000
BDX65A	TO-3	NS	80	80	12A	2·5	5A	1000
BDY20	TO-3	NS	60	100	15A	1·1	4A	20-70
BF115	TO-72(28)	NS	30	50	30			45-165
BF167	TO-72(28)	NS	30	40	25			26
BF173	TO-72(28)	NS	25	40	25			37
BF177	TO-39	NS	60	100	50			20
BF178	TO-39	NS	115	185	50			20
BF179	TO-39	NS	115	250	50			20
BF180	TO-72(25)	NS	20	30	20			13
BF184	TO-72(28)	NS	20	30	30			75-750
BF185	TO-72(28)	NS	20	30	30			34-140
BF194	SOT 25/1	NS	20	30	30			65-220
BF195	SOT 25/1	NS	20	30	30			35-125
BF200	TO-72(25)	NS	20	30	20			15
BF336	TO-39	NS	180	185	100			20-60
BF337	TO-39	NS	200	300	100			20-60
BF338	TO-39	NS	225	250	100			20-60
BFY50	TO-39	NS	35	80	1A	2	150	30
BFY51	TO-39	NS	30	60	1A	·35	150	40
BFY52	TO-39	NS	20	40	1A	·35	150	60
MJ2501	TO-3	PS	80	80	10A	2	5A	1000
MJ2955	TO-3	PS	60	70	15A	1·1	4A	20-70
MJ3001	TO-3	NS	80	80	10A	2	5A	1000
MJE2955	90·05	PS	60	70	10A	1·1	4A	20-70
MJE3055	90·05	NS	60	70	10A	1·1	4A	20-70
MU9610	152	NS	30	40	2A	0·4	1·5A	80-400
MU9611	152·01	NS	30	40	2A	0·4	1·5A	80-400
MU9660	152	PS	30	40	2A	0·4	1·5A	80-400
MU9661	152·01	PS	30	40	2A	0·4	1·5A	80-400
NSD106	TO-202(35)	NS	100	140		2·9	100	50-150
NSD206	TO-202(35)	PS	100	100		2·1	100	50-150
OC26	TO-3	PG	30	50	3·5A	·7	3A	30-100

IC mA	F1 MHz	IC mA	Ptot mW	Use	Comparable types
100	200	10	800	O/P	2N3642
2	300	10	500	S.S. amp.	BC107,BC207,BC147
2	300	10	500	S.S. amp.	BC108,BC208,BC148
2	300	10	500	Low noise s. sig.	BC109,BC209,BC149
2	300	10	500	Low noise, high gain	BC109C,BC149C
150	130	500	1W	Audio O/P	BC639
150	130	500	1W	Audio O/P	BC640
150	130		1W	Audio O/P	MU9610,TT801
150	130		1W	Audio O/P	MU9660,TT800
10	250	50	350	G.P.	BC212
10	200	50	350	G.P.	BC212
10	200	50	350	G.P.	BC213
150	250	500	8W	G.P. O/P	BD139
150	75	500	8W	G.P. O/P	BD140
150	250	500	8W	G.P. O/P	40409
150	75	500	8W	G.P. O/P	40410
1·5A	7	1·5A	36W	High gain darl. O/P	BD266
1·5A	7	1·5A	36W	High gain darl. O/P	BD267
3A	7		60W	High gain darl. O/P	
3A	7		60W	High gain darl. O/P	
8A	7	5A	117W	Darl. O/P	
8A	7	5A	117W	Darl. O/P	
4A	1	4A	115	Power O/P	2N3055
1	230	1	145	V.H.F. amp.	
4	350	4	130	T.V. I.F. amp.	
7	550	5	230	T.V. I.F. amp.	
15	120	10	795	T.V. video amp.	BF336
30	120	10	1·7W	T.V. video amp.	BF336
20	120	10	1·7W	T.V. video amp.	BF338
2	675	2	150	U.H.F. amp.	BF200
1	300	1	145	H.F. amp.	
1	220	1	145	H.F. amp.	BF195
1	260	1	250	H.F. amp.	
1	200	1	250	H.F. amp.	BF185
3	650	3	150	V.H.F. amp.	BF180
30	130		3W	Video amp.	
30	130		3W	Video amp.	
30	130		3W	Video amp.	
150	60	50	2·86W	G.P.	
150	50	50	2·86W	G.P.	
150	50	50	2·86W	G.P.	
5A			150W	Darl. O/P	
4A	4	500	115W	High power O/P	2N4908,2N4909,2N5871
5A			150W	Darl. O/P	
4A	2	500	90W	High power O/P	TIP2955
4A	2	500	90W	High power O/P	TIP3055
350	70	250	1W	O/P	TT801
350	70	250	1W	O/P	TT801
350	70	250	1W	O/P	TT800
350	70	250	1W	O/P	TT800
100	80	50		Driver–O/P	
100	150	50		Driver–O/P	
1A	3	500	32W	G.P. O/P	AD149

Type	Case	POL MAT	Vce	Vcb	IC mA	Vces	IC mA	Hfe
OC28	TO-3	PG	60	100	10A	·4	10A	20-55
OC44N	TO-1	PG	5	15	10			45-225
OC45	GT-3	PG	5	15	10			25-125
OC70	GT-3	PG	10	30	50			30
OC71	GT-3	PG	10	30	50			30-75
OC72	GT-6	PG	16	32	250			45-120
OC74N	TO-1	PG	10	20	300	6	300	60-150
OC75	GT-3	PG	10	30	50			60-130
TIP31B	TOP-66	NS	80	80	3A	1.2	3A	20
TIP32B	TOP-66	PS	80	80	3A	1.2	3A	20
TIP2955	TOP-3	PS	70	100	15A	1.1	4A	20
TIP3055	TOP-3	NS	70	100	15A	1.1	4A	20
2N301	TO-3	PG	32	40	3A			50
2N706A	TO-18	NS	15	25	200			20
2N2926	TO-92(74)	NS	25	25	100			150
2N3053	TO-39	NS	40	60	700	1.4	150	50-250
2N3054	TQ-66	NS	55	90	4A	1	200	25
2N3055	TO-3	NS	60	90	15A	1.1	4A	20
2N3563	TO-106	NS	12	30	50			20-200
2N3564	TO-106	NS	15	30	100	3	20	20-500
2N3565	TO-106	NS	25	30	50	35	1	150-600
2N3566	TO-105	NS	30	40	200	1	100	150-600
2N3567	TO-105	NS	40	80	500	25	150	40-120
2N3568	TO-105	NS	60	80	500	25	150	40-120
2N3569	TO-105	NS	40	80	500	25	150	100-300
2N3638	TO-105	PS	25	25	500	25	50	30
2N3638A	TO-105	PS	25	25	500	25	50	100
2N3640	TO-106	PS	12	12	80	2	10	30-120
2N3641	TO-105	NS	30	60	500	22	150	40-120
2N3642	TO-105	NS	45	60	500	22	150	40-120
2N3643	TO-105	NS	30	60	500	22	150	100-300
2N3644	TO-105	PS	45	45	500	1	300	115-300
2N3645	TO-105	PS	60	60	500	1	300	115-300
2N3702	TO-92(74)	PS	25	40	200	25	50	60-300
2N3904	TO-92	NS	40	60	200			100-300
2N4250	TO-106	PS	40	40	100	25	10	250-400
2N4258	TO-106	PS	12	12	50	5	50	30-120
2N4292	TO-92	NS	15	30	50	6	10	20
2N4403	TO-92	PS	40	40	600			100-300
2N5589	MT-71C	NS	18	36	600			5
2N5590	MT-72C	NS	18	36	2A			5
2N5591	MT-72C	NS	18	36	4A			5
2N5871	TO-3	PS	60	60	7A	1	4A	20-100
40250	TO-66	NS	50	50	4A	1.5	1.5A	25
40408	TO-5	NS	80		700	1.4	150	40-200
40409	TO-39(H)	NS	80		700	1.4	150	50-250
40410	TO-39(H)	PS	80		700	1.4	150	50-250

IC mA	Ft MHz	IC mA	Ptot mW	Use	Comparable types
1A	2	1A	30W	H.C. switch	ASZ15
1	7·5	1	85	R.F. amp.	AF125,AF135,AF172
1	3	3	85	R.F. amp.	AF132,AF185,AF196
5	5		125	G.P. amp.	AC121,AC126,2N1190
3	6		125	G.P. amp.	AC126,2N2429
10	35		165	Audio O/P	AC122,AC125,AC162
50	1		550	Audio O/P	AC125,AC180,AC192
3	1		125	G.P. amp.	AC173,AC192
500	3	500	40W	Power amp–Sw	
500	3	500	40W	Power amp–Sw	
4A	8		90W	Power amp–Sw	MJE2955
4A	8		90W	Power amp–Sw	MJE3055
1A	2	1A	11W	Audio O/P	AT1138,OC26
10	200		300	High speed Sw	
2	100		200	G.P.	BC108 etc.
150	100	50	2·86W	G.P. switch	BD137
500	8	200	25W	Audio O/P	TIP31B
4A	8	1A	115W	O/P–Sw	BDY20
8	600	8	200	RF–IF amp	BF173
15	400	15	200	RF–IF amp	BF167
1	40	1	200	Low level amp	BC108,BC208
10	40	30	300	GP amp & Sw	BC183
1	60	50	300	GP amp & Sw	BC337
1	60	50	300	GP amp & Sw	
1	60	50	300	GP amp & Sw	
50	100	50	300	GP amp & Sw	BC327
50	150	50	300	GP amp & Sw	BC558
10	300	10	200	Saturated switch	
	250		350	GP amp & Sw	BC337
150	250	50	350	GP amp & Sw	BC337
150	250	50	350	GP amp & Sw	BC337
50	200	20	300	GP amp & Sw	BC327
500	200	20	300	GP amp & Sw	
50	100	50	360	GP amp & Sw	BC213
1mA			310	Low level amp.	BC167A,BF194
1	50		200	Low level amp.	BC559
10	700	10	200	Saturated Sw	
3	600	4	200	Saturated Sw	
10			310	G.P.	BC307A,2N2904
100	175→ 3W		15W	H.F. mobile R.F.	
250	175→ 10W		30W	H.F. mobile R.F.	
500	175→ 25W		70W	H.F. mobile R.F.	
2·5A	4	250	100W	Power transistor	2N5872,2N4908,MJ2955
100	1		29W	Power transistor	2N3054
200	100		1W	Power transistor	BC639
150	100		3W	Power transistor	BD139
150	100		3W	Power transistor	BD140

Common transistor and diode data

FETS

Type	Case	BV_{GSS}		$V_{GS(OFF)}$				$I_{DSS(mA)}$			
		V	$I_{G(uA)}$	Min	Max	V_{DS}	$I_{D(nA)}$	Min	Max	V_{DS}	V_{GS}
MPF102	TO-92(72)	25	10	5	8	15	2	2	20	15	0
MPF103	TO-92(72)	25	1		6	15	1	1	5	15	0
MPF104	TO-92(72)	25	1		7	15	1	2	9	15	0
MPF105	TO-92(72)	25	1		8	15	10	4	16	15	0
MPF106	TO-92(72)	25	1	5	4	15	10	4	10	15	0
2N5457	TO-92(72)	25	1	5	6	15	10	1	5	15	0
2N5458	TO-92(72)	25	1	1	7	15	10	2	6	15	0
2N5459	TO-92(72)	25	1	2	8	15	10	4	9	15	0
2N5484	TO-92(72)	25	1	3	3	15	10	1	5	15	0
2N5485	TO-92(72)	25	1	5	4	15	10	4	10	15	0
BFW10	TO-72(25)	30						8	20	10	0
BFW11	TO-72(25)	30						4	10	15	0
BFW61	TO-72(25)	25						2	20	15	0
MPF121	206	7·20			4	15		5	30	15	0
2N4342	TO-106	20			5	10		12	30	10	0

Common transistor and diode data

Power MOSFETS/DMOS and VMOS

Type	Case	Channel	P_{tot}	V_{ds}	V_{dg}	$V_{gs(th)}$
IRF120	TO-3(F)	n	40W	100V	100V	4V
IRF130	TO-3(F)	n	75W	100V	100V	4V
IRF9130	TO-3(F)	p	75W	−100V	−100V	−4V
IRF510	TO220(F)	n	20W	100V	100V	4V
IRF530	TO220(F)	n	75W	100V	100V	4V
IRF640	TO220(F)	n	125W	200V	200V	4V
IRF9520	TO220(F)	p	40W	−100V	−100V	−4V
IRF9530	TO220(F)	p	75W	−100V	−100V	−4V
VN10KM	TO92(F)	n	1W	60V	60V	2·5V max
VN1010	TO92(F)	n	1W	100V	100V	2V max
VN46AF	TO202(F)	n	12·5W	40V	40V	2V max
VN66AF	TO202(F)	n	12·5W	60V	60V	2V max
VN88AF	TO202(F)	n	12·5W	80V	80V	2V max
2SJ50	TO3(F)	p	100W	−160V	−160V	−1·5 max
2SK133	TO3(F)	n	100W	120V	120V	1·5 max

Common transistor and diode data

Unijunction transistors

Type	Case	$P_{tot(max)}$	V_{B2}–V_{B1}	I_E	Intrinsic st. rat.
TIS43	TO92(U)	300mW	35V	1·5A	0·5 to 0·82
2N2646	TO18(U)	300mW	35V	2A	0·55 to 0·75
2N2647	TO18(U)	300mW	35V	2A	0·68 to 0·8

$Y_{fs(umhos)}$ Min	Max	V_{DS}	P_{tot} MW	Use/comments
2000	7500	15	310	N/CH junction–VHF
1000	5000	15	310	N/CH junction–audio Sw
1500	5500	15	310	N/CH junction–audio Sw
2000	6000	15	310	N/CH junction–audio Sw
2500	7000	15	310	N/Ch junction–RF
1000	5000	15	310	N/CH junction–audio Sw
1500	5500	15	310	N/CH junction–audio Sw
2000	6000	15	310	N/CH junction–audio Sw
3000	6000	15	310	N/CH junction–VHF
3500	7000	15	310	N/CH junction–VHF
	6500		300	N/CH junction audio to H.F.
	6500		300	N/CH junction audio to H.F.
	6500		300	N/CH junction audio to H.F.
10000	20000	15	500	N/CH dual gate MOS VHF amp.
	6000	10	180	P/CH junction–audio, Sw

I_{gss}	I_{dss}	$g_{fs}(mS)$	$I_{d(max)}$
100nA	1mA	1500	6A
100nA	1mA	3000	12A
−100nA	−1mA	2000	−8A
500nA	0·5mA	1000	3A
500nA	1mA	3000	10A
500nA	1mA	6000	11A
−500nA	−1mA	900	−4A
−500nA	−1mA	2000	−7A
10µA	10µA	200	0·5A
10µA	10µA	200	0·5A
10µA	10µA	250	2A
10µA	10µA	250	2A
10µA	10µA	250	2A
−10µA	−10µA	1000	−7A
10µA	10µA	1000	7A

Common transistor and diode data

Triacs

Type	Case	PIV	$I_{T(rms)}$	V_{GT}	I_{GT}
TRI400-0·35	TO92(TRI)	400V	0·35A	2V	5mA
C206D	TO202(TRI)	400V	3A	2V	5mA
C226D	TO202(TRI)	400V	8A	2·5V	50mA
C246D	TO202(TRI)	400V	15A	2·5V	50mA

Common transistor and diode data

Thyristors

Type	Case	PIV	$I_{T(rms)}$ max	V_{GT}	I_{GT}
C106D	TO202(TH)	400V	4A	0·8V	0·2mA
2N3525	TO66(TH)	400V	5A	2V	15mA
2N4443	TO126(TH)	400V	5A	1·5V	30mA
BTX18-400	TO5(TH)	500 V	1A	2V	5mA

(continued on page 50)

Thyristors

Some confusion exists over the use of the term *thyristor*. Here it is taken as a generic title, the *silicon controlled rectifier* (s.c.r.) being one particular type. An s.c.r. with its equivalent circuit and symbol is shown below. With G open-circuit Q_1 is cut off, so the device will not conduct unless V_{AK} is made sufficiently positive for it to avalanche. If the gate is made positive I_{C1} flows. Now I_{C1} is base current for Q_2 and I_{C2} is base current for Q_1. Therefore I_{C1} brings on Q_2 and the cumulative action makes both transistors saturate, i.e. the voltage across the device falls to a minimum and it is in the condition of a closed switch. Once the s.c.r. is on, the gate voltage is not required to sustain it. In fact the gate cannot be used to turn it off, and this must be done by reducing V_{AK} to a very small voltage.

To switch a thyristor on without any gate voltage the device must be made to avalanche. Such a device, which will avalanche in either direction in a controlled manner, is the *bi-directional diode thyristor* or *diac*. A gated version of this is the *bi-directional triode thyristor* or *triac*, which will conduct in either direction when gated with a pulse of the appropriate polarity. In this way it performs as a pair of thyristors connected in inverse parallel.

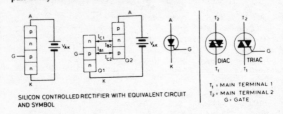

SILICON CONTROLLED RECTIFIER WITH EQUIVALENT CIRCUIT AND SYMBOL

T_1 : MAIN TERMINAL 1
T_2 : MAIN TERMINAL 2
G : GATE

Pro Electron system of semiconductor type labelling

The Pro Electron system of semiconductor labelling, used by most European manufacturers, describes a device by means of a code comprising two letters followed by a serial number. The letters define the semiconductor material used and the device's general function, as listed below:

First letter	Semiconductor material
A	Germanium
B	Silicon
C	Gallium arsenide or similar
D	Indium antimonide or similar
R	Cadmium sulphide or similar

Second letter	General function
A	Detection diode, high speed, diode, mixer diode
B	Varicap diode
C	Audio frequency, non-power, transistor
D	Audio frequency power transistor
E	Tunnel diode
F	Radio frequency, non-power, transistor
G	Miscellaneous
L	Radio frequency power transistor
N	Photo-coupler
P	Radiation (e.g., light) detecting device
Q	Radiation source
R	Switching device, non-power
S	Switching transistor, non-power
T	Switching device, power
U	Switching transistor, power
X	Multiplier diode
Y	Rectifying diode or similar device
Z	Voltage reference or regulating diode

The serial number defines the device's particular application, and will consist of either: three numbers (which shows the device is intended for use primarily in consumer applications), or; a letter followed by two numbers (which shows the device is intended for use primarily in industrial or professional environments).

Range numbers

Where variants of a device exist, the above code is addended with a further code (separated by a hyphen) to identify the specific device type within the range. Two classes of device are affected:

(a) Rectifer diodes and thyristors; the group of figure indicate either the repetitive peak inverse voltage, V_{RRM}, or the repetitive peak off-state voltage, V_{DRM}, whichever is the lowest.

(b) Voltage regulator diodes and transient suppression diodes; a first letter (voltage regulator diodes only) indicates operating voltage tolerance, where:

$$A = \pm 1\%$$
$$B = \pm 2\%$$
$$C = \pm 5\%$$
$$D = \pm 10\%$$
$$E = \pm 15\%$$

and a group of figures indicate the typical operating voltage (or the maximum recommended stand-off voltage, in the case of transient suppressor diodes).

In all cases, a final letter (R) may be used, to indicate a reverse polarity version (i.e., one with a stud anode).

Common transistor and diode data (continued)

Rectifiers/diodes

Type	Mat	V_R	$I_F(A)$	V_F	$I_F(A)$	$I_R(\mu A)$	V_R
A14P	S	1000	2·5	1·25	2·5	0·5	1000
A15A	S	100	5	1·1	5	5	100
BYX21L/200R	S	75	25	1·2	25	1·1	75
EM4005	S	50	1	1·1	1	5	50
EM401	S	100	1	1·1	1	5	100
EM404	S	400	1	1·1	1	5	400
EM410	S	1000	1	1·1	1	5	1000
1N4001	S	50	1	1·1	1	5	50
1N4002	S	100	1	1·1	1	5	100
1N4004	S	400	1	1·1	1	5	400
1N4007	S	1000	1	1·1	1	5	1000
1N5408	S	1000	3	1	3	5	1000
1N5059(A14B)	S	200	2·5	1·25	2·5	0·2	200
1N5060(A14D)	S	400	2·5	1·25	2·5	0·2	400
1N5061(A14M)	S	600	2·5	1·25	2·5	0·2	600
1N5062(A14N)	S	800	2·5	1·25	2·5	0·2	800
MR110	S	100	10				
MR410	S	400	10				

Common transistor and diode data

Diodes

Type	Case	V_R	$I_F(mA)$	$C_d(pF)$	V_F	$I_F(mA)$
Germanium						
AA119	DO-7	30	100	1·2	2·2	10
OA90	DO-7	20	45		1·5	10
OA91	DO-7	90	150		1·9	10
OA95	DO-7	90	150		1·5	10
Silicon						
BA100	DO-7	60	90	25	96	10
BA102	DO-7	20		20-45	C_d ratio 1·4 @ 4/10 V/VV	
BA114	DO-7		20		7	1
OA200	DO-7	50	160	25	96	10
OA202	DO-7	150	160	25	96	10
1N914A	DO-35	75	75	4	1	10
1N4148	SD-5	75	75	4	1	10
50822800	DO-7	70	15	2	41	1

Use

Transient protected (controlled avalanche)
G.P. rectifier
Automobile H. duty
G.P. rectifier
G.P. rectifier
G.P. rectifier
G.P. rectifier
G.P. rectifier
G.P. rectifier
G.P. rectifier
G.P. rectifier
Transient protected (controlled avalanche)
Transient protected (controlled avalanche)
Transient protected (controlled avalanche)
Transient protected (controlled avalanche)
G.P. stud mount
G.P. stud mount

$I_R(\mu A)$	V_R	$T_r(nS)$	Use	Comparable types
150	30		AM/FM detection	
			Point contact	
450	20		G.P.–point contact	OA70,OA80
180	75		G.P.–point contact	OA71,OA79,OA81
110	75		G.P.–point contact	
10	60		G.P.–alloyed	
			Variable capacitance	
			Bias stabilizer	
1	50		Small signal–alloyed	
1	150		Small signal–alloyed	
5	75	4	Small signal–switching	1N4148
·025	20	4	Small signal–switching	1N014A
0·2	50	0·1	Schottky (hot carrier)	
			UHF detector, mixer, switch	

Bridge rectifier data

Type	Case	PIV	$V_{IN(rms)max}$	$V_{F(max)}$	$I_{F(ave)}$
Vm28	1	200V	140V	1·9V at 1A	0·9A
Vm48	1	400V	280V	1·9V at 1A	0·9A
Vm88	1	800V	560V	1·9V at 1A	0·9A
Wo05	2	50V	35V	2V at 1A	1A
Wo2	2	200V	140V	2V at 1A	1A
Wo4	2	400V	280V	2V at 1A	1A
Wo8	2	800V	560V	2V at 1A	1A
BY164	3	60V	42V	2V at 1A	1A
So05	4	50V	35V	2V at 1A	2A
So4	4	400V	280V	2V at 1A	2A
SKB2/02L5A	3	200V	140V	1·8V at 1A	1·6A
SKB2/04L5A	3	400V	280V	1·8V at 1A	1·6A
KBLo2	5	200V	140V	1·2V at 1A	3A
KBLo8	5	800V	560V	1·2V at 1A	3A
Ko1	6	100V	70V	2·1V at 10A	25A
Ko2	6	400V	280V	2·1V at 10A	25A
KBPC3502	6	200V	140V	1·2V at 17·5A	35A
KBPC3506	6	600V	420V	1·2V at 17·5A	35A

Voltage regulator data

Type	Case	$I_{out(max)}$	V_{out}	$V_{in(range)}$	Load reg.
78L05	2A	100mA	5V	7 to 25V	0·2%
79L05	2B	−100mA	−5V	7 to 25V	0·2%
78L12	2A	100mA	12V	14·5 to 35V	0·2%
79L12	2B	−100mA	−12V	14·5 to 35V	0·2%
78L15	2A	100mA	15V	17·5 to 35V	0·3%
79L15	2B	−100mA	−15V	17·5 to 35V	0·3%
78L24	2A	100mA	24V	27 to 35V	0·4%
79L24	2B	−100mA	−24V	27 to 35V	0·4%
7805	1A	1A	5V	7 to 25V	0·2%
7905	1B	−1A	−5V	7 to 25V	0·2%
7812	1A	1A	12V	14·5 to 30V	0·4%
7912	1B	−1A	−12V	14·5 to 30V	0·4%
7815	1A	1A	15V	17·5 to 30V	0·5%
7915	1B	−1A	−15V	17·5 to 30V	0·5%
7824	1A	1A	24V	27 to 38V	0·6%
7924	1B	−1A	−24V	27 to 38V	0·6%
LM309K	4A	1·2A	5V	7 to 35V	1%
78H05	4B	5A	5V	8 to 25V	0·2%
78H12	4B	5A	12V	15 to 25V	0·2%
78HG	5A	5A	5 to 24V	8 to 40V	1%
79HG	5B	5A	−2 to −24V	8 to 40V	0·7%
317K	4B	1·5A	1·2 to 37V	4 to 40V	0·1%
338K	4B	5A	1·2 to 32V	4 to 35V	0·1%
396K	4C	10A	1·25 to 15V	4 to 25V	0·15%
4195NB	6	±50mA	±15V	±18 to 30V	0·6%
78MGU1C	3A	500mA	5V to 30V	8 to 40V	1%
79MGU1C	3B	−500mA	−3 to −30V	7 to 30V	1%

Bridge rectifier encapsulations

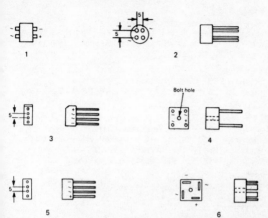

1   2

3

4

5   6

Voltage regulator encapsulations

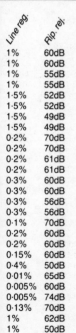

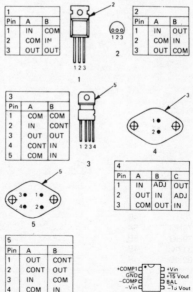

Line reg.	Rip. rej.
1%	60dB
1%	60dB
1%	55dB
1%	55dB
1·5%	52dB
1·5%	52dB
1·5%	49dB
1·5%	49dB
0·2%	70dB
0·2%	70dB
0·2%	61dB
0·2%	61dB
0·3%	60dB
0·3%	60dB
0·3%	56dB
0·3%	56dB
0·1%	70dB
0·2%	60dB
0·2%	60dB
0·15%	60dB
0·4%	50dB
0·01%	65dB
0·005%	60dB
0·005%	74dB
0·13%	70dB
1%	62dB
1%	50dB

1

Pin	A	B
1	IN	COM
2	COM	IN
3	OUT	OUT

1 2 3

2

Pin	A	B
1	IN	OUT
2	COM	IN
3	OUT	COM

3

Pin	A	B
1	COM	IN
2	IN	CONT
3	OUT	OUT
4	CONT	IN
5	COM	IN

1 2 3 4

4

Pin	A	B	C
1	IN	ADJ	OUT
2	OUT	IN	ADJ
3	COM	OUT	IN

5

Pin	A	B
1	OUT	CONT
2	CONT	OUT
3	IN	COM
4	COM	IN
5	ISOL	ISOL

+COMP
GND
−COMP
−Vin

+Vin
+15 Vout
BAL
−15 Vout

6

Zener diodes

BZY88C series
Tolerance: ±5% Maximum dissipation: 500 mW
Range values: 2·7V; 3V; 3·3V; 3·6V; 3·9V; 4·3V; 4·7V; 5·1V; 5·6V;
6·2V; 6·8V; 7·5V; 8·2V; 9·1V; 10V; 11V; 12V; 13V; 15V; 16V;
18V; 20V; 22V; 24V; 27V; 30V

BZX 85 series
Tolerance: ±5% Maximum dissipation: 1·3W
Range values: 2·7V; 3·0V; 3·3V; 3·6V; 3·9V; 4·3V; 4·7V; 5·1V;
5·6V; 6·2V; 6·8V

BZX 61 series
Tolerance: ±5% Maximum dissipation: 1·3W
Range values: 4·7V; 5·1V; 5·6V; 6·2V; 6·8V; 7·5V; 8·2V; 9·1V;
10V; 11V; 12V; 13V; 15V; 16V; 18V; 20V; 22V; 24V; 27V; 30V;
33V; 36V; 39V; 43V; 47V; 51V; 56V; 62V; 68V; 75V

1N5333 series
Tolerance: ±5% Maximum dissipation: 5W
Range values: 3·3V; 3·9V; 4·7V; 5·6V; 6·8V; 8·2V; 9·1V; 10V;
12V; 15V; 24V

Transistor and diode encapsulations

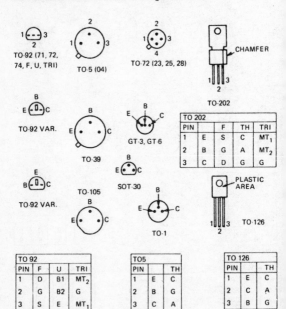

TO 202				
PIN		F	TH	TRI
1	E	S	C	MT$_1$
2	B	G	A	MT$_2$
3	C	D	G	G

TO 92				
PIN	F	U	TRI
1	D	B1	MT$_2$
2	G	B2	G
3	S	E	MT$_1$

TO5		
PIN		TH
1	E	C
2	B	G
3	C	A

TO 126		
PIN		TH
1	E	C
2	C	A
3	B	G

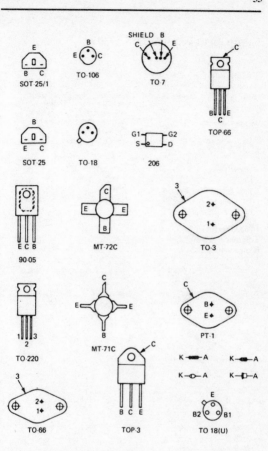

PIN		71	PIN	72 (STD)		PIN		74	PIN	T (25)	FET N (25)
	T	FET		T	FET		T	FET	1	E	S
1	C	G	1	C	G	1	B	S	2	B	D
2	E	D	2	B	D	2	C	G	3	C	G
3	B	S	3	E	S	3	E	D	4	GND	CASE

PIN	T (28)	FET P (23)	TO 3			TO 66			TO 220		
			Pin		F	Pin		TH	Pin		F
1	B	S	1	E	G	1	E	C	1	B	G
2	E	G	2	B	S	2	B	G	2	C	D
3	C	D	3	C	D	3	C	A	3	E	S
4	GND	CASE									

BIPOLARS	FETS	DIODES	
E : EMITTER	S : SOURCE	A : ANODE	G P : GENERAL PURPOSE
B : BASE	G : GATE	K : CATHODE	S S : SMALL SIGNAL
C : COLLECTOR	D : DRAIN		SW : SWITCH
NG : NPN GERMANIUM	N CH : N CHANNEL		O P : OUTPUT
PG : PNP GERMANIUM	P CH : P CHANNEL		R F : RADIO FREQUENCY
NS : NPN SILICON			H F : HIGH FREQUENCY
PS : PNP SILICON			V H F : VERY HIGH FREQUENCY

Component symbols (BS 3939)

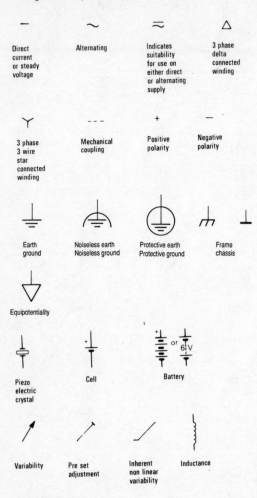

—	Direct current or steady voltage
~	Alternating
≂	Indicates suitability for use on either direct or alternating supply
△	3 phase delta connected winding

Y	3 phase 3 wire star connected winding
- - -	Mechanical coupling
+	Positive polarity
—	Negative polarity

Earth ground

Noiseless earth Noiseless ground

Protective earth Protective ground

Frame chassis

Equipotentiality

Piezo electric crystal

Cell

Battery   or 6V

Variability

Pre set adjustment

Inherent non linear variability

Inductance

SWITCHES AND CONTACTS

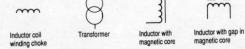

Inductor coil winding choke

Transformer

Inductor with magnetic core

Inductor with gap in magnetic core

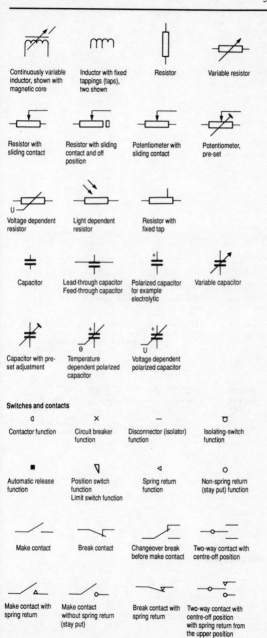

Continuously variable inductor, shown with magnetic core

Inductor with fixed tappings (taps), two shown

Resistor

Variable resistor

Resistor with sliding contact

Resistor with sliding contact and off position

Potentiometer with sliding contact

Potentiometer, pre-set

Voltage dependent resistor

Light dependent resistor

Resistor with fixed tap

Capacitor

Lead-through capacitor Feed-through capacitor

Polarized capacitor for example electrolytic

Variable capacitor

Capacitor with pre-set adjustment

Temperature dependent polarized capacitor

Voltage dependent polarized capacitor

Switches and contacts

Contactor function

Circuit breaker function

Disconnector (isolator) function

Isolating-switch function

Automatic release function

Position switch function Limit switch function

Spring return function

Non-spring return (stay put) function

Make contact

Break contact

Changeover break before make contact

Two-way contact with centre-off position

Make contact with spring return

Make contact without spring return (stay put)

Break contact with spring return

Two-way contact with centre-off position with spring return from the upper position

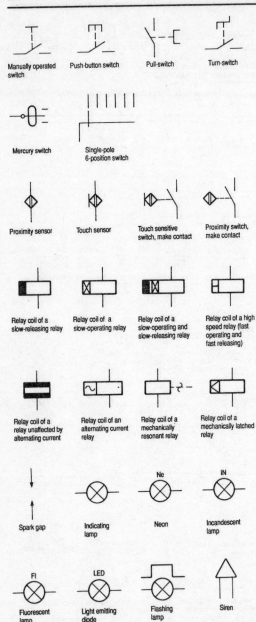

Manually operated switch

Push-button switch

Pull-switch

Turn-switch

Mercury switch

Single-pole 6-position switch

Proximity sensor

Touch sensor

Touch sensitive switch, make contact

Proximity switch, make contact

Relay coil of a slow-releasing relay

Relay coil of a slow-operating relay

Relay coil of a slow-operating and slow-releasing relay

Relay coil of a high speed relay (fast operating and fast releasing)

Relay coil of a relay unaffected by alternating current

Relay coil of an alternating current relay

Relay coil of a mechanically resonant relay

Relay coil of a mechanically latched relay

Spark gap

Indicating lamp

Neon

Incandescent lamp

Fluorescent lamp

Light emitting diode

Flashing lamp

Siren

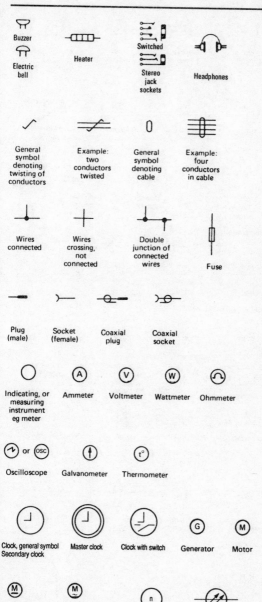

Buzzer

Electric bell

Heater

Switched

Stereo jack sockets

Headphones

General symbol denoting twisting of conductors

Example: two conductors twisted

General symbol denoting cable

Example: four conductors in cable

Wires connected

Wires crossing, not connected

Double junction of connected wires

Fuse

Plug (male)

Socket (female)

Coaxial plug

Coaxial socket

Indicating, or measuring instrument eg meter

Ammeter

Voltmeter

Wattmeter

Ohmmeter

Oscilloscope

Galvanometer

Thermometer

Clock, general symbol Secondary clock

Master clock

Clock with switch

Generator

Motor

Direct current motor

Alternating current motor

Tachometer

Optical fibre

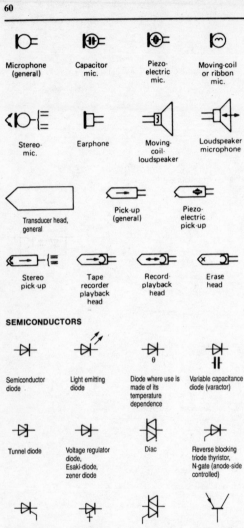

Microphone (general)

Capacitor mic.

Piezo-electric mic.

Moving-coil or ribbon mic.

Stereo-mic.

Earphone

Moving-coil loudspeaker

Loudspeaker microphone

Transducer head, general

Pick-up (general)

Piezo-electric pick-up

Stereo pick-up

Tape recorder playback head

Record-playback head

Erase head

SEMICONDUCTORS

Semiconductor diode

Light emitting diode

Diode where use is made of its temperature dependence

Variable capacitance diode (varactor)

Tunnel diode

Voltage regulator diode, Esaki-diode, zener diode

Diac

Reverse blocking triode thyristor, N-gate (anode-side controlled)

Reverse blocking triode thyristor, P-gate (cathode-side controlled)

Turn-off triode thyristor, gate not specified

Bidirectional triode thyristor Triac

PNP transistor

NPN transistor with collector connected to the envelope

Unijunction transistor with P-type base

Unijunction transistor. N-type base

Junction field effect transistor with N-type channel

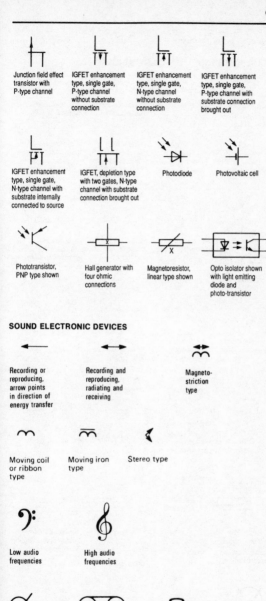

Junction field effect transistor with P-type channel

IGFET enhancement type, single gate, P-type channel without substrate connection

IGFET enhancement type, single gate, N-type channel without substrate connection

IGFET enhancement type, single gate, P-type channel with substrate connection brought out

IGFET enhancement type, single gate, N-type channel with substrate internally connected to source

IGFET, depletion type with two gates, N-type channel with substrate connection brought out

Photodiode

Photovoltaic cell

Phototransistor, PNP type shown

Hall generator with four ohmic connections

Magnetoresistor, linear type shown

Opto isolator shown with light emitting diode and photo-transistor

SOUND ELECTRONIC DEVICES

Recording or reproducing, arrow points in direction of energy transfer

Recording and reproducing, radiating and receiving

Magneto-striction type

Moving coil or ribbon type

Moving iron type

Stereo type

Low audio frequencies

High audio frequencies

Disk

Tape or film

Drum

Radiocommunications symbols

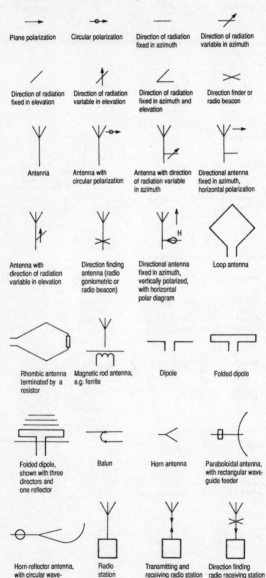

Plane polarization

Circular polarization

Direction of radiation fixed in azimuth

Direction of radiation variable in azimuth

Direction of radiation fixed in elevation

Direction of radiation variable in elevation

Direction of radiation fixed in azimuth and elevation

Direction finder or radio beacon

Antenna

Antenna with circular polarization

Antenna with direction of radiation variable in azimuth

Directional antenna fixed in azimuth, horizontal polarization

Antenna with direction of radiation variable in elevation

Direction finding antenna (radio goniometric or radio beacon)

Directional antenna fixed in azimuth, vertically polarized, with horizontal polar diagram

Loop antenna

Rhombic antenna terminated by a resistor

Magnetic rod antenna, e.g. ferrite

Dipole

Folded dipole

Folded dipole, shown with three directors and one reflector

Balun

Horn antenna

Paraboloidal antenna, with rectangular wave-guide feeder

Horn-reflector antenna, with circular wave-guide feeder

Radio station

Transmitting and receiving radio station

Direction finding radio receiving station

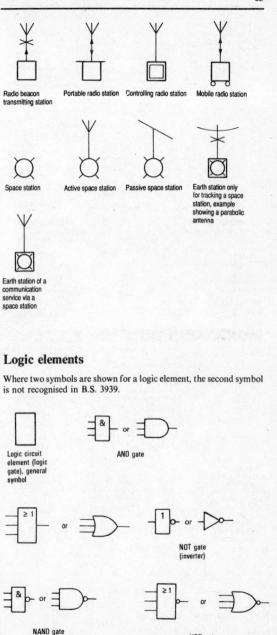

Radio beacon transmitting station

Portable radio station

Controlling radio station

Mobile radio station

Space station

Active space station

Passive space station

Earth station only for tracking a space station, example showing a parabolic antenna

Earth station of a communication service via a space station

Logic elements

Where two symbols are shown for a logic element, the second symbol is not recognised in B.S. 3939.

Logic circuit element (logic gate), general symbol

AND gate

NOT gate (inverter)

NAND gate

NOR gate

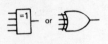 or

Exclusive OR gate

Logic identity gate; produces a logic 1 output if, and only if, all inputs are the same

Wired connection where a number of elements are wired together to achieve the effect of an AND or an OR operation without the use of an explicit element

Wire AND connection

Amplifier for logic diagrams

Symbol grouping to save space

Schmitt trigger

RS bistable element

Delay element, general symbol; this element produces a logic 1 output a set period of time after its input has changed from logic 0 to logic 1 and changes back to a logic 0 output a set period of time after its input has reverted to logic 0

Common control block; to make diagram clearer, inputs common to a number of related elements may be shown connected to a common control block

Direction of data flow should normally be from top to bottom. This symbol is used to indicate exceptions to the normal flow direction

Input/output polarity indicator indicating that the logic 1 state is the less positive level, ie negative logic is in force at this point

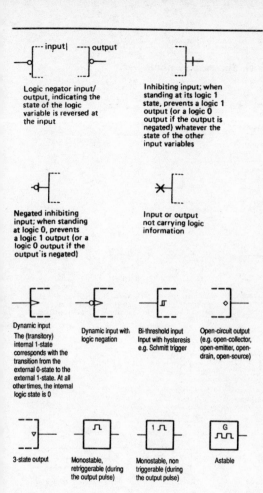

Logic negator input/
output, indicating the
state of the logic
variable is reversed at
the input

Inhibiting input; when
standing at its logic 1
state, prevents a logic 1
output (or a logic 0
output if the output is
negated) whatever the
state of the other
input variables

Negated inhibiting
input; when standing
at logic 0, prevents
a logic 1 output (or a
logic 0 output if the
output is negated)

Input or output
not carrying logic
information

Dynamic input
The (transitory)
internal 1-state
corresponds with the
transition from the
external 0-state to the
external 1-state. At all
other times, the internal
logic state is 0

Dynamic input with
logic negation

Bi-threshold input
Input with hysteresis
e.g. Schmitt trigger

Open-circuit output
(e.g. open-collector,
open-emitter, open-
drain, open-source)

3-state output

Monostable,
retriggerable (during
the output pulse)

Monostable, non
triggerable (during
the output pulse)

Astable

Synchronously
starting

Block diagram symbols

Pulse-position or pulse-phase modulation

Pulse-frequency modulation

Pulse-amplitude modulation

Pulse-interval modulation

Pulse-duration modulation

Pulse-code modulation, where the asterisk is replaced by details of the code

Equipment, general symbol

G

Non-rotating generator, general symbol

$\begin{array}{c} G \\ \sim \\ 500\ Hz \end{array}$

Sine-wave generator (non-rotating)

$\begin{array}{c} G \\ 500\ Hz \end{array}$

Sawtooth generator (non-rotating)

Pulse generator (non-rotating)

Variable frequency sine-wave generator (non-rotating)

Noise generator (non-rotating)

Changer, general symbol

Rectifier

Inverter

DC converter

Frequency changer

Frequency multiplier

Frequency divider

Pulse inverter

Amplifier

Rectifier equipment

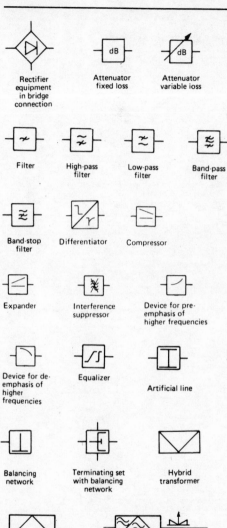

Rectifier equipment in bridge connection

Attenuator fixed loss

Attenuator variable loss

Filter

High-pass filter

Low-pass filter

Band-pass filter

Band-stop filter

Differentiator

Compressor

Expander

Interference suppressor

Device for pre-emphasis of higher frequencies

Device for de-emphasis of higher frequencies

Equalizer

Artificial line

Balancing network

Terminating set with balancing network

Hybrid transformer

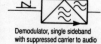

Modulator, demodulator or discriminator

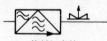

Modulator, double sideband output

Demodulator, single sideband with suppressed carrier to audio

Frequency spectrum symbols

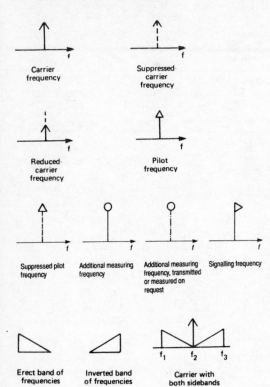

Carrier
frequency

Suppressed
carrier
frequency

Reduced
carrier
frequency

Pilot
frequency

Suppressed pilot
frequency

Additional measuring
frequency

Additional measuring
frequency, transmitted
or measured on
request

Signalling frequency

Erect band of
frequencies

Inverted band
of frequencies

Carrier with
both sidebands

f_1 f_2 f_3

Carrier with
both sidebands

f_1 f_2 f_3 f_4 f_5

Single-sideband
suppressed
carrier

f_1 f_2

Equipment marking symbols (BS 6217)

Battery check

Positioning of cell

a.c./d.c. converter, rectifier, substitute power supply

Variability

Plus; positive polarity

Minus; negative polarity

On (power)

Off (power)

Stand-by

On/off (push-push)

On/off (push button)

Lamp; lighting; illumination

Bell

Horn

Air impeller (blower, fan)

Fuse

Earth (ground)

Noiseless (clean) earth ground

Protective earth (ground)

Frame or chassis

Equipotentiality

Movement in one direction

Movement in both directions

Movement limited in both directions

Action away from reference point

Action towards a reference point

Action in both directions away from a reference point

Action in both directions towards a reference point

Non-simultaneous action away from and towards a reference point

Simultaneous action away from and towards a reference point

Direct current

Alternating current

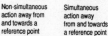

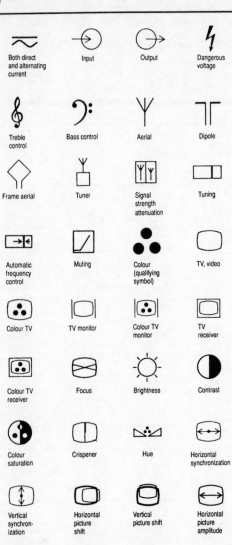

Both direct and alternating current

Input

Output

Dangerous voltage

Treble control

Bass control

Aerial

Dipole

Frame aerial

Tuner

Signal strength attenuation

Tuning

Automatic frequency control

Muting

Colour (qualifying symbol)

TV, video

Colour TV

TV monitor

Colour TV monitor

TV receiver

Colour TV receiver

Focus

Brightness

Contrast

Colour saturation

Crispener

Hue

Horizontal synchronization

Vertical synchronization

Horizontal picture shift

Vertical picture shift

Horizontal picture amplitude

Vertical picture amplitude

Picture size adjustment

Horizontal linearity

Vertical linearity

Monophonic	Stereophonic	Balance	Omni-directional microphone
Bidirectional microphone	Unidirectional microphone	Earphone	Headphones
Stereo headphones	Headset	Loudspeaker	Loudspeaker microphone
Microphone	Stereophonic microphone	Amplifier	Music
Pick-up for disc records	Stereophonic pick-up for disc records	Piezo-electric pick-up, crystal or ceramic	Dynamic pick-up
Telephone adapter	High-pass filter	Low-pass filter	Tape recorder
Magnetic tape stereo sound recorder	Recording on tape	Play-back or reading from tape	Erasing from tape
Monitoring at the input	Monitoring from tape after recording on tape	Monitoring during play-back	Recording lock on tape recorders

72

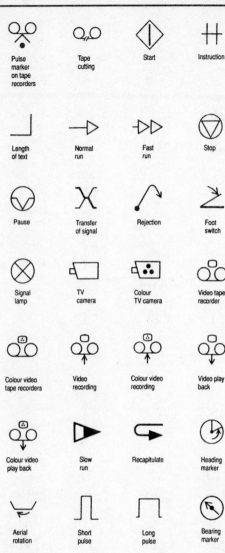

Pulse marker on tape recorders	Tape cutting	Start	Instruction
Length of text	Normal run	Fast run	Stop
Pause	Transfer of signal	Rejection	Foot switch
Signal lamp	TV camera	Colour TV camera	Video tape recorder
Colour video tape recorders	Video recording	Colour video recording	Video play back
Colour video play back	Slow run	Recapitulate	Heading marker
Aerial rotation	Short pulse	Long pulse	Bearing marker
Ship's head-up presentation	North up presentation	Anti-sea clutter	Anti-rain clutter

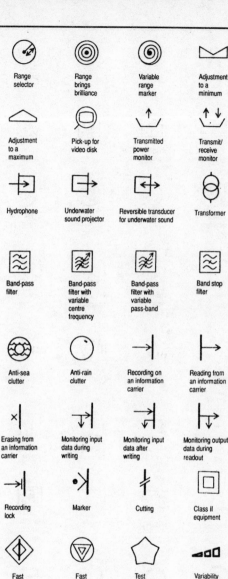

Range selector	Range brings brilliance	Variable range marker	Adjustment to a minimum
Adjustment to a maximum	Pick-up for video disk	Transmitted power monitor	Transmit/ receive monitor
Hydrophone	Underwater sound projector	Reversible transducer for underwater sound	Transformer
Band-pass filter	Band-pass filter with variable centre frequency	Band-pass filter with variable pass-band	Band stop filter
Anti-sea clutter	Anti-rain clutter	Recording on an information carrier	Reading from an information carrier
Erasing from an information carrier	Monitoring input data during writing	Monitoring input data after writing	Monitoring output data during readout
Recording lock	Marker	Cutting	Class II equipment
Fast start	Fast stop	Test voltage	Variability in steps
Sound	Clock	Rejection filter	Rectifier

Teacher	Student	Group of students	All students
Frame adjustment	Graphical recorder	Printer	d.c./a.c. converter
Variable band-stop filter	Gyro indicator	Gyro indicator setting	Gyro-compass true bearing
Relative bearing	Bearing ruler setting	Phase calibration	Angle calibration
Sense aerial switch	Speak	Listen	Morse key
Link unit	Travelling wave tube amplifier	Signalling sender	Signalling receiver
Demodulator	Modulator	Modem	Principal control panel
'On' for a part of equipment	'Off' for a part of equipment	Stand-by state for a part of equipment	In position of a bi-stable push control

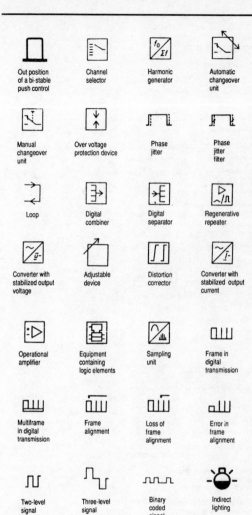

Out position of a bi-stable push control	Channel selector	Harmonic generator	Automatic changeover unit
Manual changeover unit	Over voltage protection device	Phase jitter	Phase jitter filter
Loop	Digital combiner	Digital separator	Regenerative repeater
Converter with stabilized output voltage	Adjustable device	Distortion corrector	Converter with stabilized output current
Operational amplifier	Equipment containing logic elements	Sampling unit	Frame in digital transmission
Multiframe in digital transmission	Frame alignment	Loss of frame alignment	Error in frame alignment
Two-level signal	Three-level signal	Binary coded signal	Indirect lighting
Low intensity lighting	Hand-held switch		

Op-amp data

Bipolar op-amps

Device type	OP07	OP27	11	165	301A	308	324	348	531
Supply voltage range (V_s)	±3 to ±18	±4 to 18	±2·5 to ±20	±6 to ±18	±5 to ±18	±5 to ±18	3 to 32 ±1·5 to ±16	±10 to ±18	±5 to ±22
Max. differential input voltage	±30	±0·7	1	±15	30	30	32	24	15
Max. input V either input to earth	±22	±18	—	V_s	15	15	16	12	15
Operating temperature range	0–70	0–70	0–70	−40-150 (junc.)	0–70	0–70	0–70	0–70	0–70
Output short circuit duration	indef.	indef.	indef.	indef.	indef.	—	—	indef.	indef.
Max. total power dissipation		500	500	20(W)	500	500	625	500	300
Typical characteristics at 25°C, 2 kΩ load									
Large signal open loop V. gain	132	123	109	80	88	102	100	96	96
Input resistance	33	4	10^5	500	2	40	10	2·5	20
Differential input offset voltage	0·06	0·03	0·2	2	2	10	2	1	2
Differential input offset current	0·8	12	0·001	20	3	1·5	5	4	50
Input bias current	±2·2	±15	0·04	200	70	<7	45	30	400
Common mode rejection ratio	120	100	130	70	90	100	70	90	100
Supply voltage rejection ratio	0·16	2	0·2	1000	16	16	—	15	10
Slew	0·17	2·8	0·3	6	0·4	—	—	0·6	35
Input offset voltage temp. coeff.	0·5	0·4	2	—	6	—	7	—	—
Input offset current temp. coeff.	12p	—	10f	—	20p	2p	10p	—	0·6n
Full power bandwidth	—	—	—	—	10	10	6	10	500
Output voltage swing	±13	±13	±12	24	±14	±13	28 or ±14	±12	±15

Op-amp data

F.E.T. op-amps

Max. ratings	Device type	3130E	355	3140E 3240E
	Package	8-pin d.i.l.	8-pin d.i.l.	d.i.l.
Supply voltage range (V_s)		+6 to +16V or ±3 to ±8V	±4 to ±18V	+4 to +36V or ±2 to ±18V
Max. differential input voltage		±8V	±30V	±8V
Max. input voltage either input with respect to earth		±V_s	±V_s	±V_s
Operating temperature range		0°–70°C	0°–70°C	0°–70°C
Max. total power dissipation		630mW	500mW	630mW
Output short circuit duration		indefinite	indefinite	indefinite
Typical characteristics at 25°C V_s = +15V				
Open loop voltage gain		110dB	106dB	100dB
Input resistance		$1·5 \times 10^{12}\,\Omega$	$10^{12}\,\Omega$	$10^{12}\,\Omega$
Input offset voltage		8mV	3mV	5mV
Input offset current		0·5pA	10pA	0·5pA
Input bias current		5pA	30pA	10pA
Common mode rejection ratio		80dB	100dB	90dB
Supply voltage rejection ratio		300μV/V	10μV/V	100μV/V
Slew rate		10V/μs	5V/μs	9V/μs
Input offset voltage temp. coeff.		10μV/°C	5μV/°C	8μV/°C
Input bias current temp. coeff.				Doubles for every +20°C approx.
Full-power bandwidth		120kHz	60kHz	110kHz
Output voltage swing $R_L = 1$kΩ		—	—	—
$R_L = 2$kΩ		13V (V_s = 15V)	—	13V (V_s = 15V)
$R_L = 10$kΩ		—	±13V	—

709	725CN	741 741N	741S	747	748	759	4558	5532	5534	5539	Units
±9 to ±18	±4 to ±22	±5 to ±18	±5 to ±18	±7 to ±18	±7 to ±18	7 to 36 ±3·5 to ±18	±3 to ±18	±3 to ±20	±3 to ±20	±8 to ±12	V
5	5	30	30	30	30	30	30	—	—	—	V
10	15	15	15	15	15	V_s	15	13	13	—	V
0–70	0–70	0–70	0–70	0–70	0–70	0–125 (junc.)	0–70	0–70	0–70	0–70	°C
5 sec.	5 sec.	indef.	indef.	indef.	indef.	indef.	indef.	indef.	indef.	—	
120	500	500	625	670	500	1300	680	1000	1000	550	mW (25°C)
93	127	106	100	106	106	106	109	100	100	52	dB
0·25	1·5	2	1	2	2	1·5	5	0·3	0·1	0·1	MΩ
2	2	1	2	1	2	1	0·5	0·5	0·5	2	mV
100	1·2	20	30	20	20	5	5	10	20	2000	nA
300	80	80	200	80	80	50	40	200	500	5000	nA
90	115	90	90	90	90	100	90	100	100	80	dB
25	20	30	10	30	30	10	30	10	10	200	μV/V
12	0·25	0·5	20	0·5	0·8	0·5	1	9	13	600	V/μs
3·3	2	5	3	—	—	—	—	—	—	—	μV/°C
0·1n	10p	0·5n	0·5n	0·5n	0·1n	—	—	—	—	—	A/°C
—	10	10	200	10	10	—	—	100	95	48000	kHz
±14	±10	±13	±13	±13	±13	±12·5	±13	±16	±16	+2·3 to −2·7	V

BIFET op-amps

351 353	064	071,072,074, 081,082,084	091,092
8-pin	14-pin		
d.i.l.	d.i.l.	d.i.l.	d.i.l.
±5 to ±18V	±2 to ±18V	±3 to ±18V	3V to 36V
±30V	±30V	±30V	36V
±V_s	±V_s	±V_s	36V
0°–70°C	0°–70°C	0°–70°C	0°–70°C
500mW	680mW	680mW	1150mW
indefinite	indefinite	indefinite	indefinite
110dB	76dB	106dB	106dB
$10^{12}\,\Omega$	$10^{12}\,\Omega$	$10^{12}\,\Omega$	$10^{12}\,\Omega$
5mV	3mV	3mV (071,072,074) 5mV (081,082,084)	5mV
25pA	5pA	5pA	5nA
50pA	30pA	30pA	10nA
100dB	76dB	76dB	90dB
30μV/V	18μV/V	158μV/V	90dB
13V/μs	3·5V/μs	13V/μs	0·6V/μs
10μV/°C	20μV/°C	20μV/°C	10μV/°C
150kHz	40kHz	150kHz	9kHz
—	—	—	—
—	—	—	26V
±13·5V	±13·5V	±13·5V	27V

Logic terms

Astable Type of multivibrator circuit, producing a square wave oscillation.

Asynchronous Operation not dependent on clock pulses.

Bistable Type of multivibrator circuit, having two stable states.

Buffered Capable of driving external circuits, isolated from previous stage.

Clock Source of regular voltage pulses, used to synchronise systems.

Decoder Device capable of translating a BCD input to separate control line inputs (also known as a demultiplexer).

Dual Two, twin.

Edge triggered Operation of device takes place on rising (or falling) part of input pulse.

Enable Over-ride input.

Fan-out Number of devices that can be placed in parallel on output.

Flip-flop Two-state device, changes state when clocked.

Hex Six.

Latch Retains previous input state until over-ridden.

Monostable Type of multivibrator circuit, with one stable state.

Multiplexer Samples many inputs in sequence, gives one output.

Multivibrator Circuit having two output states, each of which may or may not be stable. Oscillators of astable, bistable, or monostable types can be built with multivibrators.

Octal Eight.

One-shot Gives single output pulse of defined duration from variable input pulse.

Open collector TTL output which needs external pull-up resistor, can be used to wire OR outputs.

Parity Check bit added to data, can be odd or even parity. In odd parity sum of data 1s + parity 1 is odd.

Propagation delay Time taken for signal to pass through a device, limits highest frequency of operation.

Quad Four.

Quiescent Stable state not driving a load.

Schmitt trigger Circuit with hysteresis.

Synchronous Operation dependent on clock pulses.

Basic logic symbols and truth tables

Logic symbols are to the Mil Std-806B specification, as they are in more general use than those of B.S.3939. Positive logic convention used, i.e. 1 = high, 0 = low.

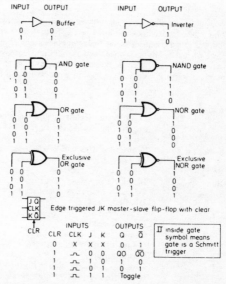

- ⎍ High level pulse, data is transferred on falling edge of pulse.

- QO The level of Q before indicated output conditions were established.

Toggle Each output changes to its complement on each active transition (pulse) of clock.

Medium scale integrated logic symbols and terminology

Medium scale integrated (MSI) logic elements are represented by rectangular blocks with appropriate external AND/OR gates when necessary. A small circle at an external input means that the specific input is active Low, i.e., it produces the desired function, in conjunction with other inputs, if its voltage is the lower of the two logic levels in the system. A circle at the output indicates that when the function designated is True, the output is Low. Generally, inputs are at the top and left and outputs appear at the bottom and right of the logic symbol. An exception is the asynchronous Master

Reset in some sequential circuits which is always at the left-hand bottom corner.

Inputs and outputs are generally labelled with mnemonic letters. Those used in this book are listed below. Note that an active Low function labelled outside of the logic symbol is given a bar over the label, while the same function inside the symbol is labelled without the bar. When several inputs or outputs use the same letter, subscript numbers starting with zero are used in an order natural for device operation.

Label	Meaning
A, B, C, D etc.	Data inputs (binary weighted where applicable: $A=1$; $B=2$; $C=4$; $D=5$ etc.)
a, b, c, d etc.	Segment outputs of a seven-segment decoder driver
BCD	Binary coded decimal
BI	Blanking input
$C_{in, out}$	Carry in or out. Sometimes may be labelled CI, CY
CE	Clock enable
CF	Cascade feedback
CEP	Count enable parallel input
CER	Count enable ripple input
CK	Clock input
CP	Clock pulse, generally a high-to-low transition. An active high clock (no circle) means outputs change on low-to-high clock transition
CS	Chip select
D, J, K, R, S	Data inputs to JK, SR and D flip-flops, latches, registers and counters
DIS	Disable 3-state output
EN	Enable device, generally active low
GND	Ground (0 volts) terminal (TTL)
I/O	Input/output
INC	Increment
INH	Inhibit
LE	Latch enable
LT	Lamp test
MR	Master reset, asynchronously resets all outputs to zero, overriding all other inputs. Generally active low
OEN	Output enable
OF	Overflow
PE	Parallel enable, a control input used to synchronously load information in parallel into an otherwise autonomous circuit (generally active low)
PH	Phase input for liquid crystal displays
P/S	Parallel/serial mode control input

Q, Q̄	General term, and complement, for output of sequential circuit. May have a letter indicating weighting
QP	Phase pulse output
R	Reset
RBI	Ripple blanking input
RBO	Ripple blanking output
RC, C, R	Capacitor and resistor timing on monostables
RCO	Ripple carry output
S	Preset input of flip-flop
$S_{1, 2 \text{ etc}}$	Sum outputs
$S_{in, out}$	Serial inputs, outputs of shift register
SDL	Serial data in left shift
SDR	Serial data in right shift
SF	Source follower output
SQ	Serial output
SR	Synchronous reset
ST	Strobe input
T	Trigger input
TC	Terminal count output (1111 for up binary counters, 1001 for up decimal counters, or 0000 for down counters)
U/D	Up/down mode control input
VCO	Voltage controlled oscillator
VI	Input to voltage controlled oscillator
VO	Voltage controlled oscillator output
V_{CC}	Positive supply terminal
V_{DD}	Positive supply terminal (CMOS)
V_{EE}	Negative supply terminal (CMOS)
V_{SS}	0 volts supply terminal (CMOS)
W	User-selected positive or negative logic
WE	Write enable
X	Data inputs to selector
Z, O, F	General term for outputs of combinational circuits. May have a letter indicating weighting
⎍	Schmitt trigger device or function

Comparison of logic families

Since RTL was introduced in the early 1960s, there has been a steady progression in technology; the design engineer now has a wide choice of integrated circuit ranges and operating parameters.

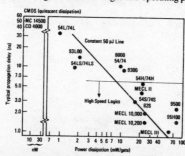

Speed/power characteristics of major logic lines

It is apparent that speed/power comparisons are not sufficient in themselves. Other important parameters to be considered are noise immunity, supply voltage requirements and fan out.

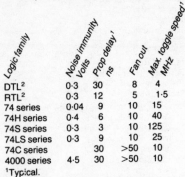

Logic family	Noise immunity Volts	Prop delay[1] ns	Fan out	Max. toggle speed[1] MHz
DTL[2]	0·3	30	8	4
RTL[2]	0·3	12	5	1·5
74 series	0·04	9	10	15
74H series	0·4	6	10	40
74S series	0·3	3	10	125
74LS series	0·3	9	10	25
74C series		30	>50	10
4000 series	4·5	30	>50	10

[1]Typical.
[2]Not recommended for new designs.

Power supply requirements

Each logic type has different power supply requirements and since system economics can be greatly affected by the cost of power supplies it is important to establish exact power supply parameters.

Logic family	Supply voltage Nominal V	Supply voltage Min. V	Supply voltage Max. V	Power diss. per package mW (typ)	Decoupling and other requirements
RTL	3·6	3·24	3·96	20	No special precautions
DTL	5·0	4·5	5·5	30	No special precautions
74 series	5·0	4·75	5·25	40	0·1 µF
74H series	5·0	4·75	5·25	60	decoupling capacitor
74S series	5·0	4·75	5·25	40	for every 8 packages
74LS series	5·0	4·75	5·25	8	
74C series	5·0	4·75	5·25	2	
4000 series	—	3·0	18·0	0·01	No special precautions

With the exception of the 74C series of devices, all series in the 74 family are of transistor-transistor-logic (TTL) construction. The 74C series (which is of CMOS construction) is pin compatible with all 74 family members and therefore the generic TTL title usually includes it.

TTL 74 family and CMOS 4000 family devices have generally superseded all other logic types.

TTL data

All devices are listed by generic family number, e.g. 7400. Certain devices may only be available, however, as members of as few as one series of the 74 family. Readers are referred to relevant data books for further details.

Selection by device number

Device	Description
7400	Quad 2-input Positive NAND Gate
7401	Quad 2-input Positive NAND Gate (open collector o/p)
7401A	Quad 2-input Positive NAND Gate (open collector o/p)
7402	Quad 2-input Positive NOR Gate (open collector o/p)
7403	Quad 2-input Positive NAND Gate (open collector o/p)
7404	Hex Inverter
7405A	Hex Inverter (open collector o/p)
7406	Hex Inverter/Buffer 30V o/p
7407	Hex Buffer 30V o/p
7408	Quad 2-input Positive AND Gate
7409	Quad 2-input Positive AND Gate
7410	Triple 3-input Positive NAND Gate
7411	Triple 3-input AND Gate
7412	Triple 3-input NAND Gate (open collector o/p)
7413	Dual 4-input Schmitt Trigger
7414	Schmitt Hex Inverter Buffer
7415	Triple 3-input AND Gate with Open Collector Output
7416	Hex Inverter/Buffer 15V o/p
7417	Hex Buffer 15V o/p
7420	Dual 4-input Positive NAND Gate
7421	Dual 4-input AND Gate
7422	Dual 4-input NAND Gate with Open Collector Output
7425	Dual 4-input NOR Gate with Strobe
7426	Quad 2-input High Voltage Interface NAND Gate
7427	Triple 3-input NOR Gate
7428	Quad 2-input NOR Buffer (Fan Out 30)
7430	8-input Positive NAND Gate
7432	Quad 2-input OR Gate
7433A	Quad 2-input NOR Buffer 15V
7437	Quad 2-input NAND Buffer
7438A	Quad 2-input NAND Buffer 15V
7440	Dual 4-input Buffer NAND Gate
7441A	BCD-to-Decimal Decoder/Nixie Driver
7442	BCD-to-Decimal Decoder
7445	BCD-to-Decimal Decoder/Driver 30V output o/c
7446A	BCD-to-Seven Segment Decoder/Driver 30V/40mA
7447	BCD-to-Seven Segment Decoder/Driver 15V/20mA
7447A	BCD-to-Seven Segment Decoder/Driver 15V/40mA
7448	BCD-to-Seven Segment Decoder/Driver
7449	BCD-to-7-segment driver with Open Collector Output
7450	Expandable Dual 2 wide, 2 i/p AND-OR-INVERT Gate
7451	Dual 2 wide, 2 i/p AND-OR-INVERT Gate
7453	Expandable 4 wide, 2 i/p AND-OR-INVERT Gate
7454	4 wide, 2 i/p AND-OR-INVERT Gate
7455	2 wide, 4 i/p AND-OR-INVERT Gate
7460	Dual 4-input Expander
7464	4-2-3-2-input AND-OR-Invert Gate
7470	Positive Edge-triggered J-K Flip Flops
7472	J-K Master-Slave Flip Flops (AND inputs)
7473	Dual J-K Master-Slave Flip Flops
7474	Dual D-Type Edge Triggered Flip Flops
7475	4-bit bistable latch = Quad bistable latch
7476	Dual J-K Master-Slave Flip Flops + preset and clear
7478	Dual J-K Flip-flop with Preset, Common Clear and Clock

7481	16-bit Active Element Memory
7482	2-bit Binary Full Adder
7483A	4-bit Full Adder with Carry
7484	16-bit Active Element Memory
7485	4-bit Comparator
7486	Quad 2-input Exclusive OR Gate
7489	64-bit RAM (16 × 4W)
7490	Decade Counter
7491	8-bit Shift Registers
7492	Divide-by-twelve Counter
7493	4-bit Binary Counter
7494	4-bit Shift Registers (Parallel-In, Serial-Out)
7495	4-bit Right Shift, Left Shift Register
7496	5-bit Shift Registers (Dual Para-In, Para-Out)
74100	8-bit Bistable Latch
74107	Dual J-K Master Slave Flip Flop
74109	Dual Positive Edge Triggered Flip-flop with Preset and Clear
74112	Dual Negative Edge Triggered J-K Flip-flop with Preset and Clear
74113	Dual Negative Edge Triggered J-K Flip-flop with Preset
74114	Dual Negative Edge Triggered J-K Flip-flop with Preset and Clear
74121	Monostable Multivibrator
74122	Monostable Multivibrator with reset
74123	Dual Monostable Multivibrator with reset
74124	Universal Pulse Generator
74125	Quad Buffer with 3-state Active Low Enable Output
74126	Quad Buffer with 3-state Active High Enable Output
74128	Quad Line Driver
74132	Quad 2-input Schmitt NAND
74133	13-input NAND
74137	Demultiplexer
74138	3 line to 8 line Decoder/Demultiplexer
74139	Dual 2-to-4 Line Multiplexer
74141	BCD-to-Decimal Decoder/Driver
74145	BCD-to-Seven Segment Decoder/Driver 15V output
74147	10-line Priority Decimal to 4-line BCD Priority Encoder
74148	8-to-3 Octal Priority Encoder
74150	16-bit Data Selector
74151	8-bit Data Selector (with strobe)
74153	Dual 4 to 1 line Data Selector 1 MPX
74154	4 line to 16 line Decoder
74155	Dual 2-to-4 line Decoder/DeMPX (totem pole output)
74156	Dual 2-to-4 line Decoder/DeMPX (open collector output)
74157	Quad 2 line to 1 line Selector
74158	Quad 2-input Inverting Multiplexer
74160	Synchronous Decade Counter
74161	Asynchronous Binary Counter with Reset
74162	Synchronous Decade Counter
74163	Synchronous Binary Counter
74164	8-bit Shift Register, Serial In-Parallel Out
74165	8-bit Shift Register, Parallel In-Serial Out
74169	4-stage Synchronous Bidirectional Counter
74173	4-bit D-Type Register
74174	Hex Type 'D' Flip Flop
74175	Quad 'D' Flip Flop with common reset
74180	8-bit Odd/Even Parity Generator/Checkers

74181	4-bit Arithmetic Logic Out
74182	Carry-Look-Ahead Unit
74190	Synchronous Up/Down Decade Counter (Single Clock Unit)
74191	Synchronous Up/Down 4-bit Binary Counter (Single Clock Unit)
74192	Synchronous 4-bit Up/Down Counter
74193	Synchronous 4-bit Up/Down Counter
74194	4-bit Universal Shift Register
74195	Synchronous 4-bit Parallel Shift Register with J-K inputs
74196	50Mhz Presettable Decade Counter/Latch (Bi-Quinary)
74197	4-bit Presettable Ripple Counter
74200	256-bit Random Access Memory (RAM)
74221	Dual Monostable Multivibrator
74240	Octal Inverting Buffer with 3-state Outputs
74241	Octal Buffer with 3-state Outputs
74242	Octal Bus Inverting Transceiver
74243	Octal Bus Transceiver
74244	Octal Buffer with 3-state Outputs
74245	Octal Bus Transceiver with 3-state Outputs
74251	Selector Multiplexer with 3-state Outputs
74253	Dual 4-input Multiplexer with 3-state Output
74256	Dual 4-bit Addressable Latch
74257	Quad 2-input Multiplexer with 3-state Output
74258	Quad 2-input Multiplexer with Inverting 3-state Output
74259	8-bit Addressable Latch
74273	8-bit Register with Clear
74280	9-bit Parity Generator/Checker
74283	4-bit Full Adder with Carry
74298	Quad 2-port Register
74299	8-bit Universal Storage Shift Register with 3-state Output
74321	Crystal Oscillator
74323	8-bit Universal Storage Shift Register with 3-state Output
74352	Dual 4-bit Inverting Multiplexer
74353	Dual 4-bit Multiplexer with 3-state Inverting Output
74354	Transparent Data Selector Multiplexer
74356	Data Selector Multiplexer
74365	Hex Buffer with 2-input NOR Enable
74366	Hex Inverting Buffer with 2-input NOR Enable
74367	Hex Buffer with 3-state Output
74368	Hex Inverting Buffer with 3-state Output
74373	Octal Latch with 3-state Output
74374	Octal D-type Flip-flop with 3-state Output
74378	Hex D-type Flip-flop
74381	4-bit Arithmetic Logic Unit
74390	Dual Decade Counter
74393	Dual 4-bit Binary Counter
74395	4-bit Cascadable Shift Register
74399	Quad, 2-part Register
74423	Retriggerable Monostable Multivibrator
74442	Quad Tridirectional Transceiver
74443	Quad Tridirectional Inverting Transceiver
74444	Quad Tridirectional Transceiver
74533	Inverting Octal D-Type Latch
74534	Inverting Octal D-type Flip Flop
74563	Octal Transparent Latch with Inverted Outputs
74564	Octal Edge-Triggered Flip Flop with Inverted Outputs
74620	Octal Bus Transceiver

74625	Voltage Controlled Oscillator
74655	Inverting Octal Buffer/Line Driver with 3-state Outputs
74657	Octal Bi-directional Transceiver with Parity
74669	4-bit Binary Counter
74670	4 × 4 Register File with 3-state Output
74673	16-bit Serial to Parallel Shift Register
74674	16-bit Parallel to Serial Shift Register
74682	8-bit Magnitude Comparator
74688	8-bit Magnitude Comparator with Totem Pole Output
741242	Quad Bus Transceiver – Inverting
741243	Quad Bus Transceiver – Non-inverting
744002	Dual 4-input NOR gates
744017	Decade Counter Divider
744020	14-bit Binary Counter
744040	12-bit Binary Counter
744049	Hex-Inverter Buffer
744050	Hex Buffer
744060	14-bit Binary Counter
744075	Triple 3-Input OR Gate
744078	8-input NOR Gate
744511	BCD-Seven Segment Latch/Decoder/Driver
744514	4-bit Latch to 1-of-16 Decoder
744538	Dual Precision Retriggerable/Resettable Monostable Multivibrator
744543	BCD- to-Seven Segment Latch/Decoder/Driver

Selection by function
Gates
AND

Quad 2-input	7408
Quad 2-input open collector o/p	7409
Triple 3-input	7411
Triple 3-input open collector o/p	7415
Dual 4-input	7421

OR

Triple 3-input	744075
Quad 2-input	7432
Exclusive OR	
Quad 2-input	7486

NAND

Quad 2-input	7400
Quad 2-input open collector o/p	7401
Quad 2-input open collector o/p	7403
Triple 3-input	7410
Dual 4-input	7420
Dual 4-input open collector o/p	7422
Quad 2-input high voltage	7426
8-input	7430
Quad 2-input buffer	7437
Dual 2-input open collector o/p	7438
Dual 4-input buffer	7440
13-input	74133

NOR

Quad 2-input	7402
Dual 4-input	744002
Dual 4-input with strobe	7425
Triple 3-input	7427

Quad 2-input buffer	**7428**
Quad 2-input buffer	**7433**
Quad 2-input exclusive	**74266**
8-input	**744078**

Schmitt

Dual 4-input NAND	**7413**
Hex inverting	**7414**
Quad 2-input NAND	**74132**

AND-OR-Invert

Dual 2-wide, 2-input	**7451**
4-wide	**7454**
2-wide, 4-input	**7455**
4-2-3-2-input	**7464**

Buffers

Hex	**744050**
Hex inverting	**744049**
Hex inverting	**7404**
Hex inverting open collector o/p	**7405**
Hex inverting open collector o/p	**7406**
Hex open collector o/p	**7407**
Hex inverting open collector o/p	**7416**
Quad 3-state active low enable	**74125**
Quad 3-state active high enable	**74126**
Hex 2-input NOR enable	**74365**
Hex inverting, 2-input NOR enable	**74366**
Hex 3-state	**74367**
Hex 3-state inverting	**74368**

Line/bus, drivers/transceivers

Quad line driver	**74128**
Octal buffer 3-state inverting	**74240**
Octal buffer 3-state	**74241**
Quad bus transceiver inverting	**74242**
Quad bus transceiver	**74243**
Quad bus transceiver, inverting	**741242**
Quad bus transceiver	**741243**
Octal buffer 3-state	**74244**
Octal bus transceiver 3-state	**74245**
Quad tridirectional transceiver true	**74442**
Quad tridirectional transceiver inverting	**74443**
Quad tridirectional transceiver	**74444**
Octal bus transceiver	**74620**
Octal bus transceiver	**74640**
Octal bus transceiver	**74643**
Octal, bi-directional transceiver with parity	**74657**
Octal buffer/line driver, inverting, 3-state o/p	**74655**
Octal, buffer/line drive, non-inverting, 3-state o/p	**74656**

Flip flops (bistables)

D-type

Dual edge triggered	**7474**
4-bit	**7475**
Hex with clear	**74174**
Inverting octal	**74534**
Quad with clear	**74175**
Octal 3-state	**74374**
Octal common enable	**74377**

Octal, edge-triggered, inverted outputs	74564
Hex	74378
Octal transparent latch	74573
Octal transparent latch inverted	74580

J-K

AND gated positive edge triggered	7470
AND gated master slave	7472
Dual with clear	7473
Dual with preset and clear	7476
Dual with preset, common clear and clock	7478
Dual with clear	74107
Dual positive edge triggered preset and clear	74109
Dual negative edge triggered preset and clear	74112
Dual negative edge triggered preset	74113
Dual negative edge triggered preset and clear	74114

Monostable multivibrators

Single	74121
Dual retriggerable with clear	74123
Dual retriggerable/resettable	744538
Dual retriggerable	744423
Dual	74221

Latches

Dual 4-bit addressable	74256
Inverting octal D-type	74533
4-bit to 1-of-16 decoder	744514
8-bit addressable	74259
8-bit register with clear	74273
Quad 2-port register	74298
Octal 3-state	74373
Octal transparent, inverted outputs	74563

Arithmetic functions

4-bit full adder with carry	7483A
4-bit magnitude comparator	7485
4-bit arithmetic logic unit	74181
4-bit arithmetic logic unit	74381
4-bit full adder with carry	74283
4 × 4 register file 3-state	74670
8-bit magnitude comparator	74682
8-bit magnitude comparator, totem-pole outputs	74688

Counters

Decade up	7490
Divide by 12	7492
4-bit binary	7493
B.C.D asynchronous reset	74160
Binary asynchronous reset	74161
B.C.D. synchronous reset	74162
Binary synchronous reset	74163
Binary up/down synchronous	74191
Decade up/down synchronous	74192
Binary up/down synchronous with clear	74193
Decade presettable ripple	74196
4-bit presettable ripple	74197
Dual decade	74390
Dual 4-bit binary	74393
4-bit binary	74669
4-stage synchronous up/down	74169

Decade counter/divider	**744017**
4-bit binary	**744020**
12-bit binary	**744040**
14-bit binary	**744060**

Shift registers

4-bit	**7495**
5-bit	**7496**
8-bit serial in parallel out	**74164**
8-bit parallel to serial	**74165**
4-bit universal	**74194**
4-bit parallel access	**74195**
4-bit D-type	**74173**
8-bit universal storage 3-state	**74299**
8-bit universal storage 3-state	**74323**
4-bit cascadable	**74395**
16-bit serial to parallel	**74673**
16-bit parallel to serial	**74674**
Quad, 2-part	**74399**

Encoders, decoders/drivers
Decoders

B.C.D.–decimal	**7442**
B.C.D.–decimal driver	**7445**
B.C.D.–7-segment driver open collector o/p	**7447**
B.C.D.–7-segment driver	**7448**
B.C.D.–7-segment driver open collector o/p	**7449**
B.C.D.-to-7-segment latch/decoder/driver	**744511**
B.C.D.-to-7-segment latch/decoder/driver	**744543**
De-multiplexer	**74137**
3-to-8 line multiplexer	**74138**
Dual 2-to-4 line multiplexer	**74139**
B.C.D.–decimal driver	**74141**
B.C.D.–decimal driver	**74145**
4-to-16 line	**74154**
Dual 1-of-4	**74155**
Dual 1-of-4 open collector o/p	**74156**

Encoders/multiplexers

Octal priority encoder 8-to-3	**74148**
8-input multiplexer	**74151**
Dual 4-input multiplexer	**74153**
Quad 2-input multiplexer	**74157**
Quad 2-input multiplexer inverting	**74158**
Parity generator/checker 9-bit odd/even	**74180**
Selector multiplexer 3-state	**74251**
Dual 4-input multiplexer 3-state	**74253**
Quad 2-input multiplexer 3-state	**74257**
Quad 2-input multiplexer 3-state inverting	**74258**
Dual 4-input multiplexer inverting	**74352**
Dual 4-input multiplexer 3-state inverting	**74353**
Data selector multiplexer transparent	**74354**
Data selector multiplexer	**74356**
10-line decimal to 4-line B.C.D.	**74147**

Miscellaneous

Crystal oscillator	**74321**
Voltage controlled oscillator	**74625**
9-bit parity generator/checker	**74280**

TTL pinouts

7400

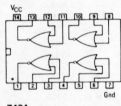

7401

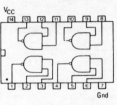

7402

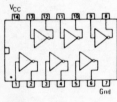

7403

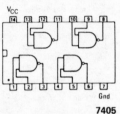

7404

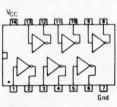

7405

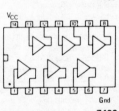

7406

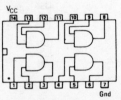

7407

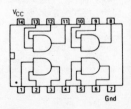

7408

7409

7410

7411

7413

7414

7415

7416

7420

7421

7422

7425

92

7426

7427

7428

7430

7432

7433

7437

7438

7440

7442

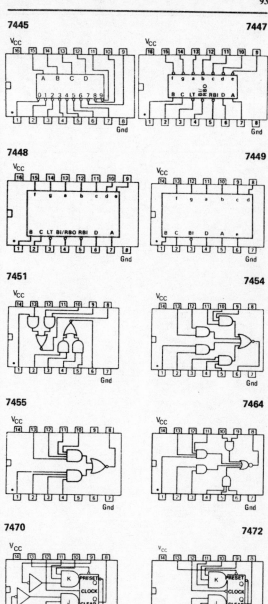

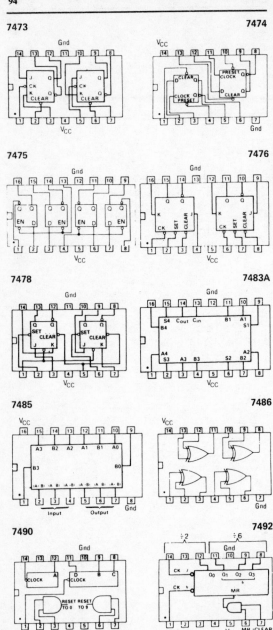

7473

7474

7475

7476

7478

7483A

7485

7486

7490

7492

7493

Gnd

| 14 | 13 | 12 | 11 | 10 | 9 | 8 |

CLOCK A   D CLOCK RESET B   C

| 1 | 2 | 3 | 4 | 5 | 6 | 7 |

V_CC

7495B

V_CC

| 14 | 13 | 12 | 11 | 10 | 9 | 8 |

PARALLEL OUTPUTS
Q_0 Q_1 Q_2 Q_3 SERIAL
CK PARALLEL
CK MODE CONTROL
SERIAL DATA IN
PARALLEL DATA INPUTS
A   B   C   D

| 1 | 2 | 3 | 4 | 5 | 6 | 7 |

Gnd

7496

Gnd

| 16 | 15 | 14 | 13 | 12 | 11 | 10 | 9 |

A   B   C   D   E
CLEAR —OUTPUTS—
CLOCK SERIAL IN
—PRESET— ENABLE
A   B   C   D   E

| 1 | 2 | 3 | 4 | 5 | 6 | 7 | 8 |

V_CC

74107

V_CC

| 14 | 13 | 12 | 11 | 10 | 9 | 8 |

K CK J CLEAR Q Q K CK J CLEAR Q

| 1 | 2 | 3 | 4 | 5 | 6 | 7 |

Gnd

74109

V_CC

| 16 | 15 | 14 | 13 | 12 | 11 | 10 | 9 |

J SET Q
CK
K
CLEAR Q
J SET Q
CK
K
CLEAR Q

| 1 | 2 | 3 | 4 | 5 | 6 | 7 | 8 |

Gnd

74112

V_CC

| 16 | 15 | 14 | 13 | 12 | 11 | 10 | 9 |

CLEAR CK K J SET Q
Q
CK CLEAR
K J SET Q Q

| 1 | 2 | 3 | 4 | 5 | 6 | 7 | 8 |

Gnd

74113

V_CC

| 14 | 13 | 12 | 11 | 10 | 9 | 8 |

J SET Q
CK
K Q
J
CK
K SET Q Q

| 1 | 2 | 3 | 4 | 5 | 6 | 7 |

Gnd

74114

V_CC

| 14 | 13 | 12 | 11 | 10 | 9 | 8 |

J SET Q
CK
K
CLEAR Q
J SET Q
CK
K
CLEAR Q

| 1 | 2 | 3 | 4 | 5 | 6 | 7 |

Gnd

74121

V_CC

| 14 | 13 | 12 | 11 | 10 | 9 | 8 |

TIMING
RC C R

A1
A2 B Q Q

| 1 | 2 | 3 | 4 | 5 | 6 | 7 |

Gnd

74123

V_CC

TIMING
R C

| 16 | 15 | 14 | 13 | 12 | 11 | 10 | 9 |

CLEAR
Q Q
CLEAR
Q Q

| 1 | 2 | 3 | 4 | 5 | 6 | 7 | 8 |

C R
TIMING
Gnd

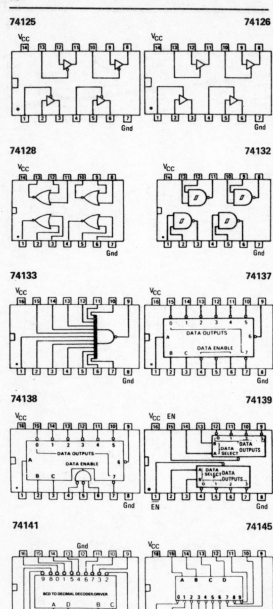

74125   74126

74128   74132

74133   74137

74138   74139

74141   74145

74147

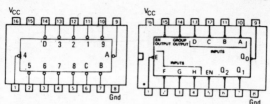

74148

74151

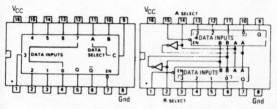

74153

74154

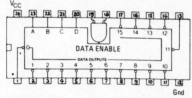

74155

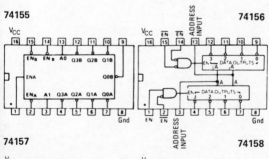

74156

74157

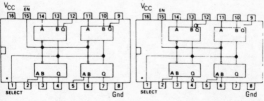

74158

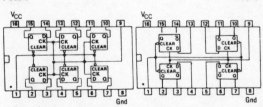

74160

V_CC
TC QA QB QC QD CER
MR
PE
CK A B C D CEP
Gnd

74161

V_CC
TC QA QB QC QD CER
MR
PE
CK A B C D CEP
Gnd

74162

V_CC
TC QA QB QC QD CER
SR
PE
CK A B C D CEP
Gnd

74163

V_CC
TC QA QB QC QD CER
SR
PE
CK A B C D CEP
Gnd

74164

V_CC
Q_8 Q_7 Q_6 Q_5
A MR
B Q_1 Q_2 Q_3 Q_4 CK
Gnd

74165

V_CC
D C B A DATA INPUT Q
LOAD
CK
E F G H Q̄
Gnd

74169

V_CC
T̄C Q_0 Q_1 Q_2 Q_3 CĒT P̄Ē
U/D̄ CP P_0 P_1 P_2 P_3 C̄ĒP
Gnd

74173

V_CC
CLEAR 1D 2D 3D 4D DATA ENABLE
OUTPUT CONTROL
1Q 2Q 3Q 4Q CK
Gnd

74174

V_CC
D CK D CK D CK
CLEAR CLEAR CLEAR
CLEAR CK CLEAR CK CLEAR CK
D Q D Q D Q
Gnd

74175

V_CC
Q CLEAR CLEAR Q
CK D D CK
CK CLEAR CLEAR CK
D Q Q D
Gnd

74180

V_{CC}

F E D C B

G

EVEN INPUT ODD INPUT

SUM OUTPUT

EVEN ODD

H

A

Gnd

74181

V_{CC}

C_{out} CARRY PROPOGATE OUTPUT

B_1 A_2 B_2 A_3 B_3

B_0 A_1

COMP OUT

A_0

F_4

MODE SELECT

CARRY GENERATE OUTPUT

FUNCTION OUTPUTS F_3

S_4 S_3 S_2 S_1

OPERAND INPUTS

C_{in} INPUT

CARRY MODE CONTROL

F_1 F_2

Gnd

74191

V_{CC}

OUTPUTS

A CK RIPPLE CLOCK MAX/ MIN LOAD C

B

D

QB QA EN UP/ DOWN QC QD

INPUTS

Gnd

74192

V_{CC}

A CLEAR BORROW CARRY LOAD C

B

D

QB QA COUNT DOWN COUNT UP QC QD

Gnd

74193

V_{CC}

A CLEAR BORROW CARRY LOAD C

B

D

QB QA COUNT DOWN COUNT UP QC QD

Gnd

74194

V_{CC}

Q_0 Q_1 Q_2 Q_3 CK

MR

SELECT S_2 S_1

SDR A B C D SDL

Gnd

74195

V_{CC}

Q_0 Q_1 Q_2 Q_3 CK

SHIFT/ LOAD

CLEAR

SERIAL INPUTS PARALLEL INPUTS

J K A B C D

Gnd

74196

V_{CC}

Q_3 D B Q_1

MR DIVIDE BY TWO CK

PE DIVIDE BY FIVE CK

Q_2 C A Q_0

Gnd

74197

V_{CC} $\overline{MR}$

QD D QB

QC C CK B A CK QA

PE

Gnd

74221

V_{CC}

R C Q

TIMING

INPUTS

CLEAR

Q

INPUTS

TIMING

Q C R

Gnd

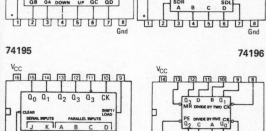

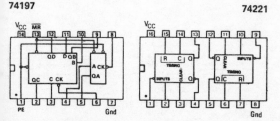

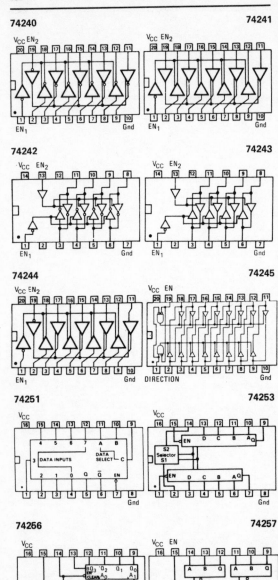

74258

V_CC
OEN
C_0 C_1 Q_C D_0 D_1 Q_D
SELECT
A_0 A_1 Q_A B_0 B_1 Q_B
Gnd

74259

V_CC
CLEAR EN DATA INPUT Q_7 Q_6 Q_5 Q_4
ADDRESS INPUTS LATCH OUTPUTS
A_0 A_1 A_2 Q_0 Q_1 Q_2 Q_3
Gnd

74266

V_CC
Gnd

74273

V_CC
Q_7 H G Q_6 Q_5 F E Q_4
MR CK
Q_0 A B Q_1 Q_2 C D Q_3
Gnd

74280

V_CC
I_5 I_4 I_3 I_2 I_1 I_0
I_6 I_7 I_8 Σ_E Σ_O
Gnd

74283

V_CC
B3 A3 S3 A4 B4 S4
S2 C_out
B2 A2 S1 A1 B1 C_in
Gnd

74298

V_CC
Q_A Q_B Q_C Q_D CK
SELECT
B_1 A_1 A_0 B_0 C_1 D_1 D_0 C_0
Gnd

74299

V_CC
SQ I/O_7 I/O_5 I/O_3 I/O_1
SDL
S_2 SELECT
S_1 SDR
OEN I/O_6 I/O_4 I/O_2 I/O_0 CK
SQ MR
Gnd

74321

V_CC   V_CC
XTAL XTAL F/2 F F^1
2   1
EXTERNAL INDUCTOR   F^1
FFQ FFD F/4 F
Gnd 1   Gnd 2

74323

V_CC
SQ I/O_7 I/O_5 I/O_3 I/O_1
SDL
S_2 SELECT
S_1 SDR
OEN I/O_6 I/O_4 I/O_2 I/O_0 9R
SQ CK
Gnd

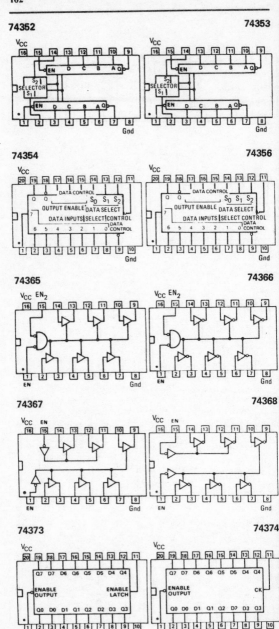

74377

V_CC

CLOCK

EN

Gnd

74378

V_CC

Q5 F E Q4 D Q3

EN

CK

Q0 A B Q1 C Q2

Gnd

74381

V_CC

A_2 B_2 A_3 B_3 C_n P G F_3 F_2

A_1 B_1 A_0 B_0 S_0 S_1 S_2 F_0 F_1

Gnd

74390

V_CC

MR
CK_0 Q_0 CK_1 Q_1 Q_2 Q_3

CK_0
MR Q_0 CK_1 Q_1 Q_2 Q_3

Gnd

74393

V_CC

MR
CK Q_0 Q_1 Q_2 Q_3

CK
MR Q_0 Q_1 Q_2 Q_3

Gnd

74395

V_CC

Q_A Q_B Q_C Q_D CK

CLEAR

CASCADE
OUTPUT

OUTPUT
CONTROL
LOAD
SHIFT

SERIAL
INPUT A B C D

Gnd

74399

V_CC

Q_d I_od I_id I_1c I_oc Q_c CP

S Q_a I_oa I_ia I_ib I_ob Q_b

Gnd

74423

V_CC

CLR

CLR

Gnd

74442, 443, 444

V_CC

C B A A1 A2 A3 A4 S_1

CS ENABLE   SELECT S_0

B1 C1 C2 B2 B3 C3 C4 B4

Gnd

74533

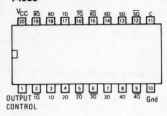

74534

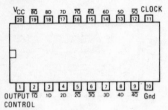

74563

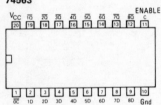

74564

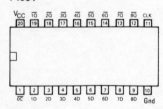

74573

74574

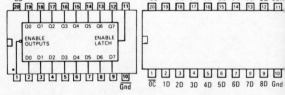

74580

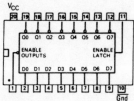

V_CC

20 19 18 17 16 15 14 13 12 11

Q0 Q1 Q2 Q3 Q4 Q5 Q6 Q7

ENABLE
OUTPUTS

ENABLE
LATCH

D0 D1 D2 D3 D4 D5 D6 D7

1 2 3 4 5 6 7 8 9 10
$\overline{Gnd}$

74620   **74625**

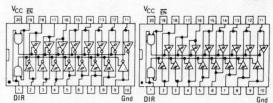

V_CC

20 19 18 17 16 15 14 13 12 11

B→A B_0 B_1 B_2 B_3 B_4 B_5 B_6

A→B ENABLE   B_7

A_0 A_1 A_2 A_3 A_4 A_5 A_6 A_7

1 2 3 4 5 6 7 8 9 10
Gnd

V_CC   V_CC Gnd

16 15 14 13 12 11 10 9

Q
IC EXT
Q

OSCILLATOR

FREQ.
CONTROL

Q
IC EXT
Q

FREQ.
CONTROL

OSCILLATOR

1 2 3 4 5 6 7 8
Gnd   V_CC Gnd

74640   **74643**

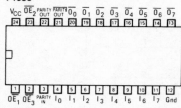

V_CC $\overline{EN}$

20 19 18 17 16 15 14 13 12 11

1 2 3 4 5 6 7 8 9 10
DIR   Gnd

V_CC $\overline{EN}$

20 19 18 17 16 15 14 13 12 11

1 2 3 4 5 6 7 8 9 10
DIR   Gnd

74655

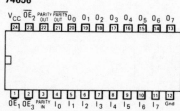

V_CC $\overline{OE}_2$ PARITY $\overline{PARITY}$ $\overline{O}_0$ $\overline{O}_1$ $\overline{O}_2$ $\overline{O}_3$ $\overline{O}_4$ $\overline{O}_5$ $\overline{O}_6$ $\overline{O}_7$
       OUT   OUT

24 23 22 21 20 19 18 17 16 15 14 13

1 2 3 4 5 6 7 8 9 10 11 12
$\overline{OE}_1$ $\overline{OE}_3$ PARITY I_0 I_1 I_2 I_3 I_4 I_5 I_6 I_7 Gnd
                  IN

74656

V_CC $\overline{OE}_2$ PARITY $\overline{PARITY}$ O_0 O_1 O_2 O_3 O_4 O_5 O_6 O_7
       OUT   OUT

24 23 22 21 20 19 18 17 16 15 14 13

1 2 3 4 5 6 7 8 9 10 11 12
OE_1 $\overline{OE}_3$ PARITY I_0 I_1 I_2 I_3 I_4 I_5 I_6 I_7 Gnd
                  IN

74657

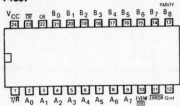

74669   **74670**

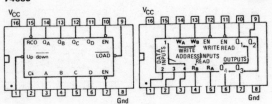

74673

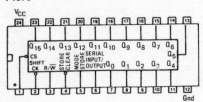

74674

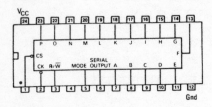

74682

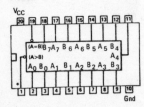

74688

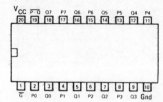

741242

741243

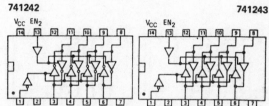

744002

744017

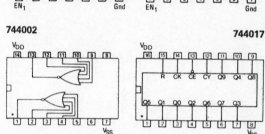

744020

744040

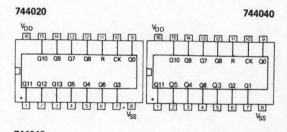

744049

744050

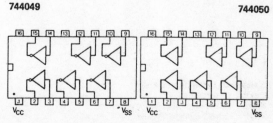

744060

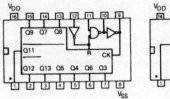

744075

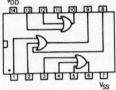

744078

744511

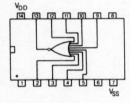

744514

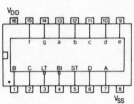

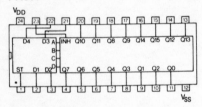

744538

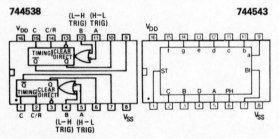

744543

CMOS data

Selection by device number

Device	Description
4000	Dual 3-input NOR gate plus Inverter
4001	Quad 2-input NOR Gate

4002	Dual 4-input NOR Gate
4006	18-Stage Static Shift Register
4007	Dual Complementary Pair Plus Inverter
4008	4-Bit full Adder with Parallel Carry
4009	Hex Buffer/Converter (Inverting)
4010	Hex Buffer/Converter (Non-Inverting)
4011	Quad 2-Input NAND Gate
4012	Dual 4-Input NAND Gate
4013	Dual 'D' Flip-Flop with Set/Reset
4014	8-Stage Static Shift Register
4015	Dual 4-Stage Static Shift Register
4016	Quad Bilateral Switch
4017	Decade Counter/Divider
4018	Presettable Divide-By-'N' Counter
4019	Quad AND-OR Select Gate
4020	14-Stage Binary Ripple Counter
4021	8-Stage Static Shift Register
4022	Divide-by-8 Counter/Divider
4023	Triple 3-Input NAND Gate
4024	7-Stage Binary Counter
4025	Triple 3-Input NOR Gate
4026	Decade Counter/Divider
4027	Dual J-K Master Slave Flip-Flop
4028	BCD-to-Decimal Decoder
4029	Presettable Up/Down Counter
4030	Quad Exclusive-OR Gate
4032	Triple Serial Adder
4035	4-Stage Parallel IN/OUT Shift Register
4038	Triple Serial Adder
4040	12/Stage Binary Ripple Counter
4042	Quad Clocked 'D' Latch
4043	Quad, 3-state R-S Latch
4044	Quad, 3-state R-S Latch
4046	Micropower Phase-Locked Loop
4047	Multivibrator, Astable/Monostable
4049	Hex Buffer/Converter (Inverting)
4050	Hex Buffer/Converter (Non-Inverting)
4051	Single 8-Channel Multiplexer
4052	Differential 4-Channel Multiplexer
4053	Triple, 2-input Analogue Multiplexer
4054	4-Line Liquid Crystal Display Driver
4056	BCD-7-Segment Decoder/Driver
4059	Programmable Divide-by-N Counter
4060	14-Stage Counter and Oscillator
4061	256-Word X 1-Bit Static Ram
4066	Quad Bilateral Switch
4068	8-Input NAND Gate
4069	Hex Inverter
4070	Quad Exclusive OR Gate
4071	Quad 2-Input OR Gate
4072	Dual, 4-input OR Gate
4073	Triple, 3-input AND Gate
4075	Triple, 3-input OR Gate
4076	Quad, 3-state D Register
4077	Quad Exclusive NOR Gate
4078	8-input NOR Gate
4081	Quad 2-Input AND Gate
4082	Dual 4-Input AND Gate
4085	Dual 2-Wide 2-Input AOI Gate

4086	Expendable 4-Wide 2-Input AOI Gate
4093	Quad 2-Input NAND Schmitt Trigger
4094	8-stage Shift Register, with Storage
4099	8-Bit Addressable Latch
40106	Hex, Inverting Schmitt Buffers
4160	Asynchronous Decade Counter with Clear
4161	Asynchronous 4-bit Binary Counter with Clear
4162	Synchronous Decade Counter with Clear
4163	Synchronous 4-bit Binary Counter with Clear
4502	Strobed Hex Inverting Buffer
4508	Dual 4-bit Latch
4510	BCD UP/DOWN Counter
4511	BCD-to-Segment Decoder/Driver
4512	8-channel Data Selector
4513	BCD-to-7-segment Latch/Driver
4514	1 to 16 Decoder (Output High)
4515	1 to 16 Decoder (Output Low)
4516	Binary UP/DOWN Counter
4518	Dual BCD UP Counter
4519	Quad, 2-input Multiplexer
4520	Dual 4-bit Binary Counter
4521	24-stage Frequency Divider
4522	BCD Programmable Divider
4526	Binary Programmable Divider
4527	BCD Rate Multiplier
4528	Dual Retriggerable Monostable
4529	Dual 4-channel Analogue Selector
4530	Dual 5-bit Majority Gate
4531	12-bit Parity Tree
4532	8-bit Priority Encoder
4536	Programmable Timer
4538	Dual Monostable Multivibrator
4539	Dual 4-bit Multiplexer
4541	Programmable Timer
4543	BCD-to-7-segment Latched LCD Driver
4551	Quad 2-input Analogue Multiplexer
4553	3-digit BCD Counter
4554	2 × 2 Binary Multiplier
4556	Dual Binary to 1-of-4 Decoder
4560	BCD Adder
4561	9's Complementer
4566	Timebase Generator
4580	4 × 4 Multiport Register
4581	4-bit Arithmetic Logic Unit
4582	Carry Look Ahead 4-bit Magnitude
4583	Dual Schmitt Gates
4585	4-bit Magnitude Comparator
4597	8-bit 3-state Bus Latch
4598	8-bit 3-state Bus Latch
4599	8-bit Addressable Latch
45100	4 × 4 Crosspoint Switch

Selection by function
Gates
AND

Triple 3-input	4073
Quad 2-input	4081

OR

Quad 2-input	4071

| Dual 4-input | 4072 |
| Triple 3-input | 4075 |

Exclusive OR

| Quad 2-input | 4070 |

NAND

Quad 2-input	4011
Dual 4-input	4012
Triple 3-input	4023
8-input	4068

NOR

Quad 2-input	4001
Dual 4-input	4002
Triple 3-input	4025
8-input	4078

Exclusive NOR

| Quad 2-input | 4077 |

Schmitt

Quad 2-input NAND	4093
Hex inverting	40106
Dual	4583

Majority

| Dual 5-bit | 4530 |

Buffers

Hex inverting	4049
Hex	4050
Hex inverting	4069
Strobed Hex inverting	4502

Flip-flops (bistables)

Dual D-type	4013
Dual J-K	4027
Quad latch	4042
Quad R-S latch 3-state	4043
Quad R-S latch 3-state	4044
Quad D register 3-state	4076
8-bit addressable latch	4099
Dual 4-bit latch	4508
4 × 4 multiport register	4580
8-bit bus latch 3-state	4597
8-bit bus latch 3-state	4598
8-bit addressable latch	4599

Counters

decade/divider	4017
divide by n	4018
14-bit binary	4020
Octal/divider	4022
7-stage binary	4024
Presettable binary/BCD, up/down	4029
12-bit binary	4040
14-bit binary	4060
Decade async. clear	4160
4-bit binary async. clear	4161
Decade sync. clear	4162
4-bit binary sync. clear	4163
BCD up/down	4510
Binary up/down	4516
Dual BCD up	4518
Dual 4-bit binary	4520
24-stage frequency divider	4521

BCD programmable divider	4522
Binary programmable divider	4526
3-digit BCD	4553

Shift registers

8-bit	4014
Dual 4-bit	4015
8-bit	4021
4-bit FIFO	4035
8-stage with storage	4094

Encoders, decoders/drivers

Decoders

BCD-decimal, binary-octal	4028
BCD-7-segment latch/driver	4511
BCD-7-segment latch/driver	4513
4-bit latch, 4-to-16 line	4514
4-bit latch, 4-to-16 line inverted outputs	4515
BCD-7-segment latched LCD driver	4543
Dual binary to 1-of-4	4556

Encoders/multiplexers

8-input analogue multiplexer	4051
Dual 4-input analogue multiplexer	4052
Triple 2-input analogue multiplexer	4053
8-channel data selector	4512
Quad 2-input multiplexer	4519
Dual 4-channel analogue selector	4529
8-bit priority encoder	4532
Dual 4-input multiplexer	4539
Quad 2-input analogue multiplexer	4551

Arithmetic functions

4-bit full adder	4008
Triple serial adder + logic	4032
Triple serial adder − logic	4038
BCD rate multiplier	4527
12-bit parity tree	4531
2 × 2 binary multiplier	4554
BCD adder	4560
9's complementer	4561
4-bit arithmetic logic unit	4581
Carry look ahead	4582
4-bit magnitude comparator	4585

Miscellaneous

Quad switch	4016
Phase locked loop	4046
Mono/astable multivibrator	4047
Quad switch	4066
Dual resettable monostable	4528
Programmable timer	4536
Dual monostable multivibrator	4538
Programmable timer	4541
Industrial timebase generator	4566
4 × 4 crosspoint switch	45100

CMOS pinouts

4001

4002

4008

4011

4012

4013

4014

4015

4016

4017

114

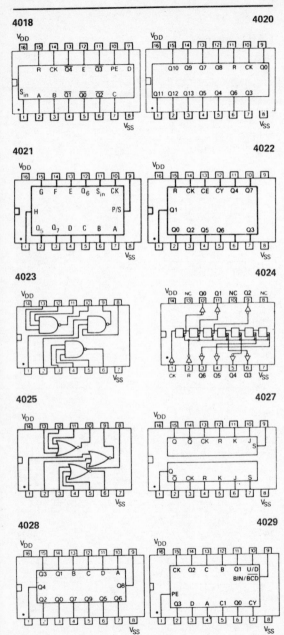

4018

4020

4021

4022

4023

4024

4025

4027

4028

4029

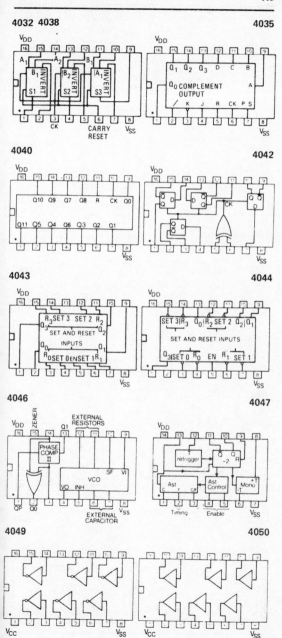

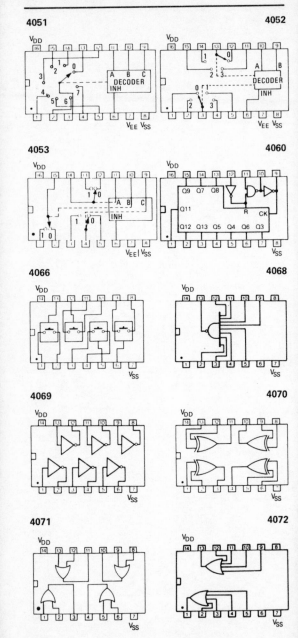

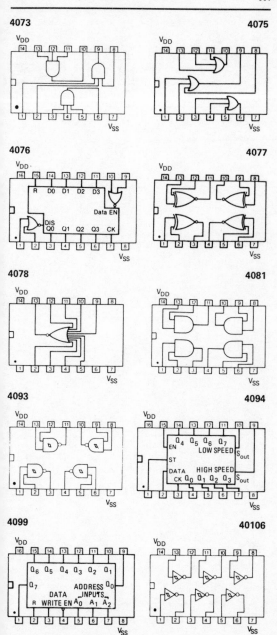

4160 4161 4162 4163

4502

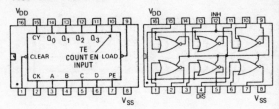

4508

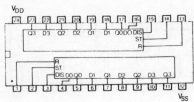

4510

4511

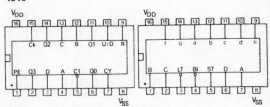

4512

4513

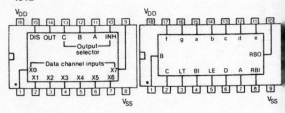

4514

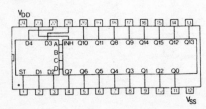

4515

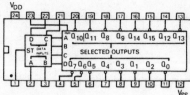

4516

V_{DD}

| 16 | 15 | 14 | 13 | 12 | 11 | 10 | 9 |

| | CK | Q2 | C | B | Q1 | U/D | R |

| | | | | | | | |

| PE | Q3 | D | A | C1 | Q0 | CY | |

| 1 | 2 | 3 | 4 | 5 | 6 | 7 | 8 |

V_{SS}

4518

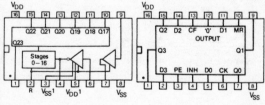

4519

V_{DD}

| 16 | 15 | 14 | 13 | 12 | 11 | 10 | 9 |

| | A_4 | CONTROL | Q_3 | Q_2 | Q_1 | Q_0 | |

| | B_4 | | | | | CONTROL | |

| | A_3 | B_3 | A_2 | B_2 | A_1 | B_1 | |

| 1 | 2 | 3 | 4 | 5 | 6 | 7 | 8 |

V_{SS}

4520

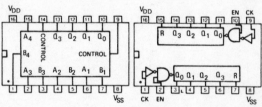

4521

V_{DD}

| 16 | 15 | 14 | 13 | 12 | 11 | 10 | 9 |

| | Q22 | Q21 | Q20 | Q19 | Q18 | Q17 | |

| Q23 | | | | | | | |

| | Stages 0–16 | | | | | | |

| 1 | 2 | 3 | 4 | 5 | 6 | 7 | 8 |

R V_{SS}^1 V_{DD}^1 V_{SS}

4522

V_{DD}

| 16 | 15 | 14 | 13 | 12 | 11 | 10 | 9 |

| | Q2 | D2 | CF | '0' | D1 | MR | |

| | | | OUTPUT | | | | |

| Q3 | | | | | | Q1 | |

| | D3 | PE | INH | D0 | CK | Q0 | |

| 1 | 2 | 3 | 4 | 5 | 6 | 7 | 8 |

V_{SS}

4526

V_{DD}

| 16 | 15 | 14 | 13 | 12 | 11 | 10 | 9 |

| | Q2 | D2 | CF | '0' | D1 | MR | |

| | | | OUTPUT | | | | |

| Q3 | | | | | | Q1 | |

| | D3 | PE | INH | D0 | CK | Q0 | |

| 1 | 2 | 3 | 4 | 5 | 6 | 7 | 8 |

V_{SS}

4527

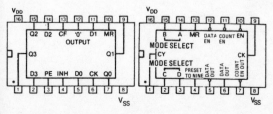

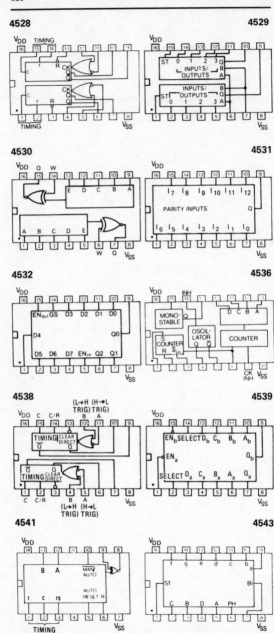

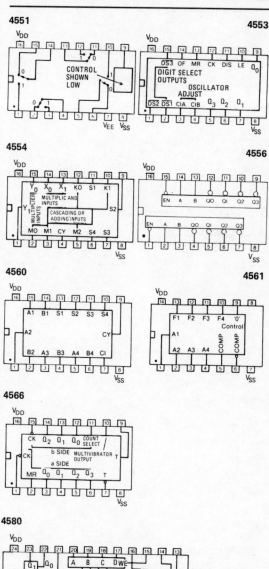

4581

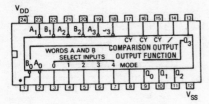

4582

4583

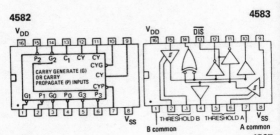

4585

4597

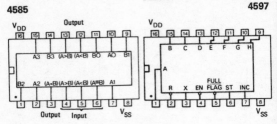

4598

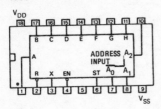

4599

45100

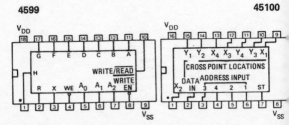

TTL and CMOS letter symbols

I_{IH} High level input current.

I_{IL} Low-level input current.

I_{OH} High-level output current.

I_O Off-state output current.

I_{OS} Short-circuit output current.

I_{CCH} Supply current output(s) high.

I_{CCL} Supply current output(s) low.

f_{max} Maximum clock frequency.

t_w Average pulse width.

I_{DD} Quiescent device current (CMOS).

I_{OL} Low level output current.

I_{IN} Input current.

I_{OZ} High impedance state output current of a 3-state output.

I_{CC} Quiescent device current (TTL).

t_h Hold time.

t_{PZX} Output enable time of a 3-state output to high or low level.

t_{PXZ} Output disable time of a 3-state output from high or low level.

t_{PD} Propagation delay time.

t_{TLH} Transition time from low to high level.

t_{THL} Transition time from high to low level.

Q_O Level of Q before the indicated steady-state input conditions were established.

$\bar{Q}_O$ Complement of Q_O.

V_{IH} High-level input voltage.

V_{IL} Low-level input voltage.

V_{T+} Positive-going threshold voltage.

V_{T-} Negative-going threshold voltage.

V_{OH} High-level output voltage.

V_{OL} Low-level output voltage.

$V_{O(ON)}$ On-state output voltage.

$V_{O(OFF)}$ Off-state output voltage.

V_{DD} DC supply voltage (CMOS).

V_{CC} DC supply voltage (TTL).

V_{SS} Ground (CMOS).

GND Ground (TTL).

V_{IN} Input voltage.

T_S Lead temperature when soldering.

P_D Package dissipation.

T_S Storage temperature range.

T_A Operating temperature range.

H High level (steady state).

L Low level (steady state).

↓ Transition from high to low.

↑ Transition from low to high.

X Irrelevant input level.

Z High impedance state of a 3-state output.

⎍ One high level pulse.

⎍ One low level pulse.

Toggle Each output changes to the complement of its previous level.

Q_n Level of Q before the most recent change.

ITU defined regions

For purposes of international allocations of frequencies the world has been divided into three regions as shown on the map.

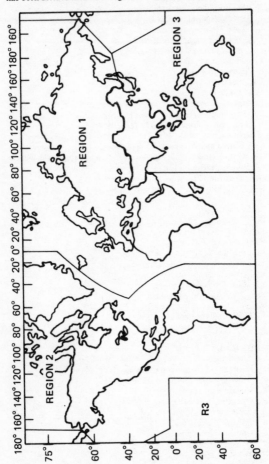

Designations of radio emissions

Radio emissions should be expressed in a three symbol code form, which defines the exact nature of carrier, signal and transmitted information. The first symbol defines the carrier, the second symbol defines the signal, and the third symbol defines the information.

First symbol

A   Double-sideband amplitude-modulated
B   Independent sideband amplitude-modulated
C   Vestigial sideband amplitude-modulated
D   Amplitude- and angle-modulated simultaneously, or in a pre-defined sequence
F   Frequency modulated
G   Phase modulated
H   Single-sideband, full carrier
J   Single-sideband, suppressed carrier
K   Amplitude-modulated pulse sequence
L   Width-modulated pulse sequence
M   Position phase modulated pulse sequence
N   Unmodulated carrier
P   Unmodulated pulse sequence
Q   Pulse sequence in which carrier is angle-modulated during the pulse period
R   Single-sideband, reduced or variable level carrier
V   Pulse sequence with a combination of carrier modulations, or produced by other means
W   Carrier is modulated by two or more of angle, amplitude, and pulse modes, simultaneously or in a defined sequence
X   Other cases

Second symbol

0   No modulating signal
1   Digital signal without modulating sub-carrier
2   Digital signal with modulating sub-carrier
3   Analogue signal
7   Two or more channels with digital signals
8   Two or more channels with analogue signals
9   Composite system with one or more channels of digital signals and one or more channels of analogue signals
X   Other cases

Third symbol

A   Aural telegraph
B   Automatic telegraph
C   Facsimile
D   Data
E   Telephony (and sound broadcasting)
F   Television
N   No information transmitted
W   Combination of any of the above
X   Other cases

Bandwidth and frequency designations

A four symbol code should be used to express bandwidth and frequency to three significant figures. A letter to denote the unit of frequency is placed in the position of the decimal point, where the letters and bandwidths are:

Letter	Bandwidth		
H	Below 1000 Hz	M	Between 1 and 999 MHz
K	Between 1 and 999 kHz	G	Between 1 and 999 GHz

So, a frequency of 120 Hz is 120H, while a frequency of 12 Hz is 12H0 etc.

General frequency allocations

VLF, LF, MF (frequency in kHz)

10·0–140·5	Fixed; maritime; navigation
140·5–283·5	Broadcast
255·0–526·5	Radio navigation; fixed
526·0–1,606·5	Broadcast
1,606·5–1,800·0	Maritime and land mobile; fixed
1,810·0–1,850·0	Amateur (shared in UK)
1,850–2,000	Amateur
1,850–2,045	Fixed; mobile
2,045–2,173·5	Maritime mobile; fixed
2,160–2,170	Radiolocation
2,173·5–2,190·5	Mobile
2,190·5–2,194	Maritime
2,194–2,625	Fixed; mobile
2,300–2,498	Broadcast
2,625–2,650	Maritime mobile
2,650–2,850	Fixed; mobile
2,850–3,155	Aero mobile

HF (frequency in kHz)

3,155–3,400	Fixed; mobile
3,200–3,400	Broadcast
3,400–3,500	Aero mobile
3,500–3,800	Amateur, fixed; mobile
3,800–4,000	Amateur (region 2 only)
3,800–3,900	Fixed; mobile
3,800–3,950	Aero mobile
3,950–4,000	Fixed; broadcast
4,000–4,063	Fixed; maritime mobile
4,063–4,438	Maritime mobile
4,438–4,650	Fixed; mobile
4,650–4,750	Aero mobile
4,750–5,060	Fixed; mobile; broadcast
5,060–5,480	Fixed; mobile
5,450–5,730	Aero mobile
5,730–5,950	Fixed; mobile
5,950–6,200	Broadcast
6,200–6,525	Maritime mobile
6,525–6,765	Aero mobile
6,765–7,000	Fixed; mobile
7,000–7,100	Amateur
7,100–7,300	Amateur (region 2 only)
7,100–7,300	Broadcast (regions 1 and 3)
7,300–8,195	Fixed
8,100–8,815	Maritime mobile
8,815–9,040	Aero mobile
9,040–9,500	Fixed
9,500–10,000	Broadcast
10,000–10,100	Aero mobile
10,100–11,175	Fixed
10,100–10,150	Amateur
11,175–11,400	Aero mobile
11,400–11,650	Fixed
11,650–12,050	Broadcast

12,050–12,230	Fixed	
12,230–13,200	Maritime mobile	
13,200–13,360	Aero mobile	
13,360–13,600	Fixed	
13,600–13,800	Broadcast	
13,800–14,000	Fixed	
14,000–14,350	Amateur	
14,350–15,000	Fixed	
15,000–15,100	Aero mobile	
15,100–15,600	Broadcast	
15,600–16,360	Fixed	
16,360–17,410	Maritime mobile	
17,410–17,550	Fixed	
17,550–17,900	Broadcast	
17,900–18,030	Aero mobile	
18,030–18,068	Fixed	
18,068–18,168	Amateur	
18,168–18,780	Fixed	
18,780–18,900	Maritime mobile	
18,900–19,680	Fixed	
19,680–19,800	Maritime mobile	
19,800–21,000	Fixed	
21,000–21,450	Amateur	
21,450–21,850	Broadcast	
21,850–21,870	Fixed	
21,870–22,000	Aero mobile	
22,000–22,855	Maritime mobile	
22,855–23,200	Fixed; mobile	
23,200–23,350	Aero mobile	
23,350–24,890	Fixed; mobile	
24,890–24,990	Amateur	
25,010–25,070	Fixed; mobile	
25,070–25,210	Maritime mobile	
21,210–25,550	Fixed; mobile	
25,550–25,670	Radio astronomy	
25,670–26,100	Broadcast	
26,100–26,175	Maritime mobile	
26,175–28,000	Fixed; mobile	
28,000–29,700	Amateur	
29,700–30,000	Fixed; mobile	

VHF, UHF (frequencies in MHz)

30·0–50·0	Fixed; mobile
47·0–68·0	Broadcast (TV)
50·0–52·0	Amateur (UK)
50·0–54·0	Amateur (regions 2 and 3)
68·0–74·8	Fixed; mobile
70·0–70·5	Amateur (UK)
74·8–75·2	Aero navigation
75·2–87·5	Fixed; mobile
87·5–108	Broadcast (FM)
108–118	Aero navigation
118–137	Aero mobile
137–138	Spacecraft; satellites
138–144	Aero mobile; space research
144–146	Amateur
146–148	Amateur (regions 2 and 3 only)

146–174	Fixed; mobile
156–174	Maritime mobile
174–230	Broadcast (TV)
220–225	Amateur (USA)
230–328·6	Fixed; mobile
328·6–335·4	Aero navigation
335·4–400	Fixed; mobile
400–410	Space research; meteorology
410–430	Fixed; mobile
430–440	Amateur; radiolocation
440–470	Fixed; mobile
470–855	Broadcast (TV)
855–1,300	Fixed; mobile
902–928	Amateur (USA)
934–935	Citizens band (UK)
1,240–1,325	Amateur
1,300–1,350	Aero navigation
1,350–1,400	Fixed; mobile
1,400–1,429	Space (uplink); fixed
1,429–1,525	Fixed; mobile
1,525–1,600	Space (downlink)
1,600–1,670	Space (uplink)
1,670–1,710	Space (downlink)
1,710–2,290	Fixed; mobile
2,290–2,300	Space (downlink); fixed
2,300–2,450	Amateur; fixed
2,310–2,450	Amateur (UK)
2,300–2,500	Fixed; mobile
2,500–2,700	Fixed; space (downlink)
2,700–3,300	Radar
3,300–3,400	Radiolocation; amateur
3,400–3,600	Fixed; space (uplink)
3,600–4,200	Fixed; space (downlink)
4,200–4,400	Aero navigation
4,400–4500	Fixed; mobile
4,500–4,800	Fixed; space (downlink)
4,800–5,000	Fixed; mobile
5,000–5,850	Radio navigation; radar
5,650–5,850	Amateur
5,850–7,250	Fixed; space (uplink)
7,250–7,900	Fixed; space (downlink)
7,900–8,500	Fixed; mobile; space
8,500–10,500	Radar; navigation
10,000–10,500	Amateur
10,700–12,700	Space (downlink); fixed
12,700–15,400	Space (uplink); fixed
17,700–20,000	Space (up/down); fixed
24,000–24,250	Amateur

Classes of radio stations

AL	Aeronautical radionavigation land station
AM	Aeronautical radionavigation mobile station
AT	Amateur station
AX	Aeronautical fixed station
BC	Broadcasting station, sound

BT	Broadcasting station, television
CA	Cargo ship
CO	Station open to official correspondence exclusively
CP	Station open to public correspondence
CR	Station open to limited public correspondence
CV	Station open exclusively to correspondence of a private agency
DR	Directive antenna provided with a reflector
EA	Space station in the amateur-satellite service
EB	Space station in the broadcasting-satellite service (sound broadcasting)
EC	Space station in the fixed-satellite service
ED	Space telecommand space station
EE	Space station in the standard frequency-satellite service
EF	Space station in the radiodetermination-satellite service
EG	Space station in the maritime mobile-satellite service
EH	Space research space station
EJ	Space station in the aeronautical mobile-satellite service
EK	Space tracking space station
EM	Meteorological-satellite space station
EN	Radionavigation-satellite space station
EO	Space station in the aeronautical radionavigation-satellite service
EQ	Space station in the maritime radionavigation-satellite service
ER	Space telemetering space station
ES	Station in the intersatellite service
EU	Space station in the land mobile-satellite service
EV	Space station in the broadcasting-satellite service (television)
EW	Space station in the earth exploration-satellite service
EX	Experimental station
EY	Space station in the time signal-satellite service
FA	Aeronautical station
FB	Base station
FC	Coast station
FL	Land station
FP	Port station
FR	Receiving station only, connected with the general network of telecommunication channels
FS	Land station established solely for the safety of life
FX	Fixed station
GS	Station on board a warship or a military or naval aircraft
LR	Radiolocation land station
MA	Aircraft station
ME	Space station
ML	Land mobile station
MO	Mobile station
MR	Radiolocation mobile station
MS	Ship station
ND	Non-directional antenna
NL	Maritime radionavigation land station
OD	Oceanographic data station
OE	Oceanographic data interrogating station
OT	Station open exclusively to operational traffic of the service concerned
PA	Passenger ship
RA	Radio astronomy station
RC	Non-directional radio beacon
RD	Directional radio beacon
RG	Radio direction-finding station
RM	Maritime radionavigation mobile station

RT	Revolving radio beacon
SM	Meteorological aids station
SS	Standard frequency and time signal station
TA	Space operation earth station in the amateur-satellite service
TB	Fixed earth station in the aeronautical mobile-satellite service
TC	Earth station in the fixed-satellite service
TD	Space telecommand earth station
TE	Transmitting earth station
TF	Fixed earth station in the radiodetermination-satellite service
TG	Mobile earth station in the maritime mobile-satellite service
TH	Earth station in the space research service
TI	Earth station in the maritime mobile-satellite service at a specified fixed point
TJ	Mobile earth station in the aeronautical mobile-satellite service
TK	Space tracking earth station
TL	Mobile earth station in the radiodetermination-satellite service
TM	Earth station in the meteorological-satellite service
TN	Earth station in the radionavigation-satellite service
TO	Mobile earth station in the aeronautical radionavigation-satellite service
TP	Receiving earth station
TQ	Mobile earth station in the maritime radionavigation-satellite service
TR	Space telemetering earth station
TS	Television, sound channel
TT	Earth station in the space operation service
TU	Mobile earth station in the land mobile-satellite service
TV	Television, vision channel
TW	Earth station in the earth exploration-satellite service
TX	Fixed earth station in the maritime radionavigation-satellite service
TY	Fixed earth station in the land mobile-satellite service
TZ	Fixed earth station in the aeronautical radionavigation-satellite service

Radio wavebands

Frequency band	Frequency	Wavelength	Waveband definition
v.l.f.	3 to 30 kHz	100,000 to 10,000 m	myriametric
l.f.	30 to 300 kHz	10,000 to 1,000 m	kilometric
m.f.	300 to 3,000 kHz	1,000 to 100 m	hectometric
h.f.	3 to 30 MHz	100 to 10 m	decametric
v.h.f.	30 to 300 MHz	10 to 1 m	metric
u.h.f.	300 to 3,000 MHz	1 to 0·1 m	decimetric
s.h.f.	3 to 30 GHz	10 to 1 cm	centimetric
e.h.f.	30 to 300 GHz	1 to 0·1 cm	millimetric
e.h.f.	300 to 3,000 GHz	0·1 to 0·01 cm	decimillimetric

Standard frequency and time transmissions

Frequency (MHz)	Wavelength (m)	Code	Station location	Country	Power (kW)
60 kHz	5000	MSF	Rugby	England	—
—	—	WWVB	Colorado	USA	—
75 kHz	4000	HBG	—	Switzerland	—
77·5 kHz	3871	DCF77	Mainflingen	DDR	—
1·5	200	HD210A	Guayaquil	Ecuador	—
2·5	120	MSF	Rugby	England	0·5
—	—	WWV	Fort Collins	USA	2·5
—	—	WWVH	Kekaha	Hawaii	5
—	—	ZLF	Wellington	New Zealand	—
—	—	RCH	Tashkent	USSR	1
—	—	JJY	—	Japan	—
—	—	ZUO	Olifantsfontein	South Africa	—
3·33	90·09	CHU	Ottawa	Canada	3
3·81	78·7	HD201A	Guayaquil	Ecuador	—
4·5	66·67	VNG	Victoria	Australia	—
4·996	60·05	RWM	Moscow	USSR	5
5	60	MSF	Rugby	England	0·5
—	—	WWVB	Fort Collins	USA	10
—	—	WWVH	Kekaha	Hawaii	10
—	—	ATA	New Delhi	India	—
—	—	LOL	Buenos Aires	Argentina	2
—	—	IBF	Turin	Italy	5
—	—	RCH	Tashkent	USSR	1
—	—	JJY	—	Japan	—
—	—	ZUO	Olifantsfontein	South Africa	—
5·004	59·95	RID	Irkutsk	USSR	1
6·10	49·2	YVTO	Caracas	Venezuela	—
7·335	40·9	CHU	Ottawa	Canada	10
7·5	40	VNG	Lyndhurst	Australia	5
7·6	39·4	HD210A	Guayaquil	Ecuador	—
8	37·5	JJY	—	Japan	—
8·1675	36·73	LQB9	Buenos Aires	Argentina	5
9996	30·01	RWM	Moscow	USSR	—
10	30	MSF	Rugby	England	0·5
—	—	WWVB	Fort Collins	USA	10
—	—	WWVH	Kekaha	Hawaii	10
—	—	BPM	Xian	China	—
—	—	ATA	New Delhi	India	—
—	—	JJY	—	Japan	—
—	—	LOL	Buenos Aires	Argentina	2
—	—	RTA	Novosibirsk	USSR	5
—	—	RCH	Tashkent	USSR	1
10·004	29·99	RID	Irkutsk	USSR	1
12	25	VNG	Lyndhurst	Australia	10
14·67	20·45	CHU	Ottawa	Canada	3
14·996	20·01	RWM	Moscow	USSR	8
15	20	WWVB	Fort Collins	USA	10
—	—	WWVH	Kekaha	Hawaii	10
—	—	LOL	Buenos Aires	Argentina	2
—	—	RTA	Novosibirsk	USSR	5
—	—	BPM	Xian	China	—
—	—	ATA	New Delhi	India	—
—	—	JJY	—	Japan	—
15·004	19·99	RID	Irkutsk	USSR	1
16·384	18·31	—	Allouis	France	2000
15·55	17·09	LQC20	Buenos Aires	Argentina	5
20	15	WWVB	Fort Collins	USA	2·5
100	3	ZUO	Olifantsfontein	South Africa	—

Standard frequency formats

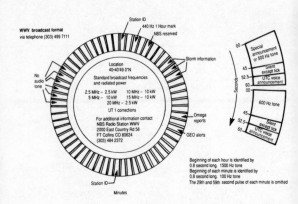

WWV broadcast format
via telephone (303) 499 7111

Station ID
440 Hz 1 Hour mark
NBS reserved

Location
40°40'49 0"N

Standard broadcast frequencies
and radiated power

2.5 MHz – 2.5 kW   10 MHz – 10 kW
5 MHz – 10 kW   15 MHz – 10 kW
20 MHz – 2.5 kW

UT 1 corrections

For additional information contact
NBS Radio Station WWV
2000 East Country Rd 58
FT Collins CO 80624
(303) 484 2372

No audio tone

Storm information

Omega reports

GEO alerts

Station ID

Minutes

00 — Special announcement or 500 Hz tone
45 —
52.5 — Silent except tick
60 — UTC voice announcement
00 — 600 Hz tone
45 —
52.5 —
60 — UTC voice announcement
Silent except tick

Seconds

Beginning of each hour is identified by
0.8 second long. 1500 Hz tone
Beginning of each minute is identified by
0.8 second long. 100 Hz tone
The 29th and 59th second pulse of each minute is omitted

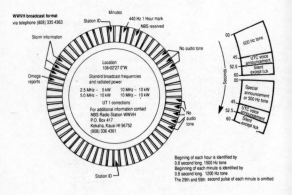

WWVH broadcast format
via telephone (808) 335 4363

Minutes
Station ID
440 Hz 1 Hour mark
NBS reserved

Storm information

No audio tone

Location
106°02'27 0"W

Standrd broadcast frequencies
and radiated power

2.5 MHz – 5 kW   10 MHz – 10 kW
5.0 MHz – 10 kW   10 MHz – 10 kW

UT 1 corrections

For additional information contact
NBS Radio Station WWVH
P.O. Box 417
Kekaha, Kauai HI 96752
(808) 336 4361

Omega reports

No audio tone

Station ID

00 — 600 Hz tone
45 —
52.5 — UTC voice announcement
60 — Silent except tick
00 — Special announcement or 500 Hz tone
45 —
52.5 — UTC voice announcement
60 — Silent except tick

Seconds

Begining of each hour is identified by
0.8 second long. 1500 Hz tone
Beginning of each minute is identified by
0.8 second long. 1200 Hz tone
The 29th and 59th second pulse of each minute is omitted

MSF Rugby
Time is inserted in the 60 kHz transmission in two ways, illustrated below.

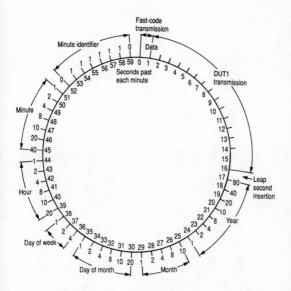

Slow code time and date information is transmitted between the 17th and 59th seconds of the minute-long cycle, in normal BCD coding.
Fast code time and date BCD coded information is inserted into a 500 ms window in the first second of each minute-long cycle, as illustrated below.

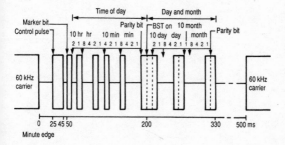

The electromagnetic wave spectrum

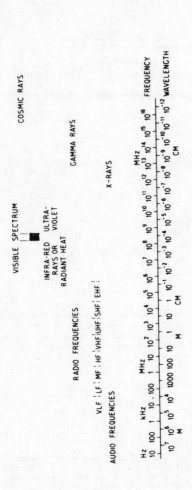

The ionosphere

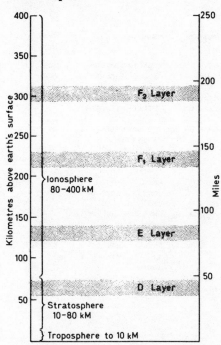

UK broadcasting bands

Frequency band	Frequency	Use
Long wave	150–285 kHz (2000–1053 m)	AM radio
Medium wave	525–1605 kHz (571–187 m)	AM radio
Band II (VHF)	88–97·6 MHz and 102–104·5 MHz	FM radio
Band IV (UHF)	470–582 MHz (channels 21 to 34)	TV
Band V (UHF)	614–854 MHz (channels 39 to 68)	TV
Band VI (SHF)	11·7–12·5 GHz (channels 1 to 40)	satellite TV

Band II is being extended to cover 88–108 MHz. However, due to existing use of the band at certain frequencies, this cannot be completed until 1990 (97·6–102 MHz) or 1996 (104·6–108 MHz).

The Beaufort scale

Force	Specification	Description	Speed (kmh^{-1})
0	Calm	Smoke rises vertically	Less than 1
1	Light air	Smoke drift shows wind direction	1–5
2	Light breeze	Wind can be felt on face	6–11
3	Gentle breeze	Leaves/twigs in constant motion	12–19
4	Moderate breeze	Dust blown about/small branches move	20–29
5	Fresh breeze	Small trees sway	30–39
6	Strong breeze	Large branches move	40–50
7	Near gale	Whole trees move, hard to walk	51–61
8	Gale	Twigs break, very hard to walk	62–74
9	Strong gale	Slight structural damage occurs, chimneys, slates blown off	75–87
10	Storm	Trees uprooted, considerable structural damage	88–101
11	Violent storm	Widespread damage	102–117
12	Hurricane	Catastrophic damage	>119

Overall rating for telephony

Symbol		Operating condition	Quality
5	Excellent	Signal quality unaffected	Commercial
4	Good	Signal quality slightly affected	
3	Fair	Signal quality seriously affected. Channel usable by operators or by experienced subscribers	Marginally commercial
2	Poor	Channel just usable by operators	Not commercial
1	Unusable	Channel unusable by operators	

Boundaries of sea areas
As used in BBC and BT weather forecasts

Stations whose latest reports are broadcast in the 5 minute forecasts on Radio 2 (200 kHz) at 0033, 0633 and 1755 (daily), 1155 (Sundays) and 1355 (weekdays).

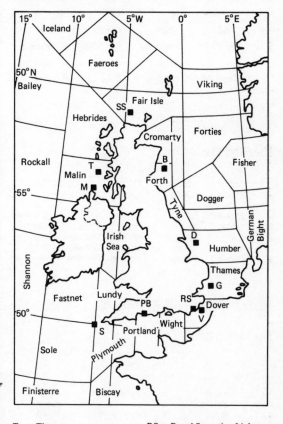

T	Tiree	RS	Royal Sovereign Light-tower
SS	Sule Skerry Lighthouse	PB	Portland Bill
B	Bell Rock Lighthouse	S	Scilly (St Mary's)
D	Dowsing light-vessel	Va	Valentia
G	Galloper light-vessel	R	Ronaldsway
V	Varne light-vessel	M	Malin Head Lighthouse

The SINPFEMO code

	S	*I*	*N*	*P*
		Degrading effect of:		
Rating scale	Signal strength	Interference (QRM)	Noise (QRN)	Propagation disturbance
5	Excellent	Nil	Nil	Nil
4	Good	Slight	Slight	Slight
3	Fair	Moderate	Moderate	Moderate
2	Poor	Severe	Severe	Severe
1	Barely audible	Extreme	Extreme	Extreme

The SINPO code

Rating scale	*S* Signal strength	*I* Interference (QRM)	*N* Noise (QRN)	*P* Propagation disturbance	*O* Overall readability (QRK)
5	Excellent	Nil	Nil	Nil	Excellent
4	Good	Slight	Slight	Slight	Good
3	Fair	Moderate	Moderate	Moderate	Fair
2	Poor	Severe	Severe	Severe	Poor
1	Barely audible	Extreme	Extreme	Extreme	Unusable

The SIO code

Rating scale	*S* Signal strength	*I* Interference	*O* Overall merit
4	Good	Nil or very slight	Good
3	Fair	Moderate	Fair
2	Poor	Heavy	Unusable

The SIO code is based on the SINPO code but in a simplified form. Using the SIO code is perfectly acceptable, however.

F	E Modulation:	M	O
Frequency of fading	Quality	Depth	Overall rating
Nil	Excellent	Maximum	Excellent
Slow	Good	Good	Good
Moderate	Fair	Fair	Fair
Fast	Poor	Poor or nil	Poor
Very fast	Very poor	Continuously overmodulated	Unusable

BBC AM radio stations

Radio 1	kHz	m	kW		kHz	m	kW
Barnstaple	1053	285	1	Lisnagarvey	1089	275	10
Barrow	1053	285	1	Londonderry	1053	285	1
Bexhill	1053	285	2	Moorside	1089	275	150
Bournemouth	1485	202	2	Edge			
Brighton	1053	285	2	Postwick	1053	285	10
Brookmans	1089	275	150	Redmoss	1089	275	2
Park				Redruth	1089	275	2
Burghead	1053	285	20	Stagshaw	1053	285	50
Droitwich	1053	285	150	Start Point	1053	285	100
Dundee	1053	285	1	Tywyn	1089	275	1
Enniskillen	1053	285	1	Wallasey	1107	271	0·5
Fareham	1089	275	1	Washford	1089	275	50
Folkestone	1053	285	1	Westerglen	1089	275	50
Hull	1053	285	1	Whitehaven	1089	275	1

Radio 2	kHz	m	kW		kHz	m	kW
Barrow	693	433	1	Lisnagarvey	909	330	10
Bexhill	693	433	1	Londonderry	909	330	1
Bournemouth	909	330	0·25	Moorside	909	330	200
Brighton	693	433	1	Edge			
Brookmans	909	330	150	Postwick	693	433	10
Park				Redmoss	693	433	1
Burghead	693	433	25	Redruth	909	330	2
Clevedon	909	330	50	Stagshaw	693	433	50
Droitwich	693	433	150	Start Point	693	433	50
Enniskillen	693	433	1	Tywyn	990	303	1
Exeter	909	330	1	Westerglen	909	330	50
Fareham	909	330	1	Whitehaven	909	330	1
Folkestone	693	433	1				

Radio 3	kHz	m	kW		kHz	m	kW
Bournemouth	1197	251	0·5	Cambridge	1197	251	0·2
Brighton	1215	247	1	Droitwich	1215	247	50
Brookmans	1215	247	50	Enniskillen	1197	251	1
Park				Fareham	1215	247	1
Burghead	1215	247	20	Hull	1215	247	0·3

	kHz	m	kW		kHz	m	kW
Lisnagarvey	1215	247	10	Redmoss	1215	247	2
Londonderry	1215	247	1	Redruth	1215	247	2
Moorside	1215	247	100	Torbay	1197	251	1
Edge				Tywyn	1215	247	0·5
Newcastle	1215	247	2	Washford	1215	247	60
Plymouth	1215	247	1	Westerglen	1215	247	50
Postwick	1215	247	1				

Radio 4

	kHz	m	kW		kHz	m	kW
Burghead	198	1515	50	Londonderry	720	417	0·25
Carlisle	1485	202	1	Newcastle	603	498	2
Droitwich	198	1515	500	Plymouth	774	388	1
Enniskillen	774	388	1	Redmoss	1449	207	2
Lisnagarvey	720	417	10	Redruth	756	397	2
London	720	417	0·75	Westerglen	198	1515	50
(Lots Road)							

Radio Scotland

	kHz	m	kW		kHz	m	kW
Burghead	810	370	100	Redmoss	810	370	5
Dumfries	585	513	2	Westerglen	810	370	100

Radio Ulster

	kHz	m	kW		kHz	m	kW
Enniskillen	873	344	1	Londonderry	792	379	1
Lisnagarvey	1341	224	100				

Radio Wales

	kHz	m	kW		kHz	m	kW
Forden	882	340	1				
Llandrindod Wells	1125	267	1				
Penmon	882	340	10	Washford	882	340	100
Tywyn	882	340	5	Wrexham	657	457	2

UK CB radio

27 MHz band: 27·60125 to 27·99125 MHz.
   40 channels at 10 kHz spacing.
   Max. e.r.p. 2W; max. transmitter output 4W.
   Aerial: single rod or wire, 1·5m overall length, base loaded. If
      mounted higher than 7m, transmitter output to be reduced at
      least 10dB.
   Modulation: F.M. only, deviation ± 2·5 kHz max.

934 MHz band: 934·025 to 934·975 MHz.
   20 channels at 50kHz (may be reduced to 25 kHz later). If
      synthesizer used spacing may be 25 kHz on precise channel
      frequencies specified.
   Max. e.r.p. 25W; max. transmitter output 8 W; if aerial integral,
      max. e.r.p. 3W.
   Aerial: may have up to four elements, none exceeding 17cm. If
      mounted higher than 10m, transmitter output to be reduced at
      least 10dB.
   Modulation: FM only, deviation ± 5·0 kHz max.

Spurious emissions: For both bands, not exceeding 0·25μW, except
for specified frequency bands where the limit is 50nW.

For full specifications see publication MPT 1320 (27 MHz) and
MPT 1321 (934 MHz) from HMSO.

BBC VHF/FM radio stations

Notes: **Stereo services:** all services are stereo except where (m) is shown against a frequency.
Polarisation: H indicates horizontal polarisation; M indicates mixed polarisation; V indicates vertical polarisation.

England, Isle of Man, and Channel Islands	Radio 1	Radio 1 and 2	Radio 3	Radio 4	Polarisation	Maximum effective radiated power
Belmont	—	88·8	90·9	93·1	M	16 kW
Holme Moss	—	89·3	91·5	93·7	M	250 kW
	98·8	—	—	—	M	60 kW
Kendal	—	89·0	91·2	93·4	M	100 W
Morecambe Bay	—	90·0	92·2	94·4	H	4 kW
Olivers Mount	—	89·9	92·1	94·3	M	250 kW
Pendle Forest	—	90·2	92·6	94·6	M	1 kW
Sheffield (Crosspool)	—	89·9	92·1	94·3	M	320 W
Stanton Moor	—	89·8	92·0	94·2	M	1·2 kW
Wensleydale	—	88·3	90·5	92·7	H	27 W
Wharfedale	—	88·4	90·6	92·8	M	40 W
Windermere	—	88·3	90·5	92·7	M	64 W
Les Platons (CI)	—	91·1	94·8	97·1	M	16 kW
Manningtree*	—	88·1	90·3	92·5	M	4·2 kW
North Hessary Tor	—	88·1	90·3	92·5	H	60 kW
Okehampton	—	88·7	90·9	93·1	M	70 W
St Thomas (Exeter)	—	89·0	91·2	93·4	M	55 W
Oxford	—	89·5	91·7	93·9	M	46 kW
Peterborough	—	90·1	92·3	94·5	M	40 kW
*Bow Brickhill**	98·2	88·6	90·8	93·0	M	9·4 kW
Cambridge (Madingley)	—	88·9	91·1	93·3	M	260 W
Pontop Pike	—	88·5	90·7	92·9	M	60 kW
Chatton	—	90·1	92·3	94·5	M	5·6 kW
Fenham	—	89·8	92·0	94·2	V	42 W
Weardale	—	89·7	91·9	94·1	H	100 W
Whitby	—	89·6	91·8	94·0	M	40 W
Redruth	—	89·7	91·9	94·1	M	17 kW
Isles of Scilly	—	88·8	91·0	93·2	M	60 W
Ridge Hill	—	88·6	90·8	93·0	M	10 kW
Rowridge	—	88·5	90·7	92·9	M	60 kW
*Newhaven**	99·3	89·7	91·9	94·1	M	100 W
Ventnor	—	89·4	91·7	93·8	H	20 W
Sandale	—	88·1	90·3	92·5	H†	120 kW
(see also Scotland)					M*	250 kW
Douglas (IOM)	—	88·4	90·6	92·8	M	11 kW
Sutton Coldfield	—	88·3	90·5	92·7	M	250 kW
	98·4	—	—	—	M	25 kW
Churchdown Hill	—	89·0	91·2	93·4	M	72 W
Ludlow	—	89·6	91·8	94·0	M	5 W
Northampton	—	88·9	91·1	93·3	M	123 W
Swingate (Dover)	—	90·0	92·4	94·4	M	11 kW

England, Isle of Man, and Channel Islands	Radio 1	Radio 1 and 2	Radio 3	Radio 4	Polarisation	Maximum effective radiated power
Tacolneston	—	89·7	91·9	94·1	M	250 kW
Wenvoe	98·7*	89·9	92·1	94·3	M	250 kW
Barnstaple	—	88·5	90·7	92·9	M	1 kW
Bath	—	88·8	91·0	93·2	M	82 W
Ilchester Crescent	—	89·3	91·5	93·7	M	1·3 kW
Winter Hill	—	88·6	90·8	93·0	M	4 kW
Wrotham	—	89·1	91·3	93·5	M	250 kW
Brighton (Whitehawk Hill)	—	90·1	92·3	94·5	M	600 W
Caterham	—	89·7	91·9	94·1	V	15 W
Crystal Palace	104·8	—			M	2 kW
Guildford	—	88·1	90·3	92·5	M	3 kW
High Wycombe	—	89·9	92·1	94·3	M	50 W
Kenley	—	88·4	90·6	92·8	V	25 W
Mickelham*	—	89·7	91·9	94·1	V	50 W
Wooburn*	—	88·3	90·5	92·7	M	50 W

Northern Ireland	Radio 1	Radio 1 and 2	Radio 3	Radio 4	Radio Ulster	Polarisation	Maximum effective radiated power
Brougher Mountain	—	89·4	91·6	—	93·8	M	9·8 kW
Divis	—	90·1	92·3		94·5†	H	60 kW
				94·5*	96·0*	H	60 kW
Ballycastle	—	88·8	91·0	93·2	95·1	M	100 W
Kilkeel	—	89·4	91·6	—	93·8	H	25 W
Larne	—	89·1	91·3	—	93·5	M	100 W
Rostrevor Forest (m)	—	88·6	90·8	—	93·0	M	64 W
Limavady	—	89·6	91·8	94·0	95·4	M	3·4 kW
Londonderry	—	88·7	90·9	—	93·1f	M	31 kW

f = Radio Foyle

Wales	Radio 1	Radio 1 and 2	Radio 3	Radio 4	R. Cymru	Polarisation	Maximum effective radiated power
Blaenplwyf	—	88·7	90·9	—	93·1	M	60 kW†
						M	250 kW*
Dolgellau (m)	—	90·1	92·3	—	94·5	H	16 W
Ffestiniog	—	88·1	90·3	—	92·5	H	49 W

Wales

	Radio 1	Radio 1 and 2	Radio 3	Radio 4	R. Cymru	Polarisation	Maximum effective radiated power
Llandyfriog	—	90·1	92·3	—	94·5	M	87 W
Machynlleth	—	89·4	91·6	—	93·8	H	60 W
Mynydd Pencarreg	—	89·7	91·9	—	94·1	M	384 W
Haverfordwest	—	89·3	91·5	—	93·7	H	10 kW
Llanddona	—	89·8	92·0	—	94·2	M	21 kW
Betws-y-Coed (m)	—	88·2	90·4	—	92·6	H	10 W
Llangollen	—	88·9	91·1	—	93·3	M	15·6 kW
Llandinam	—	90·1	92·3	—	94·5	M	20 W
Llanfyllin	—	89·1	91·3	—	93·5	M	7·2 W
Llanrhaeadr-ym-Mochnant	—	89·8	92·0	—	94·2	M	50 W
Long Mountain	—	89·6	91·8	—	94·0	H	24 W
Wenvoe	98·7	89·9	92·1	94·3	96·8	M	250 kW
Aberdare	—	89·2	91·4	—	93·6	M	42 W
Abergavenny	—	88·7	90·9	—	93·1	H	17 W
Blaenavon	—	88·5	90·7	—	92·9	V	10 W
Brecon	—	88·8	91·1	—	93·3	H	10 W
Carmarthen	—	88·9	91·1	—	93·3	M	10 W
Carmel	—	88·4	90·6	—	92·8	M	3·2 kW
Ebbw Vale	—	88·4	90·6	—	92·8	H	10 W
Kilvey Hill	—	89·5	91·7	—	93·9	M	920 W
Llandrindod Wells	—	89·1	91·3	—	93·5	H	1·5 kW
Llanidloes	—	88·1	90·3	—	92·5	H	5 W
Pontypool	—	89·2	91·4	—	93·6	M	50 W
*Ton Pentre**	—	88·8	91·0	—	100·6	M	5 W
Varteg Hill	—	88·9	91·1	—	93·3	M	48 W

Radio Gwent (opt-out from R Wales)

	Radio 1	Radio 1 and 2	R. Gwent	Radio 4	R. Cymru	Polarisation	Maximum effective radiated power
Blaenavon	—	—	95·1	—	—	V	10 W
Christchurch	—	—	95·9	—	—	M	500 W

Scotland

	Radio 1	Radio 1 and 2	Radio 3	Radio 4	Radio Scotland	Polarisation	Maximum effective radiated power
Ashkirk	—	89·1	91·3	—	93·5t	H	18 kW
Innerleithen	—	89·5	91·7	—	93·9t	M	20 W
Peebles	—	88·4	90·6	—	92·8t	M	20 W
Black Hill	98·6	89·9	92·1	95·8	94·3	M	250 kW
Bressay	—	88·3	90·5	—	92·7aoz	M	43 kW
Darvel	—	89·5	91·7	—	93·9	M	10 kW
Forfar	—	88·3	90·5	—	92·7	M	17 kW
Pitlochry (m)	—	89·2	91·4	—	93·6	H	200 W
Fort William (m)	—	89·3	91·5	—	93·7h	H	1·5 kW
					98·9‡	H	1·5 kW

Scotland	Radio 1	Radio 1 and 2	Radio 3	Radio 4	Radio Scotland	Polarisation	Maximum effective radiated power
Ballachulish (m)	—	88·1	90·3	—	92·5h	H	15 W
					97·7‡	H	15 W
Glengorm (m)	—	89·5	91·7	—	93·9h	M	4·6 kW
					99·1‡	M	4·6 kW
Kinlochleven (m)	—	89·7	91·9	—	94·1h	M	10 W
					99·3‡	M	10 W
Mallaig (m)	—	88·1	90·3	—	92·5h	H	14 W
					97·7‡	H	14 W
Oban (m)	—	88·9	91·1	—	93·3h	M	3·6 kW
					98·5‡	M	3·6 kW
Keelylang Hill	—	89·3	91·5	—	93·7ao	M	41 kW
Kirk o'Shotts†**	—	89·9	92·1	—	94·3	H	120 kW
Bowmore (m)	—	88·1	90·3	—	92·5	V	80 W
Campbeltown	—	88·4	90·6	—	92·8	M	400 W
Girvan	—	88·9	91·1	—	93·3	V	100 W
Kirkton Mailer (m)	—	89·0	91·2	—	93·4	M	964 W
Lethanhill	—	88·3	90·5	—	92·7	M	200 W
Lochgilphead	—	88·3	90·5	—	92·7	H	10 W
					97·9m‡	H	10 W
Milburn Muir	—	88·8†91·0†	—	93·2†	M	25 W
		88·3*90·5*	—	92·7*	M	25 W
Port Ellen* (m)	—	89·0	91·2	—	93·4	V	65 W
Rosneath	—	89·2	91·4	—	93·6	M	25 W
Rothesay	—	88·5	90·7	—	92·9	M	570 W
South Knapdale	—	89·3	91·5	—	93·7	H	1·1 kW
					98·9m‡	H	1·1 kW
Strachur	—	88·6	90·8	—	93·0	M	18 W
					98·2m‡	M	18 W
Meldrum	—	88·7	90·9	—	93·1a	H	60 kW
Durris	—	89·4	91·6	—	93·8a	M	2·1 kW
Tullich	—	90·1	92·3	—	94·5a	M	42 W
Melvaig (m)	—	89·1	91·3	—	93·5hn	H†	22 kW
						M*	50 kW
					98·7‡	H†	22 kW
						M*	50 kW
Penifiler (m)	—	89·5	91·7	—	93·9hn	H	6 W
					99·1‡	H	6 W
Skriaig (m)	—	88·5	90·7	—	92·9hn	H	10 kW
					98·1‡	H	10 kW
Rosemarkie	—	89·6	91·8	—	94·0h	H	12 kW
Grantown	—	89·8	92·0	—	94·6h	H	350 W
Kingussie	—	89·1	91·3	—	93·5h	H	35 W
Knock More	—	88·2	90·4	—	92·6h	M	500 W
Rumster Forest	—	90·1	92·3	—	94·5h	M	10 kW
Sandale	—	88·1	90·3	92·5	94·7d	H†	120 kW
						M*	250 kW
Cambret Hill	—	88·7	90·9	—	93·1d	H	64 W
Stranraer	—	89·7	91·9	—	94·1d	V	31 W

BBC local radio stations

	Medium frequency (AM)		
	kHz	metres	kW
Bedfordshire	1161	258	0·08
Luton	630	476	0·3
Bristol	1548	194	5
Taunton	1323	227	1
Cambridgeshire	1026	292	0·5
Peterborough	1449	207	0·15
Cleveland	1548	194	1
Cornwall (Redruth)	630	476	2
Bodmin	657	457	0·5
Cumbria (Carlisle)	756	397	1
Whitehaven	1458	206	0·5
Derby	1116	269	0·5
Devon (Exeter)	990	303	1
Barnstaple	801	375	2
Plymouth	855	351	1
Torbay	1458	206	2
Essex	1530	196	0·1
Chelmsford	765	392	0·5
Manningtree	729	411	0·2
Furness	837	358	1
Guernsey	1116	269	0·5
Humberside	1485	202	1
Jersey	1026	292	1
Kent (Hoo)	1035	290	0·5
Littlebourne	774	388	0·7
Rusthall	1602	187	0·25
Lancashire (Blackburn)	855	351	1
Oxcliffe	1557	193	0·25
Leeds	774	388	0·5
Leicester	837	358	0·7
Lincolnshire	1368	219	2
London	1458	206	50
Manchester	1458	206	5
Merseyside	1485	202	2
Newcastle	1458	206	2
Norfolk (Norwich)	855	351	1
West Lynn	873	344	0·25

KEY TO PAGES 141–144

* Proposed but not in service at date of publication.
† To be discontinued.
m Transmits presently in mono.
** To be replaced by Black Hill.
‡ Service carries Radio Scotland Medium-Wave programmes.
Opt-out service:
a R/Aberdeen   t R/Tweed
h R/Highland   z R/Shetland
n R/nan Eilean
o R/Orkney

	Medium frequency (AM)		
	kHz	metres	kW
Northampton	1107	271	0·5
Nottingham	1521	197	1
Clipstone	1584	189	1
Oxford	1485	202	0·5
Sheffield	1035	290	1
Shropshire	756	397	1
Woofferton	1584	189	0·3
Solent (Fareham)	999	300	1
Bournemouth	1359	221	0·85
Stoke-on-Trent	1503	200	1
Sussex (Brighton	1485	202	1
Bexhill	1161	258	1
Duxhurst	1368	219	0·5
WM (Birmingham)	1458	206	5
Wolverhampton	828	362	0·2
York (Fulford)	666	450	0·5
Scarborough	1260	238	0·5

	VHF (FM)		
	MHz	kW	Polarisation
Bedfordshire	103·8	0·02	Mixed
Sandy Heath	95·5	1	Mixed
Zouches Farm	103·8	0·5	Mixed
Bow Brickhill	104·5	2·2	Mixed
Bristol (Main)	95·5	9	Mixed
Town	104·4	1	Mixed
Bath	104·6	0·08	Mixed
Cambridgeshire			
Cambridge	96·0	1	Mixed
Peterborough	95·7	5	Mixed
Cleveland	95	5	Horizontal
Whitby	95·8	0·04	Horizontal
Cornwall (Redruth)	103·9	17	Mixed
Caradon Hill	95·2	4·3	Mixed
Isles of Scilly	96·0	0·06	Mixed
Cumbria	95·6	15	Mixed
Derby (Main)	104·5	5·5	Mixed
Town	94·2	0·01	Vertical
Stanton Moor	95·3	1·2	Mixed
Devon: (N. Hessary Tor)	103·4	10	Mixed
Exeter St. Thomas	95·8	0·4	Mixed
Huntshaw Cross	94·8	0·7	Mixed
Okehampton	96·0	0·07	Mixed
Essex	103·5	12·0	Mixed
Manningtree	104·9	5	Mixed
South Benfleet	95·3	1·2	Mixed
Furness	96·1	3·2	Mixed
Kendal	95·2	0·1	Mixed
Windermere	104·2	0·065	Mixed
Gloucestershire	104·7	4	Mixed
Stroud	95·0	0·2	Mixed
Guernsey	93·2	1	Mixed
Hereford and Worcester	94·7	2	Mixed
Great Malvern	104·0	2	Mixed

| | VHF(FM) | | |
	MHz	kW	Polarisation
Humberside	95·9	9	Mixed
Jersey	88·8	4	Mixed
Kent (Wrotham)	96·7	9	Mixed
Dover	104·2	10	Mixed
Lancashire (Blackburn)	95·5	1·6	Mixed
Lancaster	104·5	2	Mixed
Winter Hill	103·9	2	Mixed
Leeds	92·4	5·6	Mixed
Wharfedale	95·3	0·04	Mixed
Leicester	95·1	0·3	Mixed
Lincolnshire	94·9	6·0	Mixed
London	94·9	2	Mixed
Manchester	95·1	5·6	Mixed
Merseyside	95·8	7·5	Mixed
Newcastle (Pontop Pike)	95·4	3·5	Horizontal
Chatton	96·0	5·6	Mixed
Fenham	104·4	0·05	Vertical
Norfolk	95·1	5·7	Mixed
Great Massingham	104·4	4·2	Mixed
Northampton	104·2	4	Mixed
Geddington	103·6	0·8	Mixed
Nottingham	103·8	0·3	Mixed
Fishponds Hill	95·5	2	Mixed
Mapperley Ridge	103·8	1	Mixed
Oxford	95·2	5·8	Mixed
Sheffield (Main)	104·1	4·4	Mixed
Town	88·6	0·32	Mixed
Shropshire	96·0	5	Mixed
Ludlow	95·0	0·01	Mixed
Solent	96·1	5	Horizontal
Stoke-on-Trent	94·6	6	Mixed
Suffolk	103·9	5	Mixed
Great Barton	104·6	2	Mixed
Surrey and Berkshire	104·6	4	Mixed
Henley	94·6	0·2	Mixed
High Wycombe	104·9	0·05	Mixed
Sussex (Brighton)	95·3	1·2	Mixed
Heathfield	104·5	10	Mixed
Reigate	104·0	4	Mixed
Newhaven	95·0	0·1	Mixed
Warwickshire	94·8	1·3	Mixed
Lark Stoke	103·7	1·3	Mixed
Wiltshire	104·3	0·6	Mixed
Blunsdon	103·6	0·5	Mixed
WM	95·6	11·4	Mixed
York	103·7	2	Vertical
Scarborough	95·5	0·25	Mixed
Woolmoor	104·3	0·5	Vertical

Independent local radio stations

Station	Medium wave Site	(kHz)	(m)	(kW)	VHF Site	(MHz)	(kW)
Radio Aire **Leeds**	Morley	828	362	0·12	Morley	96·3	0·6
Beacon Radio **Wolverhampton and Black Country Shrewsbury and Telford**	Sedgley	990	303	0·09	Turners Hill The Wrekin	97·2 103·1	1·0
BRMB Radio **Birmingham**	Langley Mill	1152	261	3·0	Lichfield	96·4	2·0
Radio Broadland **Great Yarmouth and Norwich**	Brundall	1152	260	0·83	Stoke Holy Cross	102·4	3·3
Capital Radio **London – General and Entertainment**	Saffron Green	1548	194	97·5	Croydon	95·8	4·0

Station	MW Tx	kHz	m	kW	FM Tx	MHz	kW
Chiltern Radio							
Luton	Lewsey Farm	828	362	0·2	Dunstable	97·6	0·42
Bedford	Kempston	792	378	0·27	Sandy Heath	96·9	0·89
Northampton	Kings Heath	1557	193	0·76	Northampton	96·6	4·0
Radio City							
Liverpool	Rainford	1548	194	4·4	Allerton Park	96·7	8·2
Radio Clyde							
Glasgow	Dechmont Hill	1152	261	3·6	Black Hill	102·5	20·0
County Sound Radio							
Guildford	Peasmarsh	1476	203	0·5	Guildford	96·4	0·95
Devon Air Radio							
Exeter	Pearce's Hill	666	450	0·34	St Thomas	97·0	1·0
Torbay	Occombe	954	314	0·32	Beacon Hill	96·4	0·25
Downtown Radio							
Belfast	Knockbreckan	1026	293	1·7	Black Mountain	97·4	1·0
Omagh and Enniskillen					Broughton Mountain	96·6	10·0
Londonderry					Londonderry	102·4	10·0
Limavady					Limavady	96·4	2·0
Essex Radio							
Southend	Rayleigh	1431	210	0·35	Benfleet	96·3	1·4
Chelmsford	Bakers Wood	1359	220	0·28	Bakers Wood	102·6	0·4

Station	Medium wave				VHF		
	Site	(kHz)	(m)	(kW)	Site	(MHz)	(kW)
Radio Forth							
Edinburgh	Colinswell	1548	194	2·2	Craigkelly	97·3	1·3
GWR							
Bath					Bath	103·0	0·08
Bristol	Mangotsfield	1260	238	1·6	Dundry	96·3	0·6
Swindon	Blunsdon	1161	258	0·16	Blunsdon	97·2	0·36
West Wiltshire	Naish Hill	936	321	0·18	Naish Hill	102·6	0·5
Radio Hallam							
Sheffield and Rotherham	Skew Hill	1548	194	0·74	Tapton Hill	97·4	0·4
					Rotherham	96·1	0·05
Barnsley	Ardsley	1305	230	0·15	Ardsley	102·9	0·5
Doncaster	Crimpsall	990	303	0·25	Clifton	103·4	1·5
Hereward Radio							
Peterborough	Gunthorpe	1332	225	0·6	Gunthorpe	102·7	1·2
Invicta Radio							
Maidstone and Medway	Hoo St Werburgh	1242	242	0·32	Bluebell Hill	103·1	0·63
					Dunkirk	102·8	0·35
East Kent	Littlebourne	603	497	0·1	Wye (Ashford)	96·1	0·2
					Dover	97·0	0·5
					Thanet	95·0	0·27

LBC (London Broadcasting Company) **London News and Information**	Saffron Green	1152	261	23·5	Croydon	97·3	4·0
Leicester Sound **Leicester**	Freemen's Common	1260	238	0·29	Anstey Lane	103·2	0·4
Marcher Sound **Wrexham and Deeside**	Farndon	1260	238	0·64	Wrexham	103·4	1·4
Mercia Sound **Coventry**	Shilton	1359	220	0·27	Shilton	97·0	0·5
Radio Mercury **Reigate and Crawley**	Duxhurst	1521	197	0·64	Reigate Horsham	102·7 97·5	3·6 0·03
Metro Radio **Tyne and Wear**	Greenside	1152	261	1·8	Burnhope	97·1	10·0
Moray Firth Radio **Inverness**	Tarbat Ness	1107	271	1·5	Mounteagle	97·4	2·8
North South Radio **Aberdeen**	Nigg	1035	290	0·78	Granite Hill	96·9	0·6

Station	Medium wave				VHF		
	Site	(kHz)	(m)	(kW)	Site	(MHz)	(kW)
Ocean Sound **Portsmouth** **Southampton** **Winchester**	Farlington Marshes Veals Farm	1170 1557	257 193	0.12 0.5	Fort Widley Chillerton Down Winchester	97.5 103.2 96.7	0.85 2.0 0.5
Radio Orwell **Ipswich**	Foxhall Heath	1170	257	0.28	Foxhall Heath	97.1	1.0
Pennine Radio **Bradford** **Huddersfield and Halifax**	Tyersal Lane Vicars Lot	1278 1530	235 196	0.43 0.74	Idle Vicars Lot	97.5 102.5	0.5 0.63
Piccadilly Radio **Manchester**	Ashton Moss	1152	261	1.5	Saddleworth	103.0	4.0
Plymouth Sound **Plymouth**	Plumer Barracks	1152	261	0.32	Plympton Tavistock	97.0 96.6	1.0 0.04
Red Dragon Radio **Cardiff** **Newport**	Hadfield Road Christchurch	1359 1305	221 230	0.2 0.2	Wenallt Christchurch	103.2 97.4	0.38 0.5

Station	Location	kHz	m	kW	VHF Site	MHz	kW
Red Rose Radio **Preston and Blackpool**	Longton	999	301	0·8	Winter Hill	97·3*	1·9
Saxon Radio **Bury St Edmunds**	Great Barton	1251	240	0·76	Great Barton	96·4	0·64
Severn Sound **Gloucester and Cheltenham** **Stroud**	Little Shurdington	774	388	0·14	Churchdown Hill Stroud	102·4 103·0	1·0
Signal Radio **Stoke-on-Trent**	Sideway	1170	257	0·2	Alsagers Bank	102·6	1·9
Southern Sound **Brighton** **Newhaven**	Southwick	1323	227	0·5	Brighton Newhaven	103·5 96·9	0·9
Swansea Sound **Swansea**	Winsh-wen (Jersey Road)	1170	257	0·58	Kilvey Hill	96·4	1·0
Radio Tay **Dundee** **Perth**	Greenside-Scalp Friarton Road	1161 1584	258 189	1·4 0·21	Tay Bridge Perth	102·8 96·4	1·3 0·35
Radio Tees **Teesside**	Stockton	1170	257	0·32	Bilsdale	96·6	2·0

Station	Medium wave				VHF		
	Site	(kHz)	(m)	(kW)	Site	(MHz)	(kW)
Radio Trent							
Nottingham	Trowell	999	301	0·25	Colwick Wood	96·2	0·3
Derby	Quarndon	945	317	0·2	Quarndon	102·8	0·6
Two Counties Radio (2CR)							
Bournemouth	Fern Barrow	828	362	0·27	Poole	97·2	1·0
Radio 210							
Reading	Manor Farm	1431	210	0·14	Butts Centre	97·0	0·5
Basingstoke and Andover					Hannington	102·9	4·0
Viking Radio							
Humberside	Goxhill	1161	258	0·35	High Hunsley	96·9	8·5
West Sound							
Ayr	Symington	1035	290	0·32	Darvel	96·7	0·8
					Girvan	97·5	0·15
Radio Wyvern							
Hereford	Breinton	954	314	0·16	Ridge Hill	97·6	0·78
Worcester	Cotheridge	1530	196	0·52	Malvern	102·8	1·0

BBC VHF test tone transmissions

Transmission starts about 4 minutes after the end of Radio 3 programmes on Mondays and Saturdays.

Time min.	Left channel	Right channel	Purpose
—	250 Hz at zero level	440 Hz at zero level	Identification of left and right channels and setting of reference level
2	900 Hz at +7 dB	900 Hz at +7 dB, antiphase to left channel	Adjustment of phase of regenerated subcarrier (see Note 4) and check of distortion with L-R signal only
6	900 Hz at +7 dB	900 Hz +7 dB, in phase with left channel	Check of distortion with L + R signal only
7	900 Hz at +7 dB	No modulation	Check of L to R cross-talk
8	No modulation	900 Hz at +7 dB	Check of R to L cross-talk
9	Tone sequence at −4 dB: 40 Hz 6·3 kHz 100 Hz 10 kHz 500 Hz 12·5 kHz 1000 Hz 14 kHz This sequence is repeated	No modulation	Check of L-channel frequency response and L to R cross-talk at high and low frequencies
11'40"	No modulation	Tone sequences as for left channel	Check of R-channel frequency response and R to L cross-talk at high and low frequencies
14'20"	No modulation	No modulation	Check of noise level in the presence of pilot

15'20" End of test transmissions

Notes
1. This schedule is subject to variation or cancellation to accord with programme requirements and essential transmission tests.
2. The zero level reference corresponds to 40% of the maximum level of modulation applied to either stereophonic channel before pre-emphasis. All tests are transmitted with pre-emphasis.
3. Periods of tone lasting several minutes are interrupted momentarily at one-minute intervals.

4. With receivers having separate controls of subcarrier phase and crosstalk, the correct order of alignment is to adjust first the subcarrier phase to produce maximum output from either the L or the R channel and then to adjust the crosstalk (or 'separation') control for minimum crosstalk between channels.
5. With receivers in which the only control of crosstalk is by adjustment of subcarrier phase, this adjustment should be made on the crosstalk checks.
6. Adjustment of the balance control to produce equal loudness from the L and R loudspeakers is best carried out when listening to the announcements during a stereophonic transmission, which are made from a centre-stage position. If this adjustment is attempted during the tone transmissions, the results may be confused because of the occurrence of standing-wave patterns in the listening room.
7. The outputs of most receivers include significant levels of the 19-kHz tone and its harmonics, which may affect signal-level meters. It is important, therefore, to provide filters with adequate loss at these frequencies if instruments are to be used for the above tests.

Engineering information about broadcast services

Information about all BBC services as well as advice on how best to receive transmissions (including television) can be obtained from:

BBC Engineering Information Department
Broadcasting House
London
W1A 1AA

Telephone number (01) 927 5040

Transmitter service maps for most main transmitters can also be supplied, but requests for maps should be accompanied by a stamped addressed A4 sized envelope.

Similarly, information about all IBA broadcast services can be obtained from:

Engineering Information Service
Independent Broadcasting Authority
Crawley Court
Winchester
Hampshire
SO21 2QA

Telephone number (0962) 822444 or (01) 584 7011 and ask for engineering information

Relevant engineering information, including information regarding newly appointed transmitters etc., is broadcast by the IBA every Tuesday at 9.15 a.m. and 12.15 p.m., on Channel 4 television.

World time

Difference between local time and coordinated universal time
The differences marked + indicate the number of hours ahead of
UTC. Differences marked − indicate the number of hours behind
UTC. Variations from summer time during part of the year are
decided annually and may vary from year to year.

	Normal time	Summer time		Normal time	Summer time
Afghanistan	+4½	+4½	(c) Ea (Ontario,		
Alaska	−9	−8	Quebec)	−5	−4
	−10	−9	(d) Ce (Manitoba)	−6	−5
Albania	+1	+2	(e) Mountain		
Algeria	UTC	+1	(Alberta)		
Andorra	+1	+1	NWT (Mountain)	−7	−6
Angola	+1	+1	(f) Pacific (Br.		
Anguilla	−4	−4	Columbia	−8	−7
Antigua	−4	−4	Yukon	−8	−7
Argentina	−3	−3	Canary Isl.	UTC	+1
Ascension Isl.	UTC	UTC	Cape Verde Isl.	−1	−1
Australia			Cayman Isl.	−5	−4
Victoria &			Central African		
New South			Republic	+1	+1
Wales	+10	+11	Chad	+1	+1
Queensland	+10	+10	Chile	−4	−3
Tasmania	+10	+11	China		
N. Territory	+9½	+9½	People's Rep.	+8	+8
S. Australia	+9½	+10½	Christmas Isl.	+7	+7
W. Australia	+8	+8	Cocos Isl.	+6½	+6½
Austria	+1	+2	Colombia	−5	−5
Azores	−1	UTC	Comoro Rep.	+3	+3
Bahamas	−5	−4	Congo	+1	+1
Bahrain	+3	+3	Cook Isl.	−10	−9½
Bangladesh	+6	+6	Costa Rica	−6	−6
Barbados	−4	−4	Cuba	−5	−4
Belau	+9	+9	Cyprus	+2	+3
Belgium	+1	+2	Czechoslovakia	+1	+2
Belize	−6	−6	Denmark	+1	+2
Benin	+1	+1	Diego Garcia	+5	+5
Bermuda	−4	−3	Djibouti	+3	+3
Bhutan	+6	+6	Dominica	−4	−4
Bolivia	−4	−4	Dom. Rep.	−4	−4
...vana	+2	+2	Easter Isl.	−6	−5
Brazil			Ecuador	−5	−5
(a) Oceanic Isl.	−2	−2	Egypt	+2	+3
(b) Ea & Coastal	−3	−3	El Salvador	−6	−6
(c) Manaos	−4	−4	Equatorial Guinea	+1	+1
(d) Acre	−5	−5	Ethiopia	+3	+3
Brunei	+8	+8	Falkland Isl.	−4	−4
Bulgaria	+2	+3	(Port Stanley)	−4	−3
Burkina Faso	UTC	UTC	Faroe Isl.	UTC	+1
Burma	+6½	+6½	Fiji	+12	+12
Burundi	+2	+2	Finland	+2	+3
Cameroon	+1	+1	France	+1	+2
Canada			Gabon	+1	+1
(a) Newfoundland	−3½	−2½	Gambia	UTC	UTC
(b) Atlantic			Germany	+1	+2
(Labrador,			Ghana	UTC	UTC
Nova Scotia)	−4	−3	Gibraltar	+1	+2

	Normal time	Summer time		Normal time	Summer time
Greece	+2	+3	Mayotte	+3	+3
Greenland			Mexico		
Scoresbysund	−1	UTC	(a) Campeche,		
Thule area	−3	−3	Quintana Roo,		
Other areas	−3	−2	Yucatan	−6	−5
Grenada	−4	−4	(b) Sonora,	−7	−7
Guadeloupe	−4	−4	Sinaloa,		
Guam	+10	+10	Nayarit, Baja'		
Guatemala	−6	−6	California Sur		
Guiana (French)	−3	−3	(c) Baja California	−8	−7
Guinea (Rep.)	UTC	UTC	Norte		
Guinea Bissau	UTC	UTC	(d) other states	−6	−6
Guyana (Rep.)	−3	−3	Micronesia		
Haiti	−5	−4	Truk, Yap	+10	+10
Hawaii	−10	−10	Ponape	+11	+11
Honduras (Rep.)	−6	−6	Midway Isl.	−11	−11
Hong Kong	+8	+8	Monaco	+1	+2
Hungary	+1	+2	Mongolia	+8	+9
Iceland	UTC	UTC	Monserrat	−4	−4
India	+5½	+5½	Morocco	UTC	UTC
Indonesia			Mozambique	+2	+2
(a) Java, Bali,			Nauru	+11½	+11½
Sumatra	+7	+7	Nepal	+5·45	+5·45
(b) Kalimantan,			Netherlands	+1	+2
Sulawesi,			Neth. Antilles	−4	−4
Timor	+8	+8	New Caledonia	+11	+11
(c) Moluccas,			New Zealand	+12	+13
We. Irian	+9	+9	Nicaragua	−6	−6
Iran	+3½	+3½	Niger	+1	+1
Iraq	+3	+4	Nigeria	+1	+1
Ireland	UTC	+1	Niue	−11	−11
Israel	+2	+3	Norfolk Isl.	+11½	+11½
Italy	+1	+2	N. Marianas	+10	+10
Ivory Coast	UTC	UTC	Norway	+1	+2
Jamaica	−5	−4	Oman	+4	+4
Japan	+9	+9	Pakistan	+5	+5
Johnston Isl.	−10	−10	Panama	−5	−5
Jordan	+2	+3	Papua N. Guinea	+10	+10
Kampuchea	+7	+7	Paraguay	−4	−3
Kenya	+3	+3	Peru	−5	−5
Kiribati	+12	+12	Philippines	+8	+8
Korea	+9	+9	Poland	+1	+2
Kuwait	+3	+3	Polynesia (Fr.)	−10	−10
Laos	+7	+7	Portugal	UTC	+1
Lebanon	+2	+3	Puerto Rico	−4	−4
Lesotho	+2	+2	Qatar	+3	+3
Liberia	UTC	UTC	Reunion	+4	+4
Libya	+1	+2	Romania	+2	+3
Lord Howe Isl.	+10½	+11½	Rwanda	+2	+2
Luxembourg	+1	+2	Samoa Isl.	−11	−11
Macau	+8	+8	S. Tomé	UTC	UTC
Madagascar	+3	+3	Saudi Arabia	+3	+3
Madeira	UTC	+1	Senegal	UTC	UTC
Malawi	+2	+2	Seychelles	+4	+4
Malaysia	+8	+8	Sierra Leone	UTC	UTC
Maldive Isl.	+5	+5	Singapore	+8	+8
Mali	UTC	UTC	Solomon Isl.	+11	+11
Malta	+1	+2	Somalia	+3	+3
Marshall Isl.	+12	+12	So. Africa	+2	+2
Martinique	−4	−4	Spain	+1	+2
Mauritania	UTC	UTC	Sri Lanka	+5½	+5½
Mauritius	+4	+4	St. Helena	UTC	UTC

	Normal time	Summer time		Normal time	Summer time
St. Kitts-Nevis	−4	−4	(c) Mountain		
St. Lucia	−4	−4	Zone*	−7	−6
St. Pierre	−3	−3	(*) Arizona	−7	−7
St. Vincent	−4	−4	(d) Pacific Zone	−8	−7
Sudan	+2	+2	USSR		
Surinam	−3½	−3½	Moscow &		
Swaziland	+2	+2	Leningrad	+3	+4
Sweden	+1	+2	Baku, Tbilisi	+4	+5
Switzerland	+1	+2	Sverdlovsk	+5	+6
Syria	+2	+3	Tashkent	+6	+7
Taiwan	+8	+8	Novobirsk	+7	+8
Tanzania	+3	+3	Irkutsk	+8	+9
Thailand	+7	+7	Yakutsk	+9	+10
Togo	UTC	UTC	Khabarovsk	+10	+11
Tonga	+13	+13	Magadan	+11	+12
Transkei	+2	+2	Petropavlovsk	+12	+13
Trinidad &			Anadyr	+13	+14
Tobago	−4	−4	Vanuatu	+11	+12
Tristan da Cunha	UTC	UTC	Vatican	+1	+2
Tunisia	+1	+1	Venezuela	−4	−4
Turks & Caicos	−4	−4	Vietnam	+7	+7
Turkey	+2	+3	Virgin Isl.	−4	−4
Tuvalu	+12	+12	Wake Isl.	+12	+12
Uganda	+3	+3	Wallis & Futuna	+11	+11
United Arab Em.	+4	+4	Yemen	+3	+3
United Kingdom	UTC	+1	Yugoslavia	+1	+2
Uruguay	−3	−3	Zaire		
USA			Kinshasa	+1	+1
(a) Eastern			Lubumbashi	+2	+2
Zone*	−5	−4	Zambia	+2	+2
(*) Indiana	−5	−5	Zimbabwe	+2	+2
(b) Central Zone	−6	−5			

International allocation of call signs

The first character or the first two characters of a call sign indicate
the nationality of the station using it.

AAA–ALZ	USA	CQA–CRZ	Portuguese
AMA–AOZ	Spain		Territories
APA–ASZ	Pakistan	CSZ–CUZ	Portugal
ATA–AWZ	India	CVA–CXZ	Uruguay
AXA–AXZ	Australia	CYA–CZZ	Canada
AYA–AZZ	Argentina	C2A–C2Z	Nauru
A2A–A2Z	Botswana	C3A–C3Z	Andorra
A3A–A3Z	Tonga	DAA–DTZ	Germany
A5A–A5Z	Bhutan	DUA–DZZ	Philippines
BAA–BZZ	China	EAA–EHZ	Spain
CAA–CEZ	Chile	EIA–EJZ	Ireland
CFA–CKZ	Canada	EKA–EKZ	USSR
CLA–CMZ	Cuba	ELA–ELZ	Liberia
CNA–CNZ	Morocco	EMA–EOZ	USSR
COA–COZ	Cuba	EPA–EQZ	Iran
CPA–CPZ	Bolivia	ERA–ERZ	USSR

ESA–ESZ	Estonia (USSR)	PZA–PZZ	Surinam
ETA–ETZ	Ethiopia	QAA–QZZ	(Service
EUA–EWZ	Belorussia		abbreviations)
	(USSR)	RAA–RZZ	(USSR)
EXA–EZZ	USSR	SAA–SMZ	Sweden
FAA–FZZ	France and	SNA–SRZ	Poland
	Territories	SSA–SSM	Egypt
GAA–GZZ	United Kingdom	SSN–STZ	Sudan
HAA–HAZ	Hungary	SUA–SUZ	Egypt
HBA–HBZ	Switzerland	SVA–SZZ	Greece
HCA–HDZ	Ecuador	TAA–TCZ	Turkey
HEA–HEZ	Switzerland	TDA–TDZ	Guatemala
HFA–HFZ	Poland	TEA–TEZ	Costa Rica
HGA–HGZ	Hungary	TFA–TFZ	Iceland
HHA–HHZ	Haiti	TGA–TGZ	Guatemala
HIA–HIZ	Dominican	THA–THZ	France and
	Republic		Territories
HJA–HKZ	Colombia	TIA–TIZ	Costa Rica
HLA–hMZ	Korea	TJA–TJZ	Cameroon
HNA–HNZ	Iraq	TKA–TKZ	France and
HOA–HPZ	Panama		Territories
HQA–HRZ	Honduras	TLA–TLZ	Central African
HSA–HSZ	Thailand		Republic
HTA–HTZ	Nicaragua	TMA–TMZ	France and
HUA–HUZ	El Salvador		Territories
HVA–HVZ	Vatican State	TNA–TNZ	Congo
HWA–HYZ	France and	TOA–TQZ	France and
	Territories		Territories
HZA–HZZ	Saudi Arabia	TRA–TRZ	Gabon
IAA–IZZ	Italy and	TSA–TSZ	Tunisia
	Territories	TTA–TTZ	Chad
JAA–JSZ	Japan	TUA–TUZ	Ivory Coast
JTA–JVZ	Mongolia	TVA–TXZ	France and
JWA–JXZ	Norway		Territories
JYA–JYZ	Jordan	TYA–TYZ	Dahomey
JZA–JZZ	West Irian	TZA–TZZ	Mali
KAA–KZZ	United States	UAA–UQZ	USSR
LAA–LNZ	Norway	URA–UTZ	Ukraine (USSR)
LOA–LWZ	Argentina	UUA–UZZ	USSR
LXA–LXZ	Luxembourg	VAA–VGZ	Canada
LYA–LYZ	Lithuania	VHA–VNZ	Australia
	(USSR)	VOA–VOZ	Canada
LZA–LZZ	Bulgaria	VPA–VSZ	British Territories
L2A–L9Z	Argentina	VTA–VWZ	India
MAA–MZZ	United Kingdom	VXA–VYZ	Canada
NAA–NZZ	United States	VZA–VZZ	Australia
OAA–OCZ	Peru	WAA–WZZ	United States
ODA–ODZ	Lebanon	XAA–XIZ	Mexico
OEA–OEZ	Austria	XJA–XOZ	Canada
OFA–OJZ	Finland	XPA–XPZ	Denmark
OKA–OMZ	Czechoslovakia	XQA–XRZ	Chile
ONA–OTZ	Belgium	XSA–XSZ	China
OUA–OZZ	Denmark	XTA–XTZ	Upper Volta
PAA–PIZ	Netherlands	XUA–XUZ	Khmer Republic
PJA–PJZ	Netherlands	XVA–XVZ	Vietnam
	West Indies	XWA–XWZ	Laos
PKA–POZ	Indonesia	XXA–XXZ	Portuguese
PPA–PYZ	Brazil		Territories

XYA–XZZ	Burma	5NA–5OZ	Nigeria
YAA–YAZ	Afghanistan	5PA–5QZ	Denmark
YBA–YHZ	Indonesia	5RA–5SZ	Malagasy
YIA–YIZ	Iraq		Republic
YJA–YJZ	New Hebrides	5TA–5TZ	Mauretania
YKA–YKZ	Syria	5UA–5UZ	Niger
YLA–YLZ	Latvia (USSR)	5VA–5VZ	Togo
YMA–YMZ	Turkey	5WA–5WZ	Western Samoa
YNA–YNZ	Nicaragua	5XA–5XZ	Uganda
YOA–YRZ	Romania	5YA–5ZZ	Kenya
YSA–YSZ	El Salvador	6AA–6BZ	Egypt
YTA–YUZ	Yugoslavia	6CA–6CZ	Syria
YVA–YYZ	Venezuela	6DA–6JZ	Mexico
YZA–YZZ	Yugoslavia	6KA–6NZ	Korea
ZAA–ZAZ	Albania	6OA–6OZ	Somali Republic
ZBA–ZJZ	British Territories	6PA–6SZ	Pakistan
ZKA–ZMZ	New Zealand	6TA–6UZ	Sudan
ZNA–ZOZ	British Territories	6VA–6WZ	Senegal
ZPA–ZPZ	Paraguay	6XA–6XZ	Malagasy
ZQA–ZQZ	British Territories		Republic
ZRA–ZUZ	South Africa	6YA–6YZ	Jamaica
ZVA–ZZZ	Brazil	6ZA–6ZZ	Liberia
2AA–2ZZ	United Kingdom	7AA–7IZ	Indonesia
3AA–3AZ	Monaco	7JA–7NZ	Japan
3BA–3BZ	Mauritius	7OA–7OZ	Yemen (PDRY)
3CA–3CZ	Equatorial Guinea	7PA–7PZ	Lesotho
3DA–3DM	Swaziland	7QA–7QZ	Malawi
3DN–3DZ	Fiji	7RA–7RZ	Algeria
3EA–3FZ	Panama	7SA–7SZ	Sweden
3GA–3GZ	Chile	7TA–7YZ	Algeria
3HA–3UZ	China	7ZA–7ZZ	Saudi Arabia
3VA–3VZ	Tunisia	8AA–8IZ	Indonesia
3WA–3WZ	Vietnam	8JA–8NZ	Japan
3XA–3XZ	Guinea	8OA–8OZ	Botswana
3YA–3YZ	Norway	8PA–8PZ	Barbados
3ZA–3ZZ	Poland	8QA–8QZ	Maldive Islands
4AA–4CZ	Mexico	8RA–8RZ	Guyana
4DA–4IZ	Phillipines	8SA–8SZ	Sweden
4JA–4LZ	USSR	8TA–8YZ	India
4MA–4MZ	Venezuela	8ZA–8ZZ	Saudi Arabia
4NA–4OZ	Yugoslavia	9AA–9AZ	San Marino
4PA–4SZ	Sri Lanka	9BA–9DZ	Iran
4TA–4TZ	Peru	9EA–9FZ	Ethiopia
4UA–4UZ	United Nations	9GA–9GZ	Ghana
4VA–4VZ	Haiti	9HA–9HZ	Malta
4WA–4WZ	Yemen (YAR)	9IA–9JZ	Zambia
4XA–4XZ	Israel	9KA–9KZ	Kuwait
4YA–4YZ	International Civil Aviation Organization	9LA–9LZ	Sierra Leone
		9MA–9MZ	Malaysia
		9NA–9NZ	Nepal
4ZA–4ZZ	Israel	9OA–9TZ	Zaire
5AA–5AZ	Libya	9UA–9UZ	Burundi
5BA–5BZ	Cyprus	9VA–9VZ	Singapore
5CA–5GZ	Morocco	9WA–9WZ	Malaysia
5HA–5IZ	Tanzania	9XA–9XZ	Rwanda
5JA–5KZ	Colombia	9YA–9ZZ	Trinidad and Tobago
5LA–5MZ	Liberia		

Amateur bands in the UK

The Schedule of frequency bands, powers, etc, which, for the sake of convenience, appear in an identical format in both the Class A and Class B licences

Frequency bands in MHz	Status of allocations in the UK to: The Amateur Service	The Amateur Satellite Service	Maximum power Carrier PEP		Permitted typ of transmiss
1·810–1·850	Available to amateurs on a basis of non interference to other services		9dBW	15dBW	Morse Telephony RTTY Data Facsimile SSTV
1·850–2·000		No allocation			Morse Telephony Data Facsimile SSTV
3·500–3·800	Primary. Shared with other services	No allocation	20dBW	26dBW	Morse Telephony RTTY Data Facsimile SSTV
7·000–7·100	Primary	Primary			
10·100–10·150	Secondary	No allocation			
14·000–14·250	Primary	Primary			
14·250–14·350		No allocation			
18·068–16·168	Available to amateurs on a basis of non interference to other services. Antennas limited to horizontal polarisation, maximum gain 0dB with respect to a half-wave dipole	No allocation	10dBW	—	Morse, A1A only
21·000–21·450	Primary	Primary	20dBW	26dBW	Morse Telephony RTTY Data Facsimile SSTV
24·890–24·990	Available to amateurs on basis of non interference to other services. Antennas limited to horizontal polarisation, maximum gain 0dB with respect to a half-wave dipole	No allocation	10dBW	—	Morse, A1A only
28·000–29·700	Primary	Primary	20dBW	26dBW	Morse Telephony
50·000–50·500	Primary	No allocation	14dBW	20dBW	Morse Telephony
70·025–70·500	Secondary basis until further notice. Subject to not causing interference to other services. Use of any frequency shall cease immediately on demand of a government official	No allocation	16dBW	22dBW	RTTY Data Facsimile SSTV
144·0–146·0*	Primary	Primary	20dBW	26dBW	
430·0–431·0	Secondary. This band is not available for use within the area bounded by: 53 N 02 E, 55 N 02 E, 53 N 03 W, and 55 N 03 W	No allocation	10dBW e.r.p.	16dBW e.r.p.	Morse Telephony RTTY Data Facsimile SSTV Television

Frequency					Types of transmission
431·0–432·0	Secondary. This band is not available for use: a) Within the area bounded by: 53 N 02 E, 55 N 02 E, 55 N 03 W, and 55 N 03 W. b) Within a 100km radius of Charing Cross. 51 30'30''N 00.07'24''W	No allocation	10dBW e.r.p.	16dBW e.r.p.	Morse Telephony RTTY Data Facsimile SSTV Television
432·0–435·0	Secondary	No allocation	20dBW	26dBW	
435·0–438·0		Secondary			
438·0–440·0		No allocation			
1240–1260	Secondary	No allocation			
1260–1270		Secondary Earth to Space only			
1270–1325		No allocation			
2310–2400					
2400–2450	Secondary. Users must accept interference from the ISM allocations in this band	Secondary. Users must accept interference from the ISM allocations in this band			
3400–3475	Secondary	No allocation			
5650–5670		Secondary Earth to Space only			
5670–5680					
5755–5765	Secondary. Users must accept interference from the ISM allocations in this band	No allocation			
5820–5830					
5830–5850		Secondary. Users must accept interference from the ISM allocations in this band. Space to Earth only			
10000–10450	Secondary	No allocation			
10450–10500		Secondary			
24000–24050	Primary. Users must accept interference from the ISM allocations in this band	Primary. Users must accept interference from the ISM allocations in this band			
24050–24250	Secondary. This band may only be used with the written consent of the Secretary of State. Users must accept interference from the ISM allocations in this band	No allocation			
47000–47200	Primary	Primary			
75500–76000					
142000–144000					
248000–250000					

*Except in accordance with clause 1(2)(c)(ii) holders of the Amateur Radio Licence (B) are not permitted to use frequencies below 144 MHz, nor may they use the type of transmission known as morse (whether sent manually or automatically).

Dipole lengths for the amateur bands

Amateur band (metres)	Dipole length (metres)
80	39
40	20·2
20	10·1
15	6·7
10	5·0

Amateur radio emission designations

The first symbol specifies the modulation of the main carrier, the second symbol the nature of the signal(s) modulating the main carrier, and the third symbol the type of information to be transmitted.

Amplitude modulation

A1A Telegraphy by on-off keying without the use of a modulating audio frequency

A1B Automatic telegraphy by on-off keying, without the use of a modulating audio frequency

A2A Telegraphy by on-off keying of an amplitude modulating audio frequency or frequencies, or by on-off keying of the modulated emission

A2B Automatic telegraphy by on-off keying of an amplitude modulating audio frequency or modulated emission

A3E Telephony, double sideband

A3C Facsimile transmission

H3E Telephony using single sideband full carrier, amplitude modulation

R3E Telephony, single sideband, reduced carrier

J3E Telephony, single sideband, suppressed carrier

A3F/

C3F Slow scan and high definition television

Frequency modulation

F1A Telegraphy by frequency shift keying without the use of a modulating frequency: one of two frequencies being emitted at any instant

F1B Automatic telegraphy by frequency shift keying without the use of a modulating frequency

F2A Telegraphy by on-off keying of a frequency modulating audio frequency or on-off keying of an f.m. emission

F2B Automatic telegraphy by on-off keying of a frequency modulating audio frequency or of an f.m. emission

F3E Telephony

F3C Facsimile transmission

F3F Slow scan and high definition television

Microwave band designation systems

MOD. discontinued system		UK IEE recommended system		New NATO designation system		USA system	
	GHz		GHz		GHz		GHz
P	0·08–0·39	A	0–0·25	L	1–2	P	0·225–0·39
L_2	0·39–1·0	B	0·25–0·5	S	2–4	L	0·39–1·55
L_1	1·0–2·5	C	0·5–1·0	C	4–8	S	1·55–5·2
S	2·5–4·1	D	1·0–2	X	7–12	X	5·2–10·9
C	4·1–7·0	E	2–3	J	12–18	K	10·9–36
X	7·0–11·5	F	3–4	K	18–26	Q	36–46
J	11·5–18·0	G	4–6	Q	26–40	V	46–56
K	18–33	H	6–8	V	40–60	W	56–100
Q	33–40	I	8–10	O	60–90		
O	40–60	J	10–20				
V	60–90	K	20–40				
		L	40–60				
		M	60–100				

International 'Q' code

Abbrev.	Question	Answer for advice
QRA	What is the name of your station?	The name of my station is ...
QRB	How far approximately are you from my station?	The approximate distance is ... miles
QRD	Where are you bound and where are you from?	I am bound for ... from ...
QRG	Will you tell me my exact frequency in kHz?	Your exact frequency is ... kHz.
QRH	Does my frequency vary?	Your frequency varies.
QRI	Is my note good?	Your note varies.
QRJ	Do you receive me badly? Are my signals weak?	I cannot receive you. Your signals are too weak.
QRK	Do you receive me well? Are my signals good?	I receive you well. Your signals are good.
QRL	Are you busy?	I am busy. Please do not interfere.
QRM	Are you being interfered with?	I am being interfered with.
QRN	Are you troubled by atmospherics?	I am troubled by atmospherics.
QRO	Shall I increase power?	Increase power.
QRP	Shall I decrease power?	Decrease power.
QRQ	Shall I send faster?	Send faster (... words per minute).
QRS	Shall I send more slowly?	Send more slowly (... words per minute).
QRT	Shall I stop sending?	Stop sending.
QRU	Have you anything for me?	I have nothing for you.
QRV	Are you ready?	I am ready.

QRX	Shall I wait? When will you call me again?	Wait (or wait until I have finished communicating with ...). I will call you at ... GMT.
QRZ	Who is calling me?	You are being called by ...
QSA	What is the strength of my signals? (1 to 5)	The strength of your signals is ... (1 to 5).
QSB	Does the strength of my signals vary?	The strength of your signals varies.
QSD	Is my keying correct? Are my signals distinct?	Your keying is indistinct. Your signals are bad.
QSL	Can you give me acknowledgement of receipt?	I give you acknowledgement of receipt.
QSM	Shall I repeat the last telegram (message) I sent you?	Repeat the last telegram (message) you have sent me.
QSO	Can you communicate with ... direct (or through the medium of ...)?	I can communicate with ... direct (or through the medium of ...).
QSP	Will you relay to ...?	I will relay to ...
QSV	Shall I send a series of V's?	Send a series of V's.
QSX	Will you listen for ... (call sign) on ... kHz?	I am listening for ... (call sign) on ... kHz.
QSZ	Shall I send each word or group twice?	Send each word or group twice.
QTH	What is your position in latitude and longitude?	My position is ... latitude ... longitude.
QTR	What is the exact time?	The exact time is ...

QSA Code (signal strength)

QSA1 . Hardly perceptible; unreadable.
QSA2 . Weak, readable now and then.
QSA3 . Fairly good; readable, but with difficulty.
QSA4 . Good; readable.
QSA5 . Very good; perfectly readable.

QRK Code (audibility)

R1 . Unreadable.
R2 . Weak signals; barely readable.
R3 . Weak signals; but can be copied
R4 . Fair signals; easily readable.
R5 . Moderately strong signals.
R6 . Good signals.
R7 . Good strong signals.
R8 . Very strong signals.
R9 . Extremely strong signals.

RST Code (readability)   (Signal strength)

1 . Unreadable.	1 . Faint, signals barely perceptible
2 . Barely readable, occasional words distinguishable.	2 . Very weak signals.
3 . Readable with considerable difficulty.	3 . Weak signals.
4 . Readable with practically no difficulty.	4 . Fair signals.
5 . Perfectly readable.	5 . Fairly good signals.
	6 . Good signals.
	7 . Moderately strong signals.
	8 . Strong signals.
	9 . Extremely strong signals.

(Tone)

1 . Extremely rough hissing note.
2 . Very rough AC note, no trace of musicality.
3 . Rough, low-pitched AC note, slightly musical.
4 . Rather rough AC note, moderately musical.
5 . Musically modulated note.
6 . Modulated note, slight trace of whistle.
7 . Near DC note, smooth ripple.
8 . Good DC note, just a trace of ripple.
9 . Purest DC note.

(If the note appears to be crystal-controlled add an X after the appropriate number.)

International Morse Code

A	dit dah	.-	N	dah dit	-.
B	dah dit dit dit	-...	O	dah dah dah	---
C	dah dit dah dit	-.-.	P	dit dah dah dit	.--.
D	dah dit dit	-..	Q	dah dah dit dah	--.-
E	dit	.	R	dit dah dit	.-.
F	dit dit dah dit	..-.	S	dit dit dit	...
G	dah dah dit	--.	T	dah	-
H	dit dit dit dit	....	U	dit dit dah	..-
I	dit dit	..	V	dit dit dit dah	...-
J	dit dah dah dah	.---	W	dit dah dah	.--
K	dah dit dah	-.-	X	dah dit dit dah	-..-
L	dit dah dit dit	.-..	Y	dah dit dah dah	-.--
M	dah dah	--	Z	dah dah dit dit	--..

Number code

1	dit dah dah dah dah	.----	6	dah dit dit dit dit	-....
2	dit dit dah dah dah	..---	7	dah dah dit dit dit	--...
3	dit dit dit dah dah	...--	8	dah dah dah dit dit	---..
4	dit dit dit dit dah	....-	9	dah dah dah dah dit	----.
5	dit dit dit dit dit	.....	0	dah dah dah dah dah	-----

Note of interrogation	dit dit dah dah dit dit	..--..
Note of exclamation	dah dah dit dah dah dah	--.---
Apostrophe	dit dah dah dah dah dit	.----.
Hyphen	dah dit dit dit dit dah	-....-
Fractional bar	dah dit dit dah dit	-..-.
Brackets	dah dit dah dah dit dah	-.--.-
Inverted commas	dit dah dit dit dah dit	.-..-.
Underline	dit dit dah dah dit dah	..--.-
Prelim. call	dah dit dah dit dah	-.-.-
Break sign	dah dit dit dit dah	-...-
End message	dit dah dit dah dit	.-.-.
Error	dit dit dit dit dit dit	......

Timing

The basic timing measurement is the dot pulse (dit), all other morse code timings are a function of this unit length:

Dot length (dit)	one unit
Dash length (dah)	three units
Pause between elements of one character	one unit
Pause between characters	three units
Pause between words	seven units

Phonetic alphabet

To avoid the possibility of the letters of a call-sign being misunderstood, it is usual to use the words given below in place of the letters. For example, G6PY would be given as G6 Papa Yankee.

Letter	Code word	Pronunciation	Letter	Code word	Pronunciation
A	Alfa	*AL* FAH	O	Oscar	*OSS* CAH
B	Bravo	*BRAH* VOH	P	Papa	PAH *PAH*
C	Charlie	*CHAR* LEE	Q	Quebec	KEH *BECK*
D	Delta	*DELL* TAH	R	Romeo	*ROW* ME OH
E	Echo	*ECK* OH	S	Sierra	SEE *AIR* RAH
F	Foxtrot	*FOKS* TROT	T	Tango	*TANG* GO
G	Golf	GOLF	U	Uniform	*YOU* NEE FORM
H	Hotel	HOH *TELL*	V	Victor	*VIK* TAH
I	India	*IN* DEE AH	W	Whiskey	*WISS* KEY
J	Juliett	*JEW* LEE *ETT*	X	X-ray	*ECKS* RAY
K	Kilo	*KEY* LOH	Y	Yankee	*YANG* KEY
L	Lima	*LEE* MAH	Z	Zulu	*ZOO* LOO
M	Mike	MIKE			
N	November	NO *VEM* BER		Syllables in italic carry the accent.	

Miscellaneous international abbreviations

C	Yes		GA	Resume sending
N	No		MN	Minute/minutes
W	Word		NW	I resume transmission
AA	All after ...		OK	Agreed
AB	All before ...		UA	Are we agreed?
AL	All that has just been sent		WA	Word after ...
			WB	Word before ...
BN	All between		XS	Atmospherics
CL	I am closing my station			

Amateur abbreviations

ABT	About		CKT	Circuit
AGN	Again		CLD	Called
ANI	Any		CO	Crystal oscillator
BA	Buffer amplifier		CUD	Could
BCL	Broadcast listener		CUL	See you later
BD	Bad		DX	Long distance
BI	By		ECO	Electron-coupled oscillator
BK	Break in			
BN	Been		ES	And
CK	Check			

FB	Fine business (good work)
FD	Frequency doubler
FM	From
GA	Go ahead, or Good afternoon
GB	Good-bye
GE	Good evening
GM	Good morning
GN	Good night
HAM	Radio amateur
HI	Laughter
HR	Hear or here
HRD	Heard
HV	Have
LTR	Later
MILS	Milliamperes
MO	Meter oscillator
ND	Nothing doing
NIL	Nothing
NM	No more
NR	Number
NW	Now
OB	Old boy
OM	Old man
OT	Old timer
PA	Power amplifier
PSE	Please
R	Received all sent
RAC	Rectified AC
RCD	Received
RX	Receiver
SA	Say
SED	Said
SIGS	Signals
SIGN	Signature
SSS	Single signal super-heterodyne
SKD	Schedule
TKS	Thanks
TMN	Tomorrow
TNX	Thanks
TPTG	Tuned plate tuned grid
TX	Transmitter
U	You
UR	You are
VY	Very
WDS	Words
WKG	Working
WL	Will
WUD	Would
WX	Weather
YF	Wife
YL	Young lady
YR	Your
73	Kind regards
88	Love and kisses

Characteristics of world UHF terrestrial television systems

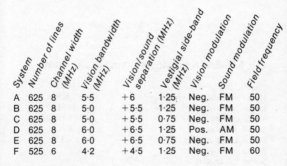

System	Number of lines	Channel width (MHz)	Vision bandwidth (MHz)	Vision/sound separation (MHz)	Vestigial side-band (MHz)	Vision modulation	Sound modulation	Field frequency
A	625	8	5·5	+6	1·25	Neg.	FM	50
B	625	8	5·0	+5·5	1·25	Neg.	FM	50
C	625	8	5·0	+5·5	0·75	Neg.	FM	50
D	625	8	6·0	+6·5	1·25	Pos.	AM	50
E	625	8	6·0	+6·5	0·75	Neg.	FM	50
F	525	6	4·2	+4·5	1·25	Neg.	FM	60

A – UK and Eire
B – Eastern Europe
C – Most of Western Europe, Australia, New Zealand
D – France
E – Russia and Eastern Europe
F – USA, most of Central and South America, Japan

European terrestrial television systems

Country	System	Colour
Austria	C	PAL
Belgium	B	PAL
Bulgaria	No UHF system	
Cyprus	C	PAL
Czechoslovakia	E	SECAM
Denmark	No UHF system	PAL
Finland	C	PAL
France	D	SECAM
Germany	C	PAL
German DR	C	SECAM
Greece	B	PAL
Holland	C	PAL
Hungary	E	SECAM
Iceland	No UHF system	
Ireland	A	PAL
Italy	C	PAL
Luxembourg	D	SECAM
Malta	B	PAL
Monaco	D	SECAM
Norway	C	PAL
Poland	E	SECAM
Portugal	C	PAL
Romania	E	PAL
Spain	C	PAL
Sweden	C	PAL
Switzerland	C	PAL
Turkey	No UHF system	
UK	A	PAL
USSR	E	SECAM
Yugoslavia	B	PAL

UK 625-line television system specification

Channel bandwidth	8 MHz
Upper sideband (vision signal)	5·5 MHz
Lower sideband (vision signal)	1·25 MHz
Vision modulation	AM negative
Sound modulation	FM
Sound deviation (max.)	± 50 kHz
Sound pre-emphasis	50 μs
Sound carrier relative to vision carrier	+
Aspect ratio	4:3
Blanking and black level	76%
White level	20% peak
Sync. level	100% peak
Video bandwidth	5·5 MHz

Field frequency	50 Hz
Line frequency	15,625 Hz
Field sync. signal	5 equalising then 5 broad pulses, followed by 5 equalising pulses in 7·5 line periods
Field sync. and flyback intervals	2 × 25 line periods
Line period (approx.)	64 μs
Line sync. pulses (approx.)	4·7 μs
Line blanking (approx.)	12 μs
Field sync. pulses (broad)	27.3 μs
Field sync. pulses (equalising)	2·3 μs
Colour subcarrier frequency	4·43361875 MHz
Burst duration	2·25 μs
Burst amplitude	equal to sync
Burst phase	180° ± 45°

UK 625-line television system field blanking details

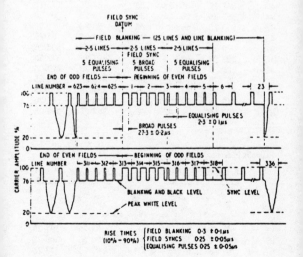

Terrestrial television channels

UK

BAND IV

Channel	Frequency (MHz) Vision	Sound	Channel	Frequency (MHz) Vision	Sound
21	471·25	477·25	28	527·25	533·25
22	479·25	485·25	29	535·25	541·25
23	487·25	493·25	30	543·25	549·25
24	495·25	501·25	31	551·25	557·25
25	503·25	509·25	32	559·25	565·25
26	511·25	517·25	33	567·25	573·25
27	519·25	525·25	34	575·25	581·25

BAND V

Channel	Frequency (MHz) Vision	Sound	Channel	Frequency (MHz) Vision	Sound
39	615·25	621·25	54	735·25	741·25
40	623·25	629·25	55	743·25	749·25
41	631·25	637·25	56	751·25	757·25
42	639·25	645·25	57	759·25	765·25
43	647·25	653·25	58	767·25	773·25
44	655·25	661·25	59	775·25	781·25
45	663·25	669·25	60	783·25	789·25
46	671·25	677·25	61	791·25	797·25
47	679·25	685·25	62	799·25	805·25
48	687·25	693·25	63	807·25	813·25
49	695·25	701·25	64	815·25	821·25
50	703·25	709·25	65	823·25	829·25
51	711·25	717·25	66	831·25	837·25
52	719·25	725·25	67	839·25	845·25
53	727·25	733·25	68	847·25	853·25

Republic of Ireland

Channel	Frequency (MHz) Vision	Sound	Channel	Frequency (MHz) Vision	Sound
IA	45·75	51·75	IF	191·25	197·25
IB	53·75	59·75	IG	199·25	205·25
IC	61·75	67·75	IH	207·25	213·25
ID	175·25	81·25	IJ	215·25	221·25
IE	183·25	189·25			

South Africa

Channel	Frequency (MHz) Vision	Sound	Channel	Frequency (MHz) Vision	Sound
4	175·25	181·25	9	215·25	221·25
5	183·25	189·25	10	223·25	229·25
6	191·25	197·25	11	231·25	237·25
7	199·25	205·25	13	247·43	253·43
8	207·25	213·25			

Australia

Channel	Frequency (MHz) Vision	Sound	Channel	Frequency (MHz) Vision	Sound
0	46·25	51·75	6	175·25	180·75
1	57·25	62·75	7	182·25	187·75
2	64·25	69·75	8	189·25	194·75
3	86·25	91·75	9	196·25	201·75
4	95·25	100·75	10	209·25	214·75
5	102·25	107·75	11	216·25	221·75
5A	138·25	143·75			

New Zealand

Channel	Frequency (MHz) Vision	Sound	Channel	Frequency (MHz) Vision	Sound
1	45·25	50·75	6	189·25	194·75
2	55·25	60·75	7	196·25	201·75
3	62·25	67·75	8	203·25	208·75
4	175·25	180·75	9	210·25	215·75
5	182·25	187·75			

USA

Channel	Frequency (MHz) Vision	Sound	Channel	Frequency (MHz) Vision	Sound
2	55·25	59·75	43	645·25	649·75
3	61·25	65·75	44	651·25	655·75
4	67·25	71·75	45	657·25	661·75
5	77·25	81·75	46	663·25	667·75
6	83·25	87·75	47	669·25	673·75
7	175·25	179·75	48	675·25	679·75
8	181·25	185·75	49	681·25	685·75

Channel	Frequency (MHz) Vision	Sound	Channel	Frequency (MHz) Vision	Sound
9	187·25	191·75	50	687·25	691·75
10	193·25	197·75	51	693·25	697·75
11	199·25	203·75	52	699·25	703·75
12	205·25	209·75	53	705·25	709·75
13	211·25	215·75	54	711·25	715·75
14	471·25	475·75	55	717·25	721·75
15	477·25	481·75	56	723·25	727·75
16	483·25	487·75	57	729·25	733·75
17	489·25	493·75	58	735·25	739·75
18	495·25	499·75	59	741·25	745·75
19	501·25	505·75	60	747·25	751·75
20	507·25	511·75	61	753·25	757·75
21	513·25	517·75	62	759·25	763·75
22	519·25	523·75	63	765·25	769·75
23	525·25	529·75	64	771·25	775·75
24	531·25	535·7	65	777·25	781·75
25	537·25	541·75	66	783·25	787·75
26	543·25	547·75	67	789·25	793·75
27	549·25	553·75	68	795·25	799·75
28	555·25	559·75	69	801·25	805·75
29	561·25	565·75	70	807·25	811·75
30	567·25	571·75	71	813·25	817·75
31	573·25	577·75	72	819·25	823·75
32	579·25	583·75	73	825·25	829·75
33	585·25	589·75	74	831·25	835·75
34	591·25	595·75	75	837·25	841·75
35	597·25	601·75	76	843·25	847·75
36	603·25	607·75	77	849·25	853·75
37	609·25	613·75	78	855·25	859·75
38	615·25	619·75	79	861·25	865·75
39	621·25	625·75	80	867·25	871·75
40	627·25	631·75	81	873·25	877·75
41	633·25	637·75	82	879·25	883·75
42	639·25	643·75	83	885·25	889·75

Aerial dimensions

Channel	Dimensions in cm A	B	C	D	E	F	G	H
UHF Groups								
A	30·1	30	24·1	23	22·8	21·1	20·4	19·9
B	26·5	21·7	18·9	18	17·8	16·5	16	15·5
C	23·2	18·2	16	15·3	15	14	13·3	12·2
D	26·1	23·5	18·4	16	15·5	14·8	13·8	13
E	27	26·5	21·1	18·6	17·9	17·6	16	15·8

Terrestrial TV aerial dimensions

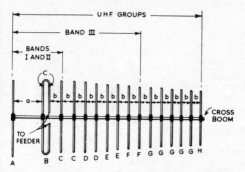

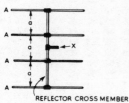

Pattern of general-purpose Yagi array to be used in conjunction with the dimensions given below.

a	b	c		Channels covered in the uhf groups are:		
			Group letter	Colour code	Channels	
10·3	10·3	1·8	A	Red	21–34
8·9	8·9	1·8	B	Yellow	39–51
7·5	7·5	1·8	C	Green	50–66
7·6	7·6	1·8	D	Blue	49–68
15·8	15·8	1·8	E	Brown	39–68

UK UHF television channels and transmitters

	ITV	Channel 4	BBC 1	BBC 2	Polarisation	Max vision erp(kW)
East of England						
Tacolneston	59	65	62	55	H	250
West Runton	23	29	33	26	V	2
Aldeburgh	23	30	33	26	V	10
Thetford	23	29	33	26	V	0·02
Little Walsingham	41	47	51	44	V	0·011
Creake	49	42	39	45	V	0·005
Wells next the sea	50	—	43	—	V	0·09
Burnham	46	—	40	—	V	0·077
Norwich (Central)	49	42	39	45	V	0·034
Bury St. Edmunds	25	32	22	28	V	0·017
Linnet Valley	23	29	33	26	V	0·016
Sudbury	41	47	51	44	H	250
Woodbridge	61	54	58	64	V	0·1
Ipswich (Stoke)	25	32	22	28	V	0·007
Wivenhoe Park	61	54	58	64	V	0·011
Felixstowe	60	67	31	63	V	0·0055
Overstrand	41	47	51	44	V	0·063
Sandy Heath	24	21	31	27	H	1000
Northampton (Dall. Park)	56	68	66	62	V	0·065
Luton	59	65	55	62	V	0·08
Kings Lynn	52	—	48	—	V	0·34
The Borders and Isle of Man						
Caldbeck	28	32	30	34	H	500
Kendal	61	54	58	64	V	2
Windermere	41	47	51	44	V	0·5
Coniston	24	31	21	27	V	0·09
Hawkshead	23	29	33	26	V	0·061
Whitehaven	43	50	40	46	V	2
Keswick	24	31	21	27	V	0·12
Threlkeld	60	53	57	63	V	0·011
Ainstable	42	49	52	45	V	0·1
Haltwhistle	59	65	55	62	V	2
Gosforth	61	54	58	64	V	0·05
Bassenthwaite	49	42	52	45	V	0·16
Pooley Bridge	46	50	48	40	V	0·013
Moffat	42	49	52	45	V	0·0065
Douglas	48	56	68	66	V	2
Beary Peark	43	50	40	46	V	0·25
Port St. Mary	61	54	58	64	V	0·25
Laxey	61	54	58	64	V	0·025
Langholm	60	53	57	63	V	0·025
Thornhill	60	53	57	63	V	0·5
Barskeoch Hill	59	65	55	62	V	2
New Galloway	23	29	33	26	V	0·1
Stranraer	60	53	57	63	V	0·25
Portpatrick	61	54	58	64	V	0·006

	ITV	Channel 4	BBC 1	BBC 2	Polarisation	Max vision erp (kW)
Cambret Hill	41	47	44	51	H	16
Creetown	61	54	58	64	V	0·032
Kirkcudbright	24	31	21	27	V	0·006
Glenluce	61	54	58	64	V	0·015
St. Bees	61	54	58	64	V	0·012
Workington	61	54	58	64	V	0·01
Bleachgreen	60	53	57	63	V	0·006
Dumfries South	46	50	40	48	V	0·023
Dentdale	60	53	57	63	V	0·052
Union Mills	52	42	39	45	V	0·012
Lowther Valley	46	50	48	40	V	0·026
Pinwherry	25	32	22	28	V	0·056
Ballantrae	61	54	58	64	V	0·0066
Lorton	60	53	57	63	V	0·05
Greystoke	60	53	57	63	V	0·011
Kirkby Stephen	60	53	57	63	V	0·012
Ravenstonedale	60	53	57	63	V	0·011
Orton	43	50	40	46	V	0·031
Sedbergh	43	50	40	46	V	0·5
Grasmere	60	53	57	63	V	0·02
Crosby Ravensworth	60	53	57	63	V	0·006
Crosthwaite	60	53	57	63	V	0·012
Minnigaff	29	23	33	26	V	0·008
Selkirk	59	65	55	62	H	50
Eyemouth	23	29	33	26	V	2
Galashiels	41	47	51	44	V	0·1
Hawick	23	29	33	26	V	0·05
Jedburgh	41	47	51	44	V	0·16
Bonchester Bridge	49	42	39	45	V	0·006
Lauder	25	32	22	28	V	0·011
Peebles	25	32	22	28	V	0·1
Innerleithen	61	54	58	64	V	0·1
Berwick-upon-Tweed	24	31	21	27	V	0·038
Stow	23	29	33	26	V	0·005
Yetholm	41	47	51	44	V	0·006

Midlands (West)

	ITV	Channel 4	BBC 1	BBC 2	Polarisation	Max vision erp (kW)
Sutton Coldfield	43	50	46	40	H	1000
Kinver	56	68	66	48	H	0·012
Kidderminster	61	54	58	64	V	2
Brierley Hill	60	53	57	63	V	10
Bromsgrove	24	21	31	27	V	4
Malvern	66	68	56	62	V	2
Lark Stoke	23	29	33	26	V	7·6
Leek	25	32	22	28	V	1
Fenton	24	21	31	27	V	10
Hartington	56	68	66	48	V	0·033
Over Norton	55	67	65	48	V	0·031
Bretch Hill	55	67	65	48	V	0·087
Icomb Hill	25	32	22	28	V	0·11
Leamington Spa	66	68	56	62	V	0·2
Allesley Park	25	32	22	28	V	0·033

	ITV	Channel 4	BBC 1	BBC 2	Polarisation	Max vision erp(kW)
Cheadle	56	68	48	66	V	0·024
Tenbury Wells	60	53	57	63	V	0·014
Redditch	25	32	22	28	V	0·0016
Ironbridge	61	54	58	64	V	0·011
Guiting Power	41	47	51	44	V	0·012
Ipstones Edge	60	53	57	63	V	0·028
Whittingslow	60	53	57	63	V	0·056
Oakamoor	24	31	21	27	V	0·011
Turves Green	62	68	56	66	V	0·012
Brailes	34	59	30	52	V	0·04
Woodford Halse	25	32	22	28	V	0·007
Winshill	56	68	66	48	H	0·006
Winchcombe	61	54	58	64	V	0·006
Oxford	60	53	57	63	H	500
Charlbury	41	47	51	44	V	0·0033
Ascott-under-Wychwood	24	31	21	27	V	0·029
The Wrekin	23	29	26	33	H	100
Clun	59	65	55	62	V	0·056
Ridge Hill	25	32	22	28	H	100
Kington	49	42	39	45	V	0·025
Garth Hill	60	53	57	63	V	0·025
Ludlow	42	49	39	45	V	0·025
Hazler Hill	41	47	51	44	V	0·025
Oakeley Mynd	49	42	39	45	V	0·05
St. Briavels	43	50	40	46	V	0·012
Peterchurch	60	53	57	63	V	0·076
Andoversford	59	65	55	62	V	0·056
New Radnor	41	47	51	44	V	0·125
Hope-under-Dinmore	60	53	63	57	V	0·0018
Upper Soudley	43	50	40	46	V	0·0017
Eardiston	61	54	58	64	V	0·006

Midlands (East)

	ITV	Channel 4	BBC 1	BBC 2	Polarisation	Max vision erp(kW)
Waltham	61	54	58	64	H	250
Ashbourne	25	32	22	28	V	0·25
Ambergate	25	32	22	28	V	0·03
Nottingham	24	31	21	27	V	2
Belper	68	62	66	56	V	0·03
Eastwood	23	29	33	26	V	0·0072
Stamford	49	42	39	45	V	0·0032
Parwich	24	31	21	27	V	0·0031
Stanton Moor	59	65	55	62	V	2
Bolehill	53	60	63	57	V	0·25
Matlock	24	31	21	27	V	0·017
Ashford-in-the-Water	23	29	33	26	V	0·011
Birchover	49	42	39	45	H	0·012

Channel Islands

	ITV	Channel 4	BBC 1	BBC 2	Polarisation	Max vision erp(kW)
Fremont Point	41	47	51	44	H	20
St. Helier	59	65	55	62	V	0·034
Les Touillets	54	52	56	48	H	2
Alderney	61	68	58	64	V	0·1

	ITV	Channel 4	BBC 1	BBC 2	Polarisation	Max vision erp(kW)
St. Peter Port	24	31	21	27	V	0·0014
Torteval	46	66	50	40	V	0·02
Gorey	23	29	54	26	V	0·006
Lancashire						
Winter Hill	59	65	55	62	H	500
Darwen	49	42	39	45	V	0·5
Pendle Forest	25	32	22	28	V	0·5
Haslingden	23	29	33	26	V	8
Elton	24	31	21	27	V	0·063
Saddleworth	49	42	52	45	V	0·5
Storeton	25	32	22	28	V	2·8
Bacup	43	53	40	46	V	0·25
Ladder Hill	23	29	33	26	V	1
Bidston	30	47	51	44	V	0·066
Birch Vale	43	53	40	46	V	0·25
Whitworth	25	32	22	28	V	0·05
Glossop	25	32	22	28	V	1
Buxton	24	31	21	27	V	1
Trawden	60	67	57	63	V	0·2
Whalley	43	53	40	46	V	0·05
Littleborough	24	31	21	27	V	0·5
North Oldham	24	31	21	27	V	0·04
Macclesfield	25	32	22	28	V	0·037
Congleton	41	47	51	44	V	0·2
Oakenhead	41	47	51	44	V	0·1
Whitewell	60	67	57	63	V	0·08
Delph	23	29	33	26	V	0·003
Lancaster	24	21	31	27	V	10
Blackburn	41	47	51	44	V	0·008
Millom Park	25	32	22	28	V	0·25
Ramsbottom	56	68	48	66	V	0·08
Dalton	43	53	40	46	V	0·025
Over Biddulph	30	48	34	67	V	0·022
Haughton Green	43	53	40	46	H	0·007
Parbold	41	47	51	44	V	0·036
Chinley	61	67	57	64	V	0·012
Dog Hill	43	53	40	46	V	0·085
Romiley	41	47	51	44	V	0·011
Bollington	24	31	21	27	V	0·021
Langley	24	31	21	27	V	0·0045
Ribblesdale	41	47	51	44	V	0·03
Backbarrow	60	50	57	63	V	0·003
West Kirby	24	31	34	27	V	0·013
Brook Bottom	61	68	58	64	V	0·006
Staveley-in-Cartmel	43	53	40	46	V	0·01
Penny Bridge	23	29	33	26	V	0·031
Cartmel	25	32	22	28	H	0·0022
Urswick	41	47	51	44	V	0·0058
Melling	60	53	57	63	V	0·025
Austwick	49	42	39	45	V	0·032
Chatburn	23	29	33	26	V	0·007

	ITV	Channel 4	BBC 1	BBC 2	Polarisation	Max vision erp(kW)
Woodnook	49	52	39	45	V	0·003
Middleton	30	48	67	34	V	0·006
Wardle	25	32	22	28	H	0·003
Norden	30	57	34	67	V	0·009
Brinscall	24	31	27	21	V	0·0008
Newchurch	24	31	27	21	H	0·004

North-east Scotland

	ITV	Channel 4	BBC 1	BBC 2	Polarisation	Max vision erp(kW)
Durris	25	32	22	28	H	500
Peterhead	59	65	55	62	V	0·1
Gartly Moor	61	54	58	64	V	2·2
Rosehearty	41	47	51	44	V	2
Balgownie	43	50	40	46	V	0·04
Tullich	59	65	55	62	V	0·07
Braemar	42	49	39	45	V	0·015
Tomintoul	43	50	40	46	V	0·0065
Banff	42	49	39	45	V	0·028
Ellon	49	42	39	45	V	0·0027
Brechin	43	50	40	46	V	0·0065
Boddam	42	49	39	45	V	0·006
Angus	60	53	57	63	H	100
Perth	49	42	39	45	V	1
Crieff	23	29	33	26	V	0·1
Cupar	41	47	51	44	V	0·02
Pitlochry	25	32	22	28	V	0·15
Kenmore	23	29	33	26	V	0·12
Blair Atholl	43	50	40	46	V	0·05
Tay Bridge	41	47	51	44	V	0·5
Killin	49	42	39	45	V	0·13
Auchtermuchty	49	42	39	45	V	0·05
Camperdown	23	29	33	26	V	0·002
Strathallan	49	42	39	45	V	0·029
Methven	25	32	22	28	V	0·006
Dunkeld	41	47	51	44	V	0·1
Balmullo	49	42	39	45	V	0·05
Balnaguard	39	45	42	49	V	0·01
Grandtully	61	54	58	64	V	0·008
Keelylang Hill (Orkney)	43	50	40	46	H	100
Pierowall	23	29	33	26	V	0·0072
Bressay	25	32	22	28	V	10
Fitful Head	49	42	39	45	V	0·094
Scalloway	59	65	55	62	V	0·029
Swinister	59	65	55	62	V	0·21
Baltasound	42	49	39	45	V	0·018
Fetlar	43	50	40	46	V	0·013
Collafirth Hill	41	47	51	44	V	0·41
Weisdale	61	54	58	64	V	0·06
Burgar Hill	24	31	21	27	V	0·0055
Rumster Forest	24	21	31	27	H	100
Ben Tongue	49	42	39	45	V	0·04
Thurso	60	53	57	63	V	0·0027

	ITV	Channel 4	BBC 1	BBC 2	Polarisation	Max vision erp(kW)
Melvich	41	47	51	44	V	0·055
Durness	53	60	57	63	V	0·007
Knock More	23	29	33	26	H	100
Grantown	41	47	51	44	V	0·35
Kingussie	43	50	40	46	V	0·091
Craigellachie	60	53	57	63	V	0·07
Balblair Wood	59	65	55	62	V	0·083
Lairg	41	47	51	44	V	0·013
Avoch	53	60	63	57	V	0·004
Eitshal (Lewis)	23	29	33	26	H	100
Scoval	59	65	55	62	V	0·16
Clettraval	41	47	51	44	V	2
Daliburgh (South Uist)	60	53	57	63	V	0·03
Skriaig	24	31	21	27	V	1
Penifiler	49	42	39	45	V	0·04
Duncraig	41	47	51	44	V	0·16
Attadale	25	32	22	28	V	0·0088
Badachro	43	50	40	46	V	0·035
Ness of Lewis	41	47	51	44	V	0·032
Ullapool	49	52	39	45	V	0·078
Kilbride (South Uist)	49	42	39	45	V	0·13
Uig	43	50	53	46	V	0·0033
Ardintoul	49	42	39	45	V	0·047
Tarbert (Harris)	49	52	39	45	V	0·047
Bruernish	43	50	40	46	V	0·0069
Poolewe	47	41	51	44	V	0·02
Lochinver	43	50	40	46	V	0·008
Rosemarkie	49	42	39	45	H	100
Auchmore Wood	25	32	22	28	V	0·1
Fort Augustus	23	29	33	26	V	0·011
Fodderty	60	53	57	63	V	0·12
Wester Erchite	24	31	21	27	V	0·016
Glen Urquhart	41	47	51	44	V	0·09
Tomatin	25	32	22	28	V	0·012
Inverness	65	59	55	62	V	0·05
Tomich	24	31	21	27	V	0·014

Wales

	ITV	Channel 4	BBC 1	BBC 2	Polarisation	Max vision erp(kW)
Wenvoe	41	47	44	51	H	500
Kilvey Hill	23	29	33	26	V	10
Rhondda	23	29	33	26	V	2·5
Mynydd Machen	23	29	33	26	V	2
Maesteg	25	32	22	28	V	0·25
Pontypridd	25	32	22	28	V	0·5
Aberdare	24	31	21	27	V	0·5
Merthyr Tydfil	25	32	22	28	V	0·13
Bargoed	24	31	21	27	V	0·3
Rhymney	60	53	57	63	V	0·15
Clydach	23	29	33	26	V	0·0035
Abertillery	25	32	22	28	V	0·28
Ebbw Vale	59	65	55	62	V	0·5

	ITV	Channel 4	BBC 1	BBC 2	Polarisation	Max vision erp(kW)
Blaina	43	50	40	46	V	0·1
Pontypool	24	31	21	27	V	0·25
Cilfrew	49	52	39	45	V	0·015
Blaenavon	60	53	57	63	V	0·15
Abergavenny	49	42	39	45	V	1
Ferndale	60	53	57	63	V	0·08
Porth	43	50	40	46	V	0·08
Wattsville	60	53	63	57	V	0·0052
Llangeinor	59	65	55	62	V	0·19
Treharris	52	68	56	48	V	0·05
Cwmafon	24	31	21	27	V	0·07
Llyswen	24	31	21	27	V	0·03
Llanhilleth	49	42	39	45	V	0·03
Gilfach Goch	24	31	21	27	V	0·05
Taff's Well	59	65	55	62	V	0·052
Ogmore Vale	60	53	57	63	V	0·1
Abertridwr	60	53	57	63	V	0·05
Ynys Owen	59	65	55	62	V	0·08
Tonypandy	59	65	55	62	V	0·02
Fernhill	59	65	62	55	V	0·0031
Mynydd Bach	61	54	58	64	V	0·25
Bedlinog	24	31	21	27	V	0·01
Machen Upper	62	68	55	65	V	0·009
Cwm Ffrwd-Oer	43	50	39	46	V	0·003
Blaenau-Gwent	60	53	57	63	V	0·0028
Pennar	43	50	40	46	V	0·1
Brecon	61	54	58	64	V	1
Sennybridge	43	50	40	46	V	0·064
Clyro	41	47	51	44	V	0·16
Crickhowell	24	31	21	27	V	0·15
Blackmill	25	32	22	28	V	0·01
Pennorth	23	29	33	26	V	0·05
Pontardawe	61	68	58	64	V	0·13
Deri	25	32	22	28	V	0·05
Cwmaman	49	42	39	45	V	0·0014
Ton Pentre	61	54	58	64	V	0·08
Trecastle	25	32	22	28	V	0·00
Monmouth	59	65	55	62	V	0·05
Cwmfelinfach	48	42	52	45	V	0·006
Llanfoist	60	53	57	63	V	0·018
Abercynon	58	54	64	66	H	0·0062
Tynewydd	59	65	55	62	V	0·02
Craig-Cefn-Parc	43	50	46	40	V	0·0063
Briton Ferry	43	50	46	40	V	0·02
Dowlais	61	54	58	64	V	0·013
Rhondda Fach	25	32	22	28	V	0·0015
Trefechan (Merthyr)	42	49	39	45	V	0·005
Crucorney	24	31	21	27	V	0·011
Tonyrefail	59	65	55	62	V	0·02
Efail Fach	49	52	39	45	V	0·0084
Llanharan	24	31	21	27	V	0·0017
Burry Port	61	54	58	64	V	0·0031
Rhondda 'B'	49	68	66	39	H	0·005

	ITV	Channel 4	BBC 1	BBC 2	Polarisation	Max vision erp(kW)
Gelli-Fendigaid	59	65	55	62	H	0·012
South Maesteg	59	65	55	62	V	0·0059
Upper Killay	24	31	21	27	V	0·004
Llanddona	60	53	57	63	H	100
Betws-y-Coed	24	31	21	27	V	0·5
Penmaen Rhos	25	32	22	28	H	0·141
Conway	43	50	40	46	V	2
Bethesda	60	53	57	63	V	0·025
Deiniolen	25	32	22	28	V	0·05
Arfon	41	47	51	44	V	3·6
Llandecwyn	61	54	58	64	V	0·3
Ffestiniog	25	32	22	28	V	1·2
Waunfawr	25	32	22	28	V	0·026
Amlwch	25	32	22	28	V	0·035
Cemaes	43	50	40	46	V	0·012
Mochdre	23	29	33	26	V	0·0017
Dolwyddelan	41	47	51	44	V	0·011
Llanengan	61	54	58	64	H	0·003
Coed Derw	41	47	51	44	V	0·025
Carmel	60	53	57	63	H	100
Llanelli	49	67	39	45	V	0·1
Ystalyfera	49	42	39	45	V	0·05
Llandrindod Wells	49	42	39	45	V	2·25
Rhayader	23	29	33	26	V	0·1
Llanwrtyd Wells	24	31	21	27	V	0·01
Builth Wells	25	32	22	28	V	0·026
Tenby	49	42	39	45	V	0·032
Cwmgors	24	31	21	27	V	0·026
Abercraf	25	32	22	28	V	0·13
Mynydd Emroch	43	50	40	46	V	0·09
Greenhill	24	31	21	27	V	0·074
Penderyn	49	42	39	45	V	0·012
Talley	49	42	39	45	V	0·0065
Llansawel	32	25	22	28	V	0·0065
Presely	43	50	46	40	H	100
Mynydd Pencarreg	61	54	58	64	V	0·12
Tregaron	56	66	62	68	V	0·015
Llandyfriog	25	32	22	28	V	0·11
St. Dogmaels	23	29	33	26	V	0·015
Trefin	25	32	22	28	V	0·056
Abergwynfi	24	31	21	27	V	0·003
Glyncorrwg	49	42	39	45	V	0·0007
Llwyn Onn	25	32	22	28	V	0·05
Dolgellau	59	65	55	62	V	0·03
Croeserw	61	54	58	64	V	0·12
Pencader	23	29	33	26	V	0·006
Llandysul	60	53	57	63	V	0·05
Broad Haven	61	54	58	64	V	0·006
Rheola	59	65	55	62	V	0·1
Newport Bay	60	67	57	63	V	0·013
Ferryside	24	31	21	27	V	0·007
Llangybi	25	32	22	28	V	0·012
Duffryn	25	32	22	28	V	0·004

	ITV	Channel 4	BBC 1	BBC 2	Polarisation	Max vision erp(kW)
Blaen-Plwyf	24	21	31	27	H	100
Machynlleth	60	53	57	63	V	0·02
Aberystwyth	61	54	58	64	V	0·023
Fishguard	61	54	58	64	V	0·056
Long Mountain	61	54	58	64	V	1
Llandinam	41	47	44	51	V	0·25
Llanidloes	25	32	22	28	V	0·005
Llanfyllin	25	32	22	28	V	0·13
Moel-y-Sant	24	31	34	27	V	0·11
Kerry	24	31	21	27	V	0·017
Carno	24	31	21	27	V	0·011
Dolybont	61	54	58	64	V	0·032
Llanbrynmair	25	32	22	28	V	0·02
Afon Dyfi	25	32	22	28	V	0·0063
Llangurig	23	29	33	26	V	0·008
Trefilan	60	53	57	63	V	0·086
Llanrhaeadr-ym-Mochnant	49	42	39	45	V	0·077
Bow Street	41	47	51	44	V	0·02
Ynys-Pennal	41	47	51	44	V	0·02
Llangadfan	25	32	22	28	V	0·0063
Tregynon	25	32	22	28	V	0·035
Corris	49	42	39	45	V	0·006
Llangynog	65	59	55	62	V	0·006
Broneirion	29	23	33	26	V	0·007
Moel-y-Parc	49	42	52	45	H	100
Llangollen	60	53	57	63	V	0·015
Glyn Ceiriog	61	54	58	64	V	0·007
Bala	23	29	33	26	V	0·2
Corwen	25	32	22	28	V	0·3
Pontfadog	25	32	22	28	V	0·0064
Cerrigydrudion	23	29	33	26	V	0·032
Wrexham-Rhos	—	67	39	—	V	0·2
Llanuwchllyn	43	50	40	46	V	0·03
Cefn-Mawr	41	47	51	44	V	0·034
Llanarmon-yn-ial	24	31	21	27	V	0·006
Llangernyw	32	25	22	28	V	0·007
Betws-yn-Rhos	24	31	21	27	V	0·013
Glyndyfrdwy	59	65	55	62	V	0·0056
Llandderfel	65	59	55	62	V	0·0065
Llanddulas	23	29	33	26	H	0·012
Pwll-Glas	23	29	33	26	V	0·007
Pen-y-Banc	24	31	21	27	V	0·004
West of England						
Mendip	61	54	58	64	H	500
Crockerton	41	47	51	44	V	0·077
Bath	25	32	22	28	V	0·25
Westwood	43	50	40	46	V	0·1
Avening	41	47	51	44	V	0·0056
Calne	24	31	21	27	V	0·05
Redcliff Bay	34	67	30	56	H	0·011

	ITV	Channel 4	BBC 1	BBC 2	Polarisation	Max vision erp(kW)
Bristol KWH	42	52	45	48	V	1
Bristol IC	43	50	40	46	V	0·5
Washford	39	68	49	66	V	0·062
Easter Compton	34	67	30	56	V	0·01
West Lavington	24	31	21	27	V	0·012
Seagry Court (Swindon)	41	47	44	51	V	0·0025
Coleford	45	39	42	52	V	0·01
Monksilver	52	42	45	48	V	0·015
Ogbourne St. George	43	50	40	46	V	0·013
Wootton Courtenay	25	32	22	28	V	0·056
Stroud	42	52	48	45	V	0·5
Cirencester	23	29	33	26	V	0·25
Nailsworth	23	29	33	26	V	0·031
Chalford	24	31	21	27	V	0·13
Roadwater	24	31	21	27	H	0·012
Marlborough	25	32	22	28	V	0·1
Upavon	23	29	33	26	V	0·07
Porlock	42	52	48	45	V	0·025
Countisbury	49	67	39	56	H	0·11
Cerne Abbas	25	32	22	28	V	0·11
Hutton	39	68	49	66	V	0·14
Bristol (Montpelier)	23	29	33	26	V	0·01
Box	43	50	40	46	V	0·0068
Dursley (Uley)	43	50	40	46	V	0·055
Slad	23	29	33	26	H	0·0028
Frome	24	31	21	27	V	0·0018
Bristol (Barton House)	24	31	21	27	H	0·011
Bruton	43	50	40	46	V	0·0015
Kewstoke	34	67	30	56	V	0·012
Burrington	59	65	55	62	H	0·103
Ubley	24	31	21	27	V	0·079
Portishead	49	68	66	39	V	0·007
Backwell	25	32	22	28	V	0·094
Tintern	24	31	21	27	V	0·006
Chiseldon	34	67	30	49	V	0·02
Chepstow	24	31	21	27	V	0·0031
Blakeney	24	31	21	27	V	0·007
Lydbrook	43	50	40	46	V	0·0075
Parkend	41	47	51	44	V	0·0017
Clearwell	68	56	66	48	V	0·01
Woodcombe	24	31	21	27	V	0·0063
Exford	41	47	51	44	V	0·008
Kilve	39	68	49	66	H	0·008
Crewkerne	43	50	40	46	V	0·0016
Carhampton	30	56	34	67	V	0·008
London						
Crystal Palace	23	30	26	33	H	1000
Guildford	43	50	40	46	V	10
Hertford	61	54	58	64	V	2
Reigate	60	53	57	64	V	10
Hemel Hempstead	41	47	51	44	V	10

	ITV	Channel 4	BBC 1	BBC 2	Polarisation	Max vision erp(kW)
Woolwich	60	67	57	63	V	0·63
High Wycombe	59	65	55	62	V	0·5
Wooburn	56	68	49	52	V	0·1
Henley-on-Thames	67	54	48	64	V	0·1
Bishops Stortford	59	49	55	62	V	0·029
Chesham	43	50	40	46	V	0·1
Welwyn	43	50	40	46	V	0·15
Gt. Missenden	61	54	58	64	V	0·085
Mickleham	58	68	61	55	V	0·09
Kenley	43	50	40	46	V	0·14
Chepping Wycombe	41	47	51	44	V	0·02
Hughenden	43	50	40	46	V	0·06
Forest Row	62	66	48	54	V	0·12
Chingford	52	48	56	50	V	0·0075
Hemel Hempstead (Town)	61	54	58	64	V	0·013
Walthamstow North	49	68	45	66	V	0·0017
Marlow Bottom	61	54	58	64	V	0·011
Cane Hill	58	68	61	54	V	0·018
New Addington	54	68	64	48	V	0·017
West Wycombe	43	67	40	46	V	0·028
Otford	60	53	57	63	V	0·031
Lea Bridge	39	59	55	62	V	0·006
Micklefield	57	67	54	64	V	0·0062
Alexandra Palace	61	54	58	64	H	0·065
Dorking	41	47	51	44	H	0·04
Caterham	59	65	55	62	V	0·035
East Grinstead	46	59	40	56	V	0·117
Biggin Hill	49	67	45	52	V	0·008
Croydon (Old Town)	52	67	49	56	V	0·033
Skirmett	41	47	51	44	V	0·13
St. Albans	57	67	49	63	V	0·022
Gravesend	59	49	55	62	V	0·011
Wonersh	52	67	48	65	V	0·025
New Barnet	59	48	55	62	V	0·007
Hammersmith	59	65	48	62	V	0·01
Central Scotland						
Black Hill	43	50	40	46	H	500
Kilmacolm	24	31	21	27	V	0·032
South Knapdale	60	53	57	63	V	1·45
Biggar	25	32	22	28	V	0·5
Abington	60	53	57	63	H	0·0051
Glasgow WC	56	66	68	62	V	0·032
Killearn	59	55	65	62	V	0·5
Callander	25	32	22	28	V	0·1
Cathcart	60	53	57	63	V	0·002
Torosay	25	32	22	28	V	20
Cow Hill	43	50	40	46	V	0·065
Netherton Braes	25	32	22	28	V	0·005
Gigha Island	41	47	51	44	V	0·06
Tarbert (Loch Fyne)	24	31	21	27	V	0·0036
Glengorm	48	54	56	52	V	1·1

	ITV	Channel 4	BBC 1	BBC 2	Polarisation	Max vision erp(kW)
Mallaig	40	50	43	46	V	0·018
Ballachulish	23	29	33	26	V	0·018
Haddington	61	54	58	64	V	0·02
Kinlochleven	59	65	55	62	V	0·012
Onich	61	54	58	64	V	0·017
Strachur	23	29	33	26	V	0·035
Spean Bridge	24	31	21	27	V	0·07
Oban	41	47	51	44	V	0·012
Bellanoch	42	49	39	45	V	0·05
Castlebay	24	31	21	27	V	0·0066
Dalmally	41	47	51	44	V	0·041
Dollar	61	54	58	64	V	0·01
Ravenscraig	24	31	21	27	V	0·02
Kirkfieldbank	60	53	57	63	V	0·0058
Tillicoultry	60	53	57	63	V	0·005
Fintry	24	31	34	27	V	0·019
Fiunary	43	50	40	46	V	0·05
Twechar	25	32	22	28	V	0·007
Strathblane	24	31	21	27	V	0·0071
Broughton	24	31	21	27	V	0·007
Leadhills	61	54	58	64	V	0·003
Glespin	61	54	58	64	V	0·006
Cumbernauld Village	61	54	58	64	V	0·008
Kelvindale	30	48	34	52	V	0·002
Strontian	39	45	42	49	V	0·014
Craigkelly	24	21	31	27	H	100
Penicuik	61	54	58	64	V	2
West Linton	23	29	33	26	V	0·025
Aberfoyle	61	54	58	64	V	0·087
Darvel	23	29	33	26	H	100
Muirkirk	41	47	51	44	V	0·1
Kirkconnel	61	54	58	64	V	0·25
West Kilbride	41	47	51	44	V	0·35
Lethanhill	60	53	57	63	V	0·25
Girvan	59	65	55	62	V	0·25
Campbeltown	60	53	57	63	V	0·13
Port Ellen	25	32	22	28	V	0·09
Bowmore	49	42	39	45	V	0·08
Millburn Muir	42	49	39	52	V	0·25
Rosneath	61	54	58	64	V	10
Rosneath	61	54	58	64	H	0·05
Millport	61	54	58	64	H	0·0027
Troon	61	54	58	64	V	0·02
Rothesay	25	32	22	28	V	2
Tighnabruaich	49	42	39	45	V	0·092
Lochwinnoch	60	53	57	63	H	0·086
New Cumnock	43	50	40	46	V	0·012
Rothesay Town	59	65	55	62	V	0·0054
Claonaig	59	65	55	62	V	0·074
Carradale	41	47	51	44	V	0·029
Ardentinny	49	52	39	45	V	0·07
Arrochar	24	31	21	27	V	0·006

	ITV	Channel 4	BBC 1	BBC 2	Polarisation	Max vision erp(kW)
Ardnadam	41	47	51	44	V	0·017
Garelochhead	41	47	51	44	V	0·012
Wanlockhead	47	41	51	44	V	0·002
Kirkoswald	25	32	22	28	V	0·032
Kirkmichael	49	52	39	45	V	0·019
Dunure	43	50	40	46	V	0·012
Holmhead	41	47	51	44	V	0·012
Largs	42	49	39	45	H	0·012
Sorn	43	50	40	46	V	0·0065
South of England						
Rowridge	27	21	31	24	H	500
Salisbury	60	53	57	63	V	10
Till Valley	43	50	46	40	V	0·075
Ventnor	49	42	39	45	V	2
Poole	60	53	57	63	V	0·1
Brighton	60	53	57	63	V	10
Shrewton	41	47	51	44	V	0·0045
Findon	41	47	51	44	V	0·05
Patcham	43	50	46	40	H	0·069
Winterborne Stickland	43	50	40	46	V	1
Corfe Castle	41	47	51	44	V	0·014
Portslade	41	47	51	44	V	0·019
Westbourne	41	47	51	44	V	0·038
Ovingdean	44	68	65	42	V	0·019
Saltdean	55	47	51	66	V	0·014
Donhead	41	47	51	44	V	0·029
Millbrook	41	47	51	44	V	0·035
Brighstone	41	47	51	44	V	0·14
Hangleton	49	42	39	45	V	0·0068
Lulworth	59	65	55	62	V	0·011
Piddletrenthide	49	42	39	45	V	0·056
Winterbourne Steepleton	45	66	39	49	V	0·012
Cheselbourne	53	60	57	63	V	0·0065
Brading	41	47	51	44	V	0·004
Luscombe Valley	49	42	39	45	V	0·008
Midhurst	58	68	61	55	H	100
Haslemere	25	32	22	28	V	0·015
Hannington	42	66	39	45	H	250
Tidworth	32	25	22	28	V	0·01
Chisbury	59	52	55	62	V	0·025
Sutton Row	25	32	22	28	V	0·25
Alton	59	52	49	62	V	0·01
Hemdean (Caversham)	56	59	49	52	V	0·022
Aldbourne	24	31	21	27	V	0·007
Lambourn	59	52	55	62	V	0·007
Luccombe (IOW)	59	34	56	62	V	0·025
Dover	66	53	50	56	H	100
Dover Town	23	30	33	26	V	0·1
Hythe	24	31	21	27	V	0·051
Chartham	24	31	21	27	V	0·1
Faversham	25	32	22	28	V	0·013

	ITV	Channel 4	BBC 1	BBC 2	Polarisation	Max vision erp(kW)
Rye	41	47	58	44	V	0·012
Newnham	24	31	21	27	V	0·035
Lyminge	25	32	22	28	V	0·0069
Horn Street	41	47	58	44	V	0·003
Elham	23	30	33	26	V	0·0035
Heathfield	64	67	49	52	H	100
Tunbridge Wells	41	47	51	44	V	10
St. Marks	60	53	57	63	V	0·051
Newhaven	43	41	39	45	V	2
Hastings	28	32	22	25	V	1
Eastbourne	23	30	33	26	V	0·125
Haywards Heath	43	41	39	45	V	0·037
Wye (Ashford)	25	32	22	28	V	0·031
East Dean	54	42	62	44	V	0·008
Hamstreet	23	30	33	26	V	0·0007
Lamberhurst	62	58	54	60	V	0·003
Mountfield	24	31	21	27	V	0·0035
Sedelscombe	23	30	33	26	V	0·007
Steyning	62	56	45	59	V	0·14
Bluebell Hill	43	65	40	46	H	30
Chatham Town	61	54	58	68	V	0·011
North-east England						
Pontop Pike	61	54	58	64	H	500
Newton	23	29	33	26	V	2
Fenham	24	31	21	27	V	2
Weardale	41	47	44	51	V	1
Alston	49	42	52	45	V	0·4
Catton Beacon	43	50	40	46	V	0·14
Morpeth	25	32	22	28	V	0·044
Bellingham	24	31	21	27	V	0·05
Humshaugh	49	42	39	45	V	0·059
Haydon Bridge	41	47	51	44	V	0·1
Shotley Field	25	32	22	28	V	0·2
Durham	43	50	40	46	V	0·015
Ireshopeburn	59	65	55	62	V	0·011
Hedleyhope	43	50	40	46	H	0·018
Seaham	41	47	51	44	V	0·059
Sunderland	43	50	40	46	V	0·013
Staithes	41	47	51	44	V	0·0017
Esh	49	42	39	45	V	0·012
Falstone	41	47	51	44	V	0·0063
Wall	43	50	40	46	H	0·025
Whitaside	41	47	51	44	V	0·015
Bilsdale	29	23	33	26	H	500
Whitby	59	65	55	62	V	0·25
Bainbridge	60	53	57	63	V	0·031
Grinton Lodge	43	50	40	46	V	0·025
Guisborough	60	53	57	63	V	0·05
Ravenscar	61	54	58	64	V	0·2
Limber Hill	43	50	40	46	V	0·05
Skinningrove	43	50	40	46	V	0·014

	ITV	Channel 4	BBC 1	BBC 2	Polarisation	Max vision erp(kW)
Romaldkirk	41	47	51	44	V	0·058
West Burton	43	50	40	46	V	0·013
Aislaby	52	49	39	45	V	0·04
Rosedale Abbey	43	50	40	46	V	0·007
Peterlee (Horden)	49	39	45	52	V	0·002
Eston Nab	43	50	40	46	V	0·02
Chatton	49	42	39	45	H	100
Rothbury	65	59	55	62	V	0·05
Northern Ireland						
Divis	24	21	31	27	H	500
Larne	49	42	39	45	V	0·5
Carnmoney Hill	43	50	40	46	V	0·1
Kilkeel	49	42	39	45	V	0·5
Newcastle	59	65	55	62	V	1
Armagh	49	42	39	45	V	0·12
Black Mountain	49	42	39	45	V	0·025
Whitehead	52	67	48	56	V	0·012
Bellair	52	67	48	56	V	0·04
Draperstown	49	42	39	45	V	0·0118
Moneymore	49	42	39	45	V	0·0067
Newry North	41	47	51	44	V	0·01
Rostrevor Forest	46	50	48	40	V	0·058
Newry South	49	42	39	45	V	0·02
Benagh	25	32	22	28	V	0·056
Cushendun	32	25	22	28	V	0·026
Cushendall	43	50	40	46	V	0·013
Glynn	61	54	58	64	V	0·0014
Newtownards	61	54	58	64	V	0·011
Banbridge	46	50	44	48	V	0·0061
Glenariff	61	54	58	64	V	0·011
Killowen Mountain	24	21	31	27	V	0·015
Bangor	59	65	62	55	V	0·003
Dromore	61	54	58	64	V	0·004
Limavady	59	65	55	62	H	100
Londonderry	41	47	51	44	V	10
Ballycastle Forest	49	42	39	45	V	0·012
Bushmills	41	47	51	44	V	0·0065
Strabane	49	42	39	45	V	2
Claudy	60	53	57	63	V	0·029
Gortnalee	24	31	21	27	V	0·032
Castlederg	65	59	55	62	V	0·011
Plumbridge	56	68	52	66	V	0·0125
Glenelly Valley	23	29	33	26	V	0·012
Ballintoy	49	42	39	45	V	0·0017
Buckna	41	47	51	44	V	0·013
Gortnageeragh	42	49	39	45	V	0·019
Muldonagh	32	25	22	28	V	0·012
Brougher Mountain	25	32	22	28	H	100
Belcoo	41	47	51	44	V	0·087
Derrygonnelly	47	66	51	44	V	0·006
Lisbellaw	59	65	55	62	V	0·0065
Ederny	62	55	65	59	V	0·06

	ITV	Channel 4	BBC 1	BBC 2	Polarisation	Max vision erp(kW)
South-west England						
Caradon Hill	25	32	22	28	H	500
St. Austell	59	65	55	62	V	0·1
Looe	43	50	40	46	V	0·005
Hartland	52	66	48	56	V	0·029
Gunnislake	43	50	40	46	V	0·04
Plympton (Plymouth)	61	54	58	64	V	2
Downderry	59	65	55	62	V	0·026
Tavistock	60	53	57	63	V	0·1
Woolacombe	42	49	39	45	V	0·006
Penaligon Downs	49	42	39	45	V	0·1
Newton Ferrers	59	65	55	62	V	0·0065
Ilfracombe	61	54	58	64	V	0·25
Combe Martin	49	42	39	45	V	0·1
Okehampton	49	42	39	45	V	0·1
Ivybridge	42	49	39	45	V	0·5
Kingsbridge	43	50	40	46	V	0·2
Penryn	59	65	55	62	V	0·022
Plymouth (North Road)	43	50	40	46	V	0·012
Slapton	55	68	48	66	V	0·125
Truro	61	54	58	64	V	0·022
Croyde	41	47	51	44	V	0·0015
Chambercombe	24	31	21	27	V	0·007
Salcombe	44	30	51	41	V	0·017
Polperro	60	53	57	63	V	0·0028
Mevagissey	43	50	40	46	H	0·0066
Lostwithiel	43	50	40	46	V	0·0063
Aveton Gifford	66	47	51	44	V	0·0015
Berrynarbor	25	32	22	28	V	0·008
Port Isaac	65	59	55	62	V	0·002
Stockland Hill	23	29	33	26	H	250
St. Thomas (Exeter)	41	47	51	44	V	0·25
Beer	59	65	55	62	V	0·0029
Tiverton	43	50	40	46	V	0·1
Bampton	45	52	39	49	V	0·03
Culm Valley	49	42	39	45	V	0·058
Bridport	41	47	51	44	V	0·1
Beaminster	59	65	55	62	V	0·02
Weymouth	43	50	40	46	V	2
Dawlish	59	65	55	62	V	0·0066
Stokeinteignhead	41	47	51	44	V	0·0063
Dunsford	39	49	45	67	V	0·006
Crediton	43	50	40	46	V	0·04
Beacon Hill	60	53	57	63	H	100
Dartmouth	41	47	51	44	V	0·01
Ashburton	24	31	21	27	V	0·003
Teignmouth	45	67	39	49	V	0·025
Coombe	24	31	21	27	V	0·0065
Newton Abbot	43	50	40	46	V	0·003
Buckfastleigh	41	47	51	44	V	0·0062
Totnes	24	31	21	27	V	0·0034
Harbertonford	49	42	39	45	H	0·0018
Sidmouth	45	67	39	49	V	0·012

	ITV	Channel 4	BBC 1	BBC 2	Polarisation	Max vision erp(kW)
Occombe Valley	24	31	21	27	V	0·0008
Torquay Town	41	47	51	44	V	0·04
Hele	43	50	40	46	H	0·006
Edginswell	45	67	39	49	V	0·004
Huntshaw Cross	59	65	55	62	H	100
Swimbridge	23	29	33	26	V	0·0066
Westward Ho	24	31	21	27	V	0·032
Chagford	24	31	21	27	V	0·012
Brushford	24	31	21	27	V	0·02
North Bovey	43	50	40	46	V	0·034
Redruth	41	47	51	44	H	100
Isles of Scilly	24	31	21	27	V	0·5
St. Just	61	54	58	64	V	0·25
Helston	61	54	58	64	V	0·01
Bossiney	61	54	58	64	V	0·0074
Boscastle	23	29	33	26	V	0·0056
Portreath	23	29	33	26	V	0·0016
Praa Sands	59	65	55	62	V	0·01
Porthleven	23	29	33	26	H	0·0016
St. Anthony-in-Roseland	23	29	33	26	V	0·0017
Gulval	23	29	33	26	V	0·26

Yorkshire

	ITV	Channel 4	BBC 1	BBC 2	Polarisation	Max vision erp(kW)
Emley Moor	47	41	44	51	H	1000
Wharfedale	25	32	22	28	V	2
Sheffield	24	21	31	27	V	5
Skipton	49	42	39	45	V	10
Chesterfield	23	29	33	26	V	2
Halifax	24	31	21	27	V	0·5
Keighley	61	54	58	64	V	10
Shatton Edge	48	54	52	58	V	1
Hebden Bridge	25	32	22	28	V	0·25
Ripponden	61	54	58	64	V	0·06
Cop Hill	25	32	22	28	V	1
Idle	24	31	21	27	V	0·25
Headingley	61	54	58	64	H	0·011
Beecroft Hill	59	65	55	62	V	1

	ITV	Channel 4	BBC 1	BBC 2	Polarisation	Max vision erp(kW)
Oxenhope	25	32	22	28	V	0·2
Calver Peak	49	42	39	45	V	0·25
Tideswell Moor	60	66	56	63	V	0·25
Hope	25	32	22	28	V	0·012
Addingham	43	50	40	46	V	0·025
Luddenden	60	67	57	63	V	0·059
Dronfield	59	65	55	62	H	0·003
Hasland	60	53	57	63	V	0·0065
Edale	60	53	57	63	V	0·004
Totley Rise	49	42	39	45	V	0·012
Cullingworth	49	68	66	39	H	0·013
Skipton Town	24	31	21	27	V	0·013
Batley	60	67	57	63	V	0·013
Heyshaw	60	53	57	63	V	0·5
Primrose Hill	60	67	57	63	V	0·028
Armitage Bridge	61	54	58	64	V	0·0065
Wincobank	59	65	55	62	V	0·0015
Holmfirth	56	68	49	66	V	0·026
Hagg Wood	59	65	55	62	V	0·033
Keighley Town	23	29	33	26	V	0·006
Sutton-in-Craven	23	29	33	26	V	0·012
Cragg Vale	61	54	58	64	V	0·025
Stocksbridge	61	54	58	64	V	0·012
Oughtibridge	59	65	55	62	V	0·02
Holmfield	59	65	55	62	V	0·022
Grassington	23	29	33	26	V	0·06
Cornholme	61	54	58	64	V	0·042
Walsden	60	67	57	63	V	0·05
Todmorden	49	42	39	45	V	0·5
Walsden South	43	53	40	46	V	0·006
Copley	59	65	55	62	V	0·0014
Kettlewell	39	45	49	42	V	0·08
Conisbrough	60	53	57	63	V	0·006
Oliver's Mount	60	53	57	63	V	1
Hunmanby	43	50	40	46	V	0·06
Bradford West	49	67	57	63	V	0·0125
Brockwell	68	49	66	39	V	0·0063
Belmont	25	32	22	28	H	500
Weaverthorpe	59	65	55	62	V	0·045

Direct broadcast by satellite (DBS) television

European allocations of satellite positions, channels and polarisations

Band	Orbital position			
	37°W	31°W	19°W	5°E
11.7–12.1 GHz RH polarised	San Marino: CH. 1, 5, 9, 13, 17 Lichtenstein: CH. 3, 7, 11, 15, 19	Eire: CH. 2, 6, 10, 14, 18 UK: CH. 4, 8, 12, 16, 20	France: CH. 1, 5, 9, 13, 17 Luxembourg: CH. 3, 7, 11, 15, 19	Turkey: CH. 1, 5, 9, 13, 17 Greece: CH. 3, 7, 11, 15, 19
11.7–12.1 GHz LH polarised	Andorra: CH. 4, 8, 12, 16, 20	Portugal: CH. 3, 7, 11, 15, 19	West Germany: CH. 2, 6, 10, 14, 18 Austria: CH. 4, 8, 12, 16, 20	Finland: CH. 2, 6, 10 Norway: CH. 14, 18 Sweden: CH. 4, 8 Denmark: CH. 12, 16, 20
12.1–12.5 GHz RH polarised	Monaco: CH. 21, 25, 29, 33, 37 Vatican: CH. 23, 27, 31, 35, 39		Belgium: CH. 21, 25, 29, 33, 37 Netherlands: CH. 23, 27, 31, 35, 39	Cyprus: CH. 21, 25, 29, 33, 37 Iceland, etc.: CH. 23, 27, 31, 35, 39
12.1–12.5 GHz LH polarised		Iceland: CH. 21, 25, 29, 33, 37 Spain: CH. 23, 27, 31, 35, 39	Switzerland: CH. 22, 26, 30, 34, 38 Italy: CH. 24, 28, 32, 36, 40	Nordic group*: CH. 22, 24, 26, 28, 30, 32, 36, 40 Sweden: CH. 34 Norway: CH. 38

* Wide beam channels: Denmark, Finland, Norway, Sweden.

World allocations of DBS satellite positions

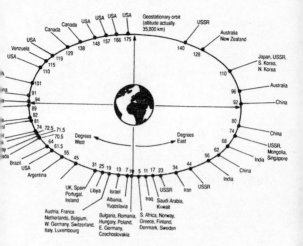

Proposed satellite television formats

Most current European satellite television programmes (non-DBS)
are broadcast as fairly standard PAL signals, FM modulated into
the satellite channel. DBS transmissions, and those from Astra
satellite, will probably be of a multiplexed analogue component
(MAC) format. In MAC, data corresponding to sound tracks and
subtitles etc., an analogue signal corresponding to chrominance and
an analogue signal corresponding to luminance are transmitted
separately in each broadcast line of the picture.

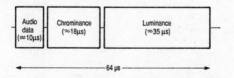

In order to achieve multiplexing of the three parts of the format,
time compression of chrominance and luminance signals occurs
before transmission, and they must be reconstituted at the receiver.
Two main variations of the MAC format have been selected for
European broadcasters, D-MAC and D2-MAC. They differ basically
in the number of data channels, and hence the overall bandwidth
required. Both modulate video signals in FM, and data signals in
duobinary FM.

	D-MAC	D2-MAC
Video	Video signal is identical in both formats	
Data rate—Horizontal interval	20·25 Mbit s^{-1}	10·125 Mbit s^{-1}
Packets per second	4100	2050
Audio channels:		
mono	6 × 15 kHz	4 × 15 kHz
stereo	3 × 15 kHz	2 × 15 kHz
other options	2 × 15 kHz with 4 Commentary channels	1 × 15 kHz with 4 Commentary channels

DBS television channels

Channel number	Frequency (GHz)	Channel number	Frequency (GHz)
1	11·72748	21	12·11108
2	11·74666	22	12·13026
3	11·76584	23	12·14944
4	11·78502	24	12·16862
5	11·80420	25	12·18780
6	11·82338	26	12·20698
7	11·84256	27	12·22616
8	11·86174	28	12·24534
9	11·88092	29	12·26452
10	11·90010	30	12·28370
11	11·91928	31	12·30288
12	11·93846	32	12·32206
13	11·95764	33	12·34124
14	11·97682	34	12·36042
15	11·99600	35	12·37960
16	12·01518	36	12·39878
17	12·03436	37	12·41796
18	12·05354	38	12·43714
19	12·07272	39	12·45632
20	12·09190	40	12·47550

Non-DBS satellite television

Positions of the main non-DBS satellites relevant to the UK

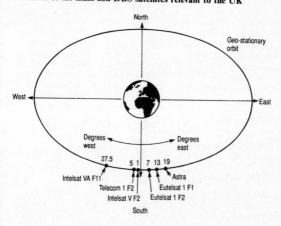

European satellite television channels broadcast via communications satellites*

Channel	Frequency (GHz)	Polarisation	Audio sub-carrier	Video standard	Satellite
3Sat	11·175	H	6·65	PAL	Eutelsat 1 F1
Anglovision	11·515	V	6·6	PAL	Intelsat VA-F11
Arts Channel	11·135	H	6·6	PAL	Intelsat VA-F11
BBC1/2	11·175	H	6·65	PAL	Intelsat VA-F11
CanalJ	12·564	V	5·8	PAL	Telecom 1 F2
Children's Channel	11·015	H	6·6	PAL	Intelsat VA-F11
CNN	11·155	V	6·65	PAL	Intelsat VA-F11
Filmnet	11·140	V	6·6	PAL	Eutelsat 1 F1
Moscow 1	3·675	—	7·0	SECAM	Gorizont-12
Moscow 2	3·	—	7·0	SECAM	Gorizont-7
Infofilm & Video	11·015	H	6·6	PAL	Intelsat F2
La Cinq	12·606	V	5·8	SECAM	Telecom 1 F2
Lifestyle	11·135	H	6·6	PAL	Intelsat VA-F11
M6	12·648	V	5·8	SECAM	Telecom 1 F2
MTV	10·975	H	6·65	PAL	Intelsat VA-F11

Channel	Frequency (GHz)	Polarisation	Audio subcarrier	Video standard	Satellite
Norsk Rikskringkasti	11·644	H	Digital	C-MAC	Eutelsat 1 F2
Premiere	11·015	H	6·6	PAL	Intelsat VA-F11
RAI-Uno	11·007	H	6·6	PAL	Eutelsat 1 F1
RTL-Plus	11·091	V	6·65	PAL	Eutelsat 1 F1
SAT1	11·507	V	6·65	PAL	Eutelsat 1 F1
Satellite Information	11·575	H	Digital	B-MAC	Intelsat VA-F11
Screensport	11·135	H	6·6	PAL	Intelsat VA-F11
Skychannel	11·650	H	6·65	PAL	Eutelsat 1 F1
Superchannel	10·674	V	6·65	PAL	Eutelsat 1 F1
SVT-2	11·178	H	Digital	C-MAC	Intelsat F2
SVT-2	11·133	H	Digital	C-MAC	Intelsat F2
Teleclub	11·987	V	6·5	PAL	Eutelsat 1 F1
TV5	11·472	H	6·65	PAL	Eutelsat 1 F1
Worldnet	11·512	H	6·65	PAL	Eutelsat 1 F1
Worldnet	11·591	H	6·6	SECAM	Eutelsat 1 F2
Worldnet	12·732	V	5·8	NTSC	Telecom 1 F2

*At the time of writing Astra had not been launched, and programme/channel plans were not finalised.

Multifrequency tones

Some push button telephones signal to the local exchange by generating a combination of two frequencies. Each row and each column of the push button keypad is connected to an oscillator of set frequency. When any push button is pressed, tones corresponding to its row and column frequencies are therefore generated. The row and column oscillator frequencies are as shown below:

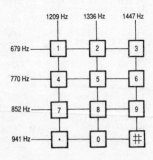

Standard PSTN tones

Tone	UK Frequency	UK Sequence	USA Frequency	USA Sequence
Number unobtainable	400 Hz	Continuous	500 + 600 Hz	Interrupted every second
Number busy	400 Hz	0·75 s on, 0·75 s off	480 + 620 Hz	Interrupted once per second
System busy	400 Hz	0·4 s on, 0·35 s off, 0·225 s on, 0·525 s off	480 + 620 Hz	Interrupted twice per second
Dial tone	50 Hz 33·3 Hz		350 + 440 Hz	
Ringing tone	400 Hz, or 400 + 450 Hz, modulated by 17, 25, or 50 Hz	0·4 s on, 0·2 s off, 0·4 s on, 2 s off	440 + 480 Hz	Interrupted once per second
Pay tone	400 Hz	0·125 s on, 0·125 s off		
Time tones	900 Hz	0·15 s on, 0·85 s off, Three times every three minutes		
Recorder warning			1400 Hz	One burst, every 15 s

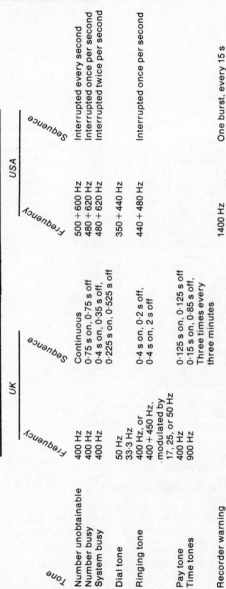

Telephone country codes – alphabetical

Country or province	Code
Algeria	213
Andorra	33 078
Anguilla	1 809 4972
Antigua	1 809 46
Antilles (Netherlands)	599
Argentina	54
Austria	43
Australia	61
Bahamas	1 809
Bahrain	973
Barbados	1 809 42
Belgium	32
Bequia	1 809 45
Bermuda	1 809 29
Botswana	267
Brazil	55
British Virgin Islands	1 809 49
Brunei	673
Burma	95
Cameroon	237
Canada	1
Cayman Islands	1 809 94
Chile	56
Costa Rica	506
Cuba	53
Cyprus	357
Czechoslovakia	42
Denmark	45
Dominica	1 809 499
Dominican Republic	1 809
Egypt	20
El Salvador	503
Ethiopia	251
Faroe Islands	45 42
Fiji	679
Finland	358
France	33
French Polynesia	689
Gambia, The	220
German Democratic Republic	37
Germany	49
Gibraltar	350
Greece	30
Grenada	1 809 444
Guatemala	502
Guyana	592
Honduras	504
Hong Kong	852
Hungary	36

Country or province	Code
Iceland	354
India	91
Indonesia	62
Iran	98
Iraq	964
Israel	972
Italy	39
Ivory Coast	225
Jamaica	1 809
Japan	81
Kenya	254
Kuwait	965
Lebanon	961
Lesotho	266
Libya	218
Liechtenstein	41 75
Luxembourg	352
Macao	853
Malawi	265
Malaysia	60
Malta	356
Mauritius	230
Mexico	52
Monaco	33 93
Montserrat	1 809 491
Morocco	212
Namibia	264
Nauru Island	674
Netherlands	31
New Zealand	64
New Caledonia	687
Nicaragua	505
Nigeria	234
Norway	47
Oman	968
Pakistan	92
Panama	507
Papua New Guinea	675
Philippines	63
Poland	48
Portugal	351
Qatar	974
Romania	40
San Marino	39 541
Saudi Arabia	966
Seychelles	248
Sierra Leone	232
Singapore	65
South Africa	27
Spain	34
Sri Lanka	94
St Kitts and Nevis	1 809 469
St Lucia	1 809 45

Country or province	Code
St Vincent	1 809 45
Swaziland	268
Sweden	46
Switzerland	41
Taiwan	886
Tanzania	255
Thailand	66
Tonga	676
Trinidad and Tobago	1 809
Tunisia	216
Turkey	90
Turks and Caicos Islands	1 809 946
Uganda	256
UK	44
United Arab Emirates	971
Uruguay	598
USA	1
USSR	7
Vatican City State	39 66982
Venezuela	58
Yemen Arab Republic	967
Yugoslavia	38
Zambia	260

Telephone country codes – numerical

Code	Country or province
1	Canada
1	USA
1 809	Bahamas
1 809	Trinidad and Tobago
1 809	Jamaica
1 809	Dominican Republic
1 809 29	Bermuda
1 809 42	Barbados
1 809 444	Grenada
1 809 45	St Lucia
1 809 45	St Vincent
1 809 45	Bequia
1 809 46	Antigua
1 809 469	St Kitts and Nevis
1 809 49	British Virgin Islands
1 809 491	Montserrat
1 809 4972	Anguilla
1 809 499	Dominica

Code	Country or province
1 809 94	Cayman Islands
1 809 946	Turks and Caicos Islands
20	Egypt
212	Morocco
213	Algeria
216	Tunisia
218	Libya
220	Gambia, The
225	Ivory Coast
230	Mauritius
232	Sierra Leone
234	Nigeria
237	Cameroon
248	Seychelles
251	Ethiopia
254	Kenya
255	Tanzania
256	Uganda
260	Zambia
264	Namibia
265	Malawi
266	Lesotho
267	Botswana
268	Swaziland
27	South Africa
30	Greece
31	Netherlands
32	Belgium
33	France
33 078	Andorra
33 93	Monaco
34	Spain
350	Gibraltar
351	Portugal
352	Luxembourg
354	Iceland
356	Malta
357	Cyprus
358	Finland
36	Hungary
37	German Democratic Republic
38	Yugoslavia
39	Italy
39 541	San Marino
39 66982	Vatican City State
40	Romania
41	Switzerland
41 75	Liechtenstein
42	Czechoslovakia
43	Austria
44	UK
45	Denmark
45 42	Faroe Islands

Code	Country or province
46	Sweden
47	Norway
48	Poland
49	Germany
502	Guatemala
503	El Salvador
504	Honduras
505	Nicaragua
506	Costa Rica
507	Panama
52	Mexico
53	Cuba
54	Argentina
55	Brazil
56	Chile
58	Venezuela
592	Guyana
598	Uruguay
599	Antilles (Netherlands)
60	Malaysia
61	Australia
62	Indonesia
63	Philippines
64	New Zealand
65	Singapore
66	Thailand
673	Brunei
674	Nauru Island
675	Papua New Guinea
676	Tonga
679	Fiji
687	New Caledonia
689	French Polynesia
7	USSR
81	Japan
852	Hong Kong
853	Macao
886	Taiwan
90	Turkey
91	India
92	Pakistan
94	Sri Lanka
95	Burma
961	Lebanon
964	Iraq
965	Kuwait
966	Saudi Arabia
967	Yemen Arab Republic
968	Oman
971	United Arab Emirates
972	Israel
973	Bahrain
974	Qatar
98	Iran

North American area codes – alphabetical

State or province	Code
Alabama	
All points	205
Alaska	
All points	907
Arizona	
All points	602
Arkansas	
All points	501
California	
Bakersfield	805
Fresno	209
Los Angeles	213
Sacramento	916
San Diego	714
San Francisco	415
San Jose	408
Santa Rosa	707
Colorado	
All points	303
Connecticut	
All points	203
Delaware	
All points	302
District of Columbia	
All points	202
Florida	
Jacksonville	904
Miami	305
Orlando	305
St Petersburg	813
Tallahassee	904
Tampa	813
Georgia	
Atlanta	404
Savannah	912
Hawaii	
All points	808
Idaho	
All points	208
Illinois	
Centralia	618
Chicago	312
Peoria	309
Rockford	815
Springfield	217
Indiana	
Evansville	612
Indianapolis	317
Sound Bend	219

State or province	Code
Iowa	
Cedar Rapids	319
Council Bluffs	712
Des Moines	515
Kansas	
Topeka	913
Wichita	316
Kentucky	
Ashland	606
Frankfort	502
Louisville	502
Louisiana	
Baton Rouge	504
New Orleans	504
Shreveport	318
Maine	
All points	207
Maryland	
All points	301
Massachusetts	
Boston	617
Falmouth	617
Lowell	617
Springfield	413
Worcester	617
Michigan	
Detroit	313
Escanaba	906
Grand Rapids	616
Lansing	517
Minnesota	
Duluth	218
Minneapolis	612
Rochester	507
Mississippi	
All points	601
Missouri	
Jefferson City	314
Kansas City	816
St Louis	314
Springfield	417
Montana	
All points	406
Nebraska	
Lincoln	402
North Platte	308
Omaha	402
Nevada	
All points	702
New Hampshire	
All points	603
New Jersey	
Atlantic City	609

State or province	Code
Camden	609
Newark	201
Paterson	201
Trenton	609
New Mexico	
All points	505
New York	
Albany	518
Binghampton	607
Buffalo	716
Elmira	607
Garden City	516
Greenport (Col Co.)	518
Hampstead	516
Ithaca	607
Mt Vernon	914
Newburgh	914
New York City	212
Nyack	914
Poughkeepsie	914
Riverhead	516
Rochester	716
Saratoga Springs	518
Syracuse	315
Utica	315
White Plains	914
North Carolina	
Asheville	704
Charlotte	704
Fayetteville	919
Raleigh	919
Winston-Salem	919
North Dakota	
All points	701
Ohio	
Akron	216
Cincinnati	513
Cleveland	216
Columbus	614
Dayton	513
Toledo	419
Youngstown	216
Oklahoma	
Oklahoma City	405
Tulsa	
Oregon	
All points	503
Pennsylvania	
Allentown (Lehigh Co.)	215
Altoona	814
Easton	215
Erie	814
Harrisburg	717

State or province	Code
Johnstown	814
Lancaster	717
Morrisville (Bucks Co.)	215
New Hope	215
Philadelphia	215
Pittsburgh	412
Reading	215
Scranton	717
Wilkes-Barre	717
Williamsport	215
Yardley	215
York	717
Rhode Island	
All points	401
South Carolina	
All points	803
South Dakota	
All points	605
Tennessee	
Chattanooga	615
Memphis	901
Nashville	615
Texas	
Amarillo	806
Austin	512
Dallas	214
El Paso	915
Fort Worth	817
Houston	713
San Antonio	512
Utah	
All points	801
Vermont	
All points	802
Virginia	
Arlington	703
Charlottesville	804
Norfolk	804
Richmond	804
Roanoke	703
Washington	
Olympia	206
Seattle	206
Spokane	509
West Virginia	
All points	304
Wisconsin	
Madison	608
Milwaukee	414
Superior	715
Wyoming	
All points	307

Canada, Mexico and the Caribbean

Country or province	Code
Bahamas	
All points	809
Canada	
Alberta	403
British Columbia	604
Manitoba	204
New Brunswick	506
Newfoundland	709
Nova Scotia	902
Ontario	
Fort William	807
Ottawa	613
Sault Marie	705
Toronto	416
Windsor	519
Quebec	
Montreal	514
Quebec	418
Trois Rivières	819
Saskatchewan	309
Mexico	
Mexico City	905
Northwest Area	903
Southern Area	905
Puerto Rico	
All points	809
Virgin Islands	
All points	809

North American area codes – numerical

Code	State or province	Area
201	New Jersey	Newark
		Paterson
202	Washington DC	All points
203	Connecticut	All points
204	Manitoba	All points
205	Alabama	All points
206	Washington	Seattle
		Olympia
207	Maine	All points
208	Idaho	All points
209	California	Fresno

Code	State or province	Area
212	New York	New York City
213	California	Los Angeles
214	Texas	Dallas
215	Pennsylvania	Allentown
		Easton
		Morrisville
		New Hope
		Philadelphia
		Reading
		Yardley
216	Ohio	Akron
		Cleveland
		Youngstown
217	Illinois	Springfield
218	Minnesota	Duluth
219	Indiana	South Bend
301	Maryland	All points
302	Delaware	All points
303	Colorado	All points
304	West Virginia	All points
305	Florida	Miami
		Orlando
306	Saskatchewan	All points
307	Wyoming	All points
308	Nebraska	North Platte
309	Illinois	Peoria
312	Illinois	Chicago
313	Michigan	Detroit
314	Missouri	St Louis
		Jefferson City
315	New York	Syracuse Utica
316	Kansas	Wichita
317	Indiana	Indianapolis
318	Louisiana	Shreveport
319	Iowa	Cedar Rapids
401	Rhode Island	All points
402	Nebraska	Lincoln
		Omaha
403	Alberta	All points
404	Georgia	All points
405	Oklahoma	Oklahoma City
406	Montana	All points
408	California	San Jose
412	Pennsylvania	Pittsburgh
413	Massachusetts	Springfield
414	Wisconsin	Milwaukee
415	California	San Francisco
416	Ontario	Toronto
417	Missouri	Springfield
418	Quebec	Quebec
419	Ohio	Toledo
501	Arkansas	All points
502	Kentucky	Louisville
		Frankfort

Code	State or province	Area
503	Oregon	All points
504	Louisiana	Baton Rouge
		New Orleans
505	New Mexico	All points
506	New Brunswick	All points
507	Minnesota	Rochester
509	Washington	Spokane
510	4 Row Twx	USA
512	Texas	Austin
		San Antonio
513	Ohio	Cincinnati
		Dayton
514	Quebec	Montreal
515	Iowa	Des Moines
516	New York	Garden City
		Hampstead
		Riverhead
517	Michigan	Lansing
518	New York	Albany
		Greenport
		Saratoga Springs
519	Ontario	London
		Windsor
601	Mississippi	All points
602	Arizona	All points
603	New Hampshire	All points
604	British Columbia	All points
605	South Dakota	All points
606	Kentucky	Ashland
		Covington
607	New York	Binghamton
		Elmira
		Ithaca
608	Wisconsin	Madison
609	New Jersey	Camden
		Trenton
		Atlantic City
610	4 Row Twx	Canada
612	Minnesota	Minneapolis
613	Ontario	Ottawa
614	Ohio	Columbus
615	Tennessee	Chattanooga.
		Nashville
616	Michigan	Grand Rapids
617	Massachusetts	Boston
		Lowell
		Worcester
		Falmouth
618	Illinois	Centralia
701	North Dakota	All points
702	Nevada	All points
703	Virginia	Arlington
		Roanoke

Code	State or province	Area
704	North Carolina	Charlotte
		Asheville
705	Ontario	North Bay
707	California	Santa Rosa
709	Newfoundland	All points
710	4 Rox Twx	USA
712	Iowa	Council Bluffs
713	Texas	Houston
714	California	San Diego
715	Wisconsin	Superior
716	New York	Rochester
		Buffalo
717	Pennsylvania	Harrisburg
		Lancaster
		Wilkes-Barre
		Scranton
		York
800	Inward Wats	All states
801	Utah	All points
802	Vermont	All points
803	South Carolina	All points
804	Virginia	Charlottesville
		Norfolk
		Richmond
805	California	Bakersfield
806	Texas	Amarillo
807	Ontario	Fort William
808	Hawaii	All points
809	Caribbean	Bahamas
		Puerto Rico
		Virgin Islands
		Bermuda
810	4 Row Twx	USA
812	Indiana	Evansville
813	Florida	Tampa
		St Petersburg
814	Pennsylvania	Altoona
		Erie
		Johnstown
815	Illinois	Rockford
816	Missouri	Kansas City
817	Texas	Fort Worth
819	Quebec	Trois Rivières
901	Tennessee	Memphis
902	Nova Scotia	All points
	Prince Edward Island	All points
903	Mexico	Northwest
904	Florida	Jacksonville
		Tallahassee
905	Mexico	Mexico City
906	Michigan	Escanaba
907	Alaska	All points
910	4 Row Twx	USA
912	Georgia	Savannah

Code	State or province	Area
913	Kansas	Topeka
914	New York	Mount Vernon
		Newburgh
		Nyack
915	Texas	El Paso
		Sweetwater
916	California	Sacramento
918	Oklahoma	Tulsa
919	North Carolina	Raleigh
		Winston-Salem

Conversion factors

To convert from column one to column two *multiply* by the conversion factor.

To convert	Into	Multiply by
acres	square feet	4.356×10^4
acres	square metres	4047
acres	square yards	4.84×10^3
acres	hectares	0.4047
ampere-hours	coulombs	3600
amperes per sq cm	amperes per sq inch	6.452
ampere-turns	gilberts	1.257
ampere-turns per cm	ampere-turns per inch	2.540
angstroms	nanometres	10^{-1}
ares	square metres	10^2
atmospheres	bars	1.0133
atmospheres	mm of mercury at 0°C	760
atmospheres	feet of water at 4°C	33.90
atmospheres	inches of mercury at 0°C	29.92
atmospheres	kg per sq metre	1.033×10^4
atmospheres	newtons per sq metre	1.0133×10^5
atmospheres	pounds per sq inch	14.70
barns	square metres	10^{-28}
bars	newtons per sq metre	10^5
bars	hectopiezes	1
bars	baryes (dyne per sq cm)	10^6
bars	pascals (newtons per sq metre)	10^5
baryes	newtons per sq metre	10^{-1}
Btu	foot-pounds	778.3
Btu	joules	1054.8
Btu	kilogram-calories	0.2520
Btu	horsepower-hours	3.929×10^{-4}
bushels	cubic feet	1.2445

To convert	Into	Multiply by
calories (I.T.)	joules	4·1868
calories (thermochem)	joules	4·184
carats (metric)	grams	0·2
Celsius (centigrade)	Fahrenheit (see pages 158–159)	
chains (surveyor's)	feet	66
circular mils	square centimetres	$5·067 \times 10^{-6}$
circular mils	square mils	0·7854
cords	cubic metres	3·625
cubic feet	cords	$7·8125 \times 10^{-3}$
cubic feet	litres	28·32
cubic inches	cubic centimetres	16·39
cubic inches	cubic feet	$5·787 \times 10^{-4}$
cubic inches	cubic metres	$1·639 \times 10^{-5}$
cubic metres	cubic feet	35·31
cubic metres	cubic yards	1·308
degrees (angle)	radians	$1·745 \times 10^{-2}$
dynes	pounds	$2·248 \times 10^{-6}$
dynes	newtons	10^{-5}
electron volts	joules	$1·602 \times 10^{-19}$
ergs	foot-pounds	$7·376 \times 10^{-8}$
ergs	joules	10^{-7}
fathoms	feet	6
fathoms	metres	1·8288
feet	centimetres	30·48
feet	varas	0·3594
feet of water at 4°C	inches of mercury at 0°C	0·8826
feet of water at 4°C	kg per sq metre	304·8
feet of water at 4°C	pounds per sq foot	62·43
fermis	metres	10^{-15}
footcandles	lumens per sq metre	10·764
footlamberts	candelas per sq metre	3·4263
foot-pounds	horsepower-hours	$5·050 \times 10^{-7}$
foot-pounds	kilogram-metres	0·1383
foot-pounds	kilowatt-hours	$3·766 \times 10^{-7}$
gallons (liq US)	gallons (liq Imp)	0·8327
gammas	teslas	10^{-9}
gausses	lines per sq inch	6·452
gausses	teslas	10^{-4}
gilberts	amperes	$7·9577 \times 10^{-1}$
grain (for humidity calculations)	pounds (avoirdupois)	$1·429 \times 10^{-4}$
grams	dynes	980·7
grams	grains	15·43
grams	ounces (avoirdupois)	$3·527 \times 10^{-2}$
grams	poundals	$7·093 \times 10^{-2}$
grams per cm	pounds per inch	$5·600 \times 10^{-3}$
grams per cu cm	pounds per cu inch	$3·613 \times 10^{-2}$
grams per sq cm	pounds per sq foot	2·0481
hectares	square metres	10^{4}
hectares	acres	2·471
horsepower (boiler)	Btu per hour	$3·347 \times 10^{4}$
horsepower (metric) (542·5 ft-lb per second)	Btu per minute	41·83
horsepower (metric) (542·5 ft-lb per second)	foot-lb per minute	$3·255 \times 10^{4}$
horsepower (metric) (542·5 ft-lb per second)	kg-calories per minute	10·54

To convert	Into	Multiply by
horsepower (550 ft-lb per second)	Btu per minute	42.41
horsepower (550 ft-lb per second)	foot-lb per minute	3.3×10^4
horsepower (550 ft-lb per second)	kilowatts	0.745
horsepower (metric) (542.5 ft-lb per second)	horsepower (550 ft-lb per second)	0.9863
horsepower (550 ft-lb per second)	kg-calories per minute	10.69
inches	centimetres	2.540
inches	feet	8.333×10^{-2}
inches	miles	1.578×10^{-5}
inches	mils	1000
inches	yards	2.778×10^{-2}
inches of mercury at 0°C	lbs per sq inch	0.4912
inches of water at 4°C	kg per sq metre	25.40
inches of water at 4°C	ounces per sq inch	0.5782
inches of water at 4°C	pounds per sq foot	5.202
inches of water at 4°C	in of mercury	7.355×10^{-2}
inches per ounce	metres per newton (compliance)	9.136×10^{-2}
joules	foot-pounds	0.7376
joules	ergs	10^7
kilogram-calories	kilogram-metres	426.9
kilogram-calories	kilojoules	4.186
kilogram-metres	joules	0.102
kilogram force	newtons	0.102
kilograms	tons, long (avdp 2240 lb)	9.842×10^{-4}
kilograms	tons, short (avdp 2000 lb)	1.102×10^{-3}
kilograms	pounds (avoirdupois)	2.205
kilograms per kilometre	pounds (avdp) per mile (stat)	3.548
kg per sq metre	pounds per sq foot	0.2048
kilometres	feet	3281
kilopond force	newtons	9.81
kilowatt-hours	Btu	3413
kilowatt-hours	foot-pounds	2.655×10^6
kilowatt-hours	joules	3.6×10^6
kilowatt-hours	kilogram-calories	860
kilowatt-hours	kilogram-metres	3.671×10^5
kilowatt-hours	pounds carbon oxidized	0.235
kilowatt-hours	pounds water evaporated from and at 212°F	3.53
kilowatt-hours	pounds water raised from 62° to 212°F	22.75
kips	newtons	4.448×10^3
knots* (naut mi per hour)	feet per second	1.688
knots	metres per minute	30.87
knots	miles (stat) per hour	1.1508
lamberts	candelas per sq cm	0.3183
lamberts	candelas per sq inch	2.054
lamberts	candelas per sq metre	3.183×10^3
leagues	miles (approximately)	3
links (surveyor's)	chains	0.01
links	inches	7.92

To convert	Into	Multiply by
litres	bushels (dry US)	2.838×10^{-2}
litres	cubic centimetres	1000
litres	cubic metres	0.001
litres	cubic inches	61.02
litres	gallons (liq Imp)	0.2642
litres	pints (liq Imp)	1.816
$\log_e$ or ln	$\log_{10}$	0.4343
lumens per sq foot	foot-candles	1
lux	lumens per sq foot	0.0929
maxwells	webers	10^{-8}
metres	yards	1.094
metres	varas	1.179
metres per min	feet per minute	3.281
metres per min	kilometres per hour	0.06
microhms per cu cm	microhms per inch cube	0.3937
microhms per cu cm	ohms per mil foot	6.015
microns	metres	10^{-6}
miles (nautical)*	feet	6076.1
miles (nautical)	metres	1852
miles (nautical)	miles (statute)	1.1508
miles (statute)	feet	5280
miles (statute)	kilometres	1.609
miles per hour	kilometres per minute	2.682×10^{-2}
miles per hour	feet per minute	88
miles per hour	kilometres per hour	1.609
millibars	inches of mercury (0°C)	0.02953
millibars	pounds per sq foot	2.089
(10^3 dynes per sq cm)		
mils	metres	2.54×10^{-5}
nepers	decibels	8.686
newtons	dynes	10^5
newtons	kilograms	0.1020
newtons	poundals	7.233
newtons	pounds (avoirdupois)	0.2248
oersteds	amperes per metre	7.9577×10
ounce-inches	newton-metres	7.062×10^{-3}
ounces (fluid)	quarts	3.125×10^{-2}
ounces (avoirdupois)	pounds	6.25×10^{-2}
pascals	newtons per sq metre	1
pascals	pounds per sq inch	1.45×10^{-4}
piezes	newtons per sq metre	10^3
piezes	sthenes per sq metre	1
pints	quarts	0.50
poises	newton-seconds per sq metre	10^{-1}
pounds of water (dist)	cubic feet	1.603×10^{-2}
pounds per inch	kg per metre	17.86
pounds per foot	kg per metre	1.488
pounds per mile (statute)	kg per kilometre	0.2818
pounds per cu foot	kg per cu metre	16.02
pounds per cu foot	pounds per cu foot	1728
pounds per sq foot	pounds per sq inch	6.944×10^{-3}
pounds per sq foot	kg per sq metre	4.882
pounds per sq inch	kg per sq metre	703.1
poundals	dynes	1.383×10^4
poundals	pounds (avoirdupois)	3.108×10^{-2}
quarts	gallons	0.25

	Into	Multiply by
	feet	16·5
	pounds (avoirdupois)	32·174
	circular mils	$1·273 \times 10^6$
	sq centimetres	6·452
	sq metres	$9·290 \times 10^{-2}$
sq miles	sq yards	$3·098 \times 10^6$
sq miles	acres	640
sq miles	sq kilometres	2·590
sq millimetres	circular mils	1973
steres	cubic metres	1
stokes	sq metres per second	10^{-4}
(temp rise, °C) × (US gal water)/minute	watts	264
tonnes	kilograms	10^3
tons, short (avoir 2000 lb)	tonnes (1000 kg)	0·9072
tons, long (avoir 2240 lb)	tonnes (1000 kg)	1·016
tons, long (avoir 2240 lb)	tons, short (avoir 2000 lb)	1·120
tons (US shipping)	cubic feet	40
torrs	newtons per sq metre	133·32
watts	Btu per minute	$5·689 \times 10^{-2}$
watts	ergs per second	10^7
watts	foot-lb per minute	44·26
watts	horsepower (550 ft-lb per second)	$1·341 \times 10^{-3}$
watts	horsepower (metric) (542·5 ft-lb per second)	$1·360 \times 10^{-3}$
watts	kg-calories per minute	$1·433 \times 10^{-2}$
watt-seconds (joules)	gram-calories (mean)	0·2389
webers per sq metre	gausses	10^4
yards	feet	3

Fractions of an inch with metric equivalents

Fractions of an inch		Decimals of an inch	mm	Fractions of an inch		Decimals of an inch	mm
	1/64	0·0156	0·397	1/4		0·2500	6·350
1/32		0·0312	0·794		17/64	0·2656	6·747
	3/64	0·0468	1·191	9/32		0·2813	7·144
1/16		0·0625	1·588		19/64	0·2969	7·541
	5/64	0·0781	1·985	5/16		0·3125	7·937
3/32		0·0938	2·381		21/64	0·3281	8·334
	7/64	0·1094	2·778	11/32		0·3438	8·731
1/8		0·1250	3·175		23/64	0·3593	9·128
	9/64	0·1406	3·572	3/8		0·3750	9·525
5/32		0·1563	3·969		25/64	0·3906	9·922
	11/64	0·1719	4·366	13/32		0·4063	10·319
3/16		0·1875	4·762		27/64	0·4219	10·716
	13/64	0·2031	5·159	7/16		0·4375	11·112
7/32		0·2187	5·556		29/64	0·4531	11·509
	15/64	0·2344	5·953	15/32		0·4687	11·906

Fractions of an inch	Decimals of an inch	mm		Fractions of an inch	Decimals of an inch	mm
31/64	0·4844	12·303		3/4	0·7500	19·050
1/2	0·5000	12·700		49/64	0·7656	19·447
33/64	0·5156	13·097		25/32	0·7813	19·843
17/32	0·5313	13·494		51/64	0·7969	20·240
35/64	0·5469	13·891		13/16	0·8125	20·637
9/16	0·5625	14·287		53/64	0·8281	21·034
37/64	0·5781	14·684		27/32	0·8438	21·431
19/32	0·5938	15·081		55/64	0·8594	21·828
39/64	0·6094	15·478		7/8	0·8750	22·225
5/8	0·6250	15·875		57/64	0·8906	22·622
41/64	0·6406	16·272		29/32	0·9062	23·019
21/32	0·6563	16·668		59/64	0·9219	23·416
43/64	0·6719	17·065		15/16	0·9375	23·812
11/16	0·6875	17·462			0·9688	24·606
45/64	0·7031	17·859		31/32		
23/32	0·7188	18·256		61/64	0·9531	24·209
47/64	0·7344	18·653		63/64	0·9844	25·003
					1·000	25·400

Code conversion tables

Dec	Octal	Hex	Binary bit pattern	ASCII character
			7 6 5 4 3 2 1	
0	0	0	0 0 0 0 0 0 0 0	NUL
1	1	1	0 0 0 0 0 0 0 1	SOH
2	2	2	0 0 0 0 0 0 1 0	STX
3	3	3	0 0 0 0 0 0 1 1	ETX
4	4	4	0 0 0 0 0 1 0 0	EOT
5	5	5	0 0 0 0 0 1 0 1	ENQ
6	6	6	0 0 0 0 0 1 1 0	ACK
7	7	7	0 0 0 0 0 1 1 1	BEL
8	10	8	0 0 0 0 1 0 0 0	BS
9	11	9	0 0 0 0 1 0 0 1	HT
10	12	A	0 0 0 0 1 0 1 0	LF
11	13	B	0 0 0 0 1 0 1 1	VT
12	14	C	0 0 0 0 1 1 0 0	FF
13	15	D	0 0 0 0 1 1 0 1	CR
14	16	E	0 0 0 0 1 1 1 0	SO
15	17	F	0 0 0 0 1 1 1 1	SI
16	20	10	0 0 0 1 0 0 0 0	DLE
17	21	11	0 0 0 1 0 0 0 1	DC1
18	22	12	0 0 0 1 0 0 1 0	DC2
19	23	13	0 0 0 1 0 0 1 1	DC3
20	24	14	0 0 0 1 0 1 0 0	DC4

Dec	Octal	Hex	Binary bit pattern							ASCII character
			7	6 5 4	3 2 1					
21	25	15	0 0 1 0 1 0 1							NAK
22	26	16	0 0 1 0 1 1 0							SYN
23	27	17	0 0 1 0 1 1 1							ETB
24	30	18	0 0 1 1 0 0 0							CAN
25	31	19	0 0 1 1 0 0 1							EM
26	32	1A	0 0 1 1 0 1 0							SUB
27	33	1B	0 0 1 1 0 1 1							ESC
28	34	1C	0 0 1 1 1 0 0							FS
29	35	1D	0 0 1 1 1 0 1							GS
30	36	1E	0 0 1 1 1 1 0							RS
31	37	1F	0 0 1 1 1 1 1							US
32	40	20	0 1 0 0 0 0 0							SPACE
33	41	21	0 1 0 0 0 0 1							!
34	42	22	0 1 0 0 0 1 0							"
35	43	23	0 1 0 0 0 1 1							#
36	44	24	0 1 0 0 1 0 0							$
37	45	25	0 1 0 0 1 0 1							%
38	46	26	0 1 0 0 1 1 0							&
39	47	27	0 1 0 0 1 1 1							'
40	50	28	0 1 0 1 0 0 0							(
41	51	29	0 1 0 1 0 0 1							)
42	52	2A	0 1 0 1 0 1 0							*
43	53	2B	0 1 0 1 0 1 1							+
44	54	2C	0 1 0 1 1 0 0							,
45	55	2D	0 1 0 1 1 0 1							—
46	56	2E	0 1 0 1 1 1 0							.
47	57	2F	0 1 0 1 1 1 1							/
48	60	30	0 1 1 0 0 0 0							0
49	61	31	0 1 1 0 0 0 1							1
50	62	32	0 1 1 0 0 1 0							2
51	63	33	0 1 1 0 0 1 1							3
52	64	34	0 1 1 0 1 0 0							4
53	65	35	0 1 1 0 1 0 1							5
54	66	36	0 1 1 0 1 1 0							6
55	67	37	0 1 1 0 1 1 1							7
56	70	38	0 1 1 1 0 0 0							8
57	71	39	0 1 1 1 0 0 1							9
58	72	3A	0 1 1 1 0 1 0							:
59	73	3B	0 1 1 1 0 1 1							;
60	74	3C	0 1 1 1 1 0 0							<
61	75	3D	0 1 1 1 1 0 1							=
62	76	3E	0 1 1 1 1 1 0							>
63	77	3F	0 1 1 1 1 1 1							?
64	100	40	1 0 0 0 0 0 0							@
65	101	41	1 0 0 0 0 0 1							A
66	102	42	1 0 0 0 0 1 0							B
67	103	43	1 0 0 0 0 1 1							C
68	104	44	1 0 0 0 1 0 0							D
69	105	45	1 0 0 0 1 0 1							E
70	106	46	1 0 0 0 1 1 0							F
71	107	47	1 0 0 0 1 1 1							G
72	110	48	1 0 0 1 0 0 0							H
73	111	49	1 0 0 1 0 0 1							I

Dec	Octal	Hex	Binary bit pattern	ASCII character
74	112	4A	1 0 0 1 0 1 0	J
75	113	4B	1 0 0 1 0 1 1	K
76	114	4C	1 0 0 1 1 0 0	L
77	115	4D	1 0 0 1 1 0 1	M
78	116	4E	1 0 0 1 1 1 0	N
79	117	4F	1 0 0 1 1 1 1	O
80	120	50	1 0 1 0 0 0 0	P
81	121	51	1 0 1 0 0 0 1	Q
82	122	52	1 0 1 0 0 1 0	R
83	123	53	1 0 1 0 0 1 1	S
84	124	54	1 0 1 0 1 0 0	T
85	125	55	1 0 1 0 1 0 1	U
86	126	56	1 0 1 0 1 1 0	V
87	127	57	1 0 1 0 1 1 1	W
88	130	58	1 0 1 1 0 0 0	X
89	131	59	1 0 1 1 0 0 1	Y
90	132	5A	1 0 1 1 0 1 0	Z
91	133	5B	1 0 1 1 0 1 1	[
92	134	5C	1 0 1 1 1 0 0	\
93	135	5D	1 0 1 1 1 0 1	]
94	136	5E	1 0 1 1 1 1 0	↑
95	137	5F	1 0 1 1 1 1 1	←
96	140	60	1 1 0 0 0 0 0	—
97	141	61	1 1 0 0 0 0 1	a
98	142	62	1 1 0 0 0 1 0	b
99	143	63	1 1 0 0 0 1 1	c
100	144	64	1 1 0 0 1 0 0	d
101	145	65	1 1 0 0 1 0 1	e
102	146	66	1 1 0 0 1 1 0	f
103	147	67	1 1 0 0 1 1 1	g
104	150	68	1 1 0 1 0 0 0	h
105	151	69	1 1 0 1 0 0 1	i
106	152	6A	1 1 0 1 0 1 0	j
107	153	6B	1 1 0 1 0 1 1	k
108	154	6C	1 1 0 1 1 0 0	l
109	155	6D	1 1 0 1 1 0 1	m
110	156	6E	1 1 0 1 1 1 0	n
111	157	6F	1 1 0 1 1 1 1	o
112	160	70	1 1 1 0 0 0 0	p
113	161	71	1 1 1 0 0 0 1	q
114	162	72	1 1 1 0 0 1 0	r
115	163	73	1 1 1 0 0 1 1	s
116	164	74	1 1 1 0 1 0 0	t
117	165	75	1 1 1 0 1 0 1	u
118	166	76	1 1 1 0 1 1 0	v
119	167	77	1 1 1 0 1 1 1	w
120	170	78	1 1 1 1 0 0 0	x
121	171	79	1 1 1 1 0 0 1	y
122	172	7A	1 1 1 1 0 1 0	z
123	173	7B	0 1 1 1 1 0 1 1	
124	174	7C	0 1 1 1 1 1 0 0	
125	175	7D	0 1 1 1 1 1 0 1	
126	176	7E	0 1 1 1 1 1 1 0	
127	177	7F	0 1 1 1 1 1 1 1	DEL

Dec	Octal	Hex	Binary bit pattern	ASCII character
128	200	80	1 0 0 0 0 0 0 0	
129	201	81	1 0 0 0 0 0 0 1	
130	202	82	1 0 0 0 0 0 1 0	
131	203	83	1 0 0 0 0 0 1 1	
132	204	84	1 0 0 0 0 1 0 0	
133	205	85	1 0 0 0 0 1 0 1	
134	206	86	1 0 0 0 0 1 1 0	
135	207	87	1 0 0 0 0 1 1 1	
136	210	88	1 0 0 0 1 0 0 0	
137	211	89	1 0 0 0 1 0 0 1	
138	212	8A	1 0 0 0 1 0 1 0	
139	213	8B	1 0 0 0 1 0 1 1	
140	214	8C	1 0 0 0 1 1 0 0	
141	215	8D	1 0 0 0 1 1 0 1	
142	216	8E	1 0 0 0 1 1 1 0	
143	217	8F	1 0 0 0 1 1 1 1	
144	220	90	1 0 0 1 0 0 0 0	
145	221	91	1 0 0 1 0 0 0 1	
146	222	92	1 0 0 1 0 0 1 0	
147	223	93	1 0 0 1 0 0 1 1	
148	224	94	1 0 0 1 0 1 0 0	
149	225	95	1 0 0 1 0 1 0 1	
150	226	96	1 0 0 1 0 1 1 0	
151	227	97	1 0 0 1 0 1 1 1	
152	230	98	1 0 0 1 1 0 0 0	
153	231	99	1 0 0 1 1 0 0 1	
154	232	9A	1 0 0 1 1 0 1 0	
155	233	9B	1 0 0 1 1 0 1 1	
156	234	9C	1 0 0 1 1 1 0 0	
157	235	9D	1 0 0 1 1 1 0 1	
158	236	9E	1 0 0 1 1 1 1 0	
159	237	9F	1 0 0 1 1 1 1 1	
160	240	A0	1 0 1 0 0 0 0 0	
161	241	A1	1 0 1 0 0 0 0 1	
162	242	A2	1 0 1 0 0 0 1 0	
163	243	A3	1 0 1 0 0 0 1 1	
164	244	A4	1 0 1 0 0 1 0 0	
165	245	A5	1 0 1 0 0 1 0 1	
166	246	A6	1 0 1 0 0 1 1 0	
167	247	A7	1 0 1 0 0 1 1 1	
168	250	A8	1 0 1 0 1 0 0 0	
169	251	A9	1 0 1 0 1 0 0 1	
170	252	AA	1 0 1 0 1 0 1 0	
171	253	AB	1 0 1 0 1 0 1 1	
172	254	AC	1 0 1 0 1 1 0 0	
173	255	AD	1 0 1 0 1 1 0 1	
174	256	AE	1 0 1 0 1 1 1 0	
175	257	AF	1 0 1 0 1 1 1 1	
176	260	B0	1 0 1 1 0 0 0 0	
177	261	B1	1 0 1 1 0 0 0 1	
178	262	B2	1 0 1 1 0 0 1 0	
179	263	B3	1 0 1 1 0 0 1 1	
180	264	B4	1 0 1 1 0 1 0 0	
181	265	B5	1 0 1 1 0 1 0 1	

Dec	Octal	Hex	Binary bit pattern	ASCII character
182	266	B6	1 0 1 1 0 1 1 0	
183	267	B7	1 0 1 1 0 1 1 1	
184	270	B8	1 0 1 1 1 0 0 0	
185	271	B9	1 0 1 1 1 0 0 1	
186	272	BA	1 0 1 1 1 0 1 0	
187	273	BB	1 0 1 1 1 0 1 1	
188	274	BC	1 0 1 1 1 1 0 0	
189	275	BD	1 0 1 1 1 1 0 1	
190	276	BE	1 0 1 1 1 1 1 0	
191	277	BF	1 0 1 1 1 1 1 1	
192	300	C0	1 1 0 0 0 0 0 0	
193	301	C1	1 1 0 0 0 0 0 1	
194	302	C2	1 1 0 0 0 0 1 0	
195	303	C3	1 1 0 0 0 0 1 1	
196	304	C4	1 1 0 0 0 1 0 0	
197	305	C5	1 1 0 0 0 1 0 1	
198	306	C6	1 1 0 0 0 1 1 0	
199	307	C7	1 1 0 0 0 1 1 1	
200	310	C8	1 1 0 0 1 0 0 0	
201	311	C9	1 1 0 0 1 0 0 1	
202	312	CA	1 1 0 0 1 0 1 0	
203	313	CB	1 1 0 0 1 0 1 1	
204	314	CC	1 1 0 0 1 1 0 0	
205	315	CD	1 1 0 0 1 1 0 1	
206	316	CE	1 1 0 0 1 1 1 0	
207	317	CF	1 1 0 0 1 1 1 1	
208	320	D0	1 1 0 1 0 0 0 0	
209	321	D1	1 1 0 1 0 0 0 1	
210	322	D2	1 1 0 1 0 0 1 0	
211	323	D3	1 1 0 1 0 0 1 1	
212	324	D4	1 1 0 1 0 1 0 0	
213	325	D5	1 1 0 1 0 1 0 1	
214	326	D6	1 1 0 1 0 1 1 0	
215	327	D7	1 1 0 1 0 1 1 1	
216	330	D8	1 1 0 1 1 0 0 0	
217	331	D9	1 1 0 1 1 0 0 1	
218	332	DA	1 1 0 1 1 0 1 0	
219	333	DB	1 1 0 1 1 0 1 1	
220	334	DC	1 1 0 1 1 1 0 0	
221	335	DD	1 1 0 1 1 1 0 1	
222	336	DE	1 1 0 1 1 1 1 0	
223	337	DF	1 1 0 1 1 1 1 1	
224	340	E0	1 1 1 0 0 0 0 0	
225	341	E1	1 1 1 0 0 0 0 1	
226	342	E2	1 1 1 0 0 0 1 0	
227	343	E3	1 1 1 0 0 0 1 1	
228	344	E4	1 1 1 0 0 1 0 0	
229	345	E5	1 1 1 0 0 1 0 1	
230	346	E6	1 1 1 0 0 1 1 0	
231	347	E7	1 1 1 0 0 1 1 1	
232	350	E8	1 1 1 0 1 0 0 0	
233	351	E9	1 1 1 0 1 0 0 1	
234	352	EA	1 1 1 0 1 0 1 0	
235	353	EB	1 1 1 0 1 0 1 1	

Dec	Octal	Hex	Binary bit pattern								ASCII character
236	354	EC	1	1	1	0	1	1	0	0	
237	355	ED	1	1	1	0	1	1	0	1	
238	356	EE	1	1	1	0	1	1	1	0	
239	357	EF	1	1	1	0	1	1	1	1	
240	360	F0	1	1	1	1	0	0	0	0	
241	361	F1	1	1	1	1	0	0	0	1	
242	362	F2	1	1	1	1	0	0	1	0	
243	363	F3	1	1	1	1	0	0	1	1	
244	364	F4	1	1	1	1	0	1	0	0	
245	365	F5	1	1	1	1	0	1	0	1	
246	366	F6	1	1	1	1	0	1	1	0	
247	367	F7	1	1	1	1	0	1	1	1	
248	370	F8	1	1	1	1	1	0	0	0	
249	371	F9	1	1	1	1	1	0	0	1	
250	372	FA	1	1	1	1	1	0	1	0	
251	373	FB	1	1	1	1	1	0	1	1	
252	374	FC	1	1	1	1	1	1	0	0	
253	375	FD	1	1	1	1	1	1	0	1	
254	376	FE	1	1	1	1	1	1	1	0	
255	377	FF	1	1	1	1	1	1	1	1	

ASCII control characters

Decimal	Hexadecimal	ASCII character	Meaning	Keyboard entry
0	00	NUL	Null	CTRL-@
1	01	SOH	Start of heading	CTRL-A
2	02	STX	Start of text	CTRL-B
3	03	ETX	End of text	CTRL-C
4	04	EOT	End of transmission	CTRL-D
5	05	ENQ	Enquiry	CTRL-E
6	06	ACK	Acknowledge	CTRL-F
7	07	BEL	Bell	CTRL-G
8	08	BS	Backspace	CTRL-H
9	09	HT	Horizontal tabulation	CTRL-I
10	0A	LF	Line feed	CTRL-J
11	0B	VT	Vertical tabulation	CTRL-K
12	0C	FF	Form feed	CTRL-L
13	0D	CR	Carriage return	CTRL-M
14	0E	SO	Shift out	CTRL-N
15	0F	SI	Shift in	CTRL-O
16	10	DLE	Data link escape	CTRL-P
17	11	DC1	Device control one	CTRL-Q
18	12	DC2	Device control two	CTRL-R
19	13	DC3	Device control three	CTRL-S

Decimal	Hexadecimal	ASCII character	Meaning	Keyboard entry
20	14	DC4	Device control four	CTRL-T
21	15	NAK	Negative acknowledge	CTRL-U
22	16	SYN	Synchronous idle	CTRL-V
23	17	ETB	End of transmission	CTRL-W
24	18	CAN	Cancel	CTRL-X
25	19	EM	End of medium	CTRL-Y
26	1A	SUB	Substitute	CTRL-Z
27	1B	ESC	Escape	CTRL-[
28	1C	FS	File separator	CTRL-\
29	1D	GS	Group separator	CTRL-]
30	1E	RS	Record separator	CTRL-^
31	1F	US	Unit separator	CTRL-—

Musical notes frequencies

The range of notes on a piano keyboard is from 27·5 Hz to 4186 Hz. Middle C (the centre note on a standard keyboard) has a frequency of 261·6 Hz. Standard pitch is A above middle C at a frequency of 440 Hz. Note that raising the pitch of a note is equivalent to doubling the frequency for each complete octave.

A	27·5	D	73·4	G	196·0	C	523·3	F	1396·9	B	3951·1		
B	30·9	E	82·4	A	220·0	D	587·3	G	1568·0	C	4186·0		
C	32·7	F	87·3	B	246·9	E	659·2	A	1760·0				
D	36·7	G	98·0	C	261·6	F	698·5	B	1975·5				
E	41·2	A	110·0	D	293·7	G	784·0	C	2093·0				
F	43·7	B	123·5	E	329·6	A	880·0	D	2344·3				
G	49·0	C	130·8	F	349·2	B	987·8	E	2637·0				
A	55·0	D	146·8	G	392·0	C	1046·5	F	2793·8				
B	61·7	E	164·8	A	440·0	D	1174·0	G	3136·0				
C	65·4	F	174·6	B	493·9	E	1318·5	A	3520·0				

Radio and electronics glossary

Absorption coefficient The ratio of the sound energy absorbed by a surface, to the total sound energy incident on it.

Access time Time interval between a received instruction to read data stored in memory and the output of the data from memory.

Accumulator 1 A secondary cell, which produces a potential difference. 2 A register within the central processing unit of a computer.

a.c. Abbreviation for alternating current.

Acoustic feedback Unwanted feedback of sound waves from the output of an acoustic system to its input, causing unpleasant audible oscillations commonly known as howling.

Acoustic wave Synonym for sound wave.

Adder Circuit in a digital computer which performs addition.

Address Number that identifies a particular item of data in memory or input/output channel of a digital computer.

Admittance Reciprocal of impedance, symbol Y. The unit of admittance is the *Siemen*.

Aerial Construction, usually of metal, which radiates or receives radio waves. Synonym for antenna.

AFC Abbreviation for automatic frequency control.

Alphanumeric Alphabetical or numerical ordering.

Alternating current An electric current which periodically changes direction.

AM Abbreviation for amplitude modulation.

Ammeter Indicating meter used to measure current.

Ampere Unit used to measure current.

Amplify Make larger, electronically.

Amplifier Electronic circuit which increases some aspect of an applied signal.

Amplifier stage A single stage of a complete piece of electronic equipment to amplify an electronic signal.

Amplitude The peak value of an alternating current.

Amplitude modulation Type of modulation in which the amplitude of a carrier signal is varied above and below its nominal amplitude, by an amount proportional to the varying amplitude of a message signal.

Analogue Term used for a non-digital signal. Some part of the analogue signal varies as the analogue of a reference.

Analogue/digital converter A circuit which converts an analogue signal to a digital one.

AND gate Logic circuit whose output is high if all of its inputs are high.

Angular frequency The frequency of a periodic wave in radians s^{-1}. Symbol ω.

Anode Positive electrode of a system.

Antenna Aerial.

Antiphase Waveforms completely out of phase, i.e., differing by $180°$.

Aspect ratio Ratio of the width of a television picture to its height. Typically 4:3.

Assembler Computer program which converts a program written in assembly code to a machine code program.

Astable multivibrator A multivibrator circuit which produces an output of two continuously alternating states, i.e., a square wave oscillator.

Asynchronous Untimed data transfer.

Attenuation Reduction in some aspect of a signal. Opposite of amplification.

Attenuator A circuit which attenuates an applied input signal.

Audio frequency Sound waves within the frequency range of the human ear, i.e., having a frequency between about 20 to 20,000 Hz.

Automatic frequency control Circuit to control the frequency of an applied signal.

Automatic gain control Circuit to control the amplitude of an applied signal.

Automatic volume control Synonym for automatic gain control.

Avalanche breakdown Phenomenon which occurs in a reverse biased semiconductor junction, in which free charge carriers within the junction multiply.

Background noise See Noise.

Balanced A transmission line with two conducting wires, each of which has the same resistance to ground, is said to be balanced.

Band 1 A coloured ring on an electronic component. 2 A specific range of communications frequencies.

Band-pass filter A filter which allows a specific range of frequencies to pass, while attenuating all other frequencies.

Band-stop filter A filter which attenuates a specific range of frequencies, while passing all other frequencies.

Bandwidth The band of frequencies a circuit passes, without the circuit's output amplitude falling by a specified fraction (usually one half) of the maximum amplitude.

Base One of the three terminals of a bipolar transistor.

BASIC A high-level computer programming language.

Bass An audio amplifier tone control which attenuates or amplifies bass (i.e. low) frequencies.

Batch processing A computing method used in large computing systems, in which a number of previously prepared programs are run in a single batch.

Battery A source of electricity, consisting of two or more cells connected together.

Baud Unit of data modulation rate, corresponding to one transmitted signalling element per second. Often incorrectly confused with data signalling rate, measured in bits per second.

Beat A periodic signal produced when two signals of similar frequency are combined. The beat is caused by interference: the frequency of the beat is defined by the difference in frequency between the two interfering signals. Synonym for heterodyne.

Bel Unit used to express power ratios in electronics. See Decibel.

Beta The common emitter, forward current transfer ratio of a transistor. Symbol: β or h_{fe}.

Bias For a transistor to operate correctly the proper potentials have to be present at its emitter, base and collector. Normally the term bias refers to the voltage applied to the base to bring the operating point to a linear part of the amplification curve. For germanium transistors this is usually 0·3 V with respect to the emitter and for silicon transistors at least 0·6 V.

Bias voltage A standing voltage applied to an electronic component.

Binary code Numerical representation which has a base of two and, therefore, only two digits: 0 and 1.

Bipolar transistor A transistor in which both types of charge carriers (i.e., electrons and holes) are used in operation.

Bistable Abbreviation of bistable multivibrator: a circuit which has two stable states. Commonly known as a flip-flop.

Bit Abbreviation of binary digit. One of the two digits (0 or 1) of binary code.

Black box Any self-contained circuit, or part of a system, which may be considered a separate entity. Because of this, a user or circuit designer does not need to understand the black box's internal operation – just its effect on external circuits.

Blocking capacitor A capacitor used in a circuit to prevent direct current flow between two parts of the circuit.

Bode diagram A graph in which gain and/or phase shift caused by a circuit, is plotted against frequency of applied signal.

Breadboard A plug-in method of temporarily assembling circuits, for design or test purposes.

Breakdown The sudden change from a high resistance to a low resistance which occurs when the breakdown voltage of a reverse-biased semiconductor junction is exceeded.

Bridge A network of components, generally arranged in a square formation.

Bridge rectifier A full-wave rectifier circuit, composed of four diodes in a bridge.

Brightness A surface's brightness is the property by which the surface appears to emit light in the direction of view. This is a subjective quantity.

Broadcast Radio or television transmission.

Bubble memory A type of computer memory device which, although solid-state, is not of semiconductor origin. Data is stored as tiny domains of magnetic polarisation.

Bucket-brigade See Charge coupled device.

Buffer Circuit interfacing two other circuits, used to prevent interference from one to the other.

Bug A computer program fault.

Bus 1 A conductor between two or more parts of a circuit, generally of high current carrying capacity. 2 A set of conductors between parts of a computer system.

Byte A group of bits, treated as a single unit of data in a computer system. Generally, though not necessarily, a byte is taken to be a group of eight bits.

Cable A set of conductors, insulated from each other but enclosed in a common outer sheath.

Capacitance The property of two isolated conductors whereby they hold an electrical charge. Symbol: C. Unit: F.

Capacitor An electronic component, which has two isolated conductive plates. A capacitor may therefore hold an electrical charge.

Carrier 1 A signal which is modulated by a message signal to allow communications e.g. amplitude modulation. 2 A hole, or electron in a semiconductor device, which carries charge.

Cathode Negative electrode of a system.

Cathode ray A beam of electrons, generated in a cathode ray tube.

Cathode ray oscilloscope An electronic test instrument which allows a signal to be displayed on its screen, as a graph of voltage against time. Abbreviated: CRO.

Cathode ray tube Glass evacuated tube allowing a beam of electrons to be generated, focused and positioned onto its face (screen). Cathode ray tubes form the display device in common TVs and cathode ray oscilloscopes. Abbreviated: CRT.

CCITT Abbreviation for International Telegraph and Telephone Consultative Committee. A body which recommends standards concerning voice and data communications systems.

Ceefax See Teletext.

Cell Device which produces a potential difference by chemical means. Two or more cells in combination form a battery.

Central processing unit The part of a digital computer that controls the computer operation. Abbreviation: CPU.

Channel 1 A communications path between a transmission source and receiver. 2 The region between the source and drain of a field effect transistor.

Charge carrier A hole or electron in a semiconductor.

Charge coupled device A semiconductor memory device comprising a number of memory cells, each of which may hold a charge. Each charge is passed along from cell to cell, earning the device the nickname bucket-brigade device. Abbreviation: CCD.

Chip 1 A small piece of semiconductor material containing a single electronic component, or an electronic circuit. A chip is found within every transistor or integrated circuit. 2 Nickname for an integrated circuit.

Clock A circuit or device which generates a periodic signal (generally a square wave) to synchronise operations of a digital system.

CMOS Abbreviation for complementary metal oxide semiconductor.

Coax Abbreviation for coaxial cable.

Coaxial cable A cable with an inner conductor comprising one or more strands of wire, and an outer conduction sheath. The conductors are insulated from each other and the whole arrangement is covered in an outer layer of insulating material.

Coil Conductor (s) wound in a number of turns.

Collector One of the three terminals of a bipolar transistor.

Colour code Method of marking an electronic component with information regarding its value, tolerance and any other aspects which may be of interest to its user.

Complementary pair Most modern transistor audio amplifiers make use of a pair of transistors, one npn and the other pnp, with similar characteristics and closely matched gains in the driver or output stage: they are referred to as a complementary pair.

Computer An automatic system, which processes information according to instructions contained in a stored program.

Conductor A material with low resistance to the flow of electric current.

CPU Abbreviation for central processing unit.

CRO Abbreviation for cathode ray oscilloscope.

Crosstalk Interference between signals of two adjacent communications channels.

CRT Abbreviation for cathode ray tube.

Current Rate of flow of electricity. Symbol: I. Unit: ampere (abbreviated: amp: A).

Cut-off frequency Frequency at which a circuit output falls to a specified fraction (usually one half) of the maximum.

Cycle Complete set of changes in a regularly repeating wave.

Darlington pair A combination of two transistors which operate as if they are a single transistor, with a gain given by the product of the individual transistors gains.

dB See decibel.

d.c. Abbreviation for direct current.

d.c. voltage Common term to mean direct voltage.

Debug The action of finding and correcting computer program faults.

Decibel Dimensionless unit expressing the ratio of two powers. Under certain conditions it may also be used to express the ratio of two voltages or currents.

Demodulation See Modulation.

Demodulator A circuit which demodulates a received, modulated signal in a communications system. Synonymous with detector.

Demultiplexer See Multiplexer.

Detector See Demodulator.

Device An electronic component or system which contains at least one active element.

Diac Bi-directional voltage breakdown diode; passes current above a certain breakdown voltage. Normally employed with a triac in an a.c. control circuit.

Dielectric A material which is an insulator and can sustain an electric field. The layer of insulating material between the conducting plates of a capacitor is a dielectric.

Dielectric constant The ratio of the capacitance of a capacitor with a dielectric, to the capacitance of the capacitor with the dielectric replaced by a vacuum. Synonymous with relative permittivity. Symbol: μ_r. See Permittivity.

Differential amplifier An amplifier which produces an output signal which is a function of the difference between its two inputs. Principle of the operational amplifier.

Differentiator A circuit which produces an output signal which is a function of the differential of its input signal.

Digital A circuit or system responding to, operating on, and producing fixed, discrete voltages. Where only two levels are used, the circuit or system is said to be binary digital.

Digital computer See Computer.

Digital multimeter A multimeter which is capable of measuring and displaying a number of electrical quantities as a decimal value.

Digital voltmeter A voltmeter which displays a measured voltage as a decimal value.

DIL Abbreviation for dual-in-line.

Diode An active electronic component with two electrodes, which allows current flow in one direction but not in the other. Many derivative types of diode exist.

Diode transistor logic Family of logic integrated circuits built using diodes and transistors. Abbreviation: DTL.

Dioptre The unit of measure of lens power; the reciprocal of the focal length, expressed in metre.

Dipole aerial Simplest type of aerial, in which a standing wave of current is symmetrical about its mid-point.

Direct current A unidirectional, constant current. Abbreviation: d.c.

Direct voltage A unidirectional, more or less constant voltage.

Distortion Extra unwanted components in the output of a system, which have been added by the system itself. There are many types of distortion.

Doping The addition of impurities to a pure semiconductor material in order to affect the numbers and types of charge carriers present. Donor impurities are added to form an n-type semiconductor. Acceptor impurities are added to form a p-type semiconductor.

Double pole switch A switch with two electrically independent switching mechanisms.

Drain One of the three connections of a field/effect transistor.

Drift A variation of an electrical property with time.

Dry battery A battery of two or more dry cells.

Dry cell A cell whose contents are in non-liquid form.

Dry joint A faulty soldered joint.

DTL Abbreviation for diode transistor logic.

Dual-in-line Standard package for integrated circuits, in which the connection pins are in two parallel rows, either side of the body.

Duplex Simultaneous operation of both channels of a communications link.

DMM Abbreviation for digital multimeter.

DVM Abbreviation for digital voltmeter.

EAROM Abbreviation for electrically alterable read only memory.

Earphone Small loudspeaker which fits into the ear.

Earth The arbitrary zero point in electrical potential.

Earth current Current which flows to earth.

Earth fault Fault occurring in a circuit or system, when a conductor is connected to earth or a low resistance occurs between the conductor and earth. Causes an unnacceptable earth current.

ECL Abbreviation for emitter coupled logic.

Edge connector A connector which is pushed onto the edge of a printed circuit board. Tracks on the printed circuit board are taken to the edge forming connections.

EEROM, E²ROM Abbreviation for electrically erasable read only memory.

EHT Abbreviation for extra high tension.

Electrically alterable read only memory See Read only memory. Abbreviation: EAROM.

Electrically erasable read only memory See Read only memory. Abbreviation: EEROM; E²ROM.

Electrode Part of a component or system which gives out or takes in charge carriers.

Electrolysis Chemical change caused by an applied current through an electrolyte.

Electrolyte material which allows conduction due to its dissociation into ions.

Electrolytic capacitor A capacitor in which the dielectric is formed by electrolytic action.

Electromagnet A component which becomes a magnet only when a current flows through it.

Electromagnetic spectrum Complete frequency range of electromagnetic energy.

Electromotive force Potential difference produced by an electrical energy source. Abbreviation: EMF. Symbol: E. Unit: volt.

Electron Atomic particle which possesses a negative charge, of magnitude 1.602×10^{-9} coulomb and a mass of 9.109×10^{-3} kg. Movement of electrons in one direction is equal to current flow in the opposite direction.

Electron beam Beam of electrons given off from an electron gun, typically in a cathode ray tube. Synonymous with cathode ray.

Electron gun Arrangement which is used to generate an electron beam in a cathode ray tube or similar.

Electronvolt The energy gained by one electron when passing across a potential difference of one volt. Symbol: eV.

Element Substance consisting of atoms of only one type.

EMF Abbreviation for electromotive force.

Emitter One of the three terminals of a bipolar transistor.

Emitter follower A single transistor amplifier whose output is between emitter and earth.

Enable Activate a circuit or device.

Encoder Circuit, system, or device producing an output which is a coded version of the input.

Energy bands Theoretical levels of energy which electrons of an atom possess.

Equalisation Process whereby the distortion produced by a system may be compensated for.

Equaliser Circuit or device which causes equalisation.

Equivalent circuit A circuit comprising simple (generally passive) elements, used to model the action of a complex circuit under specified conditions.

Erase Remove stored information.

Error Difference between the correct value of something and its actual value.

Exclusive OR gate Logic circuit with two or more inputs, whose output is high if and only if one input is high. Abbreviation: XOR.

Facsimile A picture transmission system by which pictorial images can be transmitted using an ordinary communications link. Abbreviation: fax.

Failure Ceasing of a component or system's ability to function correctly.

Failure rate The number of failures which may be assumed by a component or system, in a given time. The failure rate is given by:

$$f = \frac{1}{\text{MTBF}}$$

where MTBF is the mean time between failures.

Fall-time The time taken by a logic device or circuit to change output state from high to low.

Fan-out The maximum number of circuits which may be driven by the output of a similar circuit.

Farad Unit of capacitance. Symbol: F.

Feedback The return of some part of a circuit or system's output, to its input in such a way as to control the function of the circuit or system.

FET (field effect transistor) The f.e.t. makes use of the electric field established in a p- or n-type channel of semiconductor material to control the flow of current through the channel. The field is established by the bias applied to the gate connections and the f.e.t. is thus a voltage-controlled device. This means that it has a much higher input impedance than ordinary transistors. The main connections are the source, drain and gate but some f.e.t.s have additional connections.

Fibre optics See Optical fibre.

Field 1 Region affected by some phenomena. 2 Set of bits forming a unit of data with a specific purpose. 3 Set of lines of a displayed television picture.

Field effect transistor A unipolar transistor (i.e. with only one p-n junction). Abbreviation: FET.

Filter Circuit which passes some applied frequencies of signals while restricting others.

Fleming's left-hand rule When the thumb, first finger and middle finger of the left hand are held naturally at right angles, the thumb represents the direction of motion, the first finger represents the magnetic field, and the middle finger represents the current, I, in an electric motor.

Fleming's right-hand rule Similar to Fleming's left-hand rule, but representing a dynamo, with the right-hand.

Flicker The eye's perception of fluctuations of brightness when the fluctuations occur more rapidly than the persistance of vision.

Flicker noise See Noise.

Flip-flop Nickname for a bistable multivibrator.

Floating Term describing a part of a circuit which is not connected.

Floating-point representation Means of expressing a number with the use of a mantissa and an exponent.

Floppy disk Magnetic memory medium used by computers as auxiliary memory.

FM Abbreviation for frequency modulation.

Forward bias When a voltage is applied across a semiconductor junction, the junction is said to be forward biased when the current through the junction is the greater of the two ways. Thus, a diode is forward biased when it conducts and reverse biased when it does not conduct.

Frame One complete television picture.

Frequency Number of complete oscillations or cycles of a periodic signal in one second. Unit: hertz (Hz). Frequency is related to the wavelength (λ) of the signal by the signal velocity (v), where

$$v = f\lambda.$$

Frequency division multiplex A system in which a number of message signals are combined into one. Each message signal is modulated onto a different carrier wave frequency so that a number of frequency band channels exist. Abbreviation: FDM.

Frequency modulation Type of modulation in which the carrier frequency is varied up and down by the message signal. The carrier amplitude remains constant. Abbreviation: FM.

Frequency range Range of frequencies a circuit will operate on.

Frequency response Variation with frequency of the gain of a circuit. Drawn as a graph, usually of gain in decibels against a logarithmic scale of frequency.

Frequency spectrum A graph, chart, or table showing the frequencies of all electromagnetic waves, related to types, e.g., X-rays, radio waves, audio waves, etc.

FSD Abbreviation for full scale deflection.

Full scale deflection Maximum value displayed by measuring equipment. Abbreviation: FSD.

Full wave rectifier A circuit which rectifies both positive and negative half cycles of an applied a.c. wave.

Function generator A circuit or piece of test equipment which generates a variety of waves e.g. sine, sawtooth, square, for use in testing other circuits.

Fundamental frequency Generally the lowest sine wave frequency present in a complex periodic waveform.

Fuse Device which is intended to cause an open circuit when the current taken by a circuit goes above a specified level. Generally, a fuse is formed using a short length of fuse-wire which, at a specified frequency and voltage, will melt, i.e., 'blow' at the fuse's current rating, thus breaking the power supply connection.

Fusible link memory Type of read only memory device consisting of a matrix of fusible links. Data may be programmed into the device by 'blowing' selected links.

Gain Measure of a circuit's effect on the amplitude of an applied signal. Can be stated in terms of the ratio between output and input signals as a decimal number, or in decibels.

Gain control A control which may be used to vary the gain of a circuit.

Ganged Term used to describe variable components which are mechanically coupled so that they all vary simultaneously when a single control is varied.

Gate 1 A circuit having two or more inputs and one or more outputs. The output(s) varies as a direct result of the states of the inputs. 2 One of the terminals of a field effect transistor.

Gating signal A signal which, when applied to a gate is used to control the gate's output such as the output may be on (and produce an output signal which is some function of another input) or off (producing no output).

Geostationary orbit A satellite orbit in which the satellite lies about 36,000 km above the earth's equatorial plane, such that the satellite appears stationary to an observer on earth.

Geosynchronous orbit Similar to a geostationary orbit, but the satellite traces a figure-of-eight orbit thus appearing to move up and down in one-day cycles to an observer on earth.

Germanium Semiconductor element used in the majority of early transistors and diodes.

Giga- Unit prefix which means a multiplication factor of 10^{12}. Abbreviation: G.

Graphics Display of graphical symbols and scenes, generated by a computer.

Ground Synonym for earth. Abbreviation: Gnd.

Guard band Range of frequencies between two ranges of transmission frequencies, left unoccupied to minimise interference.

Half-adder Elementary digital circuit composed of logic gates. *See* Adder.

Half-duplex A pair of transmission channels over which two-way communications may take place, although only one channel is operational at any one time, is said to allow half-duplex communications.

Half wave rectifier A circuit which rectifies only one half of each cycle of an applied a.c. wave.

Hall effect An electromagnetic phenomenon which occurs when a current carrying conductor is placed in a magnetic field, the direction of which is perpendicular to the directions of both the current and its own magnetic field.

Ham Colloquial term denoting an amateur radio transmitting/receiving enthusiast.

Hardware Physical parts of a computer system, e.g. printer, keyboard, VDU, etc.

Harmonic A signal present in a complex periodic waveform, which is a multiple of the fundamental frequency. The second harmonic is three times etc.

Head Transducer of a magnetic recording system which allows electrical signals to be changed into a magnetic field to write data onto the medium, or converts magnetic data into electrical signals.

Headset Pair of earphones.

Heatsink Metal attachment mechanically connected to a heat producing element in a circuit (e.g. a power transistor) to ensure heat is dissipated away from the element, preventing damage by excessive heat.

Henry Unit of magnetic inductance. Symbol: H.

Hertz Unit of frequency. Equivalent to one cycle of a periodic wave which occurs in one second. Symbol: Hz.

Heterodyne Production of beats by combination of two signals which interfere. Used in a superheterodyne radio receiver to produce an intermediate frequency.

HF Abbreviation for high frequency.

h_{fe} and h_{FE} See Beta.

Hifi Acronym for high fidelity.

High fidelity Commonly used term denoting audio reproduction equipment of good quality.

High frequency Bands of radio transmissions around 10 MHz. Abbreviation: HF.

High level programming language A computer programming language which is more like human language or mathematical notation than the machine code used by the central processing unit of the computer.

High logic level Term denoting a logic 1 level (in positive logic).

High pass filter A filter which allows signal frequencies above a specific corner frequency to pass without attenuation. Signal frequencies below the corner frequencies are attenuated.

High tension Voltages in the range between about 50 V to 250 V. Abbreviation: HT.

Holding current The value of current which must be maintained to hold a thyristor in its on state. If the current through the thyristor falls below the holding current, the thyristor turns off and ceases conduction.

Hole An empty space in a semiconductor material due to a 'missing' electron. As electrons are negatively charged, holes are positive. Holes, like electrons, may be thought of as charge carriers, moving through the semiconductor material thus forming a current.

Hole current The current through a semiconductor due to the movement of holes under an applied voltage.

Howl Colloquial term for the sound caused by acoustic feedback.

HT Abbreviation for high tension.

Hum Capacitive or magnetic interference between a mains powered device such as a power supply, and local equipment such as an amplifier. Often heard in audio frequency systems as a low drone of mains supply frequency, or a harmonic of that frequency.

Hunting A system's oscillation about its desired point, caused by over-correction.

Hybrid integrated circuit An integrated circuit comprising a number of discrete components attached to a substrate and interconnected to form a circuit. *See* Integrated circuit.

Hybrid-π A type of equivalent circuit used to show transistor operation.

Hysteresis Phenomenon occurring in some circuits or systems, in which the output lags behind a changing input. A hysteresis loop is formed – a graph of output against input – which shows that the value of output depends on whether the input is increasing or decreasing in value.

Hz Abbreviation for hertz.

IC Abbreviation for integrated circuit.

IEC Abbreviation for International Electrotechnical Commission.

IEE Abbreviation for Institute of Electrical Engineers.

IEEE Abbreviation for Institute of Electrical and Electronic Engineers Inc.

IF Abbreviation for intermediate frequency.

IGFET Abbreviation for insulated gate field effect transistor.

I^2L Abbreviation for integrated injection logic.

Illuminance Luminous flux perpendicularly reaching a surface per unit area. The unit of illuminance is the lumen m^{-2} or lux.

Image frequency Unwanted input frequency to a radio, causing a spurious output. Synonym for second channel frequency.

Image interference Interference caused by an image frequency.

Impedance The opposition of a circuit to alternating current flow.

Impedance matching The matching of impedances between two circuits, to ensure maximum transfer of power from one circuit to the other.

Impulse noise Noise in an electronic system caused by a single disturbance. *See* Noise.

Impulse voltage A single, rapidly occurring, pulse of voltage. Impulses are generally unwanted, as they tend to cause impulse noise throughout the system.

Impurities Atoms in a semiconductor material, not of the semiconductor element itself. Impurities may occur naturally or may be deliberately introduced. *See* Doping.

Incandescence When a material gives off visible light due to its high temperature.

Incandescent lamp Lamp which emits light when its filament is heated by an electric current. The filament often reaches temperatures of 2,500°C and over.

Index error An error occurring in a measuring instrument such that when no measurand is present (i.e., with zero input) a non-zero reading is obtained. Synonymous with zero error.

Indirect wave Radio wave which is reflected by the ionosphere, i.e., it does not travel directly from transmitter to receiver.

Induce To cause a change in electrical or magnetic conditions in a system, by changing the electrical or magnetic conditions of another, local, system.

Inductance A constant occurring when a circuit is magnetically linked with the current flowing through it. Unit: henry.

Induction Abbreviation of electromagnetic induction or electrostatic induction.

Inductor A component which has inductance. Generally, inductors are constructed of some form of coil.

Information technology The study of the combined effects of electronics, computing and communications. Abbreviation: IT.

Infrared radiation Invisible electromagnetic radiation with wavelengths of about 730 nm to about 1 mm.

Inject To introduce charge carriers into a semiconductor junction area.

Input 1 The signal applied to a system. 2 The terminal at which the input signal is applied.

Input impedance The impedance which a circuit presents to an input signal.

Input/output Term applying to operations performed by, or devices connected to a computer, which allow the computer to receive and send out data. Abbreviation: I/O.

Instantaneous value The value of any measurand which varied with time, e.g., instantaneous voltage, instantaneous current.

Institute of Electrical and Electronics Engineers Inc A standardisation body in the USA. Abbreviated: IEEE.

Institute of Electrical Engineers A UK standardisation body. Abbreviation: IEE.

Instruction set The complete list of operations which may be performed by the central processing unit of a computer.

Insulate To prevent unwanted current flow by sheathing a conductor with non-conductive material.

Insulated gate field effect transistor Type of construction of field effect transistor, used in MOSFETs. Abbreviation: IGFET.

Insulator A non-conductor. A material with a very high resistance to flow of electric current. Current flow is assumed to be negligible.

Integrated circuit A device which contains a complete circuit. One of two main methods are used in manufacture. A *hybrid integrated circuit* is manufactured from discrete components, attached to a substrate and interconnected by layers of metallization. A monolithic integrated circuit is made by building up all components within the circuit onto a single chip of silicon. In recent usage, integrated circuit, chip, microchip, have all become synonymous. Abbreviation: IC.

Integrated injection logic A type of monolithic integrated circuit construction. Abbreviation: I^2L.

Integrator Circuit which performs the equivalent of a mathematical integration on an applied input signal.

Intelligent Any system with processing and storage capabilities, whose actions may be controlled by stored instructions, is said to be intelligent.

Intelsat Acronym of International Telecommunications Satellite Consortium.

Intensity Denoting magnetic or electric field strength.

Interactive Term used to denote computer operation where user and computer communicate in a continuous manner. Generally refers to an on-line situation.

Interference A disturbance to any signal in a system, causing additional, unwanted signals. Interference may be natural or man-made. *See* Hum, Crosstalk, Image frequency.

Interlaced scanning Scanning method used in a television system in which lines are scanned in two separate scans, even lines and odd lines.

Intermediate frequency Signal generated in a heterodyne-based radio receiver, where the received radio signal is combined with a local oscillation signal. Abbreviation: IF. *See* Heterodyne, Beats.

Internal resistance The small resistance inherent in any source of electricity. The internal resistance limits the voltage which may be produced by the electricity source under load conditions.

International Electrotechnical Commission An international standardisation body. Abbreviation: IEC.

International Radio Consultative Committee An international standardisation committee: part of the International Telecommunications Union. Abbreviation: CCIR.

International Telecommunications Union An international standardisation body. Abbreviation: ITU.

International Telegraph and Telephone Consultative Committee An international standardisation committee: part of the International Telecommunications Union. Abbreviation: CCITT.

Inversion The production of an opposite polarity in a semiconductor device, due to an applied electric field.

Inverter 1 A circuit which produces an output which is the inverse of an applied input signal. A digital inverter produces an output which is the opposite logic state to that of the input. 2 A circuit which converts a direct current to an alternating current.

I/O Abbreviation for input/output.

Ion A particle of material (an atom, molecule, group of atoms, or group of molecules) with an electric charge. Negative ions are called anions: positive ions are called cations.

ISO Abbreviation for International Standards Organisation.

Isolate To disconnect two parts of a system, ensuring that no electrical connection exists.

ITU Abbreviation for International Telecommunications Union.

Jack A connector pair (plug and socket) allowing quick and easy input or output connections, to or from a circuit or system. Many sizes and types are available.

Jam To cause interference in radio-type transmissions, rendering correct reception impossible.

JEDEC Abbreviation for Joint Electron Device Engineering Council.

JFET Abbreviation for junction field effect transistor.

JK flip flop A type of flip-flop circuit.

Johnson noise A type of noise generated by the random movement of electrons in resistive components, due to thermal activity. Synonymous with thermal noise.

Josephson junction The junction between a thin layer of insulating material and a superconducting material. A superconducting current can flow across the junction even without an applied voltage.

JUGFET Abbreviation for junction field effect transistor.

Junction 1 The boundary between two layers of material in an electronic device. 2 An electrical connection.

Junction box An enclosed container, in which wires or leads from circuits may be joined, by screw terminals or other means.

Junction capacitance Capacitance between pn junctions in a semiconductor device. Also called barrier, depletion layer or transition capacitances. See Neutralisation.

Junction field effect transistor A type of field effect transistor. Abbreviation: JFET; JUGFET.

Junction transistor Abbreviation for bipolar junction transistor.

Keyboard Part of a computer, with a typewriter-style appearance, allowing input of instructions and data to the computer.

Kilo- 1 A prefix denoting a multiple of 10^3. Abbreviation: k. 2 A prefix to a computing term, denoting a multiple of 2^{10}, i.e., 1024. Abbreviation: K.

Kirchhoff's laws Two basic laws of electricity. The first states that: the algebraic sum of all currents into and out of a point in a circuit is zero. The second states that: the algebraic sum of the products of current and resistance in each part of circuit is equal to the algebraic sum of the voltages.

Klystron An electron gun device, used as an amplifier or oscillator at high radio frequencies.

Lag The delay between one waveform and another, measured in time or as an angle. See Lead.

Lamination Thin sheet material, used to make the laminated core of a wound component, e.g., a transformer, a relay.

Land A contact on a printed circuit board.

Language Short for programming language.

Large scale integration A level of integration used in the manufacture of integrated circuits. Abbreviated: LSI.

Laser An acronym for light amplification by stimulated emission of radiation. A laser device is a source of coherent, monochromatic light. The light may not be visible but may be of ultra-violet or infra-red origin.

Latch Common name for a bistable multivibrator or flip-flop.

LCD Abbreviation for liquid crystal display.

LC network A tuned circuit containing inductance and capacitance.

Lead 1 The amount by which one waveform is in front of another, measured as a time interval or as an angle. See Lag. 2 An electrical conductor, used to make an electrical connection between two parts of a circuit or system.

Lead-acid cell A secondary cell or accumulator comprising lead metal cathodes and lead dioxide anodes, with a dilute sulphuric acid electrolyte. Lead-acid batteries, formed by a number of series connected cells are commonly used in cars.

Leading edge The portion of a pulse which signals the commencement of the pulse.

Leakage Current flow through a circuit or component due to faulty insulation.

Leakage current That current which flows due to leakage.

Leclanché cell A primary cell comprising a carbon-rod anode and a zinc cathode, with an ammonium chloride solution electrolyte. Leclanché cells with a paste-based ammonium chloride electrolyte are said to be dry and form the basis of many available cells used in common battery-powered appliances.

LED Abbreviation for light emitting diode.

Left-hand rule See Fleming's rules.

LF Abbreviation for low frequency.

Light emitting diode A semiconductor diode which emits light as the result of an electroluminescent effect. As electron and hole combine near the junction of the diode, sufficient energy is released to form light. The emitted light is of a particular frequency and so of a particular colour. Light emitting diodes of red, yellow, orange, green and blue are available, as well as infra-red varieties. Abbreviation: LED.

Light-pen A device used with a computer to produce data on a cathode ray tube screen by writing on the screen in a similar manner to writing with a conventional pen on paper. The computer locates the light-pen's position on the screen and produces an image at that point. As the light-pen is moved across the screen many images combine to form, say, a line.

Light sensitive devices Light and heat both affect the conductivity of a pn junction. Devices are available in which a pn junction is exposed to light so as to make use of this property. Light falling on the junction liberates current carriers and allows the device to conduct.

Linear Any circuit or system which produces an output directly proportional to the input at any time, is said to be a linear circuit or system.

Lines The physical paths followed by the electron beam of a television receiver's cathode ray tube across the screen. Standard UK television pictures are composed of 625 lines.

Line of flux Imaginary line in a magnetic field. The direction at any point along a line of flux is that of the magnetic flux density.

Line of force Imaginary line in an electric field, the direction of which at any point represents the field's direction at the point.

Liquid crystal display A display comprising a thin layer of liquid crystal material between two electrodes. Application of a potential difference across the electrodes causes the liquid crystal material to change in respect of light transmission. Abbreviation: LCD.

Load 1 A circuit or system which absorbs power from any other circuit or system. 2 The output power provided by a circuit or system.

Load characteristic A characteristic curve, typically for a transistor, in which the relationship between variables is plotted.

Load impedance The impedance presented to a circuit or system by its load.

Load line A line drawn on the load characteristics of a component which shows the relationship between voltage and current in the circuit.

Local oscillator An oscillator within a radio receiver operating on the superheterodyne principle.

Logic circuit A circuit which performs a logical operation such as AND, OR, NOT, NAND, NOR, EXOR.

Logic diagram A diagram showing the logic elements of a logic circuit.

Logic symbol Graphical symbol representing a logic element.

Long-tailed pair A circuit containing two transistors coupled together so that their emitters are joined with a common emitter bias resistor which provides a constant current. The long-tailed pair forms the basis of a differential amplifier.

Long wave A radio frequency wave with a wavelength between about 1 to 10 km.

Loss A dissipation of power due to the resistance of current flow.

Lossless A circuit or system which theoretically loses no power due to resistance.

Lossy A circuit or system which loses a great deal of power due to resistance.

Loudness Subjective measure of sound intensity. Although dependent on intensity it also varies with frequency and timbre of the sound.

Loudness level A comparison of a sound's loudness with a standard sound loudness. The standard sound is a sinusoidal note which has a frequency of 1,000 Hz. The unit of loudness level is the phon.

Loudspeaker A transducer which converts electrical energy into sound energy. Typically, loudspeakers are electromagnetic devices which rely on the applied electrical signal to move a coil of wire in a magnetic field. Attached to the coil is a cone of material which thus also moves with the electrical signal. The cone causes a movement of air, which the ear detects as sound.

Low frequency Radio signals in the frequency band of 30 kHz to 300 kHz, having wavelengths between 1 and 10 km. Abbreviation: LF.

Low level programming language A computer programming language which comprises instructions to the computer in machine code, i.e., binary codes which the computer can directly understand.

Low logic level Term denoting a logic 0 level (in positive logic).

Low-pass filter A filter which allows signal frequencies below a specific corner frequency to pass without attenuation. Signal frequencies above this corner frequency are attenuated.

LSI Abbreviation for large scale integration. See Integrated circuit.

Luminance A surface's luminance is the objective measure of the light emitted per unit projected area of surface, the plane of projection being perpendicular to the direction of view. The unit of luminance is the candela m^{-2}.

Luminous intensity The unit of luminous intensity is the candela (cd).

Machine code The binary codes understood by the central processing unit of a computer.

Magnet Term applied to a substance which generates a magnetic field. A magnet can be temporary or permanent.

Magnetic bubble memory See Bubble memory.

Magnetic circuit A closed path of lines of magnetic flux.

Magnetic field Space surrounding a magnet which contains a magnetic flux. A magnetic field may be represented by lines of force.

Magnetic field strength Magnetising force. Symbol: H. Unit: ampere per metre (A m^{-1}).

Magnetic flux The flux through an area in the space surrounding a magnet. Symbol: Φ. Unit: weber.

Magnetic flux density Magnetic induction. The magnetic analogue of the electric field. Symbol: B. Unit: tesla (T), or weber per square metre (w m^{-2}).

Magnetism The collection of properties exhibited by a magnet or magnets.

Mains Domestic electricity supply distributed through the National Grid system. A voltage of 240 VAC, at a frequency of 50 Hz is obtained from all domestic outlets.

Mains hum See Hum.

Make To close a circuit by means of a switch or similar component make and break: a type of switch which is automatically opened and closed, thus making and breaking the circuit, by the circuit which it forms part of.

Man-made noise See Noise.

Mark-space ratio The ratio between a pulse's duration and the time between successive pulses.

Maser An acronym for *microwave amplification by stimulated emission of radiation*. Similar to laser except radiations are part of the microwave frequency band, not light.

Mask Photographic reproduction of the circuit to be integrated into an integrated circuit chip by photographic or other means.

Matched termination A load attached to a circuit or system such that it absorbs all the power available from the circuit or system.

Mean life The mean time to failure of a component, circuit or system.

Measurand The quantity to be measured by measuring equipment.

Medium frequency Radio signals in the frequency band of 300 kHz to 3 MHz, having wavelengths between 100 m to 1 km. Abbreviation: MF.

Medium wave A radio frequency wave with a wavelength placing it in the medium frequency band.

Mega- 1 A prefix to a number, denoting a multiple of 10^6. 2 A prefix used in computing, to denote a multiple of 2^{20} (i.e., 1,048,576). Symbol: M.

Megger A portable insulation testing equipment.

Memory Any device associated with a digital circuit (particularly a computer) which is capable of storing information in digital form. Synonymous with store.

Memory location A storage element with a unique address.

Meter Any measuring equipment.

Meter movement The part of an analogue meter which indicates the measured value, typically constructed of a finely balanced moving-coil in a magnetic field. The coil rotates when a current flows through it, the amount of rotation is proportional to the value of current.

Meter resistance The internal resistance of a meter.

MF Abbreviation for medium frequency.

Micro- A prefix, denoting a multiple of 10^{-6}. Symbol: μ.

Microcomputer 1 A single integrated circuit which contains all the parts which can be combined to function as a computer, i.e., central processing unit, memory, timing and control circuits. 2 A computer which comprises an integrated circuit microprocessor. 3 A home computer.

Microphone A transducer which converts sound energy into electrical energy.

Microprocessor An integrated circuit which contains the central processing unit of a computer.

Microwave An electromagnetic wave with a frequency between infra-red and radio waves in the electromagnetic spectrum. Microwave wavelengths range from about 3 mm to 1·3 m.

Mike Abbreviation for microphone.

Milli- A prefix, denoting a multiple of 10^{-3}. Symbol: m.

Mismatch When a circuit's load does not have the same impedance as the load itself.

Mixer 1 An audio circuit to combine two or more signals. The output signal is merely the addition of the input signals. 2 A radio circuit which combines two or more signals to produce an output signal of a different frequency to the inputs.

Modem Acronym for modulator-demodulator. Any appliance which converts signals from one circuit or system to signals of another circuit or system. Typically modems are used to connect two computers via telephone circuits.

Modulation The alteration of a signal's parameter by another parameter. For instance, a carrier wave's amplitude may be modulated by a music signal. Other parameters which may be modulated include: phase, frequency, or a combination of more than one.

Monochromatic light Light of a single colour, i.e., it has only one frequency.

Monochrome television Black and white television.

Monostable multivibrator A circuit which has one stable state. On application of a triggering pulse, the output of the monostable multivibrator assumes a second state for a defined period of time, after which it returns to the stable state. Synonymous with one-shot.

Morse code Internationally agreed code for the transmission of alphanumeric symbols, in which each symbol is transmitted as a combination of short and long pulses (dots and dashes).

Morse telegraphy Electric telegraphy transmitting alphanumeric symbols as Morse code.

MOSFET Abbreviation of metal oxide semiconductor field effect transistor. A type of field effect semiconductor.

MOST Type of f.e.t. with oxide insulating layer between the metal gate and semiconductor channel. It has a higher input impedance than the junction type f.e.t.

Motorboating Term used to describe an oscillation arising in low or audio frequency amplifiers, resembling a motorboat engine.

Moving coil A device which relies on its motion due to current through a coil in a magnetic field.

Multiplex Combination of two or more signals, such that a single signal is obtained which may be transmitted and later demultiplexed back into the original signals.

Multiplexer A circuit which allows the multiplex process to take place.

Multivibrator A circuit which contains two inverters coupled so that the output of one forms the input of the other. Resistive coupling of the two inverters produces a bistable multivibrator, or flip-flop. Resistive/capacitive coupling produces a monostable multivibrator. Capacitive coupling produces an astable multivibrator.

NAND gate Logic circuit whose output is high if one or more of its inputs are low, and low if all its inputs are high.

Nano- A prefix denoting a multiple of 10^{-9}. Symbol: n.

Natural frequency The frequency at which free oscillation occurs in a resonant electrical, electronic, or mechanical system.

N-channel The conducting channel of a field-effect transistor of N-type semiconductor material. The term is also used to refer to the transistor, i.e., N-channel field-effect transistor.

Negative bias A voltage applied to an electrode of some electronic component, which is negative with respect to a fixed reference potential.

Negative feedback Type of control procedure in which all or some part of a system's output signal is fed back to the system's input terminal. Generally, by changing the amount of negative feedback the system's gain is changed. The gain may thus be controlled by choosing the required amount of negative feedback.

Negative modulation Type of modulation procedure followed in the transmission of television signals, such that a black display results from a more positive signal and a white display results from a negative signal. This principle is followed to ensure that any noise which a television receiver picks up produces a darker image and is thus less noticeable than it would be if positive modulation were used.

Neon indicator Type of indicator, relying on the gas-discharge properties of the inert gas, neon. A voltage of about 80 V is required to illuminate such indicators, and so they are typically used as indicators to display the presence of mains voltages.

Neper A dimensionless unit used to express the ratio of two signal powers. One neper equals 8·686 decibels. Symbol: Np.

Network Alternative term describing a circuit.

Neutral 1 One of the three lines of the domestic mains electric supply. 2 Descriptive term implying no overall positive or negative charge.

Neutralisation In radio frequency transistors there is a tendency for self-oscillation to occur due to the collector-base capacitance. In modern r.f. transistors this capacitance can be made very small. To overcome the effect in early r.f. transistors it was usual to use a small amount of capacitive negative feedback in each stage, this being known as neutralisation.

Nicad Abbreviation for nickel cadmium.

Nickel-cadmium cell A secondary cell, with a nickel-based anode, a cadmium cathode and a potassium hydroxide electrolyte. Abbreviation: nicad cell.

Node Any point on a transmission line, where standing wave is of zero value.

Noise Unwanted signals occurring in a electronic system, causing spurious output signals. Noise can be the result of man-made causes, or natural causes. Many different types of noise exist, named after their basic nature, e.g., thermal noise, atmospheric noise, white noise, impulse noise.

Noise factor The ratio of a device's or circuit's input signal-to-noise, to its output signal-to-noise. Synonymous with noise figure.

Noise figure See Noise factor.

Non-linear Any circuit or system which produces an output which is not directly proportional to its input at all times is said to be non-linear.

Nonvolatile memory Type of memory in which data is maintained even when power is disconnected.

NOR gate Logic circuit whose output is high if all the inputs are low. If one or more inputs are high, the output is low.

NOT gate Logic circuit whose output is always the inverse of the input. Synonymous with inverter.

NPN transistor A bipolar transistor formed by three layers of semiconductor material – the outside two layers being of N-type material, the middle layer of P-type material.

NTSC Abbreviation for National Television System Committee. An American committee, responsible for television standards. The initials NSTC are often comically described as never the same colour – referring to the constant colour changes inherent in the system.

N-type semiconductor Semiconductor material containing a higher concentration of negative charge carriers, i.e., electrons, than positive charge carriers, i.e., holes.

Numerical control Type of automatic control system in which a number generated by the controlling device is compared with a number generated by another device. The difference between the two numbers is detected by the controlling device and used to generate a control signal.

Nyquist diagram Graph of a system's performance, which may be used to determine the system's stability under untested criteria.

OCR Abbreviation for optical character reader.

Octave A difference or interval between two sounds, whereby one sound is twice the frequency of the other.

Off-line A computer peripheral which is unconnected to the computer is said to be off-line.

Ohm The unit of resistance, reactance and impedance. One ohm is the resistance between two points when a constant current of one amp flows as the result of an applied voltage of volt between the points.

Ohmic A material which follows Ohm's law is said to be ohmic.

Ohmmeter An instrument which measures resistance.

Ohmmetre The unit of electric resistivity. Symbol: Ωm.

Ohm's law Law which defines the linear relationship between the voltage applied across a material, the current produced through the material, and the resistance of the material. Ohm's law can be written:

$$V = IR$$

One shot Synonym for a monostable multivibrator.

On-line A computer peripheral which is connected to and receiving or transmitting data from or to a computer, is said to be on-line.

Opamp Abbreviation for operational amplifier.

Open circuit Term applying to a circuit or system whose output is not connected to any following circuit or system. The output is therefore unloaded. Measurements of electrical parameters at this time are said to be under open circuit or no lead conditions.

Operating point The point on a semiconductor device's characteristic curve, representing electrical parameters when defined conditions are applied to the device.

Operational amplifier An amplifier, generally in integrated circuit form, which is usable with only a few components and power supply connections.

Optical character reader A computer input peripheral which is capable of converting symbols printed on paper into digital signals.

Oracle The Independent Broadcasting authority's version of broadcast teletext.

OR gate Logic circuit whose output is high if one or more of its inputs are low.

Oscillation A-periodic variation of an electrical parameter.

Oscillator A circuit or system which produces on oscillation.

Oscilloscope Test equipment which is able to produce a visual display of one or more oscillations of voltage. Generally the device used to display the voltages is a cathode ray tube and such oscilloscopes are often referred to as cathode ray oscilloscopes (shortened to CRO).

Output 1 The part of a circuit or system which produces an output signal. 2 The signal produced by a circuit or system.

Output impedance The impedance of the output of a circuit or system.

Overall efficiency The ratio of the power absorbed by a circuit or system to the power supplied by a source.

Overdamping Damping applied to a period oscillation which prevents the oscillation from completing one cycle before stopping.

Overdriven Term, generally applied to a linear system such as an amplifier, which refers to the state when the size of input signal is such that the system's output is non-linearly related. In the case of an overdriven amplifier the output sounds harsh and is known as distorted.

Oxidation A process in the manufacture of semiconductor devices when the semiconductor base material undergoes a reaction with oxygen, to form a semiconductor oxide.

PA Abbreviation for public address system.

PABX Abbreviation for private automatic branch exchange.

Packing density The number of transistors or gates in unit area on an integrated circuit chip.

Pair Two similar conductors, insulated from each other but running in parallel, forming a transmission line. Generally, the pair is in the form of wire, e.g., twisted wire pair, coaxial cable.

PAL Abbreviation for phase alternation by line.

PAM Abbreviation for pulse amplitude modulation.

Parallel Components are said to be in parallel if current from a single source divides and flows through them then later reunites.

Parallel circuit A circuit containing two or more components connected in parallel.

Parallel plate capacitor A capacitor formed from two parallel conductive plates, between which is the dielectric.

Parallel resonant circuit A circuit containing a capacitance in parallel with an inductance, which exhibits resonance.

Parameter A criterion of an electronic component, circuit, or system. Typical parameters are voltage, current, resistance, capacitance, etc.

Parametric amplifier 1 A microwave frequency amplifier, whose reactance is varied in a regular manner. 2 An audio frequency amplifier which can amplify or attenuate specific frequency signals, while passing other signals unaltered. It is thus a bandpass/band reject filter, whose centre frequency may be adjusted.

Pascal A high level programming language.

Passive Any component which does not introduce gain is known as a passive device.

P-channel The conducting channel of a field-effect transistor of P-type material. The term is also used to refer to the transistor, i.e., P-channel field-effect transistor.

PCM Abbreviation for pulse code modulation.

PD Abbreviation for potential difference.

Peak-to-peak amplitude The difference between extreme values of a periodic oscillation.

Peak value The extreme value of a periodic oscillation.

Period The time to complete a single cycle of an oscillation. Symbol: T.

Periodic Term used to describe any variable which exhibits a regularly occurring form.

Peripheral devices Devices which connect to a computer.

Permanent memory Non-volatile memory, i.e. memory, the contents of which remain intact without a supply of power.

PFM Abbreviation for pulse frequency modulation.

Phase The amount by which a periodic variable has progressed from a reference point. Phase can be measured as an angle or in radians. Two periodic variables with the same frequency and waveform which reach corresponding stages simultaneously are said to be in phase. If this does not occur, they are said to be out of phase.

Phase alternation by line A colour television system, variations of which have been adopted throughout Europe, in which the colour signal (known as the chrominance signal) is resolved into two components and transmitted separately. The phase difference of these two components is reversed on alternate lines, a procedure which helps to reduce errors due to received phase variations. Abbreviation: PAL.

Phase difference Difference in phase between two sine waves of the same frequency.

Phase modulation Modulation in which the phase of a carrier wave is varied by an amount proportional to the amplitude of the message signal. Abbreviation: PM.

Phase shift keying Alternative name for simple phase modulation of a digital signal. Abbreviation: PSK.

Photocell A transducer which converts light to some parameter of electricity.

Photodiode A semiconductor diode device, which conducts electric current by an amount proportional to the quantity of light falling on it.

Photoresist Photosensitive material which changes in molecular ways upon exposure to light. Photoresists are used in the manufacture of semiconductors and integrated circuits and printed circuit boards.

Pick-up A transducer which converts recorded signals into electrical signals.

Pico- Prefix denoting a multiple of 10^{-12}. Symbol: p.

Picture element The smallest portion of a graphic or pictorial display system which can be resolved by the system. Often shortened to pixel.

Piezoelectric crystal A crystal which displays the piezoelectric effect.

Piezoelectric effect An effect observed in certain materials when a voltage is generated across the faces of the material as a mechanical stress is applied.

p-i-n diode A diode which contains a layer of intrinsic, i.e., pure, semiconductor between the P and N layers.

PM Abbreviation for phase modulation.

PN junction The junction between two layers of semiconductors of P-type and N-type origin.

PNP transistor A bipolar transistor formed by three layers of semiconductor materials – the outside two layers being of P-type material, the middle layer of N-type material.

Point contact device One in which the pn junction is formed at the contact between a metal 'cats-whisker' and the semiconductor material. Point contact diodes have advantages in some applications.

Polarised Term used to describe any component or device which must be inserted into a circuit a particular way round.

Positive feedback Type of control procedure in which part of the output signal of a circuit is fed back to the input terminal in such a way that the circuit regenerates the signal, resulting in greater amounts of signal fed back, resulting in further regenerates. Generally, the result of positive feedback is to form an oscillation.

Pot Abbreviation for potentiometer.

Potential Abbreviation for potential difference.

Potential difference The voltage across two points.

Potential divider A circuit consisting of a number of series components. Tapping at one of the junctions between components allows a fraction of the total applied voltage to be obtained. Synonymous with voltage divider.

Potentiometer A form of variable resistor with three contacts. A voltage is applied across the outer two (across the total resistance) and the third contact (the wiper) may be varied along the length of the resistance forming a variable voltage divider. Abbreviation: pot.

Power Rate at which energy is used up or work is done. The electrical unit of power is the watt. Abbreviation: W. Symbol: P.

Power ratio The unit of acoustical or electrical power measurement in comparison with a standard level is the bel. In practical terms, power ratios are usually expressed in decibels (dB).

Power supply A source of electrical power for electronic circuits. Usually the power supply is integral to the equipment. Abbreviation: PSU (for power supply unit).

Power transistor A transistor which operates at high values of power.

PPM Abbreviation for pulse position modulation.

Preamp Abbreviation for preamplifier.

Preamplifier Part of an amplifying system which amplifies small applied input signals, generally amplifying in terms of voltage amplitude only.

Preferred values Predetermined component values. Their use makes component manufacture relatively simple, as only a selected few values need be manufactured, not every possible value.

Prestel See Videotex.

Primary cell A cell whose structure does not allow it to be recharged.

Printed circuit board Method of manufacturing electronic products, in which all or most of the circuit is constructed on a thin board (the printed circuit board). Connections between components are formed with thin strips of copper. Abbreviation: PCB.

Printer Computer peripheral which prints characters or symbols onto paper.

Program The complete set of instructions which can control the operation of a computer.

Programmable read only memory Computer memory which may be programmed, i.e., have data written into it, once. After this it may only be read from. Abbreviation: PROM.

Programming language Any language which may be understood by computers and humans. Computers ultimately require instructions in machine code, so this is the simplest programming language. It *can* be understood by humans but not easily. Low level programming languages resemble machine code and are thus still difficult in terms of human use. High level programming languages resemble human languages and are thus easier for humans to use.

PROM Abbreviation for programmable read only memory.

P-type semiconductor Semiconductor material containing a higher concentration of positive charge carriers, i.e., holes, than negative charge carriers, i.e., electrons. In effect holes are simply a depletion of electrons, but nevertheless can be viewed as small objects which carry a charge through a semiconductor.

Public address system Sound reproduction system used to amplify sound and thus allow it to be relayed to many people over a large area. Abbreviation: PA.

Pulse A single variation in voltage or current from a zero value, to a maximum and back to zero.

Pulse amplitude modulation Pulse modulation system in which the amplitude of a pulse is modulated with respect to the amplitude of a message signal. Abbreviation: PAM.

Pulse code modulation Pulse modulation system in which pulses are produced corresponding to the message signal. Abbreviation: PCM.

Pulse modulation Any modulation system in which a train of pulses is used as the carrier. Abbreviation: PM.

Pulse position modulation Pulse modulation system in which the position of each pulse is related to the message signal. Abbreviation: PPM.

Pulse width modulation Pulse modulation system in which the width of each pulse is modulated with respect to the message signal. Abbreviation: PWM.

Push-pull Circuit operation in which two devices operate totally out of phase.

Q-factor Abbreviation for quality factor.

Quadrophonic Referring to a sound reproduction system with four separate sound channels.

Quadrature Two sine waves of the same frequency but 90° out of phase are referred to as being in quadrature.

Quality factor A variable which describes the selectivity of a circuit. It is typically used in conjunction with resonant circuits. The quality factor may be calculated from the expression:

$$Q = \frac{B}{f}$$

where Q is the quality factor, B is the bandwidth of the circuit, and f is the centre frequency of the circuit. Abbreviation: Q-factor.

Quantisation The production of a number of quantised, i.e. discrete, values which may be used to describe a continuous waveform. The best example of the use of quantisation is in the process of pulse modulation, where the sampled values are used to define some aspect of a pulse train.

Quartz A type of crystal which exhibits the phenomenon of piezoelectricity.

Quartz-crystal oscillator An oscillator which relies on the principle that crystal will vibrate at a fixed natural frequency.

Quiescent current Current which flows through any component or part of a circuit under normal conditions, when no signal is applied.

Quiescent point Point on a semiconductor's characteristic curve representing the parameters of the device when in a quiescent state.

Radar An acronym of radio direction and ranging. A system capable of locating distant objects using reflected radio waves.

Radiation Any form of energy transmitted as electromagnetic waves, or as streams of particles.

Radio The use of electromagnetic radiation within the frequency range of about 3 kHz to 300 GHz to transmit information without connecting wires.

Radiowave Any electromagnetic radiation with a frequency within the radio frequency range of about 3 kHz to 300 GHz.

RAM Abbreviation for random access memory.

Random access memory Type of computer memory which may be accessed randomly, i.e., directly (non-sequentially).

Raster Term describing the pattern of lines on a television-type display screen, which occurs at all times.

Ratings Specification sheets for transistors cover many facets of the device's operation but most parameters are needed only by the designer. The ratings which need to be known for replacement purposes are $V_{CE(max)}$, the maximum collector to emitter voltage; I_C the collector current; h_{fe}, the gain and f_t the cut-off frequency. The output power also needs to be observed.

RC Abbreviation for resistor-capacitor.

RC network Abbreviation for resistor-capacitor network. Any circuit or network which consists primarily of a resistor and a capacitor.

Reactance The part of the total impedance of a circuit, which is due to capacitance or inductance, and not to resistance. Reactance causes the current and voltage to become out of phase (in a circuit of pure resistance, current and voltage are in phase). Symbol: X. Unit: ohm.

Reactive load A load with reactance, which thus causes the applied current and voltage to be out of phase.

Reactor A component with reactance, i.e., a capacitor or inductor.

Read To retrieve information previously stored in a computer-type memory device.

Read only memory A computer-type memory device, from which information can only be read from, and not stored into. The information held in a read only memory is generally stored at the manufacture stage and is specific to the operation of the computer. Abbreviation: ROM.

Read-write head Device used to record and retrieve information to and from a magnetic memory.

Real time operation Use of a computer during the actual time a process is occurring, to monitor and control the process.

Receiver The part of a communication system which receives encoded information from a transmitter, and decodes it to the form required.

Record Any permanent or semi-permanent storage of electrical information.

Rectifier Any device which passes current in only one direction. A rectifier is thus an a.c.-to-d.c. converter.

Redundancy 1 The use of extra components in a circuit or system to ensure that breakdown of one component does not affect operation of the circuit or system. Redundancy is a method of increasing reliability. 2 Inclusion of extra information in a transmitted signal which may be eliminated without loss of essential information.

Refractive index The ratio (n) of the velocity of light in free space to that in the material.

Refresh The restoration of information stored so that the information is not lost, typically in a dynamic memory device, or in devices with a destructive read operation.

Regeneration Synonym for positive feedback.

Register One of the temporary storage locations within the central processor of a computer, used to store the results of operations and calculations performed.

Regulator A circuit or device which maintains a constant output voltage or current, regardless of input voltage or output current requirements.

Rejection band The band of frequencies which are not passed through a filter.

Relative permittivity The ratio of the difference between the permittivity of a capacitor dielectric and the permittivity of free space.

Relaxation oscillator An oscillator which relies for its operation on an increasing and decreasing current or voltage within each period of oscillation.

Relay An electrical component in which an applied voltage or current electromagnetically operates a switching mechanism. The contacts of the switch can be isolated from the electromagnet providing a means whereby separate circuits may be interfaced without the need for electrical contact. Modern relays, although providing the same function, are often of a solid state form.

Reliability The ability of a component, circuit, or system to perform its functions for a given period of time.

Reluctance The magnetic equivalent of resistance.

Repeater A device or circuit which amplifies, regenerates, or restores to its original condition a signal in a telecommunications system, which has deteriorated due to transmission over a distance.

Resistance The ability of a material to resist the flow of electric current and to convert electrical energy into heat. A material's resistance is given by the ratio of applied voltage across it to the current flow through it caused by this voltage. Symbol: R. Unit: ohm.

Resistivity The ability of a material to have a resistance dependent on the material's cross-sectional area and its length. The resistivity of a material is given by

$$\rho = \frac{RA}{L}$$

where ρ is the resistivity, R is the resistance, A the cross-sectional area, and L the length.

Resistor An electronic component which possesses resistance. A pure resistor possesses only resistance, no capacitance or inductance, but all practical resistors possess some small amount of capacitance or inductance. Usually these are sufficiently small to be negligible.

Resonance Phenomenon arising when a circuit or system is excited by an applied signal, so that a small input signal produces a relatively large output signal, at the system's resonant frequency.

Resonant frequency The frequency at which a resonant circuit naturally resonates. Symbol: ω.

Reverberation The persistence of sound inside an enclosure, due to multiple reflections from the inside surfaces of the enclosure.

Reverberation time The time required from the cessation of a sound, for the intensity to fall by 60 dB (that is, one millionth of the original value). The unit of reverberation time is the second.

Reverse bias Voltage applied to a PN junction, such that the P-type layer of semiconductor is negative with respect to the N-type layer. Synonymous with reverse voltage.

Reverse Voltage Synonym for reverse bias.

Rewrite Synonym for refresh.

RF Abbreviation for radio frequency.

Rheostat A variable resistor used specifically to alter the current flow in a circuit.

Right hand rule See Fleming's right-hand rule.

Ringing The delay which a system exhibits in returning to its quiescent state after a sharp pulse input, due to inherent resonance within the system. Generally a period of oscillation occurs, gradually dying away. Damping the system will reduce this period.

Ripple A small a.c. signal superimposed on a d.c. voltage or current, typically found on the output of a d.c. power supply, where the frequency of the ripple is mains frequency, i.e., 50 Hz or sometimes twice this frequency.

Rise time The time taken for a pulse's leading edge to rise from 10% to 90% of its final value.

RMS Abbreviation for root mean square.

ROM Abbreviation for read only memory.

Root mean square Term used to describe the effective value of an a.c. waveform. It is the square root of the mean value of the squares of the instantaneous values of the waveform. In the specific case of a sinewave, the root mean square value is equal to the peak value divided by $\sqrt{2}$. Abbreviation: RMS.

RS flip-flop See Bistable.

Rumble Unwanted noise heard in a hi-fi system, caused by mechanical vibrations in the record playing deck, of low frequency.

Sampling The extraction of portions of an electrical analogue signal, used to produce a series of discrete values.

Satellite Artificial body in orbit around the earth for purposes of communications, either one-way from the satellite to the earth, or two-way from earth to satellite and back.

Saturation When the output current of an electronic device is constant and independent of input.

Sawtooth oscillator A relaxation oscillator which produces a sawtooth shaped waveform.

Scanning Process of controlling the electron beam horizontally across and vertically down the face of a cathode ray tube device.

Schematic Circuit diagram.

Schmitt trigger Bistable circuit in which the binary output is determined by the magnitude of the input signal in such a way that the circuit exhibits hysteresis – the output changes when the input exceeds a predetermined level, and changes back when the input falls below a lower predetermined level.

Scramble Process of rendering a communications signal unintelligible at the receiver unless a descrambling circuit is used.

Screen 1 Surface of a cathode ray . 2 Shield to prevent electromagnetic interference.

SCS Acronym for silicon controlled switch.

SECAM Acronym for sequential couleur à memoire; a line-sequential colour television standard.

Secondary cell Rechargeable cell.

Secondary emission Emission of electrons from a material as the result of a bombardment by high-velocity electrons or positive ions.

Secondary voltage Voltage developed across the secondary windings of a transformer.

Selectivity Ability of a radio receiver to discriminate against carrier frequencies different to that selected.

Semiconductor device Device whose operation is based on the use of semiconductor material. In addition to transistors and diodes there is a wide range of components which make use of semiconductor effects.

Semiconductor material Material whose conductive properties depend on the addition of minute quantities of impurity atoms. Unlike normal conductors, semiconductors increase in conductivity with an increase in temperature.

Sensitivity 1 The change in output of a device per unit change in input. 2 Ability of a radio receiver to respond to weak input signals.

Sensor Transducer.

Serial transmission Communication method in which characters are transmitted in turn along a single line.

Series Components in series have one current flowing through each.

Shift register Digital store of information, in which the information is displaced one place in either direction on application of a shift pulse.

Short circuit Unwanted electrical connection between two points in a circuit.

Short wave Radiowave in the wavelength range from 10 to 100 metres.

Shunt Parallel connection.

Siemens Symbol: S. The SI unit of electrical conductance.

Signal Variable electrical parameter.

Signal generator Device which can generate a controlled signal.

Signal-to-noise ratio The ratio of the value of signal at a point in a system, compared with the value of noise at the same point. Usually expressed in decibels.

Silicon Semiconductor element, most widely used element to form semiconductor devices.

Silicon controlled rectifier Abbreviation SCR. Thyristor.

Simplex Communications channel operating in one direction only.

Sinusoidal Waveform identical in shape to a sine function.

Slew rate The rate at which the output of a circuit can be driven from one limit to the other.

Smoothing circuit Circuit designed to reduce ripple in a direct current or voltage.

Solid state circuit A circuit in which the current flows through solid material instead of through a gas or vacuum.

Super alpha pair See Darlington pair.

Synchronous Clocked.

Telecommunications The transfer of information by any electromagnetic means.

Telemetry Measurement at a distance using electromagnetic means.

Telephone Communication of speech and/or other sounds via electromagnetic means.

Television Communication of video and audio information by electromagnetic means.

Thermal runaway Semiconductor materials are very sensitive to heat – germanium much more so than silicon. Circuit design has to take account of this and many components have to be included to prevent increased current flow due to heat. Without such protection heat induced current will raise the temperature leading to a further increase in current and so on, a process known as thermal runaway which can destroy a semiconductor. See Heat sink.

Thermionic emission Electron emission from the surface of a body, due to the temperature of the body.

Thermistor A semiconductor whose resistance varies with temperature. Some have a negative temperature coefficient, that is resistance falls with an increase in temperature, others have a positive temperature coefficient. Typical applications are to provide compensation for the effects of heat on circuit operation.

Thévenin's theorem A theorem used to simplify the analysis of resistance networks.

Threshold of hearing The sound level or intensity which is just audible, for an average listener. For a pure sinusoidal tone of 1,000 Hz, it corresponds approximately to a root mean square pressure of 2×10^{-5} Pa.

Thyristor Three junction, four layer semiconductor rectifier which conducts when either the voltage across it reaches a breakdown point or when triggered by a pulse at its gate electrode. Once triggered it remains conducting until the voltage across it becomes zero.

Transducer Any device that converts one parameter into another, where one of the parameters is an electrical signal.

Transformer Device which transforms electrical energy at its input to electrical output at its output. Usually the voltages of the electrical energies differ.

Transistor Semiconductor device in which the current flowing between two electrodes may be modulated by the voltage or current applied to other electrodes.

Triac Bi-directional thyristor.

Tunnel diode A heavily doped semiconductor diode which exhibits a negative-resistance characteristic, i.e. over part of its characteristic increased forward bias leads to a reduction in the current flowing.

Type numbers The numbers in a transistor designation rarely describe anything about its characteristics. In the 2N series adjacent type numbers are frequently widely differing devices. European and British transistors are frequently coded with the first letter A (germanium) or B (silicon) followed by a second letter which indicates the type:

A	Diode	P	Photo type
C	a.f. (low power)	S	Switching (low power)
D	a.f. (power)	U	Switching (power)
E	Tunnel diode	Y	Diode (power)
F	h.f. (low power)	Z	Zener diode
L	h.f. (power)		

UHF Ultra high frequency.

Ultrasonics Sound frequencies above the limits of human ears, generally classed as above 20 kHz.

Ultraviolet radiation Electromagnetic radiation of wavelengths between visible light and X-rays.

Unijunction transistor Three terminal transistor comprising an n-type silicon bar with a base contact at each end (base 1 and base 2) and a p-type emitter region. Current flow from one base to the other is controlled by the emitter current; when the emitter voltage reaches a certain level the emitter-base 1 junction virtually short circuits. With a suitable charging circuit at the emitter the device operates as a relaxation oscillator.

Valency The ability of atoms to unite with other atoms due to the electrons that exist in the outer orbit, or valency band, being able to form a shared orbit with other atoms.

Varicap diode Varactor. When reverse biased, all pn junctions exhibit capacitance, as the depletion layer at the junction forms an insulator between the conductive regions. This property is used in the varicap, in purposes such as automatic tuning and AFC in radio receivers.

VDU Abbreviation for visual display unit.

VHF Abbreviation for very high frequency.

Voltage-dependent resistor Resistor using semiconductor material whose resistance varies with applied voltage.

Voltage drop Voltage between any two points of a circuit, due to the current flow between them.

Watt Symbol: W. SI unit of power.

Wave A periodic motion, through a medium (which may be space) in which the propagation from a point is a function of time and/or position.

White noise Noise with a wide, flat frequency response.

Word A string of bits corresponding to a unit of information in a digital circuit.

Wow Low frequency (below 10 Hz) periodic variations in the pitch of the sound output of a sound reproduction system.

Write To enter information into a storage element.

Yagi aerial Directional aerial array – most television aerials are based on the Yagi aerial.

Zener diode Voltage regulating diode. A pn junction diode which has a defined reverse breakdown voltage. Once in the breakdown region large increases in current produce negligible variation in the voltage across it.

Using LEDs

When using a light-emitting diode (LED) as an indicator, use the following formula to determine series resistance for various voltages: $R = (V - 1.7) \times 1000 \div I$, where R is resistance in ohms, V is supply voltage (d.c.!), and I is LED current in milliamps.

E.g. to operate LED at 20 mA on
6 V use 220 ohms
9 V   390
12 V   560
24 V   1.2 k

To operate a LED directly from the 240 V mains, a better scheme is to use the second circuit shown. In this, a capacitor is used as a voltage dropping element. A 1N4148 diode or similar across the LED provides the rectification required. As the voltage drop across the LED is negligible compared with the supply, capacitor current is almost always exactly equal to mains voltage divided by capacitive reactance X_c.

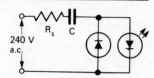

At 50 Hz, 0·47 µF will result in a LED current of about 16 mA. Resistor R_s is included to limit turn-on transients. A value of 270 ohms should be adequate.

Power supply configurations

No circuit losses are allowed for. At low voltages allow for 0·6 V diode drop.

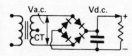

Full-wave bridge
Capacitive input filter

$V_{d.c.} = 1·41 × V_{a.c.}$

$I_{d.c.} = 0·62 × I_{a.c.}$

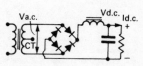

Full-wave bridge
Choke input filter

$V_{d.c.} = 0·90 × V_{a.c.}$

$I_{d.c.} = 0·94 × I_{a.c.}$

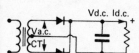

Full-wave
Capacitive input filter

$V_{d.c.} = 0·71 × V_{a.c.}$

$I_{d.c.} = 1·0 × I_{a.c.}$

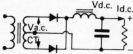

Full-wave
Choke input filter

$V_{d.c.} = 0·45 × V_{a.c.}$

$I_{d.c.} = 1·54 × I_{a.c.}$

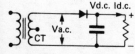

Half-wave
Capacitive input filter

$V_{d.c.} = 1·41 × V_{a.c.}$

$I_{d.c.} = 0·28 × I_{a.c.}$

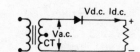

Half-wave
Resistive load

$V_{d.c.} = 0·45 × V_{a.c.}$

$I_{d.c.} = 0·64 × I_{a.c.}$

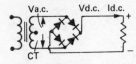

Full-wave bridge
Resistive load

$V_{d.c.} = 0.90 \times V_{a.c.}$

$I_{d.c.} = 0.90 \times I_{a.c.}$

Full-wave
Resistive load

$V_{d.c.} = 0.45 \times V_{a.c.}$

$I_{d.c.} = 1.27 \times I_{a.c.}$

Voltage multiplier circuits

Half-wave voltage doubler
C1 = peak a.c. voltage
C2 = peak a.c. voltage × 2

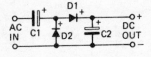

Bi-phase half wave or full wave voltage doubler
C2 and C3 = peak a.c. voltage

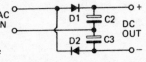

Voltage tripler
C1 = peak a.c. voltage
C2 = peak a.c. voltage
C3 = peak a.c. voltage × 2

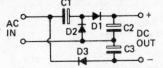

Voltage quadrupler
C1A = peak a.c. voltage
C1B = peak a.c. voltage × 3
C2A and C2B = peak a.c.
voltage × 2
D1-D4 = peak a.c. voltage
× 2

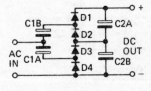

Zener diodes

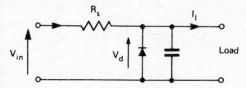

Constant load current/variable input voltage

$$\text{Series resistor } R_s = \frac{V_{in}(\text{min}) - V_d}{1 \cdot 1 \, I_L}$$

$$\text{Diode dissipation } P_d = \left(\frac{V_{in}(\text{max}) - V_d}{R_s} - I_L \right) V_d$$

Variable load current/constant input voltage

$$R_s = \frac{V_{in} - V_d}{1 \cdot 1 \, I_L(\text{max})}$$

$$P_d = \left(\frac{V_{in} - V_d}{R_s} - I_L(\text{min}) \right) V_d$$

Variable load current/variable input voltage

$$R_s = \frac{V_{in}(\text{min}) - V_d}{1 \cdot 1 \, I_L(\text{max})}$$

$$P_d = \left(\frac{V_{in}(\text{max}) - V_d}{R_s} - I_L(\text{min}) \right) V_d$$

Voltage regulators

Fixed voltage types eg 78, 79 series

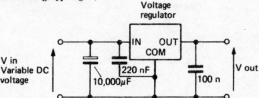

Variable voltage types eg 317, 338 series

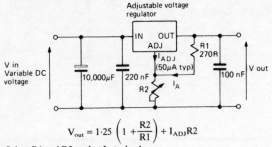

Adjustable voltage regulator

$$V_{out} = 1 \cdot 25 \left(1 + \frac{R2}{R1}\right) + I_{ADJ}R2$$

Select R1 and R2 so that $I_A > 4\,mA$

Op-amp standard circuits

A_v = closed loop a.c. gain f_o = low frequency −3dB point
e_i = input voltage R_{in} = input impedance
e_o = output voltage

  Split supply configurations–supply connections omitted for clarity

Standard op-amp

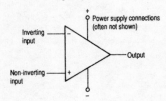

Ideal op-amp

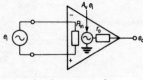

$e_o = A_v\,e_i$ $A_v = \infty$, $r_i = \infty$, $r_o = 0$.
Bandwidth $= \infty$, $e_o = 0$ if $e_i = 0$.

Inverting d.c. amplifier

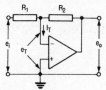

$I_T = 0, e_T = 0$, so we have a virtual ground; gain $= R_1/R_2 = e_o/e_i$; input impedance $= R_1$

Non-inverting d.c. amplifier

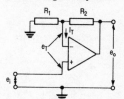

$I_T = 0, e_T = 0$, so we have a virtual ground; gain $= (R_1 + R_2)/R_1$. Input resistance $= \infty$

Non-inverting a.c. amplifier

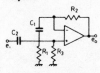

$$A_v = 1 + \frac{R_2}{R_1}; \quad R_{in} = R_2$$

$$f_o = \frac{1}{2\pi R_1 C_1} = \frac{1}{2\pi R_3 C_2}$$

Inverting a.c. amplifier

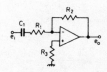

$$A_v = \frac{R_2}{R_1}; \quad R_{in} = R_1$$

$$f_o = \frac{1}{2\pi R_1 C_1}$$

Non-inverting buffer

$$A_v = 1 \quad R_{in} = R_1$$

$$f_o = \frac{1}{2\pi R_1 C_1}$$

Inverting buffer

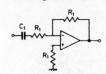

$$A_v = -1 \quad R_{in} = R_1$$

$$f_o = \frac{1}{2\pi R_1 C_1}$$

Inverting summing amplifier

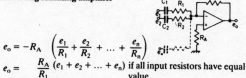

$$e_o = -R_A \left(\frac{e_1}{R_1} + \frac{e_2}{R_2} + \ldots + \frac{e_n}{R_n} \right)$$

$$e_o = \frac{R_A}{R_1} (e_1 + e_2 + \ldots + e_n) \text{ if all input resistors have equal value}$$

Difference amplifier

$$e_o = \left(\frac{R_1 + R_2}{R_3 + R_4}\right)\frac{R_4}{R_1} e_2 - \frac{R_2}{R_1} e_1$$

if $R_1 = R_3$ and $R_2 = R_4$ then

$$e_o = \frac{R_2}{R_1}(e_2 - e_1)$$

$$f_o = \frac{1}{2\pi R_1 C_1} = \frac{1}{2\pi(R_3 + R_4)C_3}$$

$R_2 = R_4$ for minimum offset error

Variable gain a.c. amplifier

$A_v = 0$ (slider at ground)

$A_{v,max} = -\dfrac{R_2}{R_1}$ (slider at positive input)

$R_{in} = \dfrac{R_1}{2}$ (minimum)

$f_o = \dfrac{1}{2\pi(\frac{1}{2}R_1)C_1}$

Single supply configurations–supply connections omitted for clarity.

Polarity switcher, or 4-quadrant gain control

$A_v = +1$ (slider at C_1)

$A_v = 0$ (slider midposition)

$A_v = -1$ (slider at ground)

$R_{in} = \dfrac{R_1}{2}$ (minimum) $f_o = \dfrac{1}{2\pi(\frac{1}{2}R_1)C_1}$

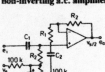

Single supply biasing of non-inverting a.c. amplifier	Single supply biasing of inverting a.c. amplifier

$A_v = 1 + \dfrac{R_2}{R_1}$ $A_v = -\dfrac{R_2}{R_1}$; $R_{in} = R_1$

$R_{in} = R_2$

$f_o = \dfrac{1}{2\pi R_2 C_1} = \dfrac{1}{2\pi R_1 C_2}$ $f_o = \dfrac{1}{2\pi R_1 C_1}$

265

Differentiating amplifier

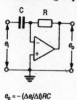

$e_0 = -(\Delta e_i/\Delta t)RC$

Integrating amplifier

$\Delta e_0/\Delta t = -e_i/RC$ input resistance $= R$

Schmitt trigger

Low-pass filter

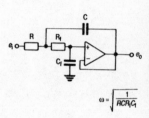

$\omega = \sqrt{\dfrac{1}{RCR_1C_1}}$

High-pass filter

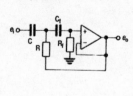

Bandpass filter

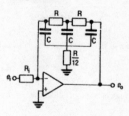

Notch filter

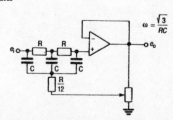

$\omega = \dfrac{\sqrt{3}}{RC}$

Bridge circuits in measurement

Bridge	Quantity measured	Equations
Wheatstone	Resistance	$R_{unknown} = \dfrac{R_1 R_3}{R_2}$
Wien	Frequency	$f = \dfrac{1}{2\pi} \sqrt{\dfrac{1}{R_3 R_4 C_1 C_2}}$
	Capacitance	$\dfrac{C_2}{C_1} = \dfrac{R_2}{R_1} - \dfrac{R_3}{R_4}$
		$C_1^2 = \dfrac{R_1}{(2\pi f)^2 (R_2 R_4 - R_1 R_3) R_3}$
		$C_2^2 = \dfrac{R_2 R_4 - R_1 R_3}{(2\pi f)^2 R_1 R_3 R_4^2}$
Scherin	Capacitance	$C_3 = \dfrac{R_1 C_2}{R_2}$
	Resistance	$R_3 = \dfrac{C_1 R_2}{C_2}$
Hay	Inductance	$L_1 = \dfrac{R_1 R_3 C_1}{1 + (2\pi f R_2 C_1)^2}$
	Resistance	$R_4 = \dfrac{R_1 R_2 R_3 (2\pi f C_1)^2}{1 + (2\pi f R_2 C_1)^2}$
Owen	Inductance	$L_1 = R_1 R_3 C_2$
	Resistance	$R_4 = \dfrac{C_2 R_3}{C_1}$
Maxwell	Industance	$L_1 = R_1 R_3 C_1$
	Resistance	$R_4 = \dfrac{R_1 R_3}{R_2}$
Resonance	Frequency	$f = \dfrac{1}{2\pi} \sqrt{\dfrac{1}{L_1 C_1}}$
	Resistance	$R_4 = \dfrac{R_1 R_3}{R_2}$

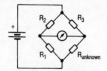

Wheatstone bridge

Wien bridge

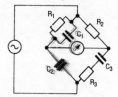

Schering bridge

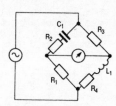

Hay bridge

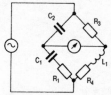

Owen bridge

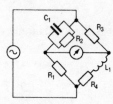

Maxwell bridge

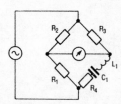

Resonance bridge

Seven-segment LED displays

Display layout

Typical truth table of seven-segment driver

d	c	b	a	A'	B'	C'	D'	E'	F'	G'	Display
0	0	0	0	0	0	0	0	0	0	1	0
0	0	0	1	1	0	0	1	1	1	1	1
0	0	1	0	0	0	1	0	0	1	0	2
0	0	1	1	0	0	0	0	1	1	0	3
0	1	0	0	1	0	0	1	1	0	0	4
0	1	0	1	0	1	0	0	1	0	0	5
0	1	1	0	1	1	0	0	0	0	0	6
0	1	1	1	0	0	0	1	1	1	1	7
1	0	0	0	0	0	0	0	0	0	0	8
1	0	0	1	0	0	0	1	1	0	0	9

The column headers shown are: Input code (d, c, b, a) | Output state (A', B', C', D', E', F', G') | Display

Interfacing logic families

B-series CMOS to standard TTL

Any B-series CMOS — 1 K — 0 V — Any standard TTL gate

CMOS to LS-TTL

Any CMOS gate — Any LS-TTL gate

TTL to CMOS

Any TTL gate — 2 K2 — +5 V — Any CMOS gate

CMOS buffer to TTL

CMOS buffers — Any standard TTL gate or up to six LS-TTL

Standard digital circuits

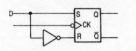

Truth table	
D_0	Q_1
0	0
1	1

D-type flip-flop and truth table

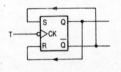

Truth table		
T_0	T_1	Q_1
0	0	Q_0
0	1	Q_0
1	0	$\overline{Q}_0$
1	1	Q_0

T-type flip-flop and truth table

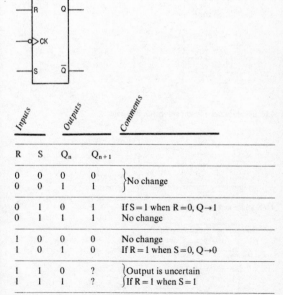

Inputs		Outputs		Comments
R	S	Q_n	Q_{n+1}	
0	0	0	0	No change
0	0	1	1	No change
0	1	0	1	If S = 1 when R = 0, Q → 1
0	1	1	1	No change
1	0	0	0	No change
1	0	1	0	If R = 1 when S = 0, Q → 0
1	1	0	?	Output is uncertain
1	1	1	?	If R = 1 when S = 1

Clocked RS flip-flop and truth table

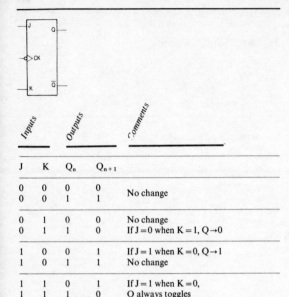

J-K flip-flop and truth table

Inputs		Outputs		Comments
J	K	Q_n	Q_{n+1}	
0	0	0	0	No change
0	0	1	1	
0	1	0	0	No change
0	1	1	0	If J = 0 when K = 1, Q → 0
1	0	0	1	If J = 1 when K = 0, Q → 1
1	0	1	1	No change
1	1	0	1	If J = 1 when K = 0,
1	1	1	0	Q always toggles

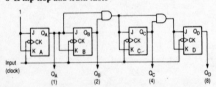

4-bit synchronous counter using J-K flip-flops

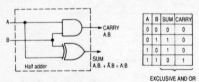

A	B	SUM	CARRY
0	0	0	0
0	1	1	0
1	0	1	0
1	1	0	1

EXCLUSIVE AND OR

Half adder and truth table

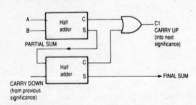

Full adder

Decibel table

The decibel figures are in the centre column: figures to the left represent decibel loss, and those to the right decibel gain. The voltage and current figures are given on the assumption that there is no change in impedance.

Voltage or current ratio	Power ratio	dB ← − + →	Voltage or current ratio	Power ratio
1·000	1·000	0	1·000	1·000
0·989	0·977	0·1	1·012	1·023
0·977	0·955	0·2	1·023	1·047
0·966	0·933	0·3	1·035	1·072
0·955	0·912	0·4	1·047	1·096
0·944	0·891	0·5	1·059	1·122
0·933	0·871	0·6	1·072	1·148
0·912	0·832	0·8	1·096	1·202
0·891	0·794	1·0	1·122	1·259
0·841	0·708	1·5	1·189	1·413
0·794	0·631	2·0	1·259	1·585
0·750	0·562	2·5	1·334	1·778
0·708	0·501	3·0	1·413	1·995
0·668	0·447	3·5	1·496	2·239
0·631	0·398	4·0	1·585	2·512
0·596	0·355	4·5	1·679	2·818
0·562	0·316	5·0	1·778	3·162
0·501	0·251	6·0	1·995	3·981
0·447	0·200	7·0	2·239	5·012
0·398	0·159	8·0	2·512	6·310
0·355	0·126	9·0	2·818	7·943
0·316	0·100	10	3·162	10·00
0·282	0·0794	11	3·55	12·6
0·251	0·0631	12	3·98	15·9
0·224	0·0501	13	4·47	20·0
0·200	0·0398	14	5·01	25·1
0·178	0·0316	15	5·62	31·6
0·159	0·0251	16	6·31	39·8
0·126	0·0159	18	7·94	63·1
0·100	0·0100	20	10·00	100·0
$3·16 \times 10^{-2}$	10^{-3}	30	$3·16 \times 10$	10^{3}
10^{-2}	10^{-4}	40	10^{2}	10^{4}
$3·16 \times 10^{-3}$	10^{-5}	50	$3·16 \times 10^{2}$	10^{5}
10^{-3}	10^{-6}	60	10^{3}	10^{6}
$3·16 \times 10^{-4}$	10^{-7}	70	$3·16 \times 10^{3}$	10^{7}
10^{-4}	10^{-8}	80	10^{4}	10^{8}
$3·16 \times 10^{-5}$	10^{-9}	90	$3·16 \times 10^{4}$	10^{9}
10^{-5}	10^{-10}	100	10^{5}	10^{10}
$3·16 \times 10^{-6}$	10^{-11}	110	$3·16 \times 10^{5}$	10^{11}
10^{-6}	10^{-12}	120	10^{6}	10^{12}

Laws

Ampere's Rule Refers to the deflection direction of a magnetic pointer that is influenced by a current; an analogy being that if a person is assumed to be swimming with the current and facing the indicator, the north-seeking pole is deflected towards the left hand, the south pole being deflected in an opposite direction.

Ampere's Theorem The magnetic field from current flowing in a circuit is equivalent to that due to a simple magnetic shell, the outer edge coinciding with the electrical conductor with such strength that it equals that current strength.

Baur's Constant That voltage necessary to cause a discharge through a determined insulating material 1 mm thick. The law of dielectric strength is that breakdown voltage necessary to cause a discharge through a substance proportional to a 2/3 power of its thickness.

Coulomb's Law Implies that the mechanical force between two charged bodies is directly proportionate to the charges and inversely so to the squares of the distance separating them.

Faraday's Laws That of induction is that the e.m.f. induced in a circuit is proportional to the rate of change in the lines of force linking it. That of electrolysis is (1) That the quantity of a substance deposited in defined time is proportional to the current. (2) That different substances and quantities deposited by a single current in a similar time are proportional to the electro-chemical equivalents. The Faraday Effect states that when a light beam passes through a strong magnetic field the plane of polarisation is rotated.

Fleming's Rules By placing the thumb and first two fingers at right-angles respectively, the forefinger can represent the direction of magnetic field; the second finger, current direction; the thumb, motion direction. Use of the right hand in this way represents the relation in a dynamo; use of the left hand represents the relation in a motor.

Hall Effect If an electric current flows across the lines of flux of a magnetic field, an e.m.f. is observed at right-angles to the primary current and to the magnetic field. When a steady current flows in a magnetic field, e.m.f. tendencies develop at right-angles to the magnetic force and to the current, proportionately to the product of the current strength, the magnetic force and the sine of the angle between the direction of quantities.

Joule's Law As a formula this is I^2Rt joules. It refers to that heat developed by the current (I) which is proportional to the square of I multiplied by R and t, letting R = resistance and t = time. If the formula is seen as $JH = RI^2t$ it equals EIt, letting J = joules equivalent of heat, and H = the number of heat units.

Kerr Effect Illustrates that an angle of rotation is proportional to a magnetisation intensity and applies to the rotation of polarisation plane of plain polarised light as reflected from the pole of a magnet. The number (a constant) varies for different wavelengths and materials, making necessary the multiplication of magnetisation intensity in order to find the angle of rotation forming the effect.

Lambert's Cosine Law For a surface receiving light obliquely, the illumination is proportional to the cosine of the angle which the light makes with the normal to the surface.

Lenz's Law That induced currents have such a direction that the reaction forces generated have a tendency to oppose the motion or action producing them.

Maxwell's Law (*a*) Any two circuits carrying current tend so to dispose themselves as to include the largest possible number of lines of force common to the two. (*b*) Every electro-magnetic system tends to change its configuration so that the exciting circuit embraces the largest number of lines of force in a positive direction.

Maxwell's Rule Maxwell's *unit tubes* of electric or magnetic induction are such that a *unit pole* delivers 4π unit tubes of force.

Miller Circuit A form of circuit in which the time-constant of a resistance-capacitance combination is multiplied by means of the Miller effect on the capacitance. Named after John M. Miller.

Miller Effect Implies that the grid input impedance of a valve with a load in the anode circuit is different from its input impedance with a zero anode load. Should the load in the anode be resistance, the input impedance is purely capacitive. If the load impedance has a reactive component, the input impedance will have a resistive component. In pre-detector amplification, with a.v.c. to signal grids, the capacity across the tuned grid circuits tends to vary with the signal strength, evidencing detuning, the effect causing a charge (electrostatic) to be induced by the anode on the grid.

Planck's Constant Quanta of energy radiated when atomic electrons transfer from one state to another, assuming both to be *energy states* with electro-magnetic radiation. The constant (*h*) is given the value of $6·626 \times 10^{-34}$ joule second. h is usually coupled to the symbol (v) to represent the frequency of the radiated energy in hertz. That is, the frequency of the radiated energy is determinable by the relation $W_1 - W_2$, this equalling hv. W_1 and W_2 equal the values of the internal energy of the atom in initial and final stages. This constant is also known as the *Quantum Theory*.

Sabine's Relation For an auditorium whose boundaries comprise areas $A_1, A_2, A_3 \dots$ etc., of absorption coefficient $\alpha_1, \alpha_2, \alpha_3 \dots$ etc., the reverberation time, t, is given by

$$t = \frac{0·16V}{\Sigma\alpha A}$$

where V is the auditorium's volume, and $\Sigma\alpha A = \alpha_1 A_1 + \alpha_1 A_1 + \dots$ etc.

Snell's Law For light incident on the boundary between two media, the ratio of the sine of the angle of incidence to the sine of the angle of refraction is a constant; equal to the inverse ratio of the refractive indices of the two media.

Thévenin's Theorem The current through a resistance R connected across any two points A and B of an active network (i.e. a network containing one or more sources of e.m.f.) is obtained by dividing the p.d. between A and B, with R disconnected, by $(R+r)$, where r is the resistance of the network measured between points A and B with R disconnected and the sources of e.m.f. replaced by their internal resistances.

CCITT recommendations

Series	Description
A	CCITT organisation
B	Means of expression
C	Telecommunications statistics
D	Tariff principles for leased circuits
E	Telephones, quality of service and tariffs
F	Telegraph, quality of service and tariffs
G	Line transmission
H	Non-telephone signal transmission
J	Television and sound programme transmission
K	Protection against interference
L	Protection of cable sheaths and poles
M	Telephone, telegraph and data transmission maintenance
N	Television and sound programme transmission maintenance
O	Measuring equipment specification
P	Telephone transmission quality
Q	Telephone signalling and transmission
R	Telegraph transmission
S	Alphabetic telegraph and data terminal equipment
T	Facsimile transmission
U	Telegraph switching
V	Data transmission via public switched telephone networks
X	Data transmission via public data networks

Connectors and connections

Data interchange by modems

When transmitting and receiving data across telephone or other circuits, the equipment which actually generates and uses the data (e.g., a computer or VDU terminal) is known as *data terminating equipment* (DTE). The equipment which terminates the telephone line and converts the basic data signals into signals which can be transmitted is known as *data circuit-terminating equipment* (DCE). As far as the user is concerned the interface between DTE and DCE is the most important. CCITT recommendation V24 defines the signal interchanges and functions between DTE and DCE; these are commonly known as the 100 series interchange circuits:

Interchange circuit		Data		Control		Timing	
Number	Name	From DCE	To DCE	From DCE	To DCE	From DCE	To DCE
101	Protective ground or earth						
102	Signal ground or common return						
103	Transmitted data		●				
104	Received data	●					

Number	Name	Data From DCE	Data To DCE	Control From DCE	Control To DCE	Timing From DCE	Timing To DCE
105	Request to send				●		
106	Ready for sending			●			
107	Data set ready			●			
108/1	Connect data set to line				●		
108/2	Data terminal ready				●		
109	Data channel received line signal detector			●			
110	Signal quality detector			●			
111	Data signalling rate selector (DTE)				●		
112	Data signalling rate selector (DCE)			●			
113	Transmitter signal element timing (DTE)						●
114	Transmitter signal element timing (DCE)					●	
115	Receiver signal element timing (DCE)					●	
116	Select standby				●		
117	Standby indicator			●			
118	Transmitted backward channel data		●				
119	Received backward channel data	●					
120	Transmit backward channel line signal				●		
121	Backward channel ready			●			
122	Backward channel received line signal detector			●			
123	Backward channel signal quality detector			●			
124	Select frequency groups				●		
125	Calling indicator			●			
126	Select transmit frequency				●		
127	Select receive frequency				●		
128	Receiver signal element timing (DTE)						●
129	Request to receive				●		
130	Transmit backward tone				●		
131	Received character timing					●	
132	Return to non-data mode				●		
133	Ready for receiving				●		
134	Received data present			●			
191	Transmitted voice answer				●		
192	Received voice answer			●			

Modem connector pin numbers

The connectors used with 100 series interchange circuits and its pin assignments are defined by international standard ISO 2110 and are (for modems following the CCITT recommendations V21, V23, V26, V26bis, V27 and V27bis) as follows:

Pin number	Interchange circuit numbers V21	V23	V26/V27
1	*1	*1	*1
2	103	103	103
3	104	104	104
4	105	105	105
5	106	106	106
6	107	107	107
7	102	102	102
8	109	109	109
9	*N	*N	*N
10	*N	*N	*N

Interchange circuit numbers

Pin number	V21	V23	V26/V27
11	126	*N	*N
12	*F	122	122
13	*F	121	121
14	*F	118	118
15	*F	*2	114
16	*F	119	119
17	*F	*2	115
18	141	141	141
19	*F	120	120
20	108/1-2	108/1-2	108/1-2
21	140	140	140
22	125	125	125
23	*N	111	111
24	*N	*N	113
25	142	142	142

Notes:
*1 Pin 1 is assigned for connecting the shields between tandem sections of shielded cables. It may be connected to protective ground or signal ground.
*F Reserved for future use.
*N Reserved for national use.

Automatic calling

A similar series of interchange circuits is defined in CCITT recommendation V25 for automatic calling answering between modems over the telephone network. This is the 200 series interchange circuits:

Interchange circuit

Number	Name	From DCE	To DCE
201	Signal ground	●	●
202	Call request		●
203	Data line occupied	●	
204	Distant station connected	●	
205	Abandon call	●	
206	Digit signal (2^0)		●
207	Digit signal (2^1)		●
208	Digit signal (2^2)		●
209	Digit signal (2^3)		●
210	Present next digit	●	
211	Digit present		●
213	Power indication	●	

RS 232C

The EIA equivalent of CCITT V24 interface is the RS 232C specification, which similarly defines the electrical interface between DTE and DCE. Although the two have different designations, they are to all practical purposes equivalent. The RS 232C interchange circuits are:

Interchange circuit

Mnemonic	Name	Data From DCE	Data To DCE	Control From DCE	Control To DCE	Timing From DCE	Timing To DCE
AA	Protective ground						
AB	Signal ground/common return						
BA	Transmitted data		●				
BB	Received data	●					
CA	Request to send				●		
CB	Clear to send			●			
CC	Data set ready			●			
CD	Data terminal ready				●		
CE	Ring indicator			●			
CF	Received line signal detector			●			
CG	Signal quality detector			●			
CH	Data signal rate selector (DTE)				●		
CI	Data signal rate selector (DCE)			●			
DA	Transmitter signal element timing (DTE)						●
DB	Transmitter signal element timing (DCE)					●	
DD	Receiver signal element timing (DCE)					●	
SBA	Secondary transmitted data		●				
SBB	Secondary received data	●					
SCA	Secondary request to send				●		
SCB	Secondary clear to send			●			
SCF	Secondary received line signal detector			●			

RS 449

The EIA RS 232C standard, although the most common, is by no means perfect. One of its main limitations is the maximum data rate – 18·2 Kbaud. Various improved interchange circuits (RS 422, RS 423) have been developed. The RS 449 standard is capable of very fast data rates (up to 2 Mbaud):

Interchange circuit

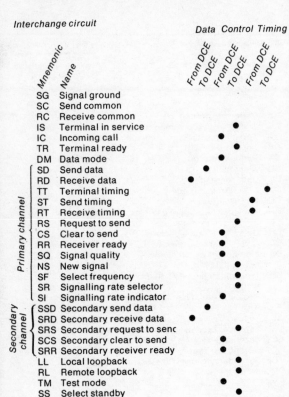

		Data From DCE	Data To DCE	Control From DCE	Control To DCE	Timing From DCE	Timing To DCE
SG	Signal ground						
SC	Send common						
RC	Receive common						
IS	Terminal in service				●		
IC	Incoming call			●			
TR	Terminal ready				●		
DM	Data mode			●			
SD	Send data		●				
RD	Receive data	●					
TT	Terminal timing						●
ST	Send timing					●	
RT	Receive timing					●	
RS	Request to send				●		
CS	Clear to send			●			
RR	Receiver ready			●			
SQ	Signal quality			●			
NS	New signal				●		
SF	Select frequency				●		
SR	Signalling rate selector				●		
SI	Signalling rate indicator			●			
SSD	Secondary send data		●				
SRD	Secondary receive data	●					
SRS	Secondary request to send				●		
SCS	Secondary clear to send			●			
SRR	Secondary receiver ready			●			
LL	Local loopback				●		
RL	Remote loopback				●		
TM	Test mode			●			
SS	Select standby				●		
SB	Standby indicator			●			

Primary channel: SD, RD, TT, ST, RT, RS, CS, RR, SQ, NS, SF, SR, SI

Secondary channel: SSD, SRD, SRS, SCS, SRR

Centronics interface
Most personal computers use the Centronics parallel data transfer
to a printer. The pin connections of the connector, abbreviations and
signal descriptions are shown.

All signals are standard TTL, although not all signals necessarily
exist in any given interface.

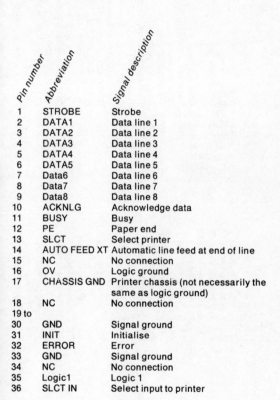

Pin number	Abbreviation	Signal description
1	STROBE	Strobe
2	DATA1	Data line 1
3	DATA2	Data line 2
4	DATA3	Data line 3
5	DATA4	Data line 4
6	DATA5	Data line 5
7	Data6	Data line 6
8	Data7	Data line 7
9	Data8	Data line 8
10	ACKNLG	Acknowledge data
11	BUSY	Busy
12	PE	Paper end
13	SLCT	Select printer
14	AUTO FEED XT	Automatic line feed at end of line
15	NC	No connection
16	OV	Logic ground
17	CHASSIS GND	Printer chassis (not necessarily the same as logic ground)
18	NC	No connection
19 to 30	GND	Signal ground
31	INIT	Initialise
32	ERROR	Error
33	GND	Signal ground
34	NC	No connection
35	Logic1	Logic 1
36	SLCT IN	Select input to printer

RS 232C/RS 449/V24 comparison

RS 232C		RS 449		V24	
AB	Signal ground	SG	Signal ground	102	Signal ground
		SC	Send common	102a	DTE common
		RC	Receive common	102b	DCE common
		IS	Terminal in service		
CE	Ring indicator	IC	Incoming call	125	Calling indicator
CD	Data terminal ready	TR	Terminal ready	108/2	Data terminal ready
CC	Data set ready	DM	Data mode	107	Data set ready
BA	Transmitted data	SD	Send data	103	Transmitted data
BB	Receive data	RD	Receive data	104	Received data
DA	Transmitter signal element Timing (DTE source)	TT	Terminal timing	113	Transmitter signal element Timing (DTE source)
DB	Transmitter signal element Timing (DCE source)	ST	Send timing	114	Transmitter signal element Timing (DCE source)
DD	Receiver signal element timing	RT	Receive timing	115	Receiver signal element timing (DCE source)
CA	Request to send	RS	Request to send	105	Request to send
CB	Clear to send	CS	Clear to send	106	Ready for sending
CF	Received line signal detector	RR	Receiver ready	109	Data channel received line signal detector
CG	Signal quality detector	SQ	Signal quality	110	Data signal quality detector
		NS	New signal		
		SF	Select frequency	126	Select transmit frequency

CH	Data signal rate selector (DTE source)	SR	Signalling rate selector	111 Data signalling rate selector (DTE source)
CI	Data signal rate selector (DCE source)	SI	Signalling rate indicator	112 Data signalling rate selector (DCE source)
				118 Transmitted backward channel data
SBA	Secondary transmitted data	SSD	Secondary send data	119 Received backward channel data
SBB	Secondary received data	SRD	Secondary receive data	120 Transmit backward channel line signal
SGA	Secondary request to send	SRS	Secondary request to send	
				121 Backward channel ready
SCB	Secondary clear to send	SCS	Secondary clear to send	122 Backward channel received line signal detector
SCF	Secondary received line signal detector	SRR	Secondary receiver ready	
				141 Local loopback
		LL	Local loopback	140 Remote loopback
		RL	Remote loopback	143 Test indicator
		TM	Test mode	116 Select standby
		SS	Select standby	117 Standby indicator
		SB	Standby indicator	

Audio connectors

The DIN standards devised by the German Industrial Standards Board are widely used for the connection of audio equipment. The connectors are shown below. The 3-way and 5-way 45° are the most common, and connections for those are listed.

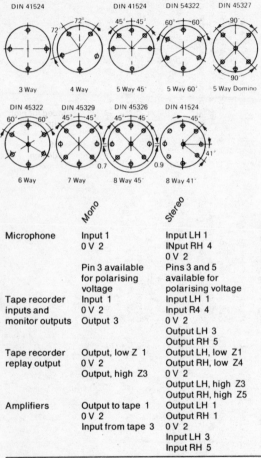

	Mono	Stereo
Microphone	Input 1	Input LH 1
	0 V 2	INput RH 4
		0 V 2
	Pin 3 available	Pins 3 and 5
	for polarising	available for
	voltage	polarising voltage
Tape recorder	Input 1	Input LH 1
inputs and	0 V 2	Input R4 4
monitor outputs	Output 3	0 V 2
		Output LH 3
		Output RH 5
Tape recorder	Output, low Z 1	Output LH, low Z1
replay output	0 V 2	Output RH, low Z4
	Output, high Z3	0 V 2
		Output LH, high Z3
		Output RH, high Z5
Amplifiers	Output to tape 1	Output LH 1
	0 V 2	Output RH 1
	Input from tape 3	0 V 2
		Input LH 3
		Input RH 5

Variations on the above exist between different manufacturers.

Coaxial connectors

A number of connectors are available for use with coaxial cables.
The most common are:

Type	Impedance (Ω)	Maximum fre. (MHz)	Max. peak voltage (V)	Notes
BNC	50	10 000	500	High quality constant
	75	10 000	500	impedance bayonet fitting connector.
Miniature				High quality constant
BNC	50	10 000	500	impedance connector.
N	50	10 000	1000	Recommended for high
	75	10 000	500	power circuits above 400 MHz.
PL259/ SO239	50	200	500	Non-constant impedance design. High vswr makes it unsuitable for use above 144 MHz.
C	75	—	—	Bayonet fitting
F	50	—	—	American cctv connector used on some 144 MHz portable transceivers. Plugs use inner conductor of cable for centre pin.
Belling Lee	75	—	—	British tv aerial connector used extensively on home-built equipment and some British commercial equipment. Main virtue is low cost but aluminium plugs can corrode when used outside.
Phono	—	—	—	American connector originally designed for audio use.
GR	50	1000	—	Constant impedance sexless connectors.

284

Videorecorder/televisions/camera connectors

Standard pin configurations for videorecorders, televisions and videocameras are shown below. Many follow standard DIN connector pinouts, but videocamera and SCART connectors differ significantly.

(a) 5-pin DIN

(b) 6-pin DIN

(c) 7-pin DIN

1,4 Audio in
2 Chassis
3,5 Audio out
 or stereo
1 L audio in
2 Chassis
3 L audio out
4 R audio in
5 R audio out

1 AV select.
 For VCR
 high = all
 outputs,
 low = all
 inputs.
 Opposite
 for TV set
2 Video in/out
3 Chassis
4 L audio in/
 out
5 12V
6 R audio in/
 out

1 L audio in
2 Chassis
3 L audio out
4 R audio in
5 R audio out
6 Remote
 control
 data
7 Chassis

(d) 8-pin DIN

(e) SCART

1 L audio in
2 Remote
 control
 data
3 R audio in
4 Chassis
 (audio)
5 Chassis
 (remote
 control)
6 Chassis
 (video)
7 Chassis
 (audio)
8 Video in

1 R audio out
2 R audio in
3 L audio out
4 Chassis
 (audio)
5 Chassis (B
 video)
6 L video in
7 B video in
8 Source
 switching

9 Chassis (G video)
10 Data bus
11 G video in
12 Data bus
13 Chassis (R
 video)
14 Chassis
 (data bus)
15 R video in

16 Fast video
 blanking
17 Chassis
 (composite
 video)
18 Chassis (fast
 video
 blanking)
19 Composite
 video out
20 Composite
 video in

SCART (BS 6552)

SCART connectors, also known as Peritelevision or Euroconnector connectors, feature two control systems which allow remote control over the television's or videorecorder's functions.

The simplest is a source switching input (pin 8) in which an external source (videorecorder, computer, etc.) can, by issuing a 12 volt signal, cause the television to switch to baseband inputs.

A more complex control system, called *domestic data bus* (D^2B), is given through pins 10 and 12, in which serial data can be passed between controlling microprocessors in the television and external equipment. No standard yet exists for D^2B.

Main low-voltage power supplies

Voltages are a.c. unless otherwise stated. Frequencies are in brackets.

Europe

Austria (50) 220/380; Vienna also has 220/440 d.c.
Azores (50) 220/380
Belgium (50) 220/380 and many others; some d.c.
Canary Islands (50) 127/220
Denmark (50) 220/380; also 220/440 d.c.
Finland (50) 220/380
France (50) 120/240, 220/380, and many others
Germany (Federal Republic) (50) 220/380; also others, some d.c.
Gibraltar (50) 240/415
Greece (50) 220/380; also others, some d.c.
Iceland (50) 220; some 220/380
Ireland (50) 220/380; some 220/440 d.c.
Italy (50) 127/220, 220/380 and others
Luxembourg (50) 110/190, 220/380
Madeira (50) 220/380; also 220/440 d.c.
Malta (50) 240/415
Monaco (50) 127/220, 220/380
Netherlands (50) 220/380; also 127/220
Norway (50) 230
Portugal (50) 220/380; some 110/190
Spain (50) 127/220; also 220/380, some d.c.
Sweden (50) 127/220, 220/380; some d.c.
Switzerland (50) 220/380

Turkey (50) 220/380; some 110/190
United Kingdom (50) 240/415 and others, some d.c.
Yugoslavia (50) 220/380

Asia
Afghanistan (50) 220/380
Burma (50) 230
Cambodia (5) 120/208; some 220/380
Cyprus (50) 240
Hong Kong (50) 220/346
India (50) 230/400 and others, some d.c.
Indonesia (50) 127/220
Iran (50) 220/380
Iraq (50) 220/380
Israel (50) 230/400
Japan (50/60) 100/200
Jordan (50) 220/380
Korea (60) 100/200
Kuwait (50) 240/415
Laos (50) 127/220; some 220/380
Lebanon (50) 110/190; some 220/380
Malaysia (50) 230/400; some 240/415
Nepal (50) 110/220
Okinawa (60) 120/240
Pakistan (50) 230/400 and others, some d.c.
Philippines (60) 110, 220, and others
Saudi Arabia (50, 60) 120/208; also 220/380, 230/400
Singapore (50) 230/400
Sri Lanka (50) 230/400
Syria (50) 115/200; some 220/380
Taiwan (60) 100/200
Thailand (50) 220/380; also 110/190
Vietnam (50) 220/380 future standard
Yemen Arab Republic (50) 220
Yemen, Peoples Democratic Republic (50) 230/400

North America
Alaska (60) 120/240
Bermuda (60) 115/230; some 120/208
Belize (60) 110/220
Canada (60) 120/240; some 115/230
Costa Rica (60) 110/220
El Salvador (60) 110/220
Guatemala (60) 110/240; some 220, 120/208
Honduras (60) 110/220
Mexico (50, 60) 127/220 and other voltages
  Mexico City (50) 125/216
Nicaragua (60) 120
Panama (60) 110/220; some 120/240, 115/230
United States (60) 120/240 and 120/208

West Indies
Antigua (60) 230/400
Bahamas (60) 115/200; some 115/220
Barbados (50) 120/208; some 110/200
Cuba (60) 115/230; some 120/208
Dominican Republic (60) 115/230
Guadeloupe (50) 127/220

Jamaica (50, some 60) 110/220
Martinique (50) 127/220
Puerto Rico (60) 120/240
Trinidad (60) 115/230
Virgin Islands (60) 120/240

South America
Argentina (50) 220/380; also 220/440 d.c.
Bolivia (50, also 60) 220 and other voltages
Brazil (50, 60) 110, 220; also other voltages and d.c. Rio de Janeiro (50) 125/216
Chile (50) 220/380; some 220 d.c.
Colombia (60) 110/220; also 120/240 and others
Ecuador (60) 120/208; also 110/220 and others
French Guiana (50) 127/220
Guyana (50, 60) 110/220
Paraguay (50) 220/440; some 220/440 d.c.
Peru (60) 220; some 110
Surinam (50, 60) 127/220; some 115/230
Uruguay (50) 220
Venezuela (60, some 50) 120/208, 120/240

Africa
Algeria (50) 127/220, 220/380
Angola (50) 220/380
Dahomey (50) 220/380
Egypt (50) 110/220 and others; some d.c.
Ethiopia (50) 220/380; some 127/220
Guinea (50) 220/380; some 127/220
Kenya (50) 240/415
Liberia (60) 120/240
Libya (50) 125/220; some 230/400
Malagasy Republic (50) 220/380; some 127/220
Mauritius (50) 230/400
Morocco (50) 115/200; also 230/400 and others
Mozambique (50) 220/380
Niger (50) 220/380
Nigeria (50) 230/400
Rhodesia (50) 220/380; also 230/400
Senegal (50) 127/220
Sierra Leone (50) 230/400
Somalia (50) 220/440; also 110, 230
South Africa (50) 220/380; also others, some d.c.
Sudan (50) 240/415
Tanganyika (50) 230/400
Tunisia (50) 220/380; also others
Uganda (50) 240/415
Upper Volta (50) 220/380
Zaire (50) 220/380

Oceania.
Australia (50) 240/415; also others and d.c.
Fiji Islands (50) 240/415
Hawaii (60) 120/240
New Caledonia (50) 220/440
New Zealand (50) 230/400

RF Cables USA RG series

RG number	Nominal impedance Z_o (ohms)	Overall diameter (inches)	Velocity factor	Attenuation (dB per 100 ft)						Capacity (pF/ft)	Maximum operating voltage RMS
				1 MHz	10 MHz	10 MHz	100 MHz	1000 MHz	3000 MHz		
RG-5/U	52·5	0·332	0·659	0·21	0·77	2·9	11·5	22·0	28·5	3000	
RG-5B/U	50·0	0·332	0·659	0·16	0·66	2·4	8·8	16·7	29·5	3000	
RG-6A/U	75·0	0·332	0·659	0·21	0·78	2·9	11·2	21·0	20·0	2700	
RG-8A/U	50·0	0·405	0·659	0·16	0·55	2·0	8·0	16·5	30·5	4000	
RG-9/U	51·0	0·420	0·659	0·16	0·57	2·0	7·3	15·5	30·0	4000	
RG-9B/U	50·0	0·425	0·659	0·175	0·61	2·1	9·0	18·0	30·5	000	
RG-10A/U	50·0	0·475	0·659	0·16	0·55	2·0	8·0	16·5	30·5	4000	
RG-11A/U	75·0	0·405	0·66	0·18	0·7	2·3	7·8	16·5	20·5	5000	
RG-12A/U	75·0	0·475	0·659	0·18	0·66	2·3	8·0	16·5	20·5	4000	
RG-13A/U	75·0	0·425	0·659	0·12	0·66	1·4	8·0	16·5	20·5	4000	
RG-14A/U	50·0	0·545	0·659	0·12	0·41	1·4	5·5	12·0	20·5	5500	
RG-16/U	52·0	0·630	0·670	0·1	0·4	1·2	6·7	16·0	29·5	6000	
RG-17A/U	50·0	0·870	0·659	0·066	0·225	0·80	3·4	8·5	30·0	11000	
RG-18A/U	50·0	0·945	0·659	0·066	0·225	0·80	3·4	8·5	30·5	11000	

Type										
RG-19A/U	50·0	1·120	0·659	0·04	0·17	0·68	3·5	7·7	30·5	14000
RG-20A/U	50·0	1·195	0·659	0·04	0·17	0·68	3·5	7·7	30·5	14000
RG-21/AU	50·0	0·332	0·659	1·4	4·4	13·0	43·0	85·0	30·0	2700
RG-29/U	53·5	0·184	0·659	0·33	1·2	4·4	16·0	30·0	28·5	1900
RG-34A/U	75·0	0·630	0·659	0·065	0·29	1·3	6·0	12·5	20·5	5200
RG-34B/U	75	0·66	0·66		0·3	1·4	5·8		21·5	6500
RG-35A/U	75·0	0·945	0·659	0·07	0·235	0·85	3·5	8·60	20·5	10000
RG-54A/U	58·0	0·250	0·659	0·18	0·74	3·1	11·5	21·5	26·5	3000
RG-55/U	53·5	0·206	0·659	0·36	1·3	4·8	17·0	32·0	28·5	1900
RG-55A/U	50·0	0·216	0·659	0·36	1·3	4·8	17·0	32·0	29·5	1900
RG-58/U	53·5	0·195	0·659	0·33	1·25	4·65	17·5	37·5	28·5	1900
RG-58C/U	50·0	0·242	0·659	0·42	1·4	4·9	24·0	45·0	30·0	1900
RG-59A/U	75·0	0·242	0·659	0·34	1·10	3·40	12·0	26·0	20·5	2300
RG-59B/U	75	0·66	0·66		1·1	3·4	12		21	2300
RG-62A/U	93·0	0·84	0·84	0·25	0·85	2·70	8·6	18·5	13·5	750
RG-74A/U	50·0	0·615	0·659	0·10	0·38	1·5	6·0	11·5	30·0	5500
RG-83/U	35·0	0·405	0·66	0·23	0·80	2·8	9·6	24·0	44·0	2000
*RG-213/U	50	0·405	0·66	0·16	0·6	1·9	8·0		29·5	5000
†RG-218/U	50	0·870	0·66	0·066	0·2	1·0	4·4		29·5	11000
‡RG-220/U	50	1·120	0·66	0·04	0·2	0·7	3·6		29·5	14000

*Formerly RG8A/U.
†Formerly RG17A/U.
‡Formerly RG19A/U.

British UR series

UR number	Nominal impedance Z₀ (ohms)	Overall diameter (inches)	Inner conductor (inches)	Capacity (pF/ft)	Maximum operating voltage RMS	Attenuation (dB per 100 ft)				Nearest RG equivalent
						10 MHz	100 MHz	300 MHz	1000 MHz	
43	52	0·195	0·032	29	2750	1·3	4·3	8·7	18·1	58/U
57	75	0·405	0·044	20·6	5000	0·6	1·9	3·5	7·1	11A/U
63*	75	0·855	0·175	14	4400	0·15	0·5	0·9	1·7	
67	50	0·405	7/0·029	30	4800	0·6	2·0	3·7	7·5	213/U
74	51	0·870	0·188	30·7	15000	0·3	1·0	1·9	4·2	218/U
76	51	0·195	19/0·0066	29	1800	1·6	5·3	9·6	22·0	58C/U
77	75	0·870	0·104	20·5	125000	0·3	1·0	1·9	4·2	164/U
79*	50	0·855	0·265	21	6000	0·16	0·5	0·9	1·8	
83*	50	0·555	0·168	21	2600	0·25	0·8	1·5	2·8	
85*	50	0·555	0·109	14	2600	0·2	0·7	1·3	2·5	
90	75	0·242	0·022	20	2500	1·1	3·5	6·3	12·3	59B/U

All the above cables have solid dielectric with a velocity factor of 0·66 with the exception of those marked with an asterisk, which are helical membrane and have a velocity factor of 0·96.

Cells and batteries

	USA size	Nominal voltage (V)	Type†	IEC equivalent	Maximum dimensions (mm)			Contacts	Current (mA)	Weight (g)
					Length (or diameter)	Width	Height			
Zinc carbon	N	1·5	D23	R1	12	—	30·1	Cap and base	1-5	7
	AAA		HP16	R03	10·5	—	45	Cap and base	0-75	8·5
	AA		HP7	R6	14·5	—	50·5	Cap and base	0-75	16·5
	AA		C7	R6	14·5	—	50·5	Cap and base	20-60	16·5
	C		SP11	R14	26·2	—	50	Cap and base	0-60	45
	C		HP11	R14	26·2	—	50	Cap and base	0-1000	45
	C		C11	R14	26·2	—	50	Cap and base	0-5	45
	D		SP2	R20	34·2	—	61·8	Cap and base	25-100	90
	D		HP2	R20	34·2	—	61·8	Cap and base	0-2000	90
		4·5	AD28	3R25	101·6	34·9	106	Socket	30-300	453·6
			1269	3R12	62	22	67	Press studs	30-300	113
		6·0	PP8	4-F100-4	65·1	51·6	200·8	Spiral springs	20-151	1100
			991	4-R25	67	67	102	Two screws	30-300	581
		9·0	PJ996	6-F22	135·7	72·2	125·4	Press studs	30-500	1470
			PP3-P	6-F22	26·5	17·5	48·5	Press studs	0-50	39
			PP3-C	6-F22	26·5	17·5	48·5	Press studs	0-50	39
			PP3	6-F22	25·5	17·5	48·5	Press studs	0-10	38
			PP4	6-F20	36	—	50	Press studs	0-10	51
			PP6	6-F50-2	46	34·5	70	Press studs	2·6-15	142
			PP7	6-F90	66	46	61·9	Press studs	5-20	198
			PP9	6-F100	66	52	81	Press studs	5-50	425
			PP10	6-F100-3	66	52	228	Socket	15-150	1250
		15·0	B154	10-F15	16	15	35	End contacts	0·1-0·5	14·2
			B121	10-F20	27	16	37	End contacts	0·1-1·0	21
		22·5	B155	15-F15	16	15	51	End contacts	0·1-0·5	20
			B122	15-F20	27	16	51	End Contacts	0·1-1·0	32

	USA size	Nominal voltage (V)	Type‡	IEC equivalent	Maximum dimensions (mm) Length (or diameter)	Width	Height	Contacts	Current (mA)	Weight (g)
Manganese alkaline	ED	1·5	MN1300*	LR20	34·2	—	61·5	Cap and base	10·00†	125
	C		MN1400*	LR14	26·2	—	50	Cap and base	5·50†	65
	AA		MN1500*	LR6	14·5	—	50·5	Cap and base	1·80†	23
	AAA		MN2400*	LR03	10·5	—	44·5	Cap and base	0·80†	13
	N		MN9100*	LR1	12	—	30·2	Cap and base	0·65†	9·6
Mercuric oxide		1·35/1·4	RM675H	NR07	11·6	—	5·4	Cap and base (button)	0·21†	2·6
			RM625N	MR9	15·6	—	6·2	Cap and base (button)	0·25†	4·3
			RM575H	NR08	11·6	—	3·5	Cap and base (button)	0·12†	1·4
			RM1H	NR50	16·4	—	16·8	Cap and base (button)	1·00†	12·0
Silver oxide		1·5	10L14	5R44	11·56	—	5·33	Cap and base (button)	0·13†	2·2
			10L124	5R43	11·56	—	4·19	Cap and base (button)	0·13†	1·7
			10L123	5R48	7·75	—	5·33	Cap and base (button)	0·08†	1·0
			10L125	5R41	7·75	—	3·58	Cap and base (button)	0·04†	0·8
Nickel cadmium	AA	1·25	NC828	—	See HP7			Button	0·28†	16·5
	C		NCC60	—	See HP11			Button	0·60†	30·0
			NCC200	—				Button	2·00†	78·0
	D		NCC400	—	See HP2			Button	4·00†	170·0
		10·0	10/225DK	(DEAC)				Button stack	0·28†	126·0
		12·0	TR7/8	(DEAC)	See PP3			Button stack	0·225†	135·0
		9·0	501RS	(DEAC)	See HP7			Press studs	0·07†	45·0
	AA	1·25	RS1-8	(DEAC)	See HP11			Press studs	0·50†	30·0
	C		RS4	(DEAC)	See HP2			Press studs	1·80†	65·0
	D			(DEAC)	See HP2			Press studs	4·00†	150·0

†Capacity in ampere hours.
‡BEREC types unless otherwise indicated.

Powers of 2

$-n$	2^{-n}	2^n	n
−1	.5	2	1
−2	.25	4	2
−3	.125	8	3
−4	.0625	16	4
−5	.03125	32	5
−6	.015625	64	6
−7	.0078125	128	7
−8	.00390625	256	8
−9	.001953125	512	9
−10	.0009765625	1 024	10
−11	.00048828125	2 048	11
−12	.000244140625	4 096	12
−13	.0001220703125	8 192	13
−14	.00006103515625	16 384	14
−15	.000030517578125	32 768	15
−16	.0000152587890625	65 536	16
−17	.00000762939453125	131 072	17
−18	.000003814697265625	262 144	18
−19	.0000019073486328125	524 288	19
−20	.00000095367431640625	1 048 576	20
−21	.000000476837158203125	2 097 152	21
−22	.0000002384185791015625	4 194 304	22
−23	.00000011920928955078125	8 388 608	23
−24	.000000059604644775390625	16 777 216	24
−25	.0000000298023223876953125	33 554 432	25
−26	.00000001490116119384765625	67 108 864	26
−27	.000000007450580596923828125	134 217 728	27
−28	.0000000037252902984619140625	268 435 456	28
−29	.00000000186264514923095703125	536 870 912	29
−30	.000000000931322574615478515625	1 073 741 824	30
−31	.0000000004656612873077392578125	2 147 483 648	31
−32	.00000000023283064365386962890625	4 294 967 296	32

Powers of 10_{16}

10^n				n	10^{-n}				
			1	0	1·0000	0000	0000	0000	
			A	1	0·1999	9999	9999	999A	$\times 16^{-1}$
			64	2	0·28F5	C28F	5C28	F5C3	$\times 16^{-2}$
			3E8	3	0·4189	374B	C6A7	EF9E	$\times 16^{-3}$
			2710	4	0·68DB	8BAC	710C	B296	$\times 16^{-4}$
		1	86A0	5	0·A7C5	AC47	1B47	8423	$\times 16^{-4}$
		F	4240	6	0·10C6	F7A0	B5ED	8D37	$\times 16^{-5}$
		98	9680	7	0·1AD7	F29A	BCAF	4858	$\times 16^{-6}$
		5F5	E100	8	0·2AF3	1DC4	6118	73BF	$\times 16^{-7}$
		3B9A	CA00	9	0·44B8	2FA0	9B5A	52CC	$\times 16^{-8}$
	2	540B	E400	10	0·6DF3	7F67	5EF6	EADF	$\times 16^{-8}$
	17	4876	E800	11	0·AFEB	FF0B	CB24	AAFF	$\times 16^{-9}$
	E8	D4A5	1000	12	0·1197	9981	2DEA	1119	$\times 16^{-9}$
	918	4E72	A000	13	0·1C25	C268	4976	81C2	$\times 16^{-10}$
	5AF3	107A	4000	14	0·2D09	370D	4257	3604	$\times 16^{-11}$
3	8D7E	A4C6	8000	15	0·480E	BE7B	9D58	566D	$\times 16^{-12}$
23	86F2	6FC1	0000	16	0·734A	CA5F	6226	F0AE	$\times 16^{-13}$
163	4578	5D8A	0000	17	0·B877	AA32	36A4	B449	$\times 16^{-14}$
DE0	B6B3	A764	0000	18	0·1272	5DD1	D243	ABA1	$\times 16^{-14}$
8AC7	2304	89E8	0000	19	0·1D83	C94F	B6D2	AC35	$\times 16^{-15}$

Powers of 16_{10}

16^n	n	16^{-n}
1	0	$0.10000\ 00000\ 00000\ 00000 \times 10$
16	1	$0.62500\ 00000\ 00000\ 00000 \times 10^{-1}$
256	2	$0.39062\ 50000\ 00000\ 00000 \times 10^{-2}$
4 096	3	$0.24414\ 06250\ 00000\ 00000 \times 10^{-3}$
65 536	4	$0.15258\ 78906\ 25000\ 00000 \times 10^{-4}$
1 048 576	5	$0.95367\ 43164\ 06250\ 00000 \times 10^{-6}$
16 777 216	6	$0.59604\ 64477\ 53906\ 25000 \times 10^{-7}$
268 435 456	7	$0.37252\ 90298\ 46191\ 40625 \times 10^{-8}$
4 294 967 296	8	$0.23283\ 06436\ 53869\ 62891 \times 10^{-9}$
68 719 476 736	9	$0.14551\ 91522\ 83668\ 51807 \times 10^{-10}$
1 099 511 627 776	10	$0.90949\ 47017\ 72928\ 23792 \times 10^{-12}$
17 592 186 044 416	11	$0.56843\ 41886\ 08080\ 14870 \times 10^{-13}$
281 474 976 710 656	12	$0.35527\ 13678\ 80050\ 09294 \times 10^{-14}$
4 503 599 627 370 496	13	$0.22204\ 46049\ 25031\ 30808 \times 10^{-15}$
72 057 594 037 927 936	14	$0.13877\ 78780\ 78144\ 56755 \times 10^{-16}$
1 152 921 504 606 846 976	15	$0.86736\ 17379\ 88403\ 54721 \times 10^{-18}$

Sounds and sound levels

Sound pressure (mPa)	Pressure ratio		Intensity ratio	Sound level (dB)	Source or description of typical sound
0·2 (datum)	1	(= 10⁰)	1	0	Sound-proof room (threshold of hearing)
0·063	3·16	(= 10⁰·⁵)	10¹	10	Rustle of leaves in a breeze
0·2	10	(= 10¹)	10²	20	Whisper
0·63	31·6	(= 10¹·⁵)	10³	30	Quiet conversation
2	100	(= 10²)	10⁴	40	Suburban home
6·3	316	(= 10²·⁵)	10⁵	50	Typical conversation
20	1000	(= 10³)	10⁶	60	Large shop
63	3160	(= 10³·⁵)	10⁷	70	City street
200	10000	(= 10⁴)	10⁸	80	Noisy office with typing
630	31600	(= 10⁴·⁵)	10⁹	90	Underground railway
2000	100000	(= 10⁵)	10¹⁰	100	Pneumatic drill at 3 m
6300	316000	(= 10⁵·⁵)	10¹¹	110	Prop aircraft taking off
20000	1000000	(= 10⁶)	10¹²	120	Jet aircraft taking off (threshold of pain)

Velocity of sound

In air at various temperatures

Temperature (°C)	Speed (ms⁻¹)
0	331·32
10	337·42
15	340·47
20	343·51
30	349·61

In liquids and solids

Material	Speed (ms⁻¹)	Material	Speed (ms⁻¹)
Alcohol	1440	Mercury	1460
Aluminium	6220	Nickel	5600
Brass	4430	Polystyrene	2670
Copper	4620	Quartz	5750
Glass	5400	Steel	6110
Lead	2430	Water	1450
Magnesium	5330		

Audible frequency range

Musical instruments

Instrument	Low (Hz)	High (Hz)
Bass clarinet	82·41	493·88
Bass tuba	43·65	349·23
Bass viola	41·20	246·94
Bassoon	61·74	493·88
Cello	65·41	987·77
Clarinet	164·81	1,567·00
Flute	261·63	3,349·30
French horn	110·00	880·00
Guitar	82·41	880·00
Oboe	261·63	1,568·00
Piano	27·50	4,186·00
Trombone	82·41	493·88
Trumpet	164·81	987·77
Viola	130·81	1,174·00
Violin	196·00	3,136·00

Human voices

Voice	Low (Hz)	High (Hz)
Alto	130·81	698·46
Baritone	98·00	392·00
Bass	87·31	349·23
Soprano	246·94	1,174·70
Tenor	130·81	493·88

Audible intensity

Musical instruments

Instrument	Range (dB)
Bass drum	35 to 115
Cymbal	40 to 110
Organ	35 to 110
Piano	60 to 100
Trumpet	55 to 95
Tympani	30 to 110
Violin	42 to 95

Stereo pickup lead colour codes

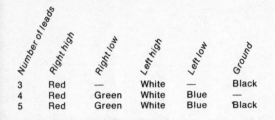

Number of leads	Right high	Right low	Left high	Left low	Ground
3	Red	—	White	—	Black
4	Red	Green	White	Blue	—
5	Red	Green	White	Blue	Black

Celsius–Fahrenheit conversion table

C	F	C	F	C	F	C	F
0	32	265	509	530	986	795	1,463
5	41	270	518	535	995	800	1,472
10	50	275	527	540	1,004	805	1,481
15	59	280	536	545	1,013	810	1,490
20	68	285	545	550	1,022	815	1,499
25	77	290	554	555	1,031	820	1,508
30	86	295	563	560	1,040	825	1,517
35	93	300	572	565	1,049	830	1,526
40	104	305	581	570	1,058	835	1,535
45	113	310	590	575	1,067	840	1,544
50	122	315	599	580	1,076	845	1,553
55	131	320	608	585	1,085	850	1,562
60	140	325	617	590	1,094	855	1,571
65	149	330	626	595	1,103	860	1,580
70	158	335	635	600	1,112	865	1,589
75	167	340	644	605	1,121	870	1,598
80	176	345	653	610	1,130	875	1,607
85	185	350	662	615	1,139	880	1,616
90	194	355	671	620	1,148	885	1,625
95	203	360	680	625	1,157	890	1,634
100	212	365	689	630	1,166	895	1,643
105	221	370	698	635	1,175	900	1,652
110	230	375	707	640	1,184	905	1,661
115	239	380	716	645	1,193	910	1,670
120	248	385	725	650	1,202	915	1,679
125	257	390	734	655	1,211	920	1,688
130	266	395	743	660	1,220	925	1,697
135	275	400	752	665	1,229	930	1,706
140	284	405	761	670	1,238	935	1,715
145	293	410	770	675	1,247	940	1,724
150	302	415	779	680	1,256	945	1,733
155	311	420	788	685	1,265	950	1,742
160	320	425	797	690	1,274	955	1,751
165	329	430	806	695	1,283	960	1,760
170	338	435	815	700	1,292	965	1,769
175	347	440	824	705	1,301	970	1,778

180	356	445	833	710	1,310	975	1,787
185	365	450	842	715	1,319	980	1,796
190	374	455	851	720	1,328	985	1,805
195	383	460	860	725	1,337	990	1,814
200	392	465	869	730	1,346	995	1,823
205	401	470	877	735	1,355	1,000	1,832
210	410	475	887	740	1,364	1,005	1,841
215	419	480	896	745	1,373	1,010	1,850
220	428	485	905	750	1,382	1,015	1,859
225	437	490	914	755	1,391		
230	446	495	923	760	1,400		
235	455	500	932	765	1,409		
240	464	505	941	770	1,418		
245	473	510	950	775	1,427		
250	482	515	959	780	1,436		
255	491	520	968	785	1,445		
260	500	525	977	790	1,454		

Temperature conversion formulae

°F to °C $\quad$ °C = 5/9 (°F − 32) $\qquad$ °R to °F $\quad$ °F = 9/4 °R + 32
°C to °F $\quad$ °F = 9/5 °C + 32 $\qquad$ °R to °C $\quad$ °C = 5/4 °R
°F to °R $\quad$ °R = 4/9 (°F − 32) $\qquad$ Absolute zero = −273·14°C.

Paper sizes

ISO standards (BS 4000)

A series

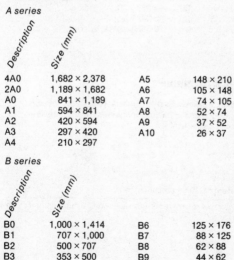

Description	Size (mm)		
4A0	1,682 × 2,378	A5	148 × 210
2A0	1,189 × 1,682	A6	105 × 148
A0	841 × 1,189	A7	74 × 105
A1	594 × 841	A8	52 × 74
A2	420 × 594	A9	37 × 52
A3	297 × 420	A10	26 × 37
A4	210 × 297		

B series

Description	Size (mm)		
B0	1,000 × 1,414	B6	125 × 176
B1	707 × 1,000	B7	88 × 125
B2	500 × 707	B8	62 × 88
B3	353 × 500	B9	44 × 62
B4	250 × 353	B10	31 × 44
B5	176 × 250		

Fuses

Fuses are sometimes coded with the use of coloured dots on the fuse body. Ratings of colour-coded fuses are as follows:

Colour	Rating		
Black	60 mA	Dark blue	1·0 A
Grey	100 mA	Light blue	1·5 A
Red	150 mA	Purple	2·0 A
Brown	250 mA	White	3·0 A
Yellow	500 mA	Black and	
Green	750 mA	white	5·0 A

Diameters of fuse wires for various amperage ratings and common materials is shown below:

Fusing current (A)	Copper		Tin		Lead	
	diameter (in)	s.w.g.	diameter (in)	s.w.g.	diameter (in)	s.w.g.
1	0·0021	47	0·0072	37	0·0081	35
2	0·0034	43	0·0113	31	0·0128	30
3	0·0044	41	0·0149	28	0·0168	27
4	0·0053	39	0·0181	26	0·0203	25
5	0·0062	38	0·0210	25	0·0236	23
10	0·0098	33	0·0334	21	0·0375	20
15	0·0129	30	0·0437	19	0·0491	18
20	0·0156	28	0·0529	17	0·0595	17

Statistical formulae

The **arithmetic mean** of a set of numbers $X_1, X_2, ..., X_N$ is their average. It is the sum of the numbers divided by the number of numbers and is denoted by $\bar{X}$

$$\bar{X} = \frac{X_1 + X_2 + X_3 ... X_N}{N} = \frac{\sum\limits_{i=1}^{N} X_1}{N}$$

The **standard deviation** is denoted by σ.

$$\sigma = \sqrt{\frac{\text{sum of squares of differences between numbers and mean}}{N}}$$

$$= \sqrt{\frac{\sum\limits_{I=1}^{N} (X_I - \bar{X})^2}{N}}$$

Particles of modern physics

Stable particles are listed below.

	Name	Symbol	Rest energy M_0/MeV	Mean lifetime τ/s	Common decay modes
Baryons	Proton	$p^\pm$	938·256(6)	stable	
	Neutron	n	939·550(5)	$9·32(14) \times 10^2$	$pe\nu$
	Lambda	Λ^0	1115·60(8)	$2·51(3) \times 10^{-10}$	$p\pi^-(65\%)n\pi^0(35\%)$
	Sigma	Σ^+	1189·4(2)	$8·02(7) \times 10^{-11}$	$p\pi^0(52\%)n\pi^+(48\%)$
		Σ^0	1192·46(12)	$< 10^{-14}$	$\Lambda\gamma$
		Σ^-	1197·32(11)	$1·49 \times 10^{-10}$	$n\pi^-$
	Xi	Ξ^0	1314·7(7)	$3·03(18) \times 10^{-10}$	$\Lambda\pi^0$
		Ξ^-	1321·25(18)	$1·66(4) \times 10^{-10}$	$\Lambda\pi^-$
	Omega	Ω^-	1672·5(5)	$1·3(4) \times 10^{-10}$	$\Xi^0\pi^-, \Xi^-\pi^0,$ $\Lambda K^-(?)$
Leptons	Photon	γ	0	stable	
	Neutrino	ν_e	0	stable	
		ν_μ	0	stable	
	Electron	$e^\pm$	0·511004(2)	stable	
	Muon	$\mu^\pm$	105·659(2)	$2·1994(6) \times 10^{-6}$	$e\nu\bar{\nu}$
Mesons	Pion	$\pi^\pm$	139·576(11)	$2·602(2) \times 10^{-8}$	$\mu\nu$
		π^0	134·972(12)	$0·84(10) \times 10^{-16}$	$\gamma\gamma(99\%)\gamma e^+e^-(1\%)$
	Kaon	$K^\pm$	493·82(11)	$1·235(4) \times 10^{-8}$	$\mu\nu(64\%)\pi^\pm\pi^0(21\%)$ $3\pi(5\%)$
		K^0	497·76(16)	$50\%K_1, 50\%K_2$	
		K_1		$8·62(6) \times 10^{-11}$	$\pi^+\pi^-(69\%)2\pi^0$ (31%)
		K_2		$5·38(19) \times 10^{-8}$	$\pi e\gamma(39\%)\pi\mu\nu(27\%)$ $3\pi^0(21\%)\pi^+\pi^-\pi^0$ (13%)
	Eta	η^0	548·8(6)		$\gamma\gamma(38\%)\pi\gamma\gamma(2\%)3\pi^0$ $(31\%)\pi^+\pi^-\pi^0(23\%)$ $\pi^+\pi^-\gamma(5\%)$

Calculus

Differentiation

The derivative of a function $y = f(t)$ is denoted by

$\dfrac{dy}{dt}$ or $\dot{y}$ if t represents time

The second derivative of $y = f(t)$ is denoted by $\dfrac{d^2y}{dt^2}$ or $\ddot{y}$ if t is time.

Useful derivatives

function $y = f(t)$		derivative $\dfrac{dy}{dt}$
1		0
t		1
t^A	$(A \neq 0)$	At^{A-1}
$\sin \omega t$	$(\omega \neq 0)$	$\omega \cos \omega t$
$\cos \omega t$	$(\omega \neq 0)$	$-\omega \sin \omega t$
$\tan at$	$(a \neq 0)$	$a \sec^2 at$
$\exp at$	$(a \neq 0)$	$a \exp at$
$\log_e at$	$(a \neq 0)$	$\dfrac{1}{t}$

Standard integrals

function $f(t)$	standard integrals $\int f(t)\, dt$
1	t
t	$\dfrac{1}{2}t^2$
$t^N (N \neq -1)$	$\dfrac{1}{N+1}\, t^{N+1}$ $(N \neq -1)$
$\dfrac{1}{T}$	$\log_e T$ $(T > 0)$
$\sin \omega t$	$-\dfrac{1}{\omega} \cos \omega t$ $(\omega \neq 0)$
$\cos \omega t$	$\dfrac{1}{\omega} \sin \omega t$ $(\omega \neq 0)$
$\exp at$ $(a \neq 0)$	$\dfrac{1}{a} \exp at$ $(a \neq 0)$
$\dfrac{1}{a^2 - t^2}$	$\dfrac{1}{2a} \log_e \left(\dfrac{a+t}{a-t}\right)(-a < t < +a)$
$\log_e(at)$	$t[\log_e(at) - 1]$

Mensuration

A and a = area; b = base; C and c = circumference; D and d = diameter; h = height; $n°$ = number of degrees; p = perpendicular; R and r = radius; s = span or chord; v = versed sine.

Square: $a = \text{side}^2$; side $= \sqrt{a}$;
diagonal $= \text{side} \times \sqrt{2}$.

Rectangle or parallelogram: $a = bp$.

Trapezoid (two sides parallel): a = mean length parallel sides × distance between them.

Triangle: $a = \frac{1}{2}bp$

Irregular figure: a = weight of template ÷ weight of square inch of similar material.

Side of square multiplied by 1·4142 equals diameter of its circumscribing circle.

A side multiplied by 4·443 equals circumference of its circumscribing circle.

A side multiplied by 1·128 equals diameter of a circle of equal area.

Circle: $a = \pi r^2 = d^2\pi/4 = 0\cdot7854d^2 = 0\cdot5cr$; $c = 2\pi r = d\pi = 3\cdot1416d = 3\cdot54\sqrt{a} = $ (approx.) $^{22}/_7 d$. Side of equal square = $0\cdot8862d$; side of inscribed square = $0\cdot7071d$; $d = 0\cdot3183c$. A circle has the maximum area for a given perimeter.

Annulus of circle: $a = (D + d)(D - d)\dfrac{\pi}{4}$

$$= (D^2 - d^2)\frac{\pi}{4}$$

Segment of circle:

a = area of sector − area of triangle

$$= \frac{4v}{3}\sqrt{(0\cdot625v)^2 + (\tfrac{1}{2}S)^2}.$$

Length of arc = $0\cdot0174533n°r$; length of

$$\text{arc} = \tfrac{1}{3}\left(8\sqrt{\frac{S^2}{4} + v^2 - s}\right);$$

approx. length of arc = $\frac{1}{3}$ (8 times chord of $\frac{1}{2}$ arc − chord of whole arc).

$$d = \frac{(\frac{1}{2}\text{ chord})}{v} + v;$$
$$\text{radius of curve} = \frac{S^2}{8V} + \frac{V}{2}.$$

Sector of circle: $a = 0\cdot5r \times$ length arc;

$$= n° \times \text{area circle} \div 360.$$

Ellipse: $a = \dfrac{\pi}{4}Dd = \pi Rr$; c (approx.)

$$= \sqrt{\frac{D^2 + d^2}{2}} \times \pi; c\text{ (approx.)} = \pi\frac{Da}{2}.$$

Parabola: $a = \frac{2}{3}bh$.
Cone or pyramid: surface

$$= \frac{\text{circ. of base} \times \text{slant length}}{2} + \text{base};$$

contents = area of base × $\frac{1}{3}$ vertical height.

Frustrum of cone:
surface = $(C + c) \times \frac{1}{2}$ slant height + ends;
contents = $0.2618h(D^2 + d^2 + Dd)$;

$$= \frac{1}{3}h(A + a + \sqrt{A \times a}).$$

Wedge: contents = $\frac{1}{6}$ (length of edge + 2 length of back)bh.
Oblique prism: contents = area base × height.
Sphere: surface = $d^2\pi = 4\pi r^2$,

$$\text{contents} = d^3 \frac{\pi}{6} = \frac{4}{3}\pi r^3.$$

Segment of sphere: r = rad. of base;

$$\text{contents} = \frac{\pi}{6}h(3r^2 + h^2); \quad r = \text{rad. of sphere};$$

$$\text{contents} = \frac{\pi}{3}h^2(3r - h).$$

Spherical zone:

$$\text{contents} = \frac{\pi}{2}h(\frac{1}{3}h^2 + R^2 + r^2); \quad \text{surface of convex part of}$$

segment or zone of sphere = πd(of sph.)$h = 2\pi rh$.

Mid. sph. zone: contents = $(r + \frac{2}{3}h^2)\dfrac{\pi}{4}$

Spheroid:

$$\text{contents} = \text{revolving axis}^2 \times \text{fixed axis} \times \frac{\pi}{6}.$$

Cube or rectangular solid contents = length × breadth × thickness.

Prismoidal formula: contents

$$= \frac{\text{end areas} + 4 \text{ times mid. area} \times \text{length}}{6}$$

Solid revolution: contents = a of generating plane × c described by centroid of this plane during revolution. Areas of similar plane figures are as the squares of like sides. Contents of similar solids are as the cubes of like sides.

Rules relative to the circle, square, cylinder, etc.:
To find circumference of a circle:
    Multiply diameter by 3.1416; or divide diameter by 0.3183.
To find diameter of a circle:
    Multiply circumference by 0.3183; or divide circumference by 3.1416.
To find radius of a circle:
    Multiply circumference by 0.15915; or divide circumference by 6.28318.
To find the side of an inscribed square:
    Multiply diameter by 0.7071; or multiply circumference by 0.2251; or divide circumference by 4.4428.
To find side of an equal square:
    Multiply diameter by 0.8862; or divide diameter by 1.1284; or multiply circumference by 0.2821; or divide circumference by 3.545.

To find area of a circle:
    Multiply circumference by ¼ of the diameter; or multiply the square of diameter by 0·7854; or multiply the square of circumference by 0·07958; or multiply the square of ½ diameter by 3·1416.
To find the surface of a sphere or globe:
    Multiply the diameter by the circumference; or multiply the square of diameter by 3·1416; or multiply 4 times the square of radius by 3·1416.

Cylinder.
    To find the area of surface:
        Multiply the diameter by 3⅐ × length.
        Capacity = 3⅐ × radius² × height.

Values and Powers of:
    $\pi = 3\cdot1415926536$, or $3\cdot1416$, or $^{22}/_7$ or $3\frac{1}{7}$;
    $\pi^2 = 9\cdot86965$; $\sqrt{\pi} = 1\cdot772453$;

$$\frac{1}{\pi} = 0\cdot31831; \quad \frac{\pi}{2} = 1\cdot570796;$$

$$\frac{\pi}{3} = 1\cdot047197.$$

Radian = 57·2958 degrees.

Table A

Fig. 1. Diagram for Table A.

Parts given	Parts to be found	Formulae
abc	A	$\cos A = \dfrac{b^2 + c^2 - a^2}{2bc}$
abA	B	$\sin B = \dfrac{b \times \sin A}{a}$
abA	C	$C = 180° - (A + B)$
aAB	b	$b = \dfrac{a \times \sin B}{\sin A}$
aAB	c	$c = \dfrac{a \sin C}{\sin A} = \dfrac{a \sin (180° - A - B)}{\sin A}$
abC	B	$B = 180° - (A + C)$

Table B

Fig. 2. Diagram for Table B.

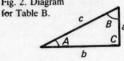

Parts given

Parts given		
$a \& c$	$\sin A = \dfrac{a}{c}$ $\cos B = \dfrac{a}{c}$ $b = \sqrt{c^2 - a^2}$	
$a \& b$	$\tan A = \dfrac{a}{b}$ $\cot B = \dfrac{a}{b}$ $c = \sqrt{a^2 + b^2}$	
$c \& b$	$\cos A = \dfrac{b}{c}$ $\sin B = \dfrac{b}{c}$ $a = \sqrt{c^2 - b^2}$	
$A \& a$	$B = 90° - A$ $b = a \times \cot A$ $c = \dfrac{a}{\sin A}$	
$A \& b$	$B = 90° - A$ $a = b \times \tan A$ $c = \dfrac{b}{\cos A}$	
$A \& c$	$B = 90° - A$ $a = c \times \sin A$ $b = c \times \cos A$	

Fig. 3. In any right-angled triangle:

$$\tan A = \frac{BC}{AC}, \quad \sin A = \frac{BC}{AB}$$
$$\cos A = \frac{AC}{AB}, \quad \cot A = \frac{AC}{BC}$$
$$\sec A = \frac{AB}{AC}, \quad \operatorname{cosec} A = \frac{AB}{BC}$$

Fig. 4. In any right-angled triangle:

$$a^2 = c^2 + b^2$$
$$c = \sqrt{a^2 - b^2}$$
$$b = \sqrt{a^2 - c^2}$$
$$a = \sqrt{b^2 + c^2}$$

Fig. 5. $c + d : a + b :: b - a : d - c$.

$$d = \frac{c + d}{2} + \frac{d - c}{2}$$
$$x = \sqrt{b^2 - d^2}$$

In Fig. 6, where the lengths of three sides only are known:

$$\text{area} = \sqrt{s(s - a)(s - b)(s - c)}$$

where $s = \dfrac{a + b + c}{2}$

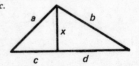

Fig. 7. In this diagram:

$a:b::b:c$ or $\dfrac{b^2}{a} = c$.

Fig. 8. In an equilateral triangle $ab = 1$, then $cd = \sqrt{0.75} = 0.866$, and $ad = 0.5$; $ab = 2$, then $cd = \sqrt{3.0} = 1.732$, and $ad = 1$; $cd = 1$, then $ac = 1.155$ and $ad = 0.577$; $cd = 0.5$, then $ac = 0.577$ and $ad = 0.288$.

Fig. 9. In a right-angled triangle with two equal acute angles, $bc = ac$, $bc = 1$, then $ab = \sqrt{2} = 1.414$; $ab = 1$, then $bc = \sqrt{0.5} = 0.707$.

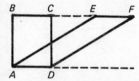

Fig. 10 shows that parallelograms on the same base and between the same parallels are equal; thus $ABCD = ADEF$.

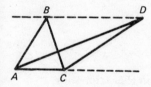

Fig. 11 demonstrates that triangles on the same base and between the same parallels are equal in area; thus, $ABC = ADC$.

Trigonometric relationships

$\sin\left(\dfrac{\pi}{2} - \alpha\right) = \cos\alpha$

$\sin(-\alpha) = -\sin\alpha$

$\sin(\pi - \alpha) = \sin\alpha$

$\sin(\pi + \alpha) = -\sin\alpha$

$\sin(2\pi - \alpha) = \sin(-\alpha) = -\sin\alpha$

$\sin(2N\pi + \alpha) = \sin\alpha$ (N an integer)

$\dfrac{\sin\alpha}{\cos\alpha} = \tan\alpha$

$$\cos\left(\frac{\pi}{2} = \alpha\right) = \sin \alpha$$

$$\cos(-\alpha) = \cos \alpha$$
$$\cos(\pi - \alpha) = -\cos \alpha$$
$$\cos(\pi + \alpha) = -\cos \alpha$$
$$\cos(2\pi - \alpha) = \cos(-\alpha) = \cos \alpha$$
$$\cos(2\pi N + \alpha) = \cos \alpha \quad (N \text{ and integer})$$

$$\tan\left(\frac{\pi}{2} - \alpha\right) = \frac{1}{\tan \alpha}$$

$$\tan(-\alpha) = -\tan \alpha$$
$$\tan(\alpha + N\pi) = \tan \alpha \quad (N \text{ an integer})$$
$$\sin^2 \alpha + \cos^2 \alpha = 1$$
$$\sin^2 \alpha = \frac{1}{2}(1 - \cos 2\alpha)$$
$$\cos^2 \alpha = \frac{1}{2}(1 + \cos 2\alpha)$$
$$\tan^2 \alpha + 1 = \sec^2 \alpha$$
$$\left.\begin{array}{l} \sin(\alpha + \beta) = \sin \alpha \cos \beta + \sin \beta \cos \alpha \\ \cos(\alpha + \beta) = \cos \alpha \cos \beta - \sin \alpha \sin \beta \\ \tan(\alpha + \beta) = \dfrac{\tan \alpha + \tan \beta}{1 - \tan \alpha \tan \beta} \end{array}\right\} \begin{array}{l} (\alpha, \beta \text{ can be positive} \\ \text{or negative}) \end{array}$$

$$\sin 2\alpha = 2 \sin \alpha \cos \alpha$$
$$\begin{aligned} \cos 2\alpha &= \cos^2 \alpha - \sin^2 \alpha \\ &= 2 \cos^2 \alpha - 1 \\ &= 1 - 2 \sin^2 \alpha \end{aligned}$$

$$\tan 2\alpha = \frac{2 \tan \alpha}{1 - \tan^2 \alpha} \quad (\tan \alpha \neq \pm 1)$$

Transistor circuits and characteristics

Basic transistor circuits showing signal source and load (R_L)	Common base	Common emitter
Characteristics		
Power gain*	Yes	Yes (highest)
Voltage gain*	Yes ($\simeq$ same CE)	Yes
Current gain*	No (less than unity)	Yes
Input impedance*	Lowest ($\simeq 50\Omega$)	Intermediate ($\simeq 1\,\text{k}\Omega$)
Output impedance*	Highest ($\simeq 1\,\text{M}\Omega$)	Intermediate ($\simeq 50\,\text{k}\Omega$)
Phase inversion	No	Yes

*Depends on transistor and other factors

Wavelength-frequency conversion table

Metres to Kilohertz

Metres	kHz	Metres	kHz	Metres	kHz
5	60,000	270	1,111	490	612·2
6	50,000	275	1,091	500	600
7	42,857	280	1,071	510	588·2
8	37,500	290	1,034	520	576·9
9	33,333	295	1,017	530	566
10	30,000	300	1,000	540	555·6
25	12,000	310	967·7	550	545·4
50	6,000	320	937·5	560	535·7
100	3,000	330	909·1	570	526·3
150	2,000	340	882·3	580	517·2
200	1,500	350	857·1	590	508·5
205	1,463	360	833·3	600	500
210	1,429	370	810·8	650	461·5
215	1,395	380	789·5	700	428·6
220	1,364	390	769·2	750	400
225	1,333	400	750	800	375
230	1,304	410	731·7	850	352·9
235	1,277	420	714·3	900	333·3
240	1,250	430	697·7	950	315·9
245	1,225	440	681·8	1,000	300
250	1,200	450	666·7	1,250	240
255	1,177	460	652·2	1,500	200
260	1,154	470	638·3	1,750	171·4
265	1,132	480	625	2,000	150

Note:—To convert kilohertz to wavelengths in metres, divide 300,000 by kilohertz.

To convert wavelengths in metres to kilohertz, divide 300,000 by the number of metres. One megahertz = 1,000,000 hertz or = 1,000 kilohertz. Thus, 30,000 kilohertz = 30 megahertz.

Common collector

Yes
No (less than unity)
Yes
Highest ($\simeq 300\,k\Omega$)
Lowest ($\simeq 300\,\Omega$)
No

Transistor testing

Although the following table cannot be used to accurately find the characteristics of an unknown transistor, if it is stepped through it *will* indicate whether the transistor is good or bad. Use of a meter with a 100 times resistance scale is assumed, which does not have a high current output.

Meter connection			Resistance	
Emitter	Base	Collector	PNP	NPN
Positive	Negative		Low	High
Negative	Positive		High	Low
	Positive	Negative	High	Low
	Negative	Positive	Low	High
Negative		Positive	High	Mid
Positive		Negative	Mid	High
Positive	Positive	Negative	High	
Positive	Negative	Negative	Low	
Negative	Negative	Positive		High
Negative	Positive	Positive		Low

Radio interference

The Radio Investigation Service of the Department of Trade and Industry now devotes its efforts against those operating radio transmitters without a licence ('pirates') and those who abuse the terms and conditions of the licence. Far less time is spent investigating complaints of interference by owners of domestic radio and electronic equipment, which is prone to pick up interference because of unsuitable internal circuit screening, poor quality design, inadequate maintenance, improper tuning and, with TV, the lack of a suitable high gain outside aerial. British Standard BS905 now provides minimum immunity standards for TV sets and will be incorporated into legislation making it an offence to manufacture, sell, hire or import TV receivers which do not comply with this standard.

Owners of TV sets, radios and other domestic equipment are expected to deal with interference problems themselves, with the assistance of the dealer, hire company or manufacturer, aided by a booklet issued by the Department of Trade and Industry and available from Post Offices.

If the DTI Radio Interference Service is called out there will be a 'call-out' fee of £21. A log detailing the interference must be provided. If this is not available or if the TV set operates from an indoor aerial the RIS will not cooperate. From 1987 the RIS will only investigate if the dealer or hirer declares that he cannot deal with the problem.

Astronomical data

Distance of earth from sun (mean) = $1\cdot496 \times 10^{11}$ m
Distance of earth from sun (at aphelion) = $1\cdot521 \times 10^{11}$ m
Distance of earth from sun (at perihelion) = $1\cdot471 \times 10^{11}$ m
Distance of moon from earth (mean) = $3\cdot844 \times 10^8$ m
Escape velocity at surface of earth = $11\cdot2$ kms^{-1}
Escape velocity at surface of moon = $2\cdot38$ kms^{-1}
Escape velocity at surface of sun = 618 kms^{-1}
Gravity at surface of earth = $9\cdot80665$ ms^{-2}
Gravity at surface of moon = $1\cdot62$ ms^{-2}
Gravity at surface of sun = 273 ms^{-2}
Land area of earth = $148\cdot8 \times 10^6$ km^2
Light year (ly) = $9\cdot4605 \times 10^{15}$ m
Mass of earth = $5\cdot977 \times 10^{24}$ kg
Mass of moon = $7\cdot349 \times 10^{22}$ kg
Mass of sun = $1\cdot99 \times 10^{30}$ kg
Mean density of earth = 5,517 kg m^{-3}
Mean density of moon = 3,340 kgm^{-3}
Mean density of sun = 1,409 kg m^{-3}
Ocean area of earth = $361\cdot3 \times 10^6$ km^2
Parsec (pc) = $3\cdot0856 \times 10^{16}$ m
Period of moon about earth (sidereal) = $27\cdot32$ mean solar days
Period of sun's rotation (with respect to earth) = $27\cdot28$ days
Period of sun's rotation (sidereal) = $25\cdot38$ days
Radius of earth: (polar) = $6,356\cdot8$ km
$\qquad\qquad\quad$ (equatorial) = $6,378\cdot2$ km
Radius of moon = 1,738 km
Radius of sun = $6\cdot960 \times 108$ m
Rotational velocity at equator of earth = 465 ms^{-1}
Sidereal day = $86,164\cdot0906$ mean solar seconds
Sidereal year = $365\cdot256$ mean solar days
Solar second (mean) = 1/86,400 of a mean solar day
Surface area of earth = $5\cdot101 \times 10^{14}$ m^2
Surface area of moon = $3\cdot796 \times 10^{13}$ m^2
Surface area of sun = $6\cdot087 \times 10^{18}$ m^2
Synodical or lunar month (mean) = $29\cdot531$ mean solar days
Tropical (civil) year = $365\cdot256$ mean solar days
Velocity of earth in orbit around sun (mean) = $29\cdot78$ kms^{-1}
Volume of earth = $1\cdot083 \times 10^{21}$ m^3
Volume of moon = $2\cdot199 \times 10^{19}$ m^3
Volume of sun = $1\cdot412 \times 10^{27}$ m^3

Resistivities of selected metals and alloys

Material	Form	Resistivity (ohm − m × 10^{-9})	Temperature (°C)	Temperature coefficient
Alumel	Solid	33·3	0	0·0012
Aluminium	Liquid	20·5	670	
	Solid	2·62	20	0·0039
Antimony	Liquid	123	800	
	Solid	39·2	20	0·0036
Arsenic	Solid	35	0	0·0042
Beryllium		4·57	20	
Bismuth	Liquid	128·9	300	
	Solid	115	20	0·004
Boron		1.8×10^{12}	0	
Brass (66 Cu 34 Zn)		3·9	20	0·002
Cadmium	Liquid	34	400	
	Solid	7·5	20	0·0038
Carbon	Diamond	5×10^{20}	15	
	Graphite	1400	20	− 0·0005
Cerium		78	20	
Cesium	Liquid	36·6	30	
	Solid	20	20	
		18.83	0	
Chromax (15 Cr, 35 Ni, balance Fe)		100	20	0·00031
Chromel	Solid	70–110	0	0·00011– 0·000054
Chromium		2·6	0	
Cobalt		9·7	20	0·0033
Constantan (55 Cu, 45 Ni)		44·2	20	+ 0·0002
Copper (commercial annealed)	Liquid	21·3	1083	
	Solid	1·7241	20	0·0039
Gallium	Liquid	27	30	
	Solid	53	0	
Germanium		45	20	
German silver (18% Ni)		33	20	0·0004
Gold	Liquid	30·8	1063	
	Solid	2·44	20	0·0034
		2·19	0	
Hafnium		32·1	20	
Indium	Liquid	29	157	
	Solid	9	20	0·00498
Iridium		5·3	20	0·0039
Iron		9·71	20	0·0052–0· 0062
Kovar A (29 Ni, 17 Co, 0·3 Mn, balance Fe)		45–85	20	

Material	Form	Resistivity (ohm – m × 10⁻⁹)	Temperature (°C)	Temperature coefficient
Lead	Liquid	98	400	
	Solid	21·9	20	0·004
PbO₂		92		
Lithium	Liquid	45	230	0·003
	Solid	9·3	20	0·005
Magnesium		4·46	20	0·004
Manganese		5	20	
Manganin (84 Cu, 12 Mn, 4 Ni)		44	20	± 0·0002
Mercury	Liquid	95·8	20	0·00089
	Solid	21·3	− 50	
Molybdenum		5·17	0	
		4·77	20	0·0033
MnO₂		6,000,000	20	
Monel metal (67 Ni, 30 Cu, 1·4 Fe, 1 Mn)	Solid	42	20	0·002
Neodymium	Solid	79	18	
Nichrome (65 Ni, 12 Cr, 23 Fe)	Solid	100	20	0·00017
Nickel	Solid	6·9	20	0·0047
Nickel–silver (64 Cu, 18 Zn, 18 Ni)	Solid	28	20	0·00026
Niobium		12·4	20	
Osmium		9	20	0·0042
Palladium		10·8	20	0·0033
Phosphor bronze (4 Sn, 0·5 P, balance Cu)		9·4	20	0·003
Platinum		10·5	20	0·003
Plutonium		150	20	
Potassium	Liquid	13	62	
	Solid	7	20	0·006
Praseodymium		68	25	
Rhenium		19·8	20	
Rhodium		5·1	20	0·0046
Rubidium		12·5	20	
Ruthenium		10	20	
Selenium	Solid	1·2	20	
Silicon		85 × 10³	20	
Silver		1·62	20	0·0038
Sodium	Liquid	9·7	100	
	Solid	4·6	20	
Steel (0·4–0·5 C, balance Fe)		13–22	20	0·003
Steel, manganese (13 Mn, 1 C, 86 Fe)		70	20	0·001
Steel, stainless (0·1 C, 18 Cr, 8 Ni, balance Fe)		90	20	

Material	Form	Resistivity (ohm – m × 10⁻⁹)	Temperature (°C)	Temperature coefficient
Strontium		23	20	
Sulfur		2×10^{23}	20	
Tantalum		13·1	20	0·003
Thallium		18·1	20	0·004
Thorium		18	20	0·0021
Tin		11·4	20	0·0042
Titanium		47·8	25	
Tungsten		5·48	20	0·0045
Tophet A (80 Ni, 20 Cr)		108	20	0·00014
Uranium		29	0	0·0021
W_2O_5		450	20	
WO_3		2×10^{11}	20	
Zinc	Liquid	35·3	420	
	Solid	6	20	0·0037
Zirconium		40	20	0·0044

Electrical properties of elements

	Symbol	Atomic number Z	Mass number Z + N	Atomic weight	Atomic radii ×10⁻¹⁰ m	Gram atomic volume (cm³)	Electro-negativity, relative scale	First ionization potential (electron volts)	Electron work function Thermionic	Electron work function Photoelectric	Electron work function Contact	Valence* involved	Electrochemical equivalent Amp-hours per gram
Actinium	Ac	89	227	227			1·1	6·9				3	0·35
Aluminium	Al	13	27	26·98	1·25	10	1·5	5·98		4·08	3·38	3	2·98
Americium	Am	95	243	243				6·05					
Antimony	Sb	51	121–123	121·75	1·41	18	2·05	8·64		4·01	4·14	5	1·1
Argon	Ar or A	18	40	39·948	1·74	24	0	15·76				n	0·67
Arsenic	As	33	75	74·92	1·21	16	2·0	9·81	5·11			5	1·79
Astatine	At	85	210	210			2·2						
Barium	Ba	56	138	137·34	1·98	38	0·9	5·21	2·11	2·48	1·73	2	0·39
Berkelium	Bk	97	247	247									
Beryllium	Be	4	9	9·012	0·89	5	1·5	9·32		3·92	3·10	2	5·94
Bismuth	Bi	83	209	208·98	1·52	21	1·9	7·29		4·25	4·17	5	0·64
Boron	B	5	11	10·81	0·88	5	2·0	8·3		4·5		3	7·43
Bromine	Br	35	79–81	79·904	1·14	23	2·85	11·81				1	0·335
Cadmium	Cd	48	114–112	112·40	1·41	13	1·7	8·99		4·07	4·0	2	0·477
Calcium	Ca	20	40	40·08	1·74	26	1·0	6·11				2	1·337
Californium	Cf	98	251	251					2·24	2·706	3·33		

Element	Symbol	Atomic number Z	Mass number Z+N	Atomic weight	Atomic radii ×10⁻¹⁰ m	Gram atomic volume (cm³)	Electro-negativity, relative scale	First ionization potential (electron volts)	Electron work function: Thermionic	Electron work function: Photoelectric	Electron work function: Contact	Valence involved	Amp-hours per gram
Carbon	C	6	12	12·011	0·77	5	2·6	11·26	4·34	4·81		4	8·93
Cerium	Ce	58	140	140·12	1·65	21	1·1	5·6	2·6	2·84		3	0·574
Cesium	Cs	55	133	132·905	2·35	71	0·7	3·89	1·81	1·92	4·46	1	0·2
Chlorine	Cl	17	35	35·453	0·99	19	3·15	12·97				1	0·756
Chromium	Cr	24	52	51·996	1·17	7	1·6	6·76	4·60	4·37	4·38	3	1·546
Cobalt	Co	27	59	58·933	1·16	7	1·8	7·86	4·40	4·20	4·21	2	0·91
Copper	Cu	29	63	63·546	1·17	7	1·9	7·72	4·26	4·18	4·46	2	0·84
Curium	Cm	96	247	247									
Dysprosium	Dy	66	164-162-163	162·50	1·59	19	1·2	5·93				3	0·495
Einsteinium	Es or E	99	254	254									
Erbium	Er	68	166-168-167	167·26	1·57	18	1·2	6·10				3	0·48
Europium	Eu	63	153-151	151·96	1·85	29	1·1	5·67				3	0·53
Fermium	Fm	100	257	257									
Fluorine	F	9	19	18·998	0·64	15	3·9	17·42				1	1·41
Francium	Fr	87	223	223			0·65						
Gadolinium	Gd	64	158-160-156	157·25	1·61	20	1·1	6·16			3·80	3	0·513
Gallium	Ga	31	69-71	69·72	1·25	12	1·6	5·99	4·12	3·80		3	1·15

Element	Symbol	Z	Mass nos.	At. wt									
Gold	Au	79	197	196.967	1.34	10	2.4	9.22	4.32	4.82	4.46	3	0.41
Hafnium	Hf	72	180–178–177	178.49	1.44	13	1.3	7.0	3.53			4	0.600
Helium	He	2	4	4.003		32	0	24.59				n	6.698
Holmium	Ho	67	165	164.93	1.58	19	1.2	6.02				3	0.488
Hydrogen	H	1	1	1.008	0.37	13	2.2	13.59				1	26.59
Indium	In	49	115	114.82	1.50	16	1.7	5.78				1	0.700
Iodine	I	53	127	126.904	1.33	26	2.65	10.45				1	0.211
Iridium	Ir	77	193–191	192.22	1.17	9	2.2	9.1		6.8		4	0.555
Iron	Fe	26	56	55.847	1.26	7	1.8	7.87	5.3		4.57	3	1.440
Krypton	Kr	36	84–86	83.80	1.89	33	0	13.99	4.25	4.33	4.40	n	0.32
Lanthanum	La	57	139	138.905	1.69	22	1.1	5.61	3.3			3	0.579
Lawrencium	Lw	103	257	257									
Lead	Pb	82	208–206–207	207.2	1.54	18	1.8	7.42	4.05		3.94	4	0.517
Lithium	Li	3	7	6.940	1.23	13	1.0	5.39	2.35		2.49	1	3.862
Lutetium	Lu	71	175	174.97	1.56	18	1.2	6.15				3	0.46
Magnesium	Mg	12	24	24.305	1.36	14	1.2	7.64	3.68		3.63	2	2.204
Manganese	Mn	25	55	54.938	1.17	7	1.5	7.43	3.83	3.76	4.14	4	1.952
Mendelevium	Md or Mv	101	256	256									
Mercury	Hg	80	202–200–199	200.59	1.44	14	1.9	10.43	4.53		4.50	2	0.267
Molybdenum	Mo	42	98–96–92–95	95.94	1.29	9	1.8	7.10	4.20	4.25	4.28	6	1.67
Neodymium	Nd	60	142–144–146	144.24	1.64	21	1.1	5.49	3.3			3	0.557
Neon	Ne	10	20	20.179	1.31	17	0	21.56				n	1.33
Neptunium	Np	93	237	237.048			1.3	5.8	5.01	4.5			
Nickel	Ni	28	58	58.71	1.15	6	1.8	7.63	5.03	4.53	4.96	2	0.913
Niobium	Nb	41	93	92.906	1.34	11	1.6	6.88	4.01		4.25		
Nitrogen	N	7	14	14.007	0.70	14	3.05	14.53	3.83		4.14		
Nobelium	No	102	254	254								5	9.57

Element	Symbol	Atomic number Z	Mass number Z + N	Atomic weight	Atomic radii $\times 10^{-10}$ m	Gram atomic volume (cm³)	Electro-negativity, relative scale	First ionization potential (electron volts)	Electron work function — Thermionic (electron volts)	Electron work function — Photoelectric	Electron work function — Contact	Valence involved	Electrochemical equivalent — Amp-hours per gram
Osmium	Os	76	192–190–189	190·2	1·26	9	2·2	8·7			4·55	4	0·56
Oxygen	O	8	16	15·999	0·66	11	3·5	13·62				2	3·35
Palladium	Pd	46	108–106–105	106·4	1·28	9	2·2	8·33	4·99	4·97	4·49	4	1·005
Phosphorus	P	15	31	30·974	1·10	17	2·15	10·48				5	4·33
Platinum	Pt	78	195–194–196	195·09	1·29	9	2·2	9·0	5·32	5·22	5·36	4	0·549
Plutonium	Pu	94	242	242				5·8					
Polonium	Po	84	209	210	1·53		2·0	8·43				6	0·766
Potassium	K	19	39	39·098	2·03	46	0·8	4·34				1	0·685
Praseodymium	Pr	59	141	140·907	1·65	21	1·1	5·42	2·7	2·24	1·60	3	0·571
Promethium	Pm	61	145	145			1·1	5·55					
Protactinium	Pa	91	231	231·036			1·5					5	0·580
Radium	Ra	88	226	226·025	2·14	45	0·9	5·28				2	0·237
Radon	Rn	86	222	222		50	0	10·75				n	0·121
Rhenium	Re	75	187–185	186·2	1·28	8	1·9	7·87	5·1	5·0	4·52	7	1·007
Rhodium	Rh	45	103	102·905	1·25		2·2	7·46	4·80	4·57		4	1·042
Rubidium	Rb	37	85–87	85·468	2·16	56	0·8	4·18			2·09	1	0·314

Ruthenium	Ru	44	102-104-101	101·07	1·24	8	2·2	7·37			4·52	4	1·054
Samarium	Sm	62	152-154-147	150·35	1·66	20.	1·1	5·63	3·2			3	0·535
Scandium	Sc	21	45	44·956	1·44	15	1·3	6·54				3	1·783
Selenium	Se	34	80-78	78·96	1·17	16	2·45	9·75		4·8	4·42	6	2·037
Silicon	Si	14	28	28·086	1·17	12	1·9	8·15	3·59	4·52	4·2	4	3·821
Silver	Ag	47	107-109	107·868	1·34	10	1·9	7·57	3·56	4·73	4·44	1	0·248
Sodium	Na	11	23	22·99	1·57	24	0·9	5·14		2·28	1·9	1	1·166
Strontium	Sr	38	88	87·62	1·92	34	1·0	5·69		2·74		2	0·612
Sulfur	S	16	32	32·064	1·04	16	2·6	10·36				6	5·01
Tantalum	Ta	73	181	180·948	1·34	11	1·3	7·88	4·19	4·14	4·1	5	0·741
Technetium	Tc	43	99	98·906				7·28					
Tellurium	Te	52	130-128-126	127·60	1·37	21	2·3	9·01		4·76	4·70	6	1·260
Terbium	Tb	65	159	158·925	1·59	19	1·2	5·98				3	0·505
Thallium	Tl	81	205-203	204·37	1·55	17	1·8	6·11		3·68	3·84	3	0·393
Thorium	Th	90	232	232·038	1·65	20	1·3	6·95	3·35	3·47	3·46	4	0·462
Thulium	Tm	69	169	168·934	1·56	18	1·2	6·18				3	0·475
Tin	Sn	50	120-118	118·69	1·40	16	1·8	7·34		4·38	4·09	4	0·903
Titanium	Ti	22	48	47·90	1·32	11	1·5	6·82	3·95	4·06	4·14	4	2·238
Tungsten	W	74	184-186-182	183·85	1·30	10	1·7	7·98	4·52	4·49	4·38	6	0·874
Uranium	U	92	238	238·029	1·42	13	1·7	6·08	3·27	3·63	4·32	6	0·676
Vanadium	V	23	51	50·94	1·22	8	1·6	6·74	4·12	3·77	4·44	5	2·63
Xenon	Xe	54	132-129-131	131·30	2·09	43	0	12·13				n	0·204
Ytterbium	Yb	70	174-172-173	173·04	1·70	25	1·2	6·25				3	0·465
Yttrium	Y	39	89	88·906	1·62	21	1·3	6·38				3	0·904
Zinc	Zn	30	64-66-68	65·38	1·25	9	1·6	9·39		3·73	3·78	2	0·820
Zirconium	Zr	40	90-94-92	91·22	1·45	14	1·6	6·84	4·21	3·82	3·60	4	1·175

* n = nonvalent

Standard wire gauge and standard drill sizes

Standard wire gauge	Standard drill size		Decimal inch equivalent	Nearest obsolete number drill
	in	mm		
50			0·0010	
49			0·0012	
48			0·0016	
47			0·0020	
46			0·0024	
45			0·0028	
44			0·0032	
43			0·0036	
42			0·0040	
41			0·0044	
40			0·0048	
39			0·0052	
38			0·0060	
37			0·0068	
36			0·0076	
35			0·0084	
34			0·0092	
33			0·0100	
32			0·0108	
31			0·0116	
30			0·0124	
		0·32	0·0126	
29			0·0136	
		0·35	0·0138	80
28			0·0148	
		0·38	0·0150	79
	$\frac{1}{64}$		0·0156	
		0·40	0·0157	78
27			0·0164	
		0·42	0·0165	
		0·45	0·0177	77
26			0·0180	
		0·48	0·0189	76
		0·50	0·0197	
25			0·0200	
		0·52	0·0205	75
		0·55	0·0217	
24			0·0220	
		0·58	0·0228	74
		0·60	0·0236	73
23			0·0240	
		0·62	0·0244	
		0·65	0·0256	72, 71
		0·68	0·0268	
		0·70	0·0276	70
22			0·0280	
		0·72	0·0283	
		0·75	0·0295	69

Standard wire gauge	Standard drill size in	Standard drill size mm	Decimal inch equivalent	Nearest obsolete number drill
		0·78	0·0307	
	$\frac{1}{32}$		0·0312	68
		0·80	0·0315	
21			0·0320	
		0·82	0·0323	67
		0·85	0·0335	66
		0·88	0·0346	
		0·90	0·0354	65
20			0·0360	
		0·92	0·0362	64
		0·95	0·0374	63
		0·98	0·0386	62
		1·00	0·0394	61, 60
19			0·0400	
		1·05	0·0413	59, 58
		1·10	0·0433	57
		1·15	0·0453	
	$\frac{3}{64}$		0·0469	56
		1·20	0·0472	
18			0·0480	
		1·25	0·0492	
		1·30	0·0512	55
		1·35	0·0532	
		1·40	0·0551	54
17			0·0560	
		1·45	0·0571	
		1·50	0·0591	53
		1·55	0·0610	
	$\frac{1}{16}$		0·0625	
		1·60	0·0630	52
16			0·0640	
		1·65	0·0650	
		1·70	0·0669	51
		1·75	0·0689	
15			0·0709	50
		1·80	0·0709	
			0·0720	
		1·85	0·0728	49
		1·90	0·0748	48
		1·95	0·0768	
	$\frac{5}{64}$		0·0781	
14			0·0781	
		2·00	0·0787	47
			0·0800	
		2·05	0·0807	46
		2·10	0·0827	45
		2·15	0·0846	
		2·20	0·0866	44
		2·25	0·0886	43
		2·30	0·0906	
13			0·0920	
		2·35	0·0925	
	$\frac{3}{32}$		0·0938	42

Standard wire gauge	Standard drill size		Decimal inch equivalent	Nearest obsolete number drill
	in	mm		
		2·40	0·0945	
		2·45	0·0965	41
		2·50	0·0984	40
		2·55	0·1004	39
		2·60	0·1024	38
12			0·1040	
		2·65	0·1043	37
		2·70	0·1063	36
		2·75	0·1083	
	7/64		0·1094	
		2·80	0·1102	35, 34
		2·85	0·1122	33
		2·90	0·1142	
11			0·1160	
		2·95	0·1161	32
		3·00	0·1181	31
		3·10	0·1220	
	1/8		0·1250	
		3·20	0·1260	
10			0·1280	
		3·30	0·1299	30
		3·40	0·1339	
		3·50	0·1378	29
	9/64		0·1406	28
		3·60	0·1417	
9			0·1440	
		3·70	0·1457	27, 26
		3·80	0·1496	25
		3·90	0·1535	24, 23
	5/32		0·1562	
		4·00	0·1575	22, 21
8			0·1600	
		4·10	0·1614	20
		4·20	0·1654	19
		4·30	0·1693	18
	11/64		0·1719	
		4·40	0·1732	17
7			0·1760	
		4·50	0·1772	16
		4·60	0·1811	15, 14
		4·70	0·1850	13
	3/16		0·1875	
		4·80	0·1890	12
6			0·1920	
		4·90	0·1929	11, 10
		5·00	0·1968	9
		5·10	0·2008	8, 7
	13/64		0·2031	
		5·20	0·2047	6, 5
		5·30	0·2087	4
5			0·2120	

Standard wire gauge	Standard drill size		Decimal inch equivalent	Nearest obsolete number drill
	in	mm		
		5·40	0·2126	3
		5·50	0·2165	
	7/32		0·2188	
		5·60	0·2205	2
		5·70	0·2244	
		5·80	0·2283	1
4			0·2320	
		5·90	0·2323	
	15/64		0·2344	A
		6·00	0·2362	B
		6·10	0·2402	C
		6·20	0·2441	D
		6·30	0·2480	
	1/4		0·2500	E
		6·40	0·2520	
3		6·50	0·2559	F
		6·60	0·2598	G
		6·70	0·2638	
	17/64		0·2656	H
		6·80	0·2677	
		6·90	0·2717	I
		7·00	0·2756	J
			0·2760	
2			0·2795	
	9/32		0·2812	K
		7·20	0·2835	
		7·30	0·2874	
		7·40	0·2913	L
		7·50	0·2953	M
	19/64		0·2969	
1		7·60	0·2992	
			0·3000	
		7·70	0·3032	N
		7·80	0·3071	
		7·90	0·3110	
	5/16		0·3125	
0		8·00	0·3150	O
		8·10	0·3189	
		8·20	0·3228	P
			0·3240	
		8·30	0·3268	
	21/64		0·3281	
		8·40	0·3307	Q
		8·50	0·3346	
		8·60	0·3386	R
		8·70	0·3425	
00	11/32		0·3438	
		8·80	0·3465	S
			0·3480	
		8·90	0·3504	
		9·00	0·3543	

Standard wire gauge	Standard drill size		Decimal inch equivalent	Nearest obsolete number drill
	in	mm		
		9·10	0·3583	T
	$\frac{23}{64}$		0·3594	
		9·20	0·3622	
		9·30	0·3661	U
		9·40	0·3701	
3/0			0·3720	
		9·50	0·3740	
			0·3750	V
		9·60	0·3780	
		9·70	0·3819	
		9·80	0·3858	W
		9·90	0·3898	
	$\frac{25}{64}$		0·3906	
		10·00	0·3937	
		10·00	0·3976	X
4/0			0·4000	
		10·20	0·4016	
		10·30	0·4055	
	$\frac{1}{32}$		0·4062	Y
		10·40	0·4094	
		10·50	0·4134	Z
		10·60	0·4173	
		10·70	0·4213	
5/0	$\frac{27}{64}$		0·4219	
		10·80	0·4252	
		10·90	0·4291	
			0·4320	
		11·00	0·4331	
		11·10	0·4370	
	$\frac{7}{16}$		0·4375	
			0·4409	

Drill sizes proceed thus;
$\frac{1}{2}$ to 2 inches in $\frac{1}{64}$ inch steps;
12·7 to 14 mm in 0·1 mm steps;
14 to 25 mm in 0·25 mm steps;
25 to 50·5 mm in 0·5 mm steps.

BSI standard metric sizes of copper winding wires

Conductor diameter			Sectional area mm²	Weight per km kg	Nominal resistance at 20°C		Current rating at 4·65 amps per mm² amps
Nom. mm	Max. mm	Min. mm			Per metre ohms	Per kg ohms	
5·000	5·050	4·950	19·63	174·6	0·0008781	0·005029	91·30
4·750	4·798	4·702	17·72	157·5	0·0009730	0·006178	82·40
4·500	4·545	4·455	15·90	141·4	0·001084	0·007666	73·95
4·250	4·293	4·207	14·19	126·1	0·001215	0·009635	65·96
4·000	4·040	3·960	12·57	111·7	0·001372	0·01228	58·43
3·750	3·788	3·712	11·04	98·19	0·001561	0·01590	51·36
3·550	3·586	3·514	9·898	87·99	0·001742	0·01980	46·03
3·350	3·384	3·316	8·814	78·36	0·001956	0·02496	40·99
3·150	3·182	3·118	7·793	69·28	0·002212	0·03193	36·24
3·000	3·030	2·970	7·069	62·84	0·002439	0·03881	32·87
2·800	2·828	2·772	6·158	54·74	0·002800	0·05115	28·63
2·650	2·677	2·623	5·515	49·03	0·003126	0·06370	25·65
2·500	2·525	2·475	4·909	43·64	0·003512	0·08048	22·83
2·360	2·384	2·336	4·374	38·89	0·003941	0·1013	20·34
2·240	2·262	2·218	3·941	35·03	0·004375	0·1249	18·32
2·120	2·141	2·099	3·530	31·38	0·004884	0·1556	16·41
2·000	2·020	1·980	3·142	27·93	0·005488	0·1965	14·61
1·900	1·919	1·881	2·835	25·21	0·006081	0·2412	13·18

| Conductor diameter | | | Sectional area mm² | Weight per km kg | Nominal resistance at 20°C | | Current rating at 4.65 amps per mm² amps |
Nom. mm	Max. mm	Min. mm			Per metre ohms	Per kg ohms	
1·800	1·818	1·782	2·545	22·62	0·006775	0·2995	11·83
1·700	1·717	1·683	2·270	20·18	0·007596	0·3764	10·55
1·600	1·616	1·584	2·011	17·87	0·008575	0·4799	9·349
1·500	1·515	1·485	1·767	15·71	0·009757	0·6211	8·217
1·400	1·414	1·386	1·539	13·69	0·01120	0·8181	7·158
1·320	1·333	1·307	1·368	12·17	0·01260	1·035	6·364
1·250	1·263	1·237	1·227	10·91	0·01405	1·288	5·706
1·180	1·192	1·168	1·094	9·722	0·01577	1·622	5·085
1·120	1·131	1·109	0·9852	8·758	0·01750	1·998	4·581
1·060	1·071	1·049	0·8825	7·845	0·01954	2·491	4·103
1·000	1·010	0·990	0·7854	6·982	0·02195	3·144	3·652
0·950	0·960	0·940	0·7088	6·301	0·02432	3·860	3·296
0·900	0·909	0·891	0·6362	5·656	0·02710	4·791	2·958
0·850	0·859	0·841	0·5675	5·045	0·03038	6·022	2·639
0·800	0·808	0·792	0·5027	4·469	0·03430	7·675	2·337
0·750	0·758	0·742	0·4418	3·928	0·03903	9·936	2·054
0·710	0·717	0·703	0·3959	3·520	0·04355	12·37	1·841
0·670	0·677	0·663	0·3526	3·134	0·04890	15·60	1·639
0·630	0·636	0·624	0·3117	2·771	0·05531	19·96	1·449
0·600	0·606	0·594	0·2827	2·514	0·06098	24·26	1·315

0.560	0.566	0.554	0.2463	2.190	0.07000	31.96	1.145
0.530	0.536	0.524	0.2206	1.961	0.07814	39.85	1.026
0.500	0.505	0.495	0.1963	1.746	0.08781	50.29	0.9130
0.475	0.480	0.470	0.1772	1.575	0.09730	61.78	0.8240
0.450	0.455	0.445	0.1590	1.414	0.1084	76.66	0.7395
0.425	0.430	0.420	0.1419	1.261	0.1215	96.35	0.6596
0.400	0.405	0.395	0.1257	1.117	0.1372	122.8	0.5843
0.375	0.380	0.370	0.1104	0.9819	0.1561	159.0	0.5136
0.355	0.359	0.351	0.09898	0.8799	0.1742	198.0	0.4603
0.335	0.339	0.331	0.08814	0.7836	0.1956	249.6	0.4099
0.315	0.319	0.311	0.07793	0.6928	0.2212	319.3	0.3624
0.300	0.304	0.296	0.07069	0.6284	0.2439	388.1	0.3287
0.280	0.284	0.276	0.06158	0.5474	0.2800	511.5	0.2863
0.265	0.269	0.261	0.05515	0.4903	0.3126	637.6	0.2565
0.250	0.254	0.246	0.04909	0.4364	0.3512	804.8	0.2283
0.236	0.240	0.232	0.04374	0.3889	0.3941	1,013.0	0.2034
0.224	0.227	0.221	0.03941	0.3503	0.4375	1,249.0	0.1832
0.212	0.215	0.209	0.03530	0.3138	0.4884	1,556.0	0.1641
0.200	0.203	0.197	0.03142	0.2793	0.5488	1,965.0	0.1461
0.190	0.193	0.187	0.02835	0.2521	0.6081	2,412.0	0.1318
0.180	0.183	0.177	0.02545	0.2262	0.6775	2,995.0	0.1183
0.170	0.173	0.167	0.02270	0.2018	0.7596	3,764.0	0.1055
0.160	0.163	0.157	0.02011	0.1787	0.8575	4,799.0	0.0935
0.150	0.153	0.147	0.01767	0.1571	0.9757	6,211.0	0.0822
0.140	0.143	0.137	0.01539	0.1369	1.20	8,181.0	0.0716
0.132	0.135	0.129	0.01368	0.1217	1.260	10,353.0	0.0636
0.125	0.128	0.122	0.01227	0.1091	1.450	12,878.0	0.0571

| Conductor diameter | | | Sectional area mm² | Weight per km kg | Nominal resistance at 20°C | | Current rating at 4·65 amps per mm² amps |
Nom. mm	Max. mm	Min. mm			Per metre ohms	Per kg ohms	
0·112	0·155	0·109	0·009852	0·08758	1·750	19,982·0	0·0458
0·100	0·103	0·097	0·007854	0·06982	2·195	31,438·0	0·0365
0·090	0·093	0·087	0·006362	0·05656	2·710	47,914·0	0·0296
0·080	0·083	0·077	0·005027	0·04469	3·430	76,751·0	0·0234
0·071	0·074	0·068	0·003959	0·03520	4·355	123,722·0	0·0184
0·063	—	—	0·003117	0·02771	5·531	199,603·0	0·0145
0·060	—	—	0·002827	0·02514	6·098	242,562·0	0·0132
0·056	—	—	0·002463	0·02190	7·000	319,635·0	0·0115
0·050	—	—	0·001963	0·01746	8·781	502,921·0	0·0091
0·045	—	—	0·001590	0·01414	10·84	766,620·0	0·0074
0·040	—	—	0·001257	0·01117	13·72	1,228,290·0	0·0058
0·036	—	—	0·001018	0·009049	16·94	1,872,030·0	0·0047
0·032	—	—	0·0008042	0·007150	21·44	2,998,601·0	0·0037
0·030	—	—	0·0007069	0·006284	24·39	3,881,286·0	0·0033
0·028	—	—	0·0006158	0·005474	28·00	5,115,090·0	0·0029
0·025	—	—	0·0004909	0·004364	35·12	8,047,663·0	0·0023

* 4·65 amps per mm² is equivalent to 3000 amps per in².
Preferred sizes shown in bold type.

Metric wire sizes: turns per 10 mm

Nominal bare diameter mm	Turns per 10 mm min	Nominal bare diameter mm	Turns per 10 mm min
5·000	1·9	0·500	18·3
4·750	2·0	0·475	19·2
4·500	2·2	0·450	20·2
4·250	2·3	0·425	21·3
4·000	2·4	0·400	22·6
3·750	2·6	0·375	24·0
3·550	2·7	0·355	25·3
3·350	2·9	0·335	26·7
3·150	3·1	0·315	28·4
3·000	3·2	0·300	29·7
2·800	3·4	0·280	31·8
2·650	3·6	0·265	33·3
2·500	3·8	0·250	35·2
2·360	4·1	0·236	37·2
2·240	4·3	0·224	39·1
2·120	4·5	0·212	41·2
2·000	4·8	0·200	43·5
1·900	5·0	0·190	45·5
1·800	5·3	1·180	47·9
1·700	5·6	0·170	50·5
1·600	5·9	0·160	53·5
1·500	6·3	0·150	56·5
1·400	6·8	0·140	60·2
1·320	7·2	0·132	63·7
1·250	7·5	0·125	67·1
1·180	8·0	0·112	74·6
1·120	8·4	0·100	82·6
1·060	8·8	0·090	90·9
1·000	9·4	0·080	102·0
0·950	9·9	0·071	113·6
0·900	10·4	0·063	128·2
0·850	11·0	0·060	133·3
0·800	11·6	0·056	142·9
0·750	12·4	0·050	161·3
0·710	13·0	0·045	178·6
0·670	13·8	0·040	200·0
0·630	14·6	0·036	222·2
0·600	15·3	0·032	250·0
0·560	16·4	0·030	263·2
0·530	17·3	0·028	285·7
		0·025	322·6

Preferred sizes shown in bold type.

Copper wire data (SWG)

Standard wire gauge	Diameter in inches	Resistance in ohms per yard	Resistance in ohms per pound	Pounds per ohm	Weight in pounds per 1000 yards	Yards per pound	Turns per inch — Enamel covered	Turns per inch — Single silk covered	Turns per inch — Double silk covered	Turns per inch — Single cotton covered	Turns per inch — Double cotton covered
10	0·128	0·001868	0·0120	83·3	148·8	6·67		7·64	7·55	7·35	7·04
11	0·116	0·002275	0·0200	50·0	122·2	8·16		8·41	8·30	8·06	7·69
12	0·104	0·002831	0·0280	35·7	98·22	10·23		9·35	9·22	8·93	8·48
13	0·092	0·003617	0·0550	18·1	76·86	13·00		10·5	10·4	10·0	9·43
14	0·080	0·004784	0·0820	12·2	58·12	17·16		12·1	11·8	11·4	10·6
15	0·072	0·005904	0·1400	7·14	47·08	21·23		13·3	13·1	12·5	11·6
16	0·064	0·007478	0·2021	4·95	37·20	26·86	15·0	14·9	14·6	14·1	13·2
17	0·056	0·009762	0·3423	2·38	28·48	35·00	17·1	16·9	16·5	15·9	14·7
18	0·048	0·01328	0·6351	1·56	20·92	47·66	19·8	20·0	19·4	18·5	17·2
19	0·040	0·01913	1·315	0·757	14·53	68·66	23·7	23·8	23·0	21·7	20·0
20	0·036	0·02362	2·012	0·497	11·77	85·00	26·1	26·3	25·3	23·8	21·7
21	0·032	0·02990	3·221	0·309	9·299	107·6	29·4	29·4	28·2	26·3	23·8
22	0·028	0·03905	5·498	0·181	7·120	140·6	33·3	38·5	31·8	29·4	26·3
23	0·024	0·05313	10·14	0·098	5·231	191·6	38·8	28·5	36·4	33·3	29·4
24	0·022	0·06324	14·38	0·069	4·395	228·3	42·1	42·1	40·0	35·7	31·3
25	0·020	0·07653	21·08	0·0471	3·632	275·3	46·0	46·0	43·5	38·5	33·3
26	0·018	0·09448	32·21	0·0309	2·942	340·0	50·6	50·6	47·6	41·7	35·7

27	0.0164	0.11138	46.55	0.0215	2.442	410.0	55.9	55.1	51.6	44.6	37.9
28	0.0148	0.1398	70.12	0.0141	1.989	503.0	61.4	60.4	56.2	48.1	40.2
29	0.0136	0.1655	98.65	0.0101	1.680	596.6	66.2	65.2	60.2	51.0	42.4
30	0.0124	0.1991	142.75	0.0069	1.396	716.6	73.3	72.0	67.1	54.4	44.7
31	0.0116	0.2275	185.80	0.0054	1.222	820.0	77.8	76.3	70.9	56.8	46.3
32	0.0108	0.2625	248.20	0.0040	1.059	943.3	83.0	81.3	75.2	63.3	50.5
33	0.0100	0.3061	337.50	0.0029	0.9081	1,100	88.9	87.0	80.0	66.7	52.6
34	0.0092	0.3617	471.00	0.0023	0.7686	1,300	98.0	93.4	85.5	70.4	54.9
35	0.0084	0.4338	676.50	0.0014	0.6408	1,556	106	101	91.8	80.6	61.0
36	0.0076	0.5300	1,009	0.00098	0.5254	1,903	116	110	102	86.2	64.1
37	0.0068	0.6620	1,574	0.00064	0.4199	2,380	128	120	110	92.6	67.6
38	0.0060	0.8503	2,598	0.000385	0.3269	3,056	143	133	121	100	71.4
39	0.0052	0.132	4,645	0.000217	0.2456	4,066	168	149	134	109	75.8
40	0.0048	0.328	6,360	0.000156	0.2092	4,766	180	159	142	144	78.1
41	0.0044	0.581	9,020	0.000112	0.1758	5,700	194	169	150		
42	0.0040	0.913	13,150	0.000076	0.1453	6,866	211	191	167		
43	0.0036	0.362	20,120	0.000050	0.1177	7,500	230	206	179		
44	0.0032	0.989	32,210	0.000030	0.0929	10,766	253	225	192		
45	0.0028	0.904	54,980	0.000015	0.0712	14,066	282	247	208		

Wire gauges

Number of gauge	SWG in	SWG mm	AWG or B and S in	AWG or B and S mm	BWG in	BWG mm	Gold and silver (Birmingham) in	Gold and silver (Birmingham) mm	Lancashire steel pinion wire in	Lancashire steel pinion wire mm
7/0	0·500	12·70	—	—	—	—	—	—	—	—
6/0	0·464	11·78	—	—	—	—	—	—	—	—
5/0	0·432	10·97	—	—	—	—	—	—	—	—
4/0	0·400	10·16	0·46	11·68	0·454	11·53	—	—	—	—
3/0	0·372	9·44	0·409	10·388	0·425	10·787	—	—	—	—
2/0	0·348	8·83	0·364	9·24	0·380	9·65	—	—	—	—
1/0	0·324	8·23	0·324	8·23	0·340	8·63	—	—	—	—
1	0·300	7·62	0·289	7·338	0·300	7·62	0·004	0·101	0·227	5·757
2	0·276	7·06	0·257	6·527	0·284	7·21	0·005	0·127	0·219	5·558
3	0·252	6·40	0·229	5·808	0·259	6·578	0·008	0·203	0·212	5·380
4	0·232	5·89	0·204	5·18	0·238	6·04	0·010	0·254	0·207	5·257
5	0·212	5·38	0·181	4·59	0·220	5·58	0·012	0·304	0·204	5·181
6	0·192	4·88	0·162	4·11	0·203	5·156	0·013	0·330	0·201	5·105
7	0·176	4·46	0·144	3·66	0·180	4·57	0·015	0·381	0·199	5·048
8	0·160	4·06	0·128	3·24	0·165	4·187	0·016	0·406	0·197	4·997
9	0·144	3·66	0·114	2·89	0·144	3·753	0·019	0·482	0·194	4·921
10	0·128	3·24	0·101	2·565	0·134	3·40	0·024	0·61	0·191	4·845
11	0·116	2·94	0·090	2·28	0·120	3·04	0·029	0·736	0·188	4·777

12	0·104	2·642	0·080	2·03	0·109	2·768	0·034	0·863	0·185	4·697
13	0·092	2·336	0·071	1·79	0·095	2·413	0·036	0·914	0·182	4·620
14	0·080	2·03	0·064	1·625	0·083	2·108	0·041	1·041	0·180	4·57
15	0·072	1·828	0·057	1·447	0·072	1·828	0·047	1·143	0·178	4·513
16	0·064	1·625	0·050	1·27	0·065	1·65	0·051	1·295	0·175	4·437
17	0·056	1·422	0·045	1·14	0·058	1·473	0·057	1·447	0·172	4·360
18	0·048	1·219	0·040	1·016	0·049	1·244	0·061	1·549	0·168	4·263
19	0·040	1·016	0·035	0·889	0·042	1·066	0·064	1·625	0·164	4·161
20	0·036	0·914	0·031	0·787	0·035	0·889	0·067	1·701	0·161	4·085
21	0·032	0·812	0·028	0·711	0·032	0·812	0·072	1·828	0·157	3·988
22	0·028	0·711	0·025	0·635	0·028	0·711	0·074	1·879	0·155	3·937
23	0·024	0·61	0·022	0·558	0·025	0·635	0·077	1·955	0·153	3·886
24	0·022	0·558	0·020	0·508	0·022	0·558	0·082	2·082	0·151	3·835
25	0·020	0·508	0·017	0·431	0·020	0·508	0·095	2·413	0·148	3·753
26	0·018	0·457	0·015	0·381	0·018	0·457	0·103	2·616	0·146	3·702
27	0·016	0·406	0·0148	0·376	0·016	0·406	0·113	2·87	0·143	3·626
28	0·0148	0·376	0·012	0·304	0·0148	0·376	0·120	3·04	0·139	3·528
29	0·0136	0·345	0·0116	0·29	0·0136	0·345	0·124	3·14	0·134	3·401
30	0·012	0·304	0·010	0·254	0·012	0·304	0·126	3·193	0·127	3·217
31	0·0116	0·29	0·008	0·203	0·010	0·254	0·133	3·376	0·120	3·04
32	0·0108	0·274	0·0079	0·199	0·009	0·228	0·143	3·626	0·115	2·917
33	0·010	0·254	0·007	0·177	0·008	0·203	0·145	3·677	0·112	2·840
34	0·009	0·228	0·006	0·152	0·0076	0·192	0·148	3·753	0·110	2·79
35	0·008	0·203	0·0056	0·142	0·005	0·127	0·158	4·013	0·108	2·743
36	0·0076	0·193	0·005	0·127	0·004	0·101	0·167	4·237	0·106	2·692

Metric sizes of insulated round winding wires

	Nominal conductor diameter	
Preferred metric size mm	Non-preferred metric size mm	Approximate inch equivalent
5·000		0·1969
4·750		0·1870
4·500		0·1772
4·250		0·1673
4·000		0·1575
3·750		0·1476
3·550		0·1398
3·350		0·1319
3·150		0·1240
3·000		0·1181
2·800		0·1102
2·650		0·1043
2·500		0·0984
2·360		0·0929
2·240		0·0882
2·120		0·0835
2·000		0·0787
1·900		0·0748
1·800		0·0709
1·700		0·0669
1·600		0·0630
1·500		0·0591
1·400		0·0551
1·320		0·0520
1·250		0·0492
1·180		0·0465
1·120		0·0441
1·060		0·0417
1·000		0·0394
0·950		0·0374
0·900		0·0354
0·850		0·0335
0·800		0·0315
0·750		0·0295
0·710		0·0280
	0·670	0·0264
0·630		0·0248
	0·600	0·0236
0·560		0·0220
	0·530	0·0209
0·500		0·0197
	0·475	0·0187
0·450		0·0177

Nominal conductor diameter

Preferred metric size mm	Non-preferred metric size mm	Approximate inch equivalent
	0·425	0·0167
0·400		0·01575
	0·375	0·0148
0·355		0·0140
	0·335	0·0132
0·315		0·0124
	0·300	0·0118
0·280		0·0110
	0·265	0·0104
0·250		0·0098
	0·236	0·0093
0·224		0·0088
	0·212	0·00835
0·200		0·0079
	0·190	0·0075
0·180		0·0071
	0·170	0·0067
0·160		0·0063
	0·150	0·0059
0·140		0·0055
	0·132	0·0052
0·125		0·0049
0·112		0·00441
0·100		0·00394
0·090		0·00354
0·080		0·00315
0·071		0·00280
0·063		0·00248
	0·060	0·00236
	0·056	0·00220
0·050		0·00197
	0·045	0·00177
0·040		0·00157
	0·036	0·00142
0·032		0·00126
	0·030	0·00118
	0·028	0·00110
0·025		0·00098

Index